# SHOOTING MODELS

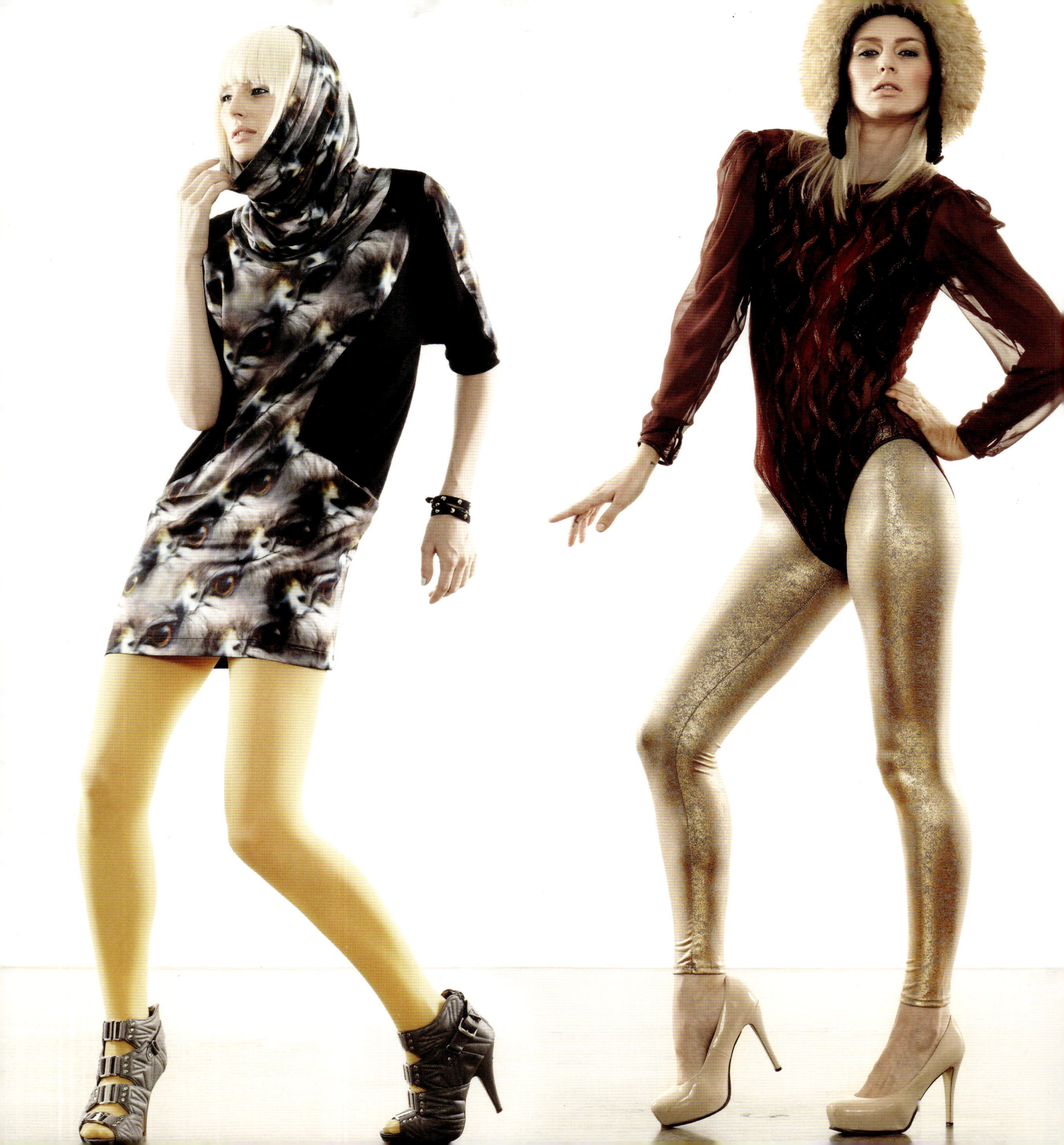

TIPS, TECHNIQUES & TESTIMONY

**FROM BOTH SIDES OF THE CAMERA**

# SHOOTING MODELS


BY INTERNATIONAL MODEL

**FRANKI FALKOW**

& PRO PHOTOGRAPHER

**ADAM DUCKWORTH**


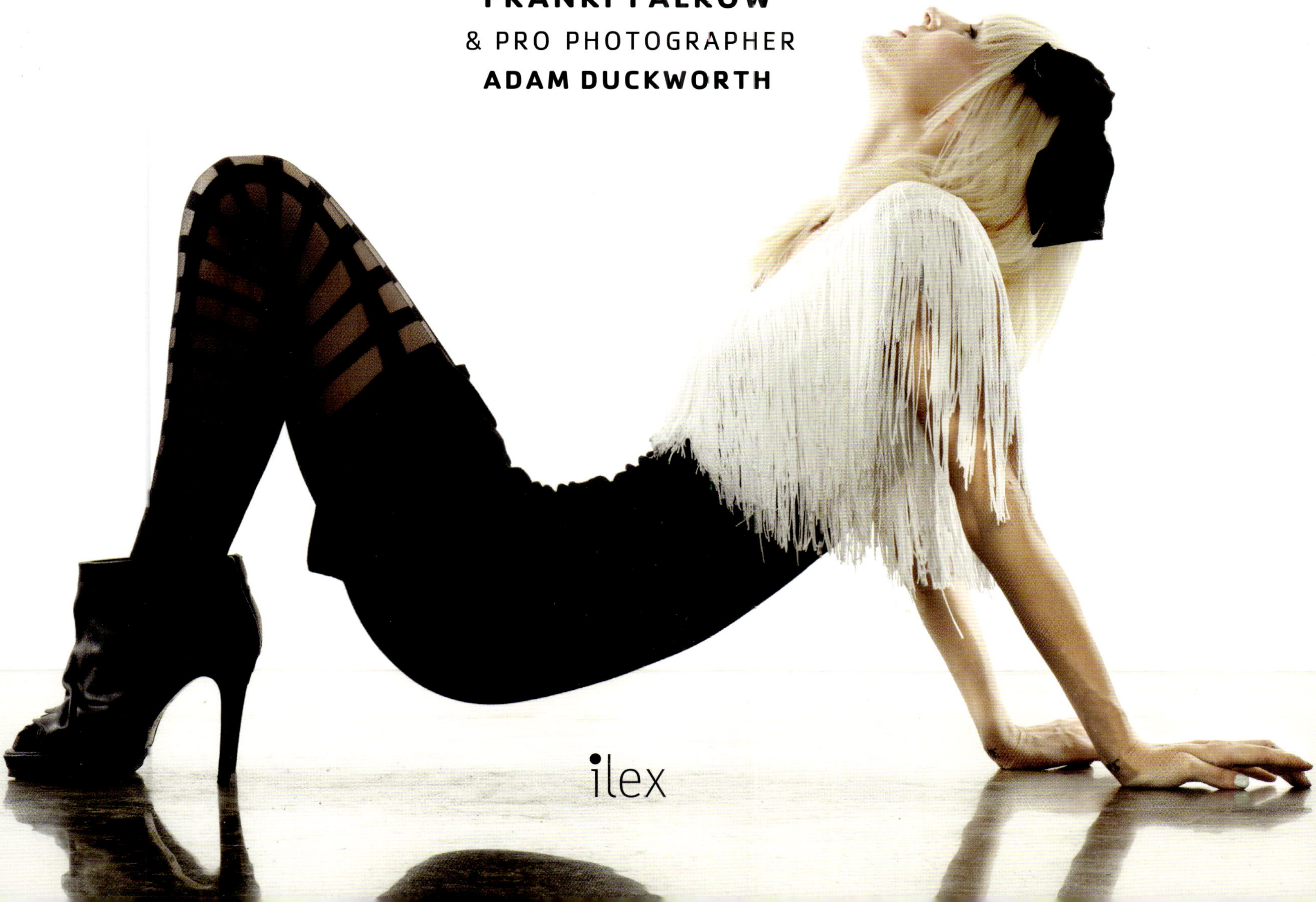

ilex

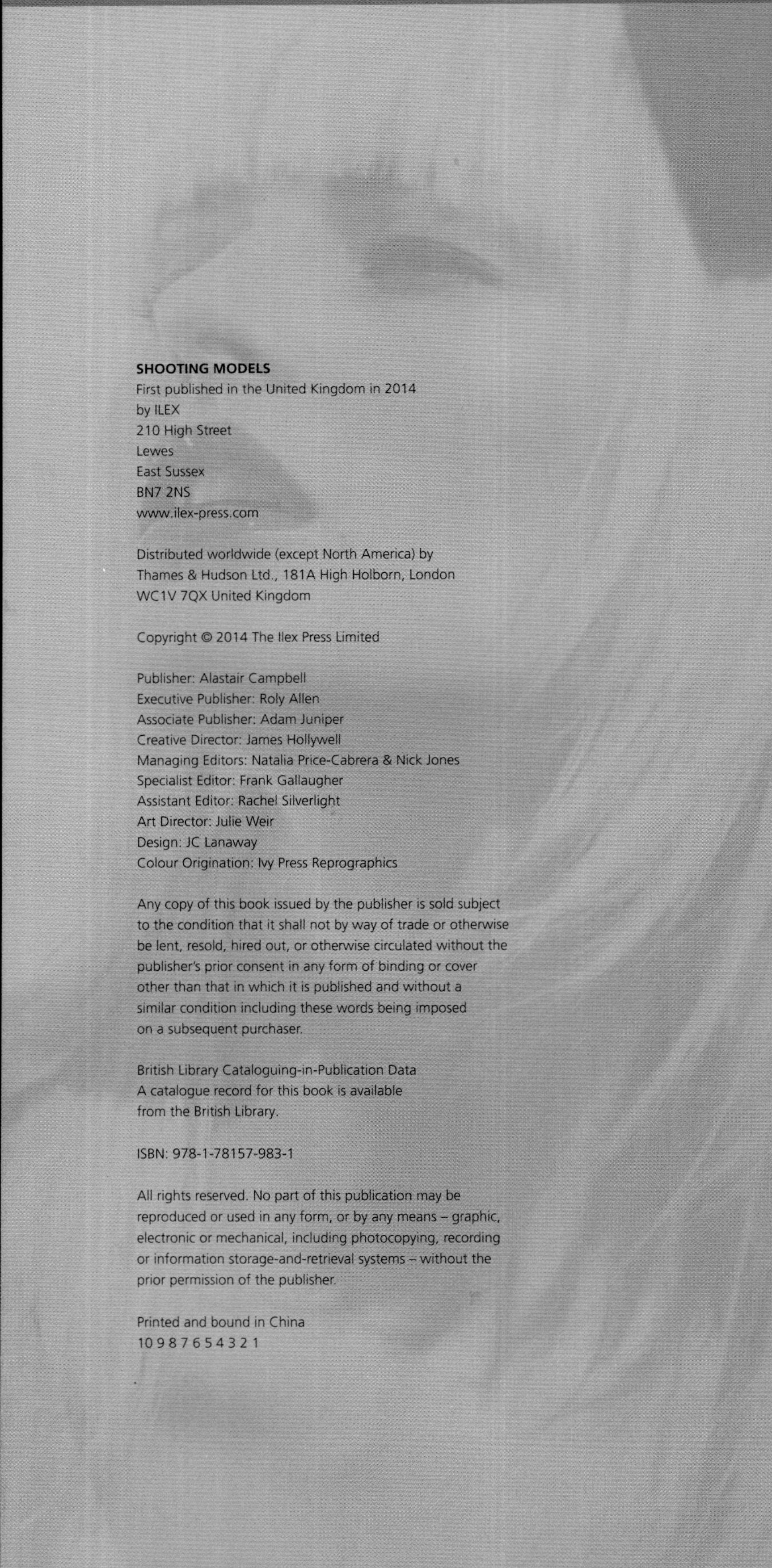

**SHOOTING MODELS**
First published in the United Kingdom in 2014
by ILEX
210 High Street
Lewes
East Sussex
BN7 2NS
www.ilex-press.com

Distributed worldwide (except North America) by
Thames & Hudson Ltd., 181A High Holborn, London
WC1V 7QX United Kingdom



Publisher: Alastair Campbell
Executive Publisher: Roly Allen
Associate Publisher: Adam Juniper
Creative Director: James Hollywell
Managing Editors: Natalia Price-Cabrera & Nick Jones
Specialist Editor: Frank Gallaugher
Assistant Editor: Rachel Silverlight
Art Director: Julie Weir
Design: JC Lanaway
Colour Origination: Ivy Press Reprographics



British Library Cataloguing-in-Publication Data
A catalogue record for this book is available
from the British Library.

ISBN: 978-1-78157-983-1



Printed and bound in China
10 9 8 7 6 5 4 3 2 1

# CONTENTS

NTENT

# INTRODUCTION

## FROM FRANKI

The world of fashion photography attracts all kinds of people. Whether it's behind the camera or in front of the lens, entering the fashion industry is the shared dream of many aspiring creatives. It's hardly surprising, as it's a modern art form that provokes stereotypes of glamorous, globetrotting individuals; impeccably cool with a look that says they're shooting top advertising campaigns and are married to a rock star. And it's exciting because, to a degree, this is true. However, if you're getting into fashion photography for fame and fortune, be prepared to work hard: you need to be dedicated and stand out from the competition if you want to make a name for yourself.

I have been modeling professionally for over ten years now. During this time I've witnessed the transition from film to digital (and back again in some cases); seen shoot budgets roller coaster from week-long trips in the Bahamas to makeshift studios in dingy office blocks; and dealt with every kind of photographer you can imagine. I've been lucky enough to shoot with some of the greats—Bruce Weber, Terry Richardson, Rankin, and Peggy Sirota—and have also worked with some not so greats. I view each time on set as a learning experience: I have had good and bad days, but no two have ever been the same!

Working in fashion has taken me all over the world, to some of the craziest locations imaginable. Photographers find inspiration all over, in places that are beautiful beyond the imagination and the ugliest holes that are the exact opposite. I've met some of the most insightful, intelligent, and on occasions eccentric people in this industry and become a better person for it. Of course, there is a financial, commercial aspect (there has to be in any business), but it's about perspective. I still model for test shoots, which means working for free, because I still love my job even after ten years. I'm not stuck in a nine-to-five with a routine as interesting as watching paint dry, and my Mondays don't suck!

I am not suggesting it's going to be easy: this is not a job for the faint of heart and there are many facets to becoming a successful fashion photographer. However, I believe one of the most common downfalls is a lack of communication skills and an ability to direct effectively. Even those who are booking regularly might not be producing their best handiwork because they are unable to work "with" their model. Photographers are, after all, directors and must learn to modify their skills to accommodate exceptionally different individuals on a daily basis. It is often forgotten that this is a "people" industry: you must be motivated by working with others and not intimidated easily. If you are going to photograph a model you cannot be frightened of talking to them.

Models are people too. You may think I'm joking saying that, but I often don't book more commercial work because I fail to resemble a "real person."

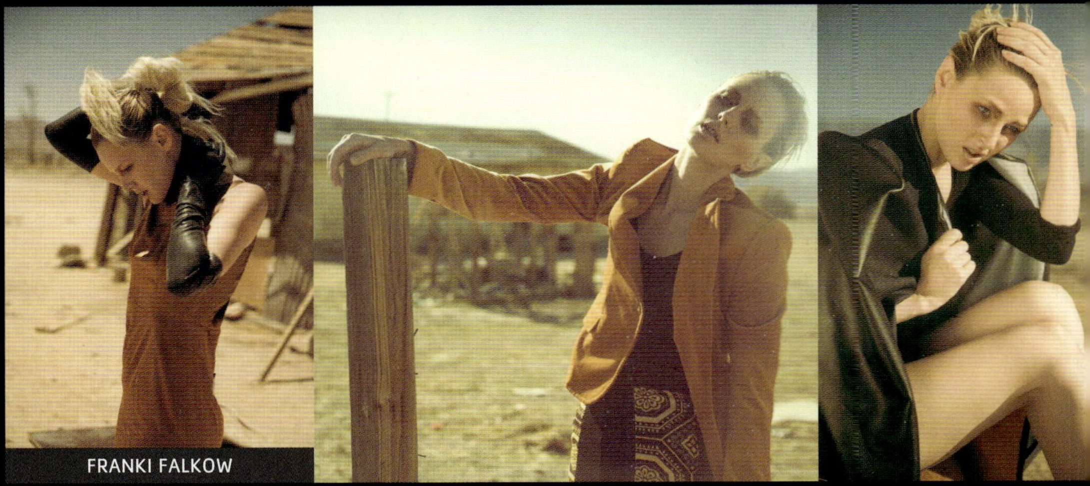

FRANKI FALKOW

Models are just the same as everyone else: they have feelings, they get nervous, they need encouragement, and they want to know if you're happy with an image. Like everyone, they benefit from positive reinforcement techniques!

There are good and bad ways to direct pose and incite emotion, and as you will learn over time, the amount of experience and talent a model has will dramatically affect how you interact with them. Throughout this book the relationship between model and photographer will be discussed from beginning to end; from finding a model, to the shoot itself, all the way through to sending off the final pictures. Although every model is different, there are certain sub-categories within the industry, and particular types of model that can be defined and examined. Whether it's editorial or commercial work, "time for print" or e-comm, the kind of shoot, the location, your team, and even how tired your model is (and how stressed you are) can affect how you communicate with those around you. This in turn affects the quality of your photography.

Photographers of all experience levels must learn to work effectively with models of all experience levels. To reinforce the importance of the relationship between model and photographer there will be interviews and testimonies from working professionals throughout this book, as well as the voice of photographer Adam Duckworth who will provide further insight and technical advice.

**FROM ADAM**

Making photos, rather than just taking photos, is what marks out an individual with the skills and potential to become a good fashion photographer. All amateurs start out taking photos—recording what's already there be it landscapes, cityscapes, friends having fun on vacation, their pets, or street reportage.

Eventually, though, with enough experience and the vision and desire to do something a little bit different, some photographers move on to making—or creating—their own images. They are not just choosing the right angle of view and lens, but controlling the lighting, collaborating with other creatives, directing the subject, and making images that try to go further than simply recording what was there. They are trying to evoke a feeling, an emotional response, or a desire.

To get to the level where a photographer can successfully do this is a fun journey, but one that can, at times, be frustrating. It is a journey where it's easy to get bogged down in the technicalities of photography, with lens choice and apertures, shutter speeds, flash durations, the inverse square law and much, much more all vying to keep a photographer concentrating on all the technical stuff at all times. Yet in essence, engaging with—and getting the best out of—your subject is by far the most important skill.

Of course, choosing and using the right kit is important, but a fashion photographer needs to become so used to dealing with the camera settings and lighting that it becomes second nature. Instead of constantly fiddling with camera dials, light meters, lighting rigs, and "chimping" every shot on the camera's LCD screen or computer screen, a great photographer can concentrate on what's really important—the subject. Whether that's a young model looking for confirmation they are doing OK, or a more experienced model looking for something more challenging, a photographer needs to be a people person; someone who intrinsically knows how to best interact with their subject, and juggle that with the demands of a client or art director looking over their shoulder on set.

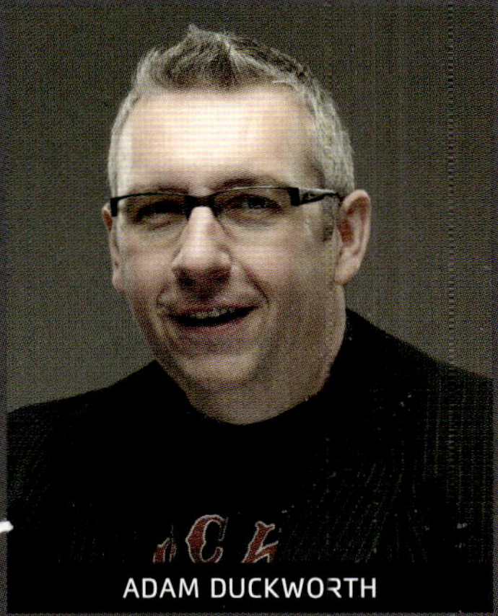
ADAM DUCKWORTH

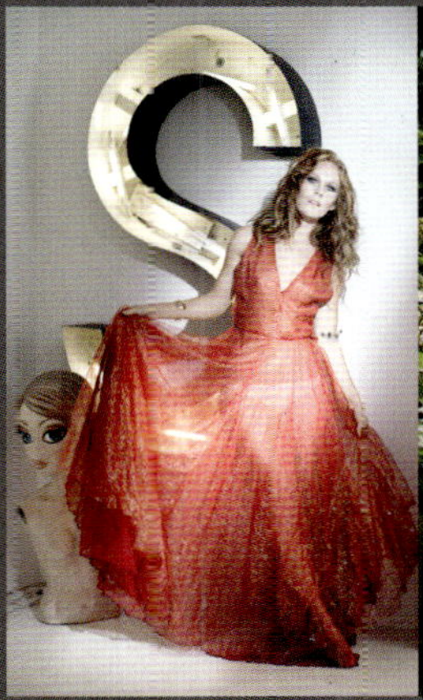

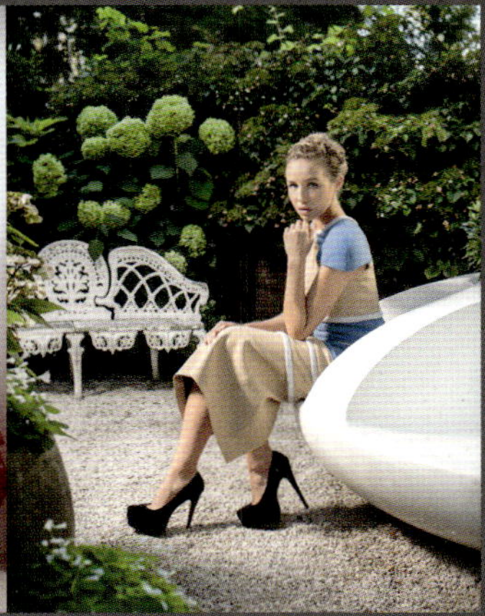

# MODEL & PHOTOGRAPHER:

## A RELATIONSHIP THROUGHOUT HISTORY

**THE HISTORY OF THE MODEL is intertwined with that of the fashion photographer, as the two are destined to be together: one simply cannot exist without the other.**

It was not until around 1910 that color photography was made available en masse, and fashion photographs began to appear frequently in publications such as *Vogue* and *La Mode*. The first modern fashion photography shoot was credited to Edward Steichen in 1911 when he photographed evening gowns for an edition of *Art et Decoration*, crushing any future ideas of simply illustrating a piece of clothing. Alongside fellow photographers such as Baron de Meyer and George Hoyningen-Huene, and later, Horst P. Horst and Cecil Beaton, a flood of creativity ensued involving the new medium. Fashion shoots were now staged and how a model was pictured began to hold meaning—a new and exciting industry had been created as the result of the relationship between artist and muse!

Escalating into the multi-billion-dollar business it is today, talents from both sides of the camera have revolutionized fashion photography, often by working together. From Twiggy in the 1960s, Christie Brinkley and Iman in the 1970s, Cindy Crawford and Elle "The Body" Macpherson in the 1980s, to "The Trinity"—Naomi Campbell, Christy Turlington, and Linda Evangelista—Kate Moss, Gisele, all the way to Tyra Banks, Liu Wen, Coco Rocha, and Cara Delevingne, iconic fashion models have helped change the shape and face of modern culture throughout the decades. That's not forgetting the boys: male models such as Jeff Aquilon, Mark Vanderloo, Tyson Beckford, and Andrej Pejic, naming only a few, have been making men feel insecure for many years!

Of course they could not have done this without the help of talented photographers: Richard Avedon, Irving Penn, Helmut Newton, David Bailey, Annie Leibovitz, Mario Testino, Patrick Demarchelier, Bruce Weber, Peter

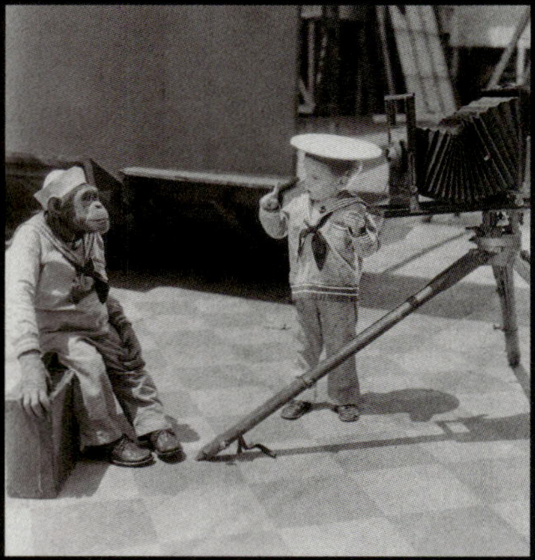

ABOVE: **FASHION FIRSTS**
Fine-art modeling can be traced back as far as Ancient Greece and the concept of the muse is thought to date back to the seventh century BC.

ABOVE: **AU PARIS**
The first photograph of a person was taken in 1839 in Paris, the "Daguerrotype." At the time fashion magazines printed pages with hand-colored pictures of clothing trends.

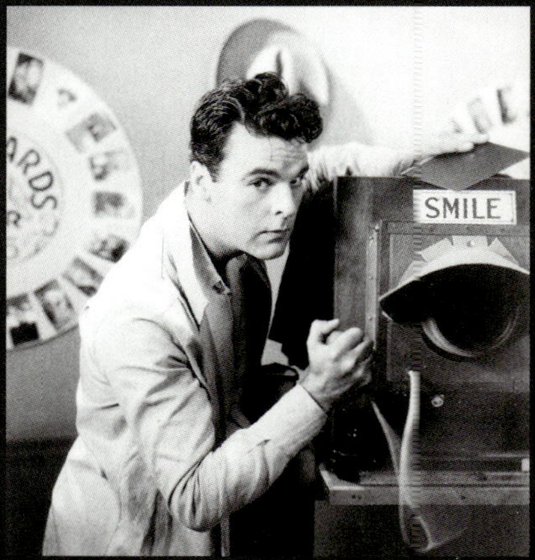


ABOVE: **TECHNICAL ADVANCES**
Color photography was developed in the early 1860s, however, it wasn't until around 1910 that fashion photographs began to appear in publications.

Lindbergh, Steven Meisel, Herb Ritts, Juergen Teller, Nick Knight, David LaChapelle, I could go on and on. They are all famous names, but you may not know what a single one of them looks like. From behind their cameras they have become known for their vision and their ability to capture moments that command an audience; images that spark an emotion. More often than not, this is created through their connection with their model.

Photographers and models frequently form life-long friendships and the photo shoot remains an intimate and artistic part of the process. You can't be a model without a photographer, and you can't be a fashion photographer without someone to take pictures of. The pair of you might really hit it off, or you may only interact with each other for a few hours. The key to winning fashion photography is creating a bond for as long as you are on set together: if both of you are happy it will show in your work.

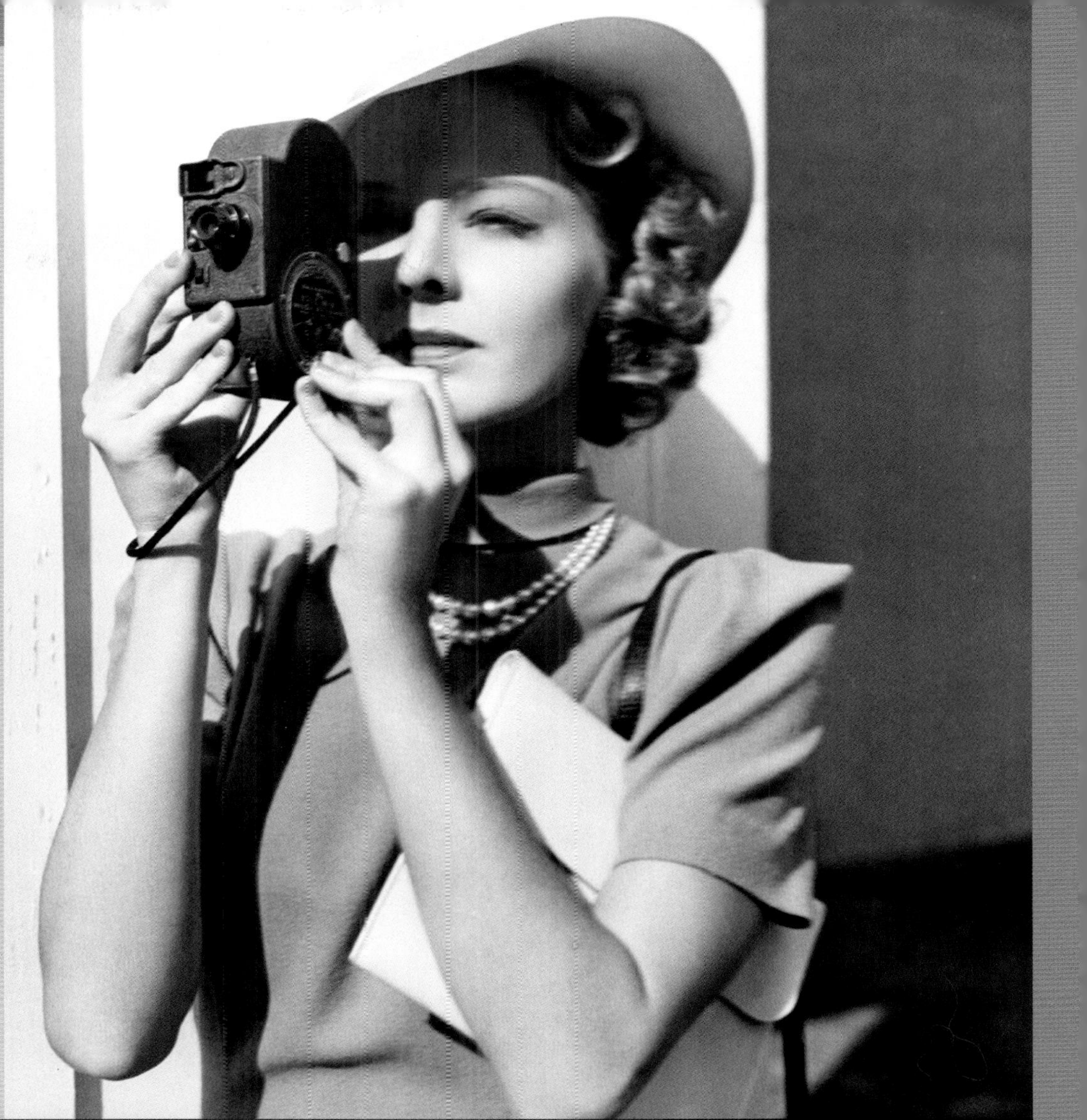

ABOVE: **BIG APPLE**
The term "Fashion Photographer" was coined in the 1950s when fashion photography was revolutionized in New York by photographers such as Richard Avedon and Irving Penn.

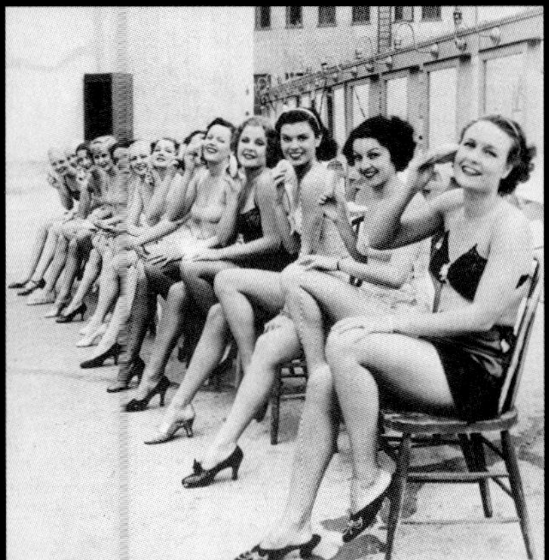

ABOVE: **MODEL LIFE**
Models came from all walks of life, from A-list society girls to ladies working as in-house mannequins in fashion stores.

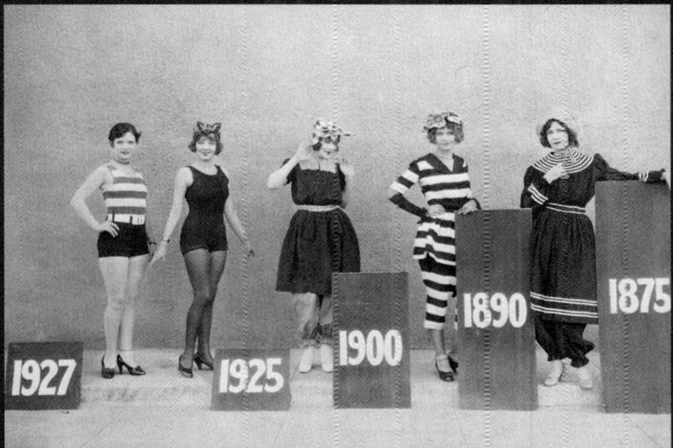


ABOVE: **OVER TIME**
The fashion industry has been hugely influential over our day-to-day lives. As it evolves so do trends and expectations, which can affect our culture as a whole.

# WHAT MAKES A MODEL?

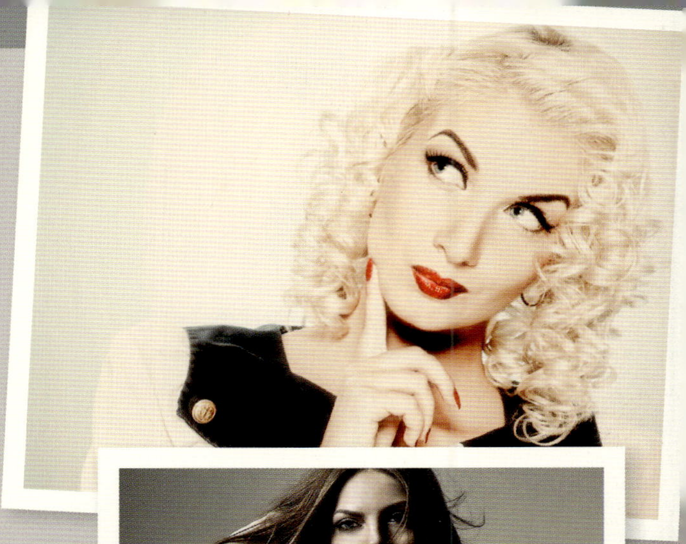

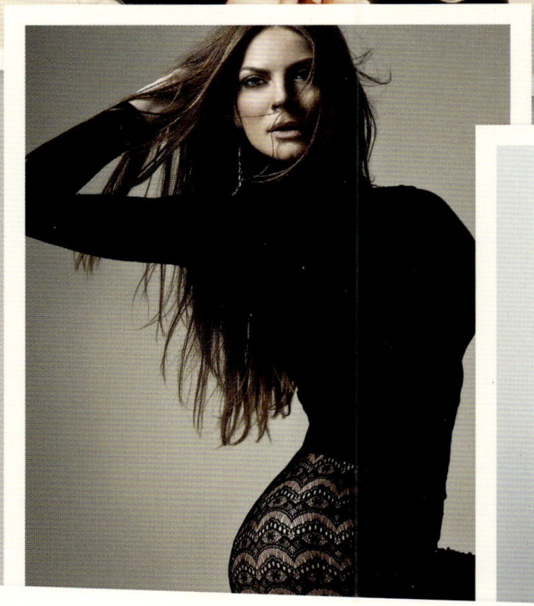

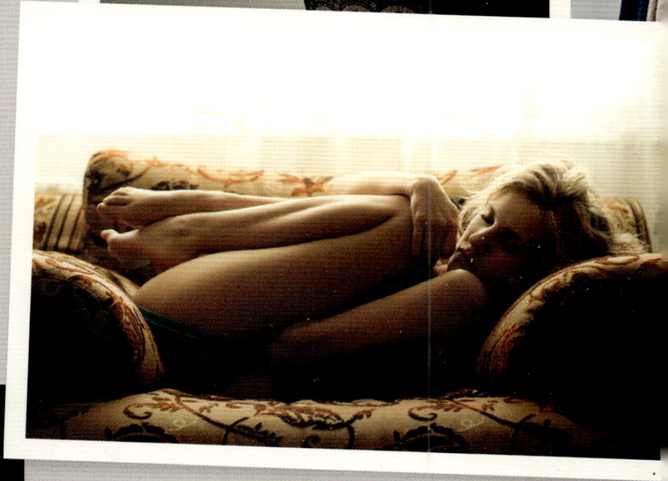

**NUMEROUS STEREOTYPES are associated with models, not all of them positive and—I can promise you—not all of them true. You might think you could spot a "real" model a mile away, and while it's true that the majority stand out in a crowd there is a lot more to modeling than good looks. Some stunning people photograph surprisingly badly and others who may not appear so "beautiful" can be incredibly photogenic. The truth is all kinds of people make successful, professional models, and that is what makes working in the industry so much fun.**

A model is someone who gets paid to be photographed, but in fashion someone can only call themselves a model when they have high-caliber agency representation. Agencies book a model's work in return for a fixed percentage of their rate, so the model is the equivalent of a financial investment. Accordingly the agencies contract under strict guidelines, assuring photographers and clients that the model meets a certain standard.

Of course this means that a model adheres to a particular aesthetic, with striking facial features, sufficient height, and a balanced figure. Though met with controversy, they must have measurements that suit the industry. This stems from culture, designers, sample sizes, and the belief that clothes hang better and with more impact on smaller frames. Thankfully the industry is evolving, and by introducing union rules—as some companies are—it is concentrating more on good health and making "strong" the new sexy.

> *Over the years I have learned that what is important in a dress is the woman who is wearing it.*
>
> **YVES SAINT LAURENT,** *fashion designer*

ABOVE: **ALL SORTS**
Models do have to have an appealing look and meet measurement requirements, but all kinds of people make the cut. Whether it is experience or representation that makes a model they certainly cannot be pigeonholed on personality.

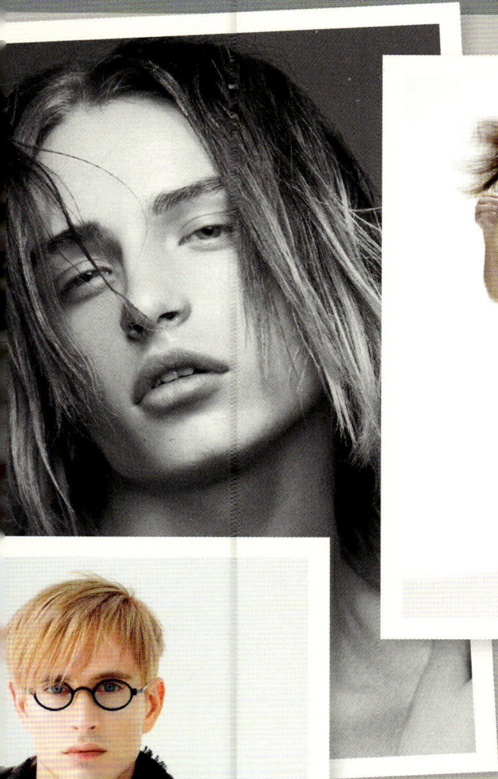

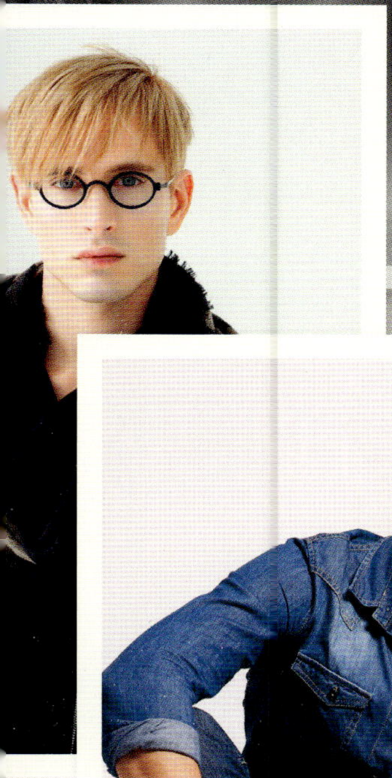

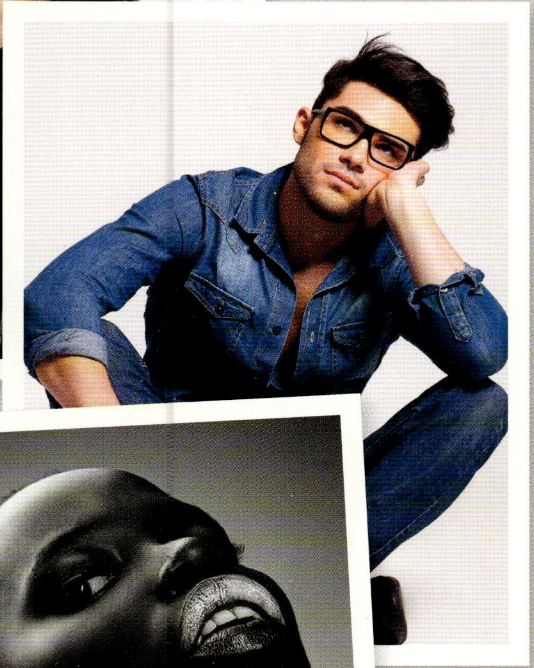

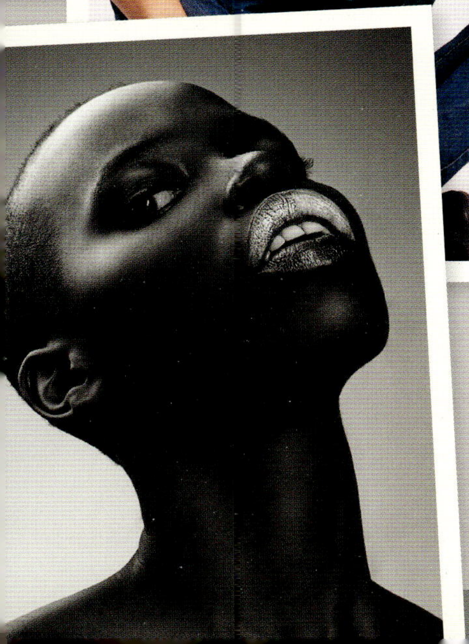

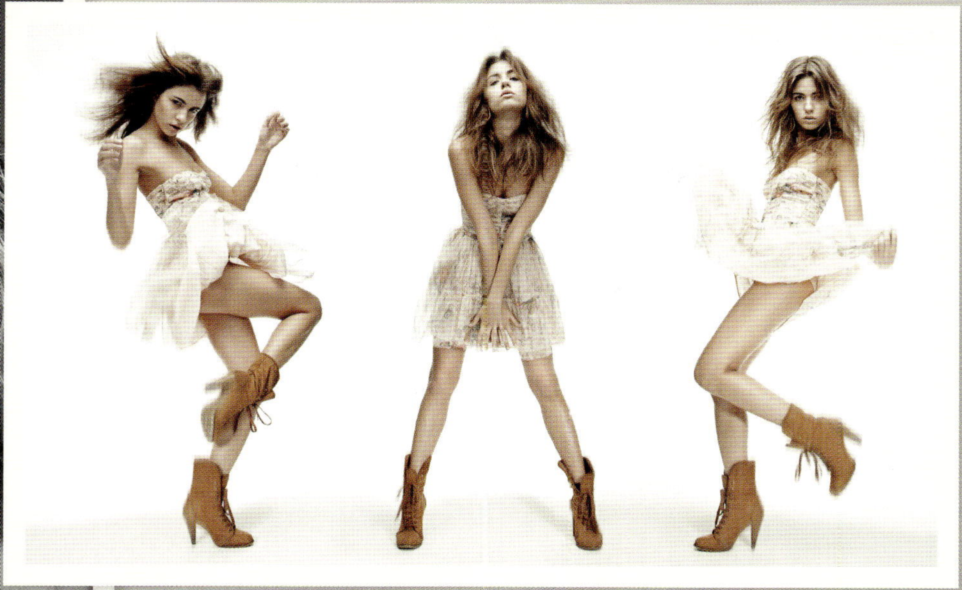

When you have to choose between ten gorgeous models, something else makes one of them stand out. Successful, profitable models are generally hard-working individuals with charm, people-skills, brains, and the versatility to work across multiple markets. Often models are well traveled, disciplined, and used to living independently from a very young age. They can also be excellent businessmen (and women)—I've heard child models negotiating overtime like they were on Wall Street!

There are all kinds of model, which we will discuss further throughout this book. Some are divas, some are laid back characters who simply wear clothes well, and others embody a particular lifestyle—maybe they live and breathe rock 'n' roll and still look bad ass even when they're wearing floral! However, the best models possess an inspirational and spontaneous energy, with enough emotional intelligence to interpret the different roles demanded of them by photographers, and enough personality to encourage someone to part with their hard-earned cash using only a facial expression. Models live unconventional lifestyles, as they are technically self-employed and only get paid when they are working. Therefore they must try to exploit themselves with dignity. They cast constantly (like going on a job interview every day) and they have to develop a thick skin to survive, as dealing with rejection is an integral part of that process. An unfortunate number are deceiving with their confidence and you must learn to spot insecurities.

**LOOKS CAN BE DECEIVING**

Never judge someone by how they appear. Just because you think someone is good looking, you can't assume that they are confident and laid back. One of the reasons people work for so long in this industry is because every day you meet different, creative, talented people. Every model you meet is an individual and every shoot is a story; your photographic experience will only improve from connecting with them.

# 01

# STARTING OUT

**PHOTOGRAPHY, ON THE WHOLE, can be rather expensive. Camera equipment, lights, lenses, computers—the list is endless. So it might deter you slightly knowing that at the beginning of your career you're going to have to work for free. A lot. However, in this chapter we are going to discuss how "Time for print" can benefit you, and how it allows you the time to practice and experiment, building your portfolio and profile. There is advice on how to start out with very little money; keeping things simple yet effective; where to find a model; and how to put together a team. With the following information and some determination on your part, it is possible to start out on a relatively small budget and still achieve great results.**

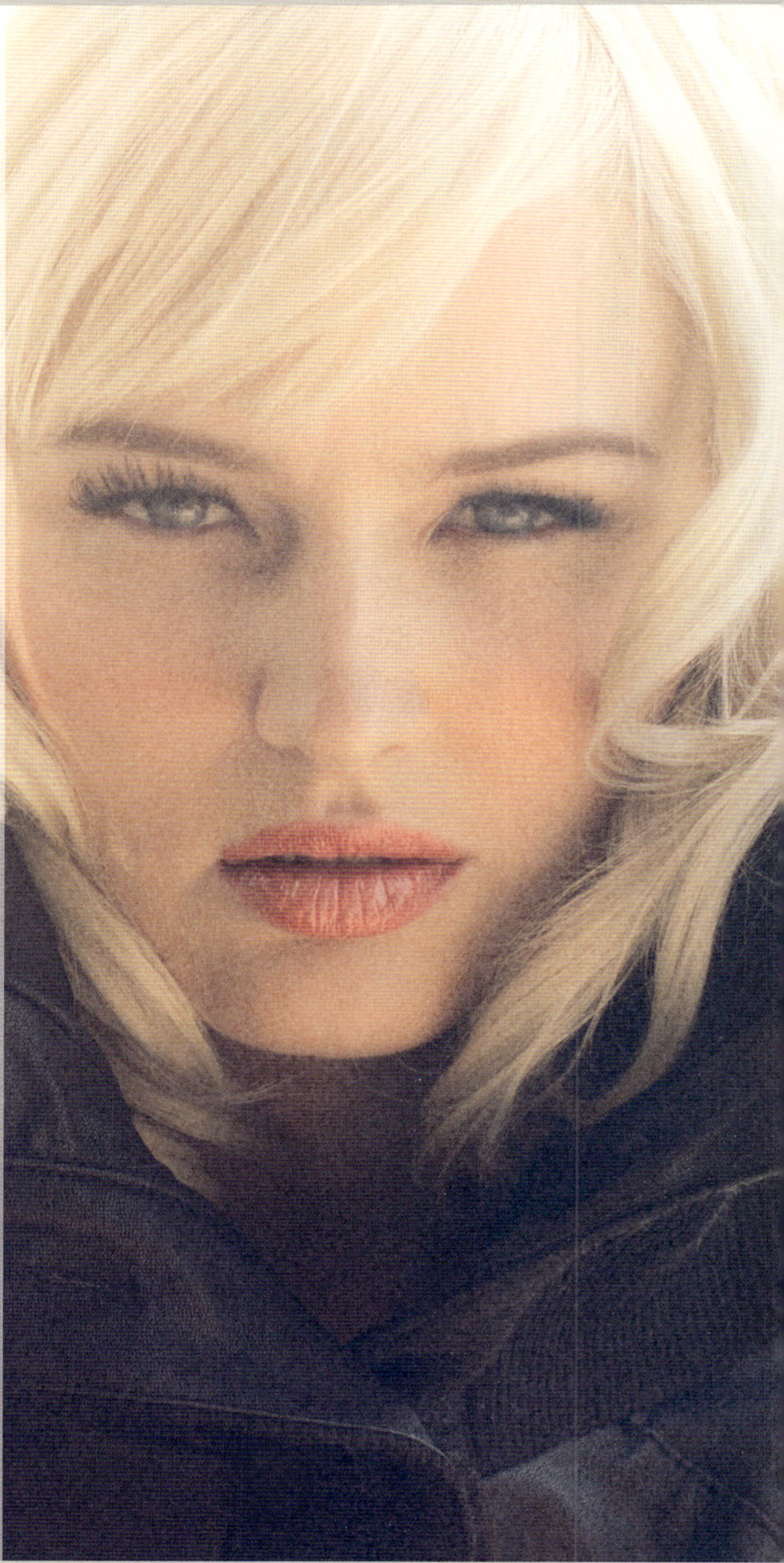

RIGHT: **START SOMEWHERE**
The idea of finding a model to shoot might seem daunting. Remember, everyone has to start somewhere. Every famous photographer had to ask their first muse to pose. It is possible.

# KEEPING IT SIMPLE

**HIGH-END ADVERTISING CAMPAIGNS and fashion editorials can run to hundreds of thousands of dollars in production costs, which is always worth remembering when you're seeking inspiration for your next shoot in *Vogue* magazine! You're going to have to start small and simple, with realistic expectations. Highlight the model in your photographs, concentrate on a single expression or emotion, and avoid over-complicating things with expensive props and sets until you're ready.**

Use what you have (you can create a studio using an old bed sheet in your lounge if necessary) or shoot outside: natural light is free and there are plenty of great alfresco backdrops with no permit costs. Shoot in your house, against walls, in gardens, and offer friends with nice apartments a bottle of wine and some flowers to use them for a few hours. Find out what equipment you can borrow and ask an attractive buddy if they don't mind you taking some shots of them. If you can't find a makeup artist or stylist, ask the model if they can do their own makeup and raid the wardrobes of your more fashionable friends. Hustle!

Your time costs nothing, but use it wisely. The best shoots all result from at least a little preparation, so explore potential locations and record the light and any safety issues. Write a brief outlining what you want to achieve, as this will center you and can be used to explain to others what you are working toward. Experimentation beforehand is priceless, as it is better to encounter problems and solve them in advance, rather than stressing out on the day and risking the shoot.

You don't need masses of equipment in the beginning, but you do need to know how to use it. Training courses can be expensive, but you can also learn the business by assisting working, professional photographers. There is competition for these positions even when you might not be paid, because not only are you gaining knowledge on the job and familiarizing yourself with the shooting environment, but there is also the opportunity to make contacts and maybe pick up work along the way.

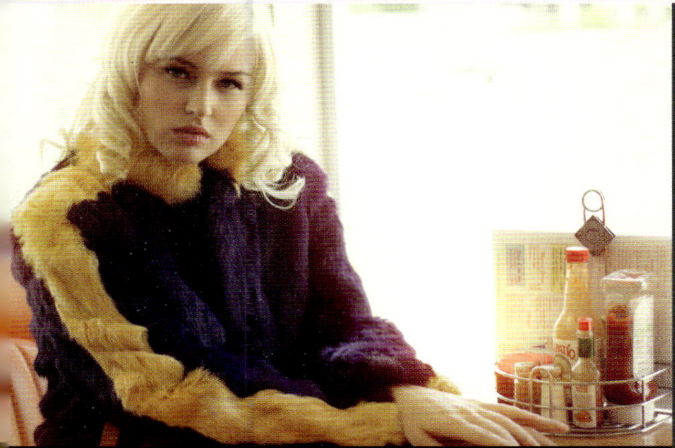

ABOVE: **USE WHAT YOU HAVE**
For this shot we stopped in at a local diner I use regularly. They often rent the space, but as they recognized me they allowed us to shoot inside for a few minutes, for free.

RIGHT: **YARD WORK**
This test shot was taken in just a few minutes in the photographer's backyard. I'm wearing my own clothes and we used a hose to wet my hair and body at the end of the day.

FAR RIGHT:
**OH, THE GLAMOUR!**
This image was taken in a studio that had been set up temporarily in the photographer's living room, using a roll of paper on stands as a make-do infinity curve for the background.

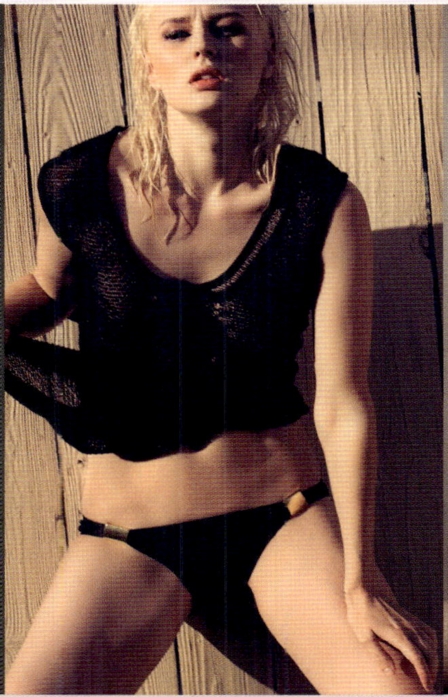

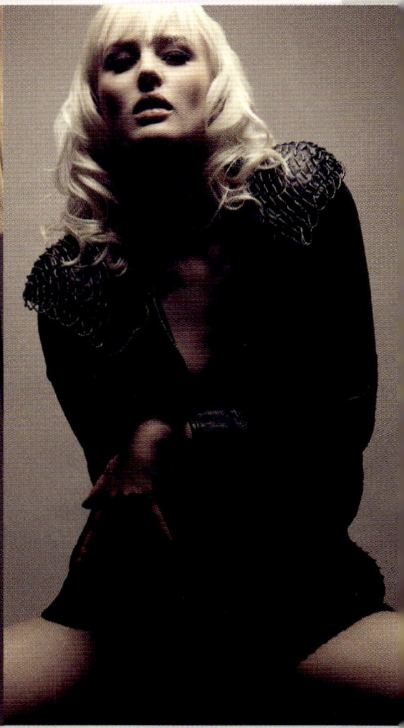

# FINDING A MODEL

**IT IS A REASSURINGLY WELL-KNOWN fact that you can't just walk into a professional modeling agency and ask them to send pretty girls round for you to take pictures of. However, it does make the process of casting and testing models more difficult at the beginning of your career. However, at that stage your focus should be on practicing and learning through experience, so take pictures of everyone and anyone who'll let you. I'm talking family, friends, sisters of friends, their dogs, cats, basically anything with eyes. If you are familiar with your subject it can create a more comfortable shooting environment, reducing any pressure and allowing you to experiment more freely.**

When you start to appeal to strangers for photo shoots make sure you appear professional. Print up-to-date business cards and keep your website current and accessible. Take control of your social media to create a strong online presence. As technology advances, your behavior and kudos across the popular networking sites becomes increasingly important and models often post booking information on their profiles.

The web has become a very powerful tool for aspiring photographers. Paid profile websites for amateur models have become increasingly well known (with varying reputations), transforming and expanding the industry. These websites allow you to create a profile, upload a limited number of images (unless you pay a fee), and then use various search criteria, such as location, measurements, experience, and nudity clauses to source models, makeup artists, hairdressers, and stylists in your area. You can advertise casting calls, correspond with fellow members, and book paid work or TFP ("time for print"). There are also extensive forums on these sites that

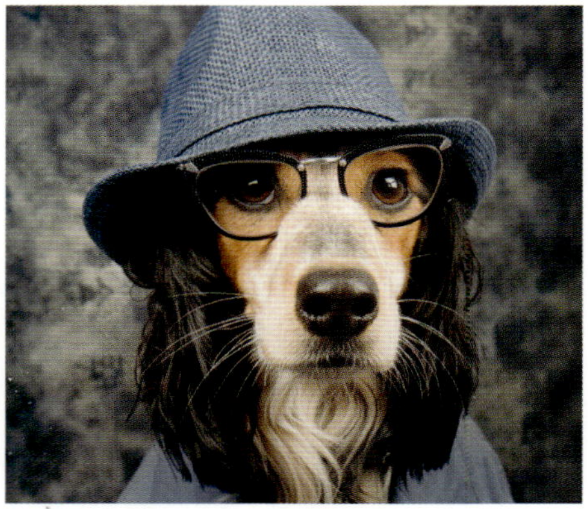

ABOVE: **SAY CHEESE**
When you're starting out, shoot everything, everybody, anywhere you can. It's all learning experience and with digital, mistakes can be deleted easily.

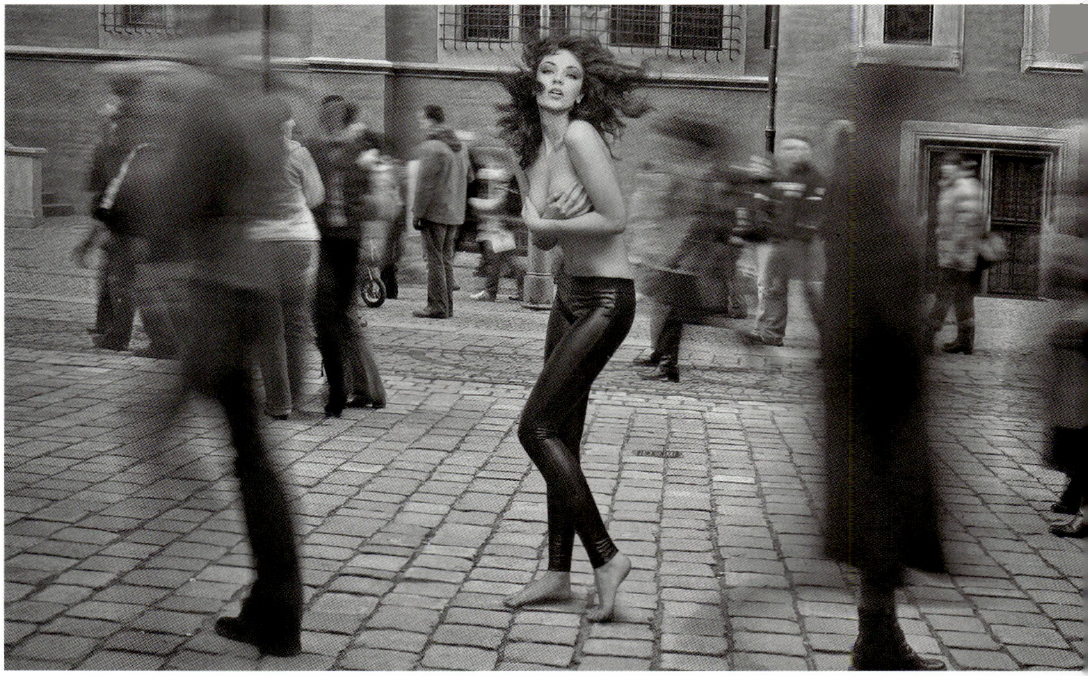

RIGHT: **LOST**
It might seem like there is so much choice online that it's difficult to find the right model. Eliminate through location and availability first, then go on instinct.

can provide answers to any industry-related questions you may have.

Websites such as these encourage equal opportunities, opening doors for passionate amateurs who would previously never have found an outlet for representation. If your interests lie in specific genres such as fine art, horror, fetish, glamour, or "alternative" you will find a number of members online with similar tastes.

However, the introduction of these sites has met with controversy across the modeling industry. There are photographers using them successfully, but there is no denying the risk of exploitation. A vast amount of sexually-charged content lacks the professionalism that an agency or client would require, and there is also a safety issue—not everyone represents themselves honestly online. Female photographers especially should be aware of the risks associated with shooting alone or inviting someone they don't know into their home.

In high fashion spheres, these websites aren't regarded in the best light. It is a blunt truth, but if you use amateur models you will produce amateur photographs. Professional models have to meet certain standards to get representation, and this is for a reason: ultimately they have to sell a lifestyle or product.

These sites can be seen as a gateway, though, especially if you're struggling to find people to pose for you. Be honest about your skill levels and communicate openly. Network, ask questions, have fun, but move on when you are ready. This is a competitive industry and it can be more obvious than you think when you're using sub-par models. Assess the kind of professional presence you are aiming for.

> *"All my early shoots were with models I met on Model Mayhem. We shot outside with natural light: the models weren't concerned and valued the safety of public places. Though one did bring her mum..."*
>
> **THOMAS COLE SIMMONDS,** *photographer*

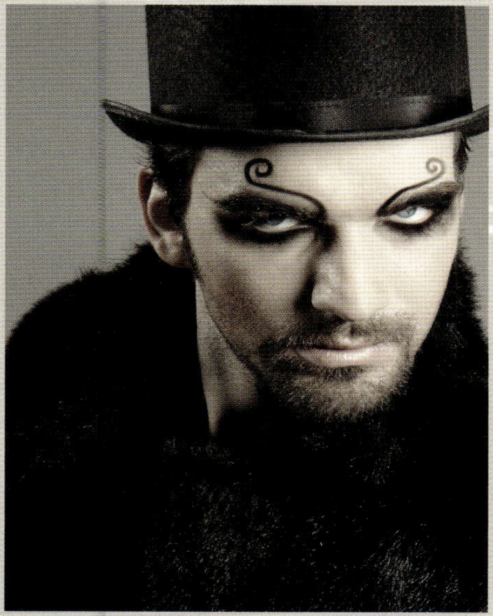

ABOVE: **BE PARTICULAR**
There is room for everyone to create what they love, no matter how others might perceive the results. Genre work can be lucrative.

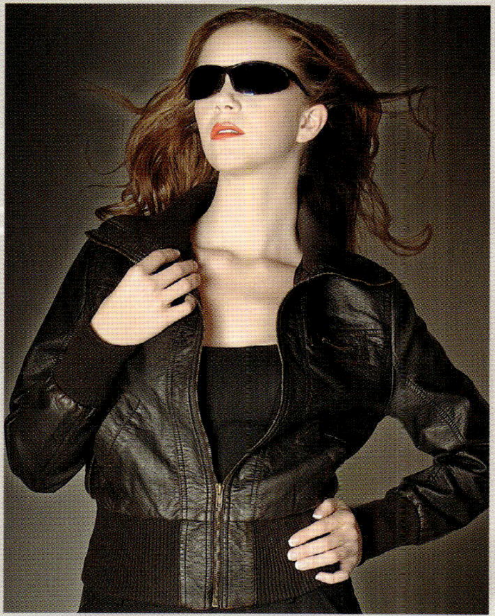

ABOVE: **UNDER PAR**
There is no denying that amateur models and photographers can create amateur pictures. The result can lead to a lack of quality control.

### INTERNET SLANG

**TFP:** "Time for print," meaning the model gives their time in exchange for portfolio pictures.

**GWC:** (Creepy) Guy With Camera. Models will steer clear of (and photographers will want to avoid being labeled as) a GWC, which is usually an amateur photographer with ulterior motives. Be careful to keep your online reputation clean as red flags travel like wild fire in this industry.

# BUILDING A PROFILE

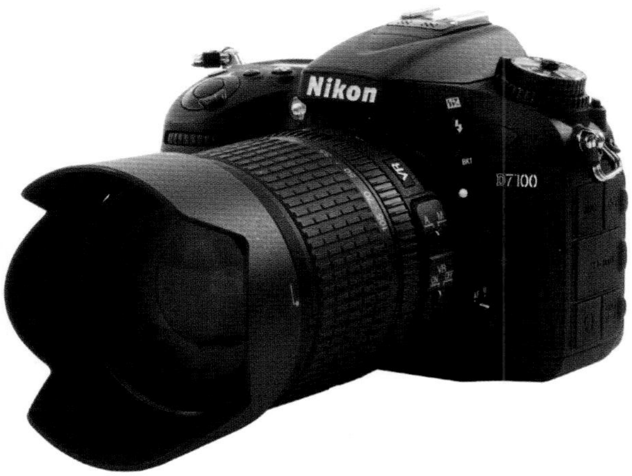


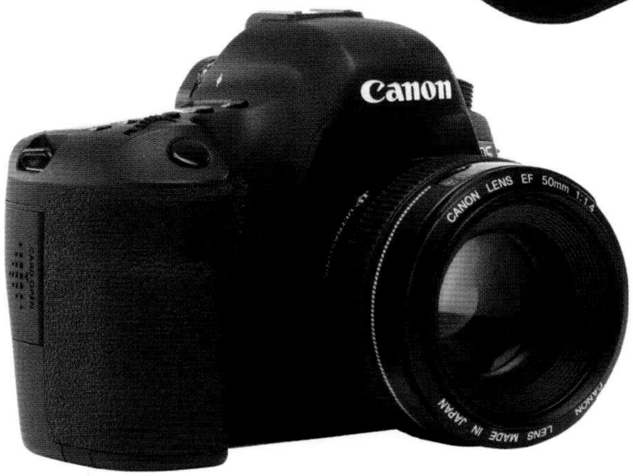


ABOVE: **NIKON D7100**
Equipped with its image-stabilized kit lens, Nikon's latest crop-sensor consumer camera—the D7100—is a fantastic and capable camera.

LEFT: **CANON EOS 6D**
The EOS 6D is Canon's first truly affordable full-frame camera. Teamed with a prime lens, it's a brilliant combination.

**ONE OF THE GREATEST THINGS about photographing models is that you don't need to invest too much in equipment, even though many of the top professionals use cameras, lenses, and lighting that cost a small fortune. Medium-format digital cameras, a bagful of leaf-shutter lenses, and a battery of studio and location lighting are all wonderful to have or to hire. However, a basic DSLR, a single zoom lens, and a reflector can also make images that are high enough quality to be used in lots of magazines. Many of the greatest fashion shots have been taken on simple equipment using just natural light.**

A modern consumer-level DSLR will have enough pixels and dynamic range to shame the top pro-spec DSLRs of just a few years ago. Models from Canon and Nikon lead the way, but other manufacturers also make great kit, too. However, as you progress you'll find more rental equipment and lenses are available for Nikon and Canon cameras, so it can be a wise choice to start here. The kit zoom lens that most cameras come with can be an adequate starting point, but a far better option is to buy a prime lens. A 50mm *f*/1.8 lens is fast, light, and inexpensive, and on a crop sensor consumer camera it becomes the equivalent of an 85mm lens—ideal for portraits. If you have a semi-pro, full-frame DSLR like a Canon EOS 6D or Nikon D700, then an 85mm *f*/1.8 lens would be a good option. These cameras and lenses cost more than crop-sensor cameras, but have better performance at higher ISO readings and are often more ruggedly built. After that, investing in good quality lenses like a 24–70mm *f*/2.8 or a 70–200mm *f*/2.8 would be a sensible move—they may be pricey, but they'll last for years.

For controlling lighting, reflectors are a great addition to your kit and can be light, portable, and cheap. A good kit to buy is a single reflector with up to five alternative covers. These usually include white for softness and subtlety; silver for efficiency and crispness; gold for warmth; silver/ gold for some warmth; and black for subtracting light, making shadows go deeper. A tripod is also a very useful accessory as it helps you get sharp images when light levels fall. Learn to use kit like this before you move on and buy more expensive equipment.

The next step would be to buy a portable flash that you could control manually, an inexpensive radio flash trigger, a lightstand, and some way of modifying the light, such as an umbrella or softbox. This off-camera flash will open up a whole new world of possibilities, especially when the natural light isn't great or you are shooting indoors.

## GETTING YOUR WORK OUT THERE

Once you have started to build up a body of work, it's essential you get it seen. When starting off, hosting your photos on web-based photo sharing sites, such as Flickr or 500px, can be a great way of getting exposure and critique. Web-based model sites such as Model Mayhem or Net Models can also be seen as useful resources as you gain more experience. However, once you start to take it more seriously, nothing compares to a proper website with your own URL.

You don't need to spend thousands of dollars on a custom-designed site. If you are relatively computer literate there are lots of inexpensive WordPress themes specially designed to show off a portfolio. For a little bit more you could buy an off-the-shelf portfolio site such as those made by Photoshelter or Creative Motion Design, which offer ease of use and lots of features. Ideally select one that's not based on Flash, as this won't work on Apple devices such as iPhones or iPads.

What's most important is that you have a cohesive body of work on there. If you want to be taken seriously as a photographer who shoots models, your site needs to be focused on that rather than hundreds of pictures of landscapes, vacations, cars, or weddings. A site about your fashion work marks you out as a fashion photographer, and ideally should have a sense of your specific shooting style, rather than a mash-up of different styles. A well written "about me" page is also essential, as statistics show it's one of the most viewed features of any website.

It's worth getting a second opinion: a website with several poor pictures can drag the overall quality down. Also, try to avoid showing lots of photos from a single shoot, as this will suggest that your work doesn't have any depth to it. If you're ready to start looking for work, then using social media such as Twitter or Facebook can be useful if you keep your accounts professional, rather than including personal ramblings. Also useful is the old-fashioned method of picking up the phone to prospective clients or agencies. Try to find the name of the person you need to speak to and target them with a card, followed-up by a call or email. If you can, arrange a face-to-face meeting where you can talk about your work and show your portfolio (either as a printed book or on a tablet computer). And always show interest in the client's needs.

### TIP
### PRINT YOUR WORK

A professionally printed portfolio can really create a great impression and make your work stand out from the rest. They may have fallen out of favor compared to web portfolios or tablet computers, but a custom-made book, embossed with your own name or logo, really makes a statement about who you are. Search the web and you'll find suppliers of portfolios that range from affordable to exotic and luxurious to suit your budget. Just remember to keep it updated often.

BELOW LEFT & RIGHT: **PROFESSIONAL RESULTS**
A couple of basic flashes, a softbox, an umbrella, and a willing friend are all you need to get truly professional results.

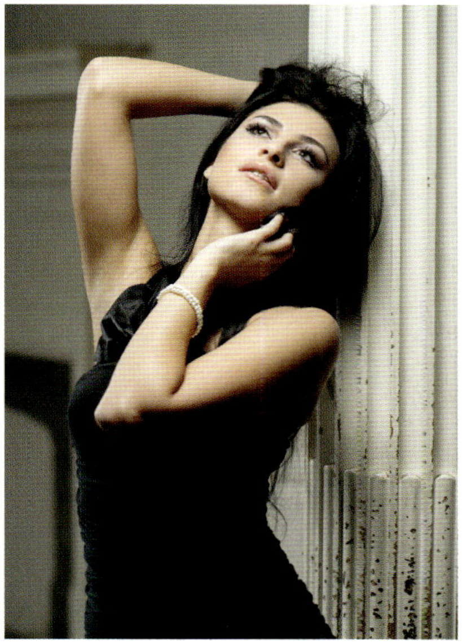

THE SCENE

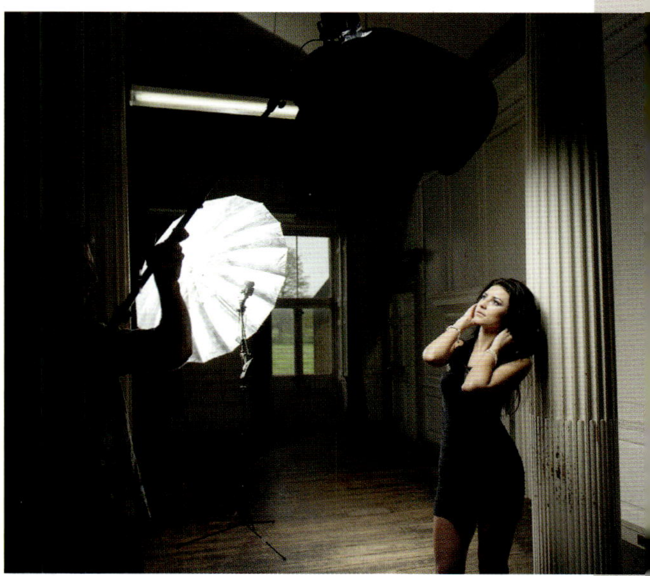

BEHIND THE SCENES

# TESTING

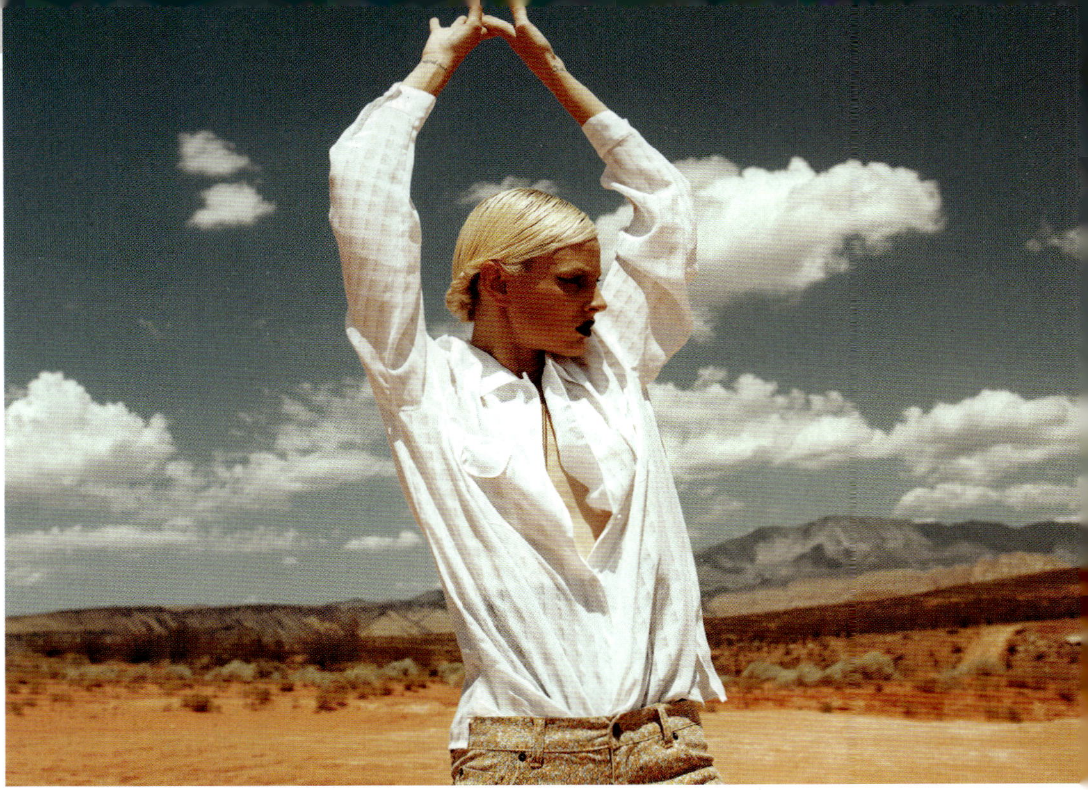

**EVERYONE WITH A CAMERA wants to get paid to take pictures of beautiful people, but the reality is that fashion photography rates work on a sliding scale. In the beginning you will be expected to shoot on a "TFP" (time for print) basis, or "Tests" as they are called in agency circles. This means that no one on the shoot gets paid: the model and team give up their time and expertise for credit and images for their portfolios. The majority of photographers and models continue to test throughout their careers as the creative process can be extremely beneficial.**

For a photographer, testing will help you build your book, or portfolio, which is essentially a marketing tool to help you establish professional relationships with agencies and get paid work from clients. Testing allows you to gain invaluable knowledge and experience, while hopefully developing a personal style that agencies and clients are looking for.

> *It helps if you're approached with respect for your time, as the amount of prep work that goes into a shoot for the stylist is at least a day on each end. It's extra nice if the photographer offers some sort of minor token compensation such as gas money or being treated to dinner afterward.*
>
> **NATALIE TOREN,** *stylist*

The beauty of a test is that you have the freedom to shoot any concept and any location you like, but ultimately try to keep a consistency to your work. Experiment with lighting to convey expression, find out what inspires you, talk to your models, and enjoy the collective creativity. Remember that your team and the model (and, if they are represented, their agency) require certain shots too, so discuss with everyone beforehand what they hope to achieve. Shoot half the shots for you, and half for them. Makeup artists and hair stylists will want their hard work featured, for example, and stylists may need a particular piece of jewelry highlighted as it's been borrowed from a store on the promise of free advertising. So be sure to listen to your team. Afterward, make sure you are prompt with sending selects and finished images—this is where many photographers ruin their reputation.

### BLACK AND WHITE

Don't just include black-and-white images when sending finished shots to the model

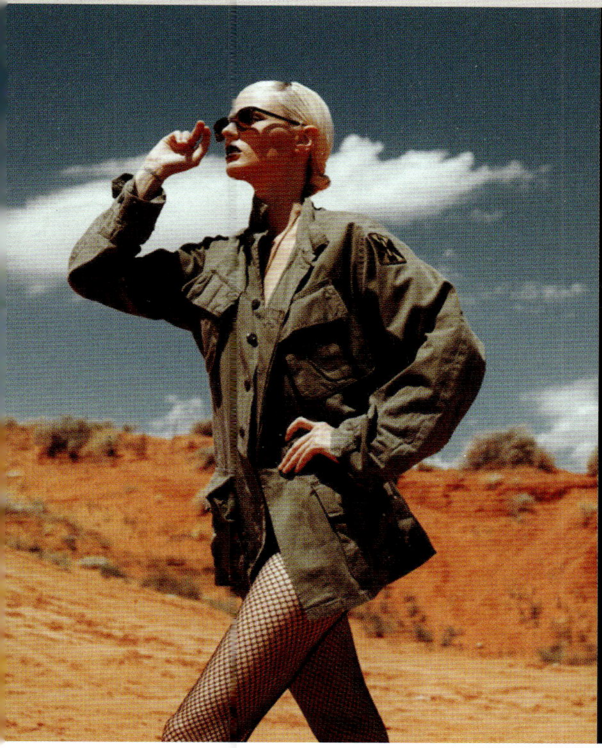

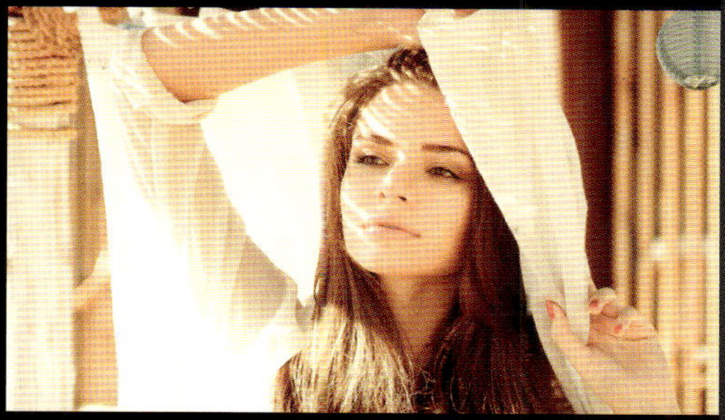

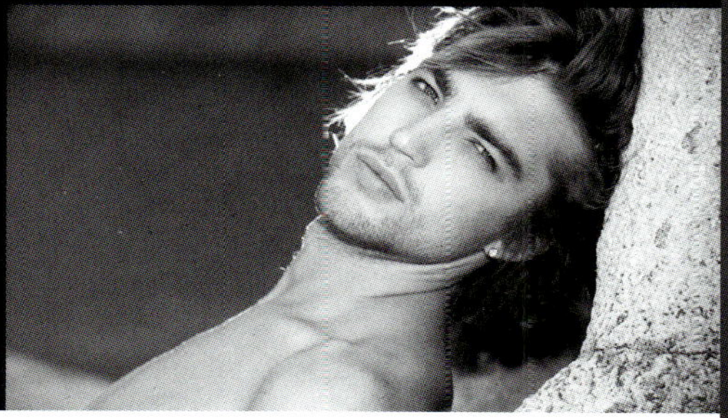

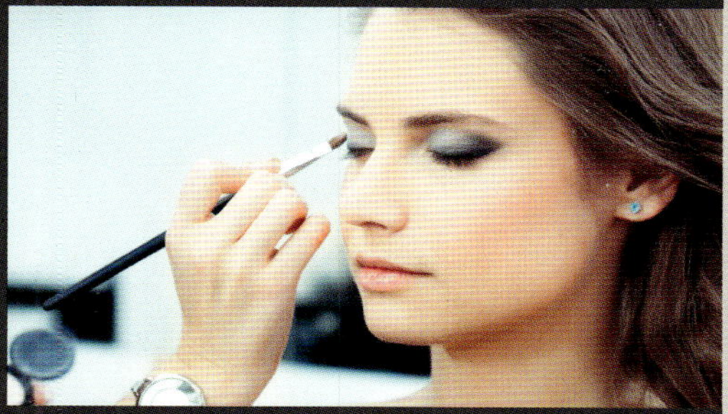

FAR LEFT & OPPOSITE: **DESERTED**
These shots were achieved in under an hour in the Utah desert. The only time we had in the heat. The clothes are from local thrift stores, and makeup and hair styled to suit the intense conditions.

LEFT: **GOOD MORNING SUNSHINE**
Whether you have purchased a full lighting set-up or have nothing to play with but the sun, keep changing things up and practicing at different times of the day.

ABOVE LEFT: **BLACK AND WHITE**
Though you should avoid shooting every frame in black and white, when testing it can be useful to forgive a multitude of fashion photography sins should they arise.

ABOVE: **READY FOR YOUR CLOSE-UP?**
Makeup artists can spend hours painting details onto a model's face. Shoot close-ups near the beginning of the shoot to highlight the work when it's fresh.

and your team. Maintain a balance, as details in the makeup can get lost without color.

## GETTING YOUR TEAM TOGETHER

The quality of your fashion photography will only meet professional standards once you employ the skills of a trained makeup artist, hair stylist, wardrobe stylist, and possibly an assistant.

As a fashion photographer you will primarily be selling clothing and accessories, so a stylist can be a crucial asset in proving your ability to shoot the product. A stylist can provide you with items from designers or borrowed from shops, as they often have extensive personal wardrobes and will have built valuable relationships with fashion houses and magazines.

Shoddy makeup and hair can often be the downfall of a shoot. Research the beauty pages in fashion magazines and online, and create mood boards of faces you like and looks that you're drawn to. In the beginning, less is generally more, so take your time and collaborate with trained individuals you connect with on a creative level. Nowadays many artists are comfortable with both hair and makeup, which will save you money in the future, although it increases preparation time on set.

A photo shoot can often be a balancing act, keeping a team motivated and communication demands energy. You will be forced to work with all kinds of people, but try to find those that work well with others, who can remain positive, and who are inspiring and understanding, even when you're chasing light or your camera has stopped working. Strong teams create strong images.

### TIP A TEAM EFFORT

It's good to work with a variety of people, but photographers will often find a team they like and stick with it. Those artists should be reliable, with range, and be willing to experiment spontaneously—you want to avoid using the same look in every shot.

# 02

# PLANNING & CASTING

IF YOU DON'T HAVE A SPECIFIC model in mind for a shoot, it's time to hold a casting, which is the modeling equivalent of an audition. In this chapter we are going to explore the casting process from beginning to end, from sourcing an appropriate location, choosing who to invite, etiquette on the day, and making a final decision. If you choose to take the plunge and start working with modeling agencies, take a look at *Approaching Agencies* on page 26 for information on how to successfully prepare and subsequently develop those relationships.

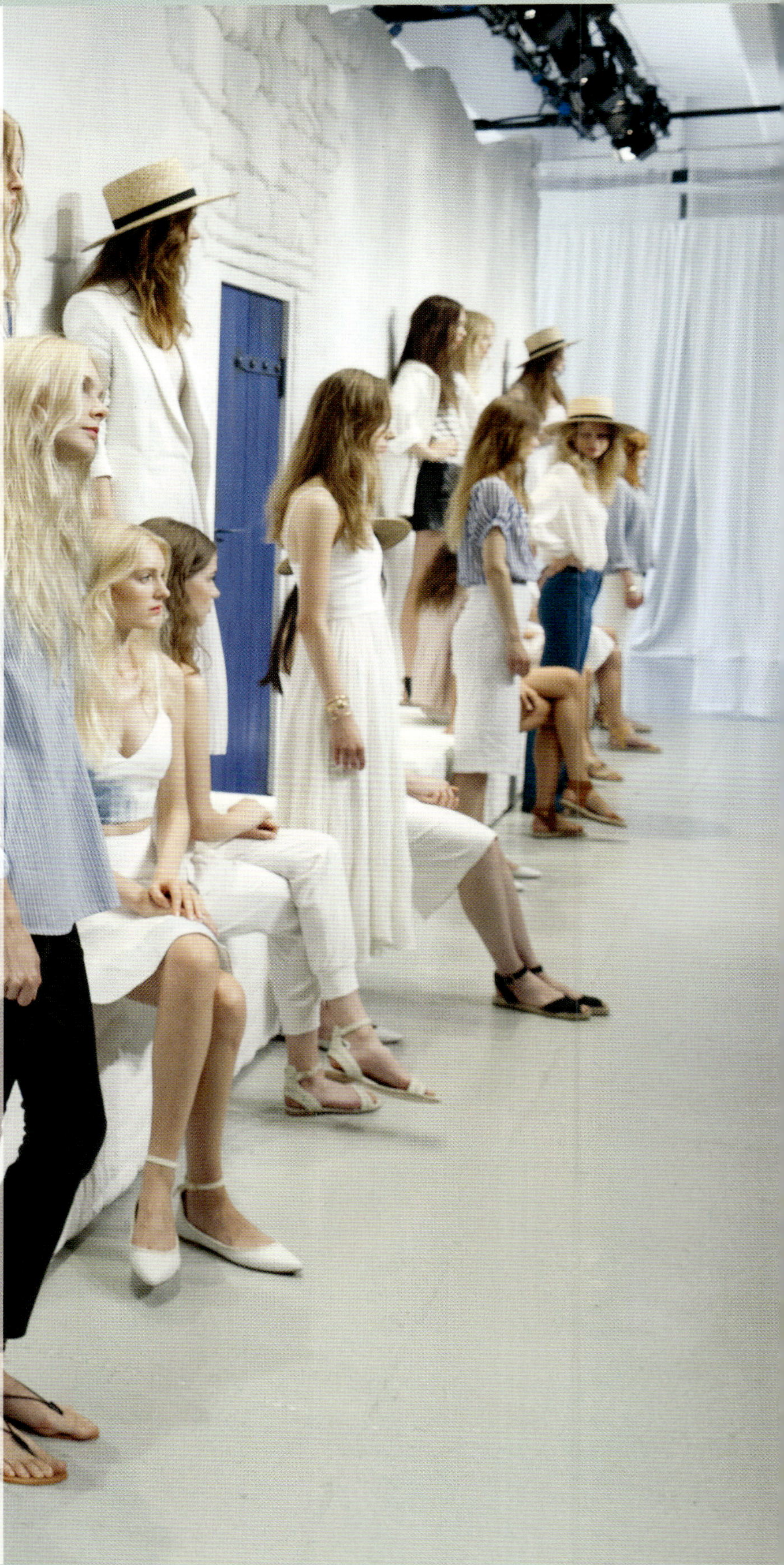

RIGHT: **CASTING FOR FREE**
You do not have to pay models to come to a casting, but be respectful that they might be paying out for gas, train tickets, and z-cards just to attend.

# THE CASTING SPACE

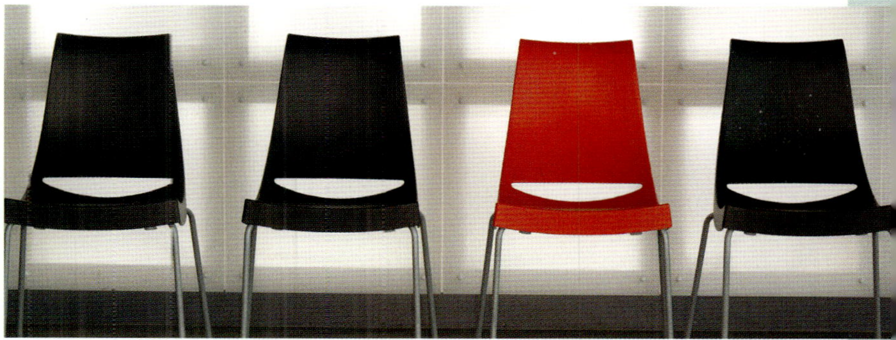

ABOVE: **FORGET A FACE?**
It will be difficult to remember everyone's face without taking photographs for future reference. Select a series of standard set-ups, such as a close-up and a full length.

So, you've decided on a project (or you've been assigned one) and now you want to find the perfect model for the job. Hang on a second, where exactly are you going to hold a casting? Is your apartment tidy? Is your flatmate sane? Location is everything when holding an effective casting session, so start by figuring out how accessible you are. Models often have multiple castings in one day and will at times dismiss castings that are difficult to get to. You can ask the models to travel to you, set up appointments at individual agencies, or consider hiring or borrowing a space closer to the nearest city and posting a casting call. Avoid coffee shops and other public places, though, as I know from experience that it can get awkward if more than one model turns up at once.

### TIP GETTING THE TIMING RIGHT

Based on the approximate number of models attending, castings can run all day or for a few hours, but providing models with a time frame will generally prevent no-shows. You can separate models by agency, age range, or maybe see girls during the first hour and guys the second.

Many models rely on public transport, so think about the nearest bus and train stops. Others may be "new faces" who drive for hours with their parents (don't be shocked if models turn up with partners, friends, or even dogs!), so make sure you are easily contactable and provide information if there are specific parking rules or gated entrances for example.

Next, what is the casting space itself like? You need a certain amount of space depending on how many models you've invited within the time frame. It is a good idea to have a "waiting area" and it's considerate to think about the number of chairs and if water and restrooms are available. I would advise providing a sheet of paper and pen so the models can start a "sign-in page" to avoid any issues with queue jumping.

Think about your position in the room. If you're expecting models to try clothing on make sure there is a private space, even if it's a makeshift screen in the corner. A well-lit white wall provides a neutral backdrop for casting shots, but make sure you have room to shoot full length. A camera and lighting set-up you're comfortable with is imperative for speed, it's embarrassing when you don't know your settings or the camera batteries are flat and a model is stood waiting. It is possible to rent studio spaces (with equipment), but obviously this comes at a price.

Timing is important, so decide beforehand how long you'd like to spend with each model. Be realistic, though: you will be browsing portfolios and conversing, which is great as you want to gauge a model's personality, but it often lasts longer than you'd expect. You'll also need to take photographs for future reference. It's usually easier to pick a few standard shots; full length, profiles, three quarters, and a close-up to save yourself time and memory.

# CASTING

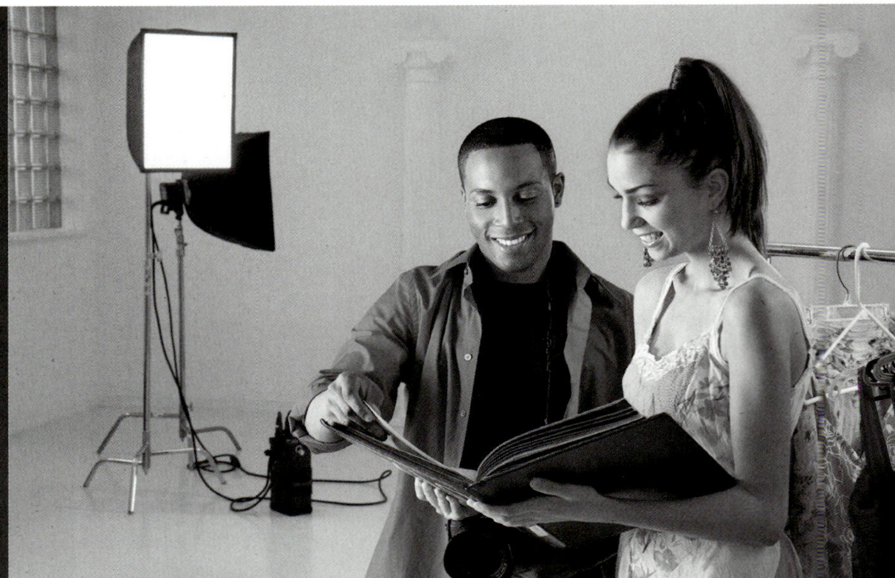

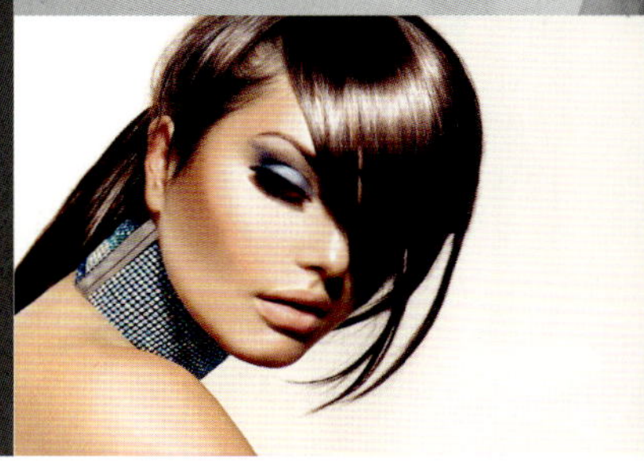

ABOVE & LEFT: **SPEED CASTING**
It might sound difficult to learn enough about a person in a meeting that could only last a few minutes to make such an important decision, but the more sessions you hold the more adept you will become at spotting positive modeling attributes at speed.

**CASTING IS THE TIME when you find the model best suited to your creative vision, or who will sell the product most effectively to its target market. Hopefully they will be fun to work with as well!**

Start by doing your research. Model portfolios are available online on both agency and freelance websites. Find faces you like and inquire about availability as models travel frequently. Don't be scared of new faces, either, especially if they have representation.

### TIP MEET & GREET

Allow yourself sufficient time to meet, greet, and briefly chat with models in castings. Try to reduce their nerves and discover something about their personality. Try blindsiding them with questions, ask them how their day is going, who is their favorite band or superhero—anything to break the ice and encourage them to reveal something about themselves that might spark an interest in you.

The key to a successful casting is to be specific. Consider what kind of model fits your idea, and if you're working with a client, what features might best highlight their product: the shape of a girl's eye for a makeup campaign, for example, or her figure for a lingerie line. Height, weight, hair, and eye color, ethnicity, age range, tattoos—these are all factors to take into account when it comes to choosing a model. Make informed decisions beforehand and you can avoid a "cattle call" where everyone and anyone might turn up.

At a typical casting I will sign in, wait my turn, greet the photographer or client, present my portfolio with z-card, possibly try on one to three outfits, pose for photographs, and where I can, throw in tidbits of my individuality—hobbies, skills, recent jobs, anything to connect with the people I'm talking to.

The majority of jobs are booked on personality. No one wants a grumpy, negative, egotistical person on their set or as part of their team. On the day of the casting watch how people act and react to events, and try to feel what kind of energy they give off. Keep it in context, though—models get nervous on castings. Work out if you'll be able to communicate easily with this person to create a shot even if the circumstances become strained.

## LONDON CALLING

The worst experience of my life was early in my career when I waited for three hours to cast with an extremely important casting director for all the high fashion brands' runways that season. I entered a room to be greeted by a lady who asked to see my ankle. I obliged and she picked up a pen and proceeded to scrawl "TOO FAT" across my card, right across my face, right in front of me. I cried, a lot. In fact, it nearly destroyed me."

Smile, talk openly, and be inviting even when you're tired. Look through a model's portfolio and take a z-card even if they are not right for the job. They took the time to cast for you, so it's all about respect. A thank you and goodbye is always appreciated, but try to avoid letting someone know they got the job in the room—you never know who's going to walk in next!

The day itself can be overwhelming, so take your time when making a decision and talk it through with your team. Overall, I would advise you choose someone you are excited to shoot and work with.

## CASTING CHECKLIST

- ✓ How did they enter the room? Confident, nervous, intimidated, smiling?
- ✓ First impression? Was there a wow factor?
- ✓ How old do they look?
- ✓ How tall?
- ✓ How is their skin?
- ✓ How strong are the facial features?
- ✓ Do they—and their body shape—meet the brief?
- ✓ Well-presented? (No worrying signs like a hangover?)
- ✓ Where do they originate from? How is their English?
- ✓ How much makeup are they wearing?
- ✓ How long have they been working? How experienced?
- ✓ How much work is in their portfolio? Do you recognize any?
- ✓ How old do they photograph (i.e. how old do they appear when photographed)?
- ✓ Have they done work previously of a similar style to your own idea?
- ✓ Do they have range?
- ✓ How do they move when they're being photographed?
- ✓ Are they photogenic?
- ✓ How do they look from various angles? Front-on, in profile?
- ✓ Do they move in between shots or are they stood stock-still?
- ✓ Are they natural and spontaneous?
- ✓ Are they capable of a range of emotions?
- ✓ Does their look fit the mood of the project? Too sexy, not sexy enough?
- ✓ Are they scared of the camera?
- ✓ Do they follow direction?
- ✓ Are they forthcoming and talkative?
- ✓ Are they trying to direct you?
- ✓ Have you seen them in swimwear (if necessary for the shoot)? Are there any tan lines or scars?
- ✓ How body-confident are they?
- ✓ Is their hair the right length for the shoot? Have you seen it down?
- ✓ Do they have any piercings or tattoos?
- ✓ How much retouching do you think will be necessary?
- ✓ Do you know anything about their personality?
- ✓ Do they seem like a team player?
- ✓ Are you having fun?
- ✓ Do they inspire your creativity?
- ✓ Have you taken a z-card? Do you have means for communication?
- ✓ This seems like a lot to learn about a person in a casting that could only last a few minutes, but the more sessions you hold, the more adept you will become at spotting positive attributes quickly.

# REMOTE CASTING

**IF YOU ARE UNABLE TO HOLD a casting or a model you are particularly interested in is not available before the shoot date, you can cast remotely. I've booked numerous jobs based purely on my portfolio, a personal recommendation, or how persuasive my booker was feeling that day. Always be polite to model bookers!**

A model's portfolio can be extremely revealing. Whether you are looking at an entire agency package or you've found a model you like online, you can tell a lot about a person from their pictures. Note their previous experience and how selective they've been with their shots—sometimes it's not about what's left in, but what's left out. Tear sheets from magazines or advertising jobs mean that the model has booked successfully in the past and may have worked with other photographers you admire. The model might have a strong style or prominent features, so determine the range displayed and how much of their work appears professional. Check for heavy retouching, unusual cropping, or harsh filters and consider how recent the shots seem. Like internet dating the last thing you want is for the person to look completely different on the day.

When casting remotely, especially for a concept that requires a certain attitude, it helps to have evidence that the model can produce the emotions and visual characters you envisage beforehand. Personally, I modify my book for each client I see, so that it is tailored more toward their brand image. I have a happy, jumpy, commercial portfolio, for example, and a moodier, sexier, editorial portfolio. Reduce the risk of miscasting by ensuring the model you've chosen will fit with the location, wardrobe, and overall vibe of the shoot.

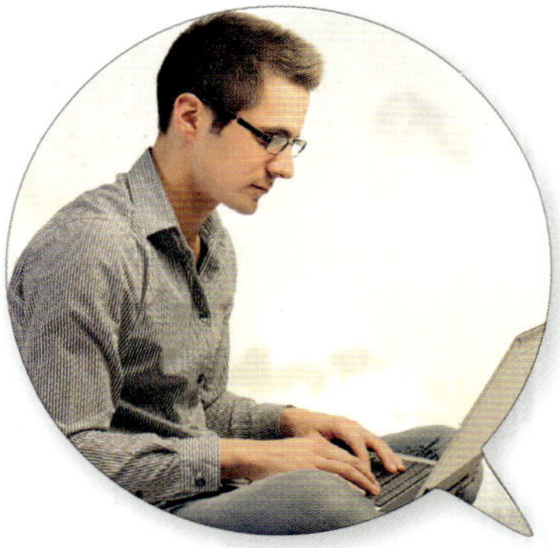

LEFT & BELOW RIGHT: **SCREEN TIME**
Casting via a web cam can be useful if you are unable to meet face to face. You can see, even if it's pixelated, whether a model can produce the emotions you need.

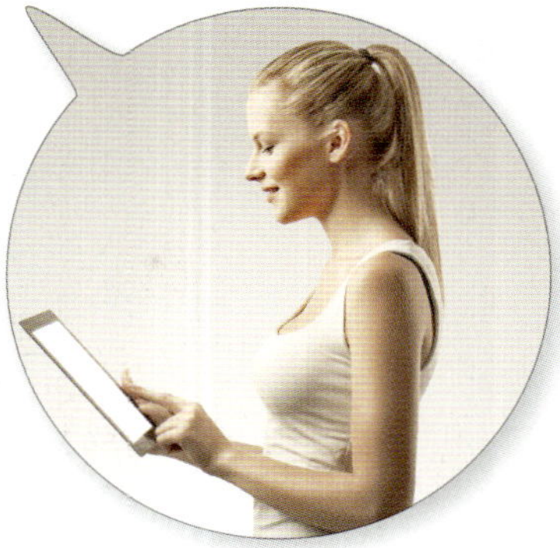

RIGHT: **FACE TIME**
Face timing can be a great way to assess your model's personality and character, while viewing their natural expressions. It gives them a chance to get to know you too and put a face to a name.

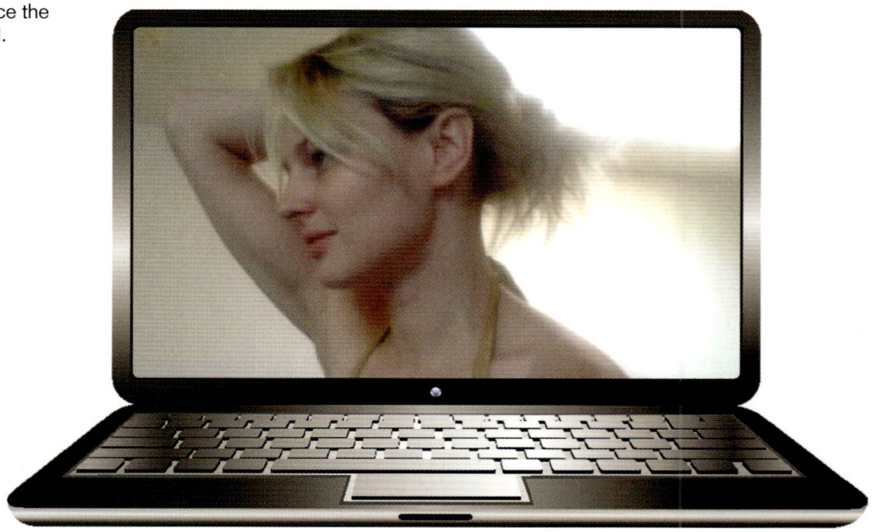

> "We approach castings differently, researching our brand's and going after people in the street that would encompass that brand. We go to their dwellings and habitations to bring a sense of authenticity. We work backward by hiring bands or DJs, or finding locations that we know will draw the right demographic. From then on we media blast out our 'events.' Within a natural environment you always notice genuine reactions and real warmth in a smile."
>
> **HEATHER SMITH,** *Smith x Union Production and Casting*

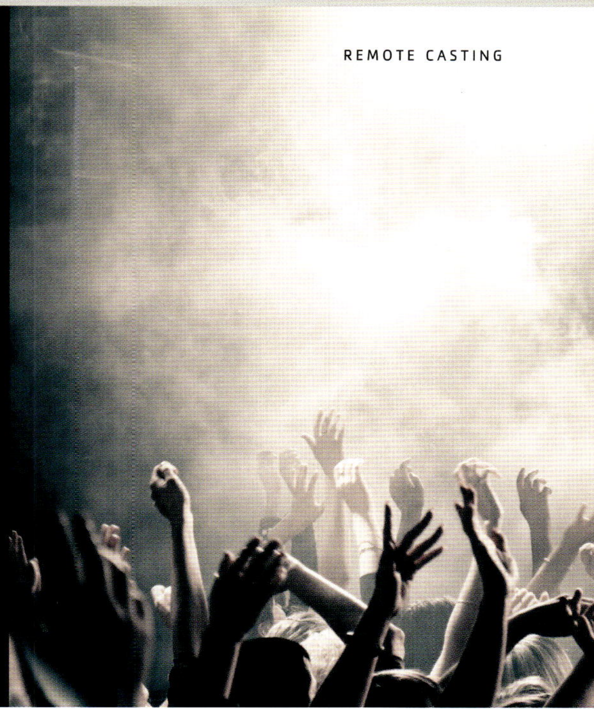

If possible, give the model the option to send you their current digitals and a casting video. Ask them to record themselves stating relevant details and showing a range of full-length, close-up, and profile shots. Online castings using a webcam are becoming more popular, especially for photographers who are setting up shoots before they travel.

## WEB CASTING

A real-time casting online, via a webcam, can reveal a lot about a model, their personality, and current stats. Remember you can take screen grabs in place of Polaroids.

All communication can indicate something about a model's character and reliability, so monitor their availability, phone etiquette, and behavior online. If you feel you need further information before a remote booking try a background check using the more popular social media websites out there.

## MODEL MEASUREMENTS

In general, an agency or individual will post their measurements online, but you should be aware that these are rarely exact. It is recognized across the industry that for high fashion women must be at least five feet nine inches tall with a dress size two to four; men, at least six feet with a jacket size 40. Commercial and fitness models can be a much wider variety of heights and shapes, and "plus size" models range in dress sizes 10 to 18 with about ten inches between waist and hips. For older models an extra 10–20 pounds or so is acceptable. Petite models of five feet six inches and above work in certain marketplaces (cosmetics, for example) and "alternative" models can vary dramatically in size and form.

### TIP MEASUREMENTS

Female models are generally a minimum of 5'9"–6' (179–182cm) with bust 34" (86cm), waist 24" (60cm), hips 34" (86cm).

Male models are generally 6'–6'2" (182–188cm) and wear a 40 regular jacket.

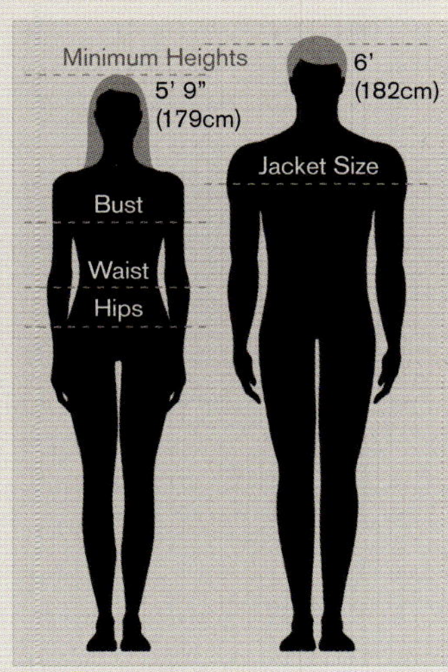

# APPROACHING AGENCIES

**AS AN ASPIRING PHOTOGRAPHER modeling agencies can be intimidating. It's as if they're the ones with all the power and they can smell the fear on you. I felt the same starting out—lots of people do—but agencies are not as impenetrable as they may seem. You are going to have to be confident, polite, and persistent to successfully develop a relationship with an agency, but in return they can offer professional, experienced models that should know how to move, in turn advancing your portfolio, furthering your career, and helping you book those bigger money jobs. A "booker" can arrange castings, provide backup in case of cancellations, and will act as a middleman throughout.**

It's a high-paced, commission-based industry, so be prepared. If you are approaching an agency with a low budget or for testing you will need a well designed website and a portfolio of a certain standard, as the bookers you will be appealing to need to be confident that it's worth their model's time to shoot with you. High-quality, professional-looking images will help convince them—not necessarily all fashion shots, but it helps. Start with simple, natural-looking pictures that highlight the model. Check agency "comp cards" and online portfolios to see what you're aiming for and remember that preferred photography styles can vary depending on the

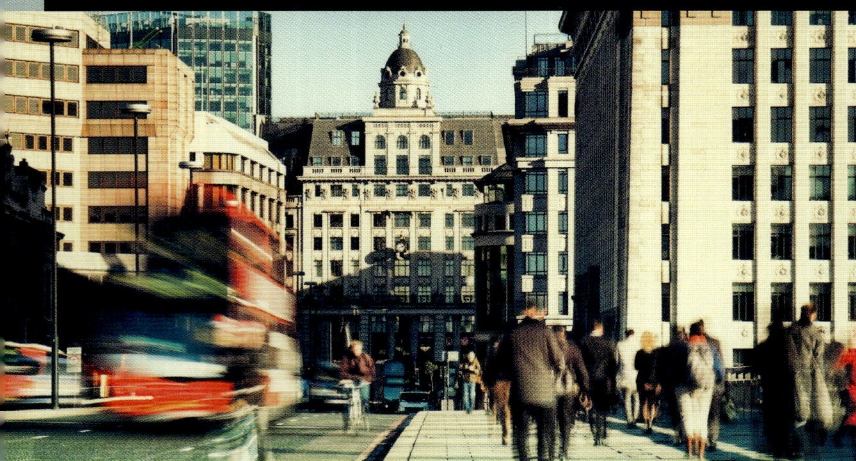

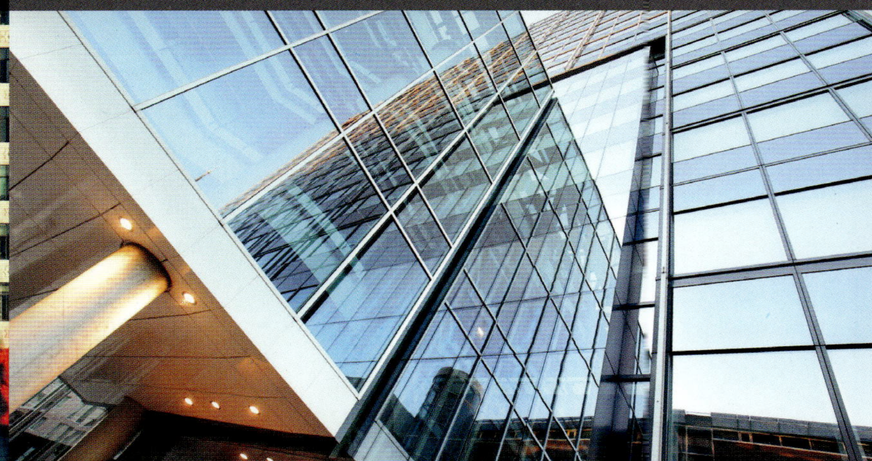

ABOVE: **CHANGE IT UP**
It can be wise to do your research and alter your portfolio to suit the preferred photography style of the agencies from city to city. Some markets are more commercial, others solely high fashion.

ABOVE: **LOCATION, LOCATION**
While you may think all agencies are located in fancy buildings on the most expensive streets, the vast majority are much more approachable. Being polite and determined will get you through most doors.

country you're in and even from city to city. It helps if you already have, or develop, a love for fashion in general, so read fashion magazines, go to shows, and meet designers; it can only improve your work.

When you're ready, research the agencies local to you—the closer the reputable ones, the better. Walk-ins are not advisable, so start calling one by one asking to speak with the booker in charge of "new faces." If they are unavailable introduce yourself as a prospective photographer and ask for the appropriate email address. Keep your email short and sweet, with a link to your website, and offer to come in and show them your print book. Some people will like your work, or you, and could be extremely supportive, others won't. It's as simple as that. Concentrate on the positives, rather than wasting time trying to please everyone. If someone is rude to you, try not to take it personally and keep your cool. You need to maintain your reputation. Be nice, as you never know who someone might be or who they might become.

If you get an appointment, be presentable and professional, and know what you're working towards. Many models are now downloading their portfolios on to electronic tablets, and while this is useful for client and editor presentations, the majority of photographers still use printed books in agency meetings. It reduces issues with light and color loss, plus a book can't run out of battery. Be confident and be prepared to keep it quick and informative. If you subsequently produce great shots with their models and receive positive feedback regarding your shoot, your options will only increase.

> *"It's hard to beat someone who never gives up.*
>
> **BABE RUTH,** *baseball player*

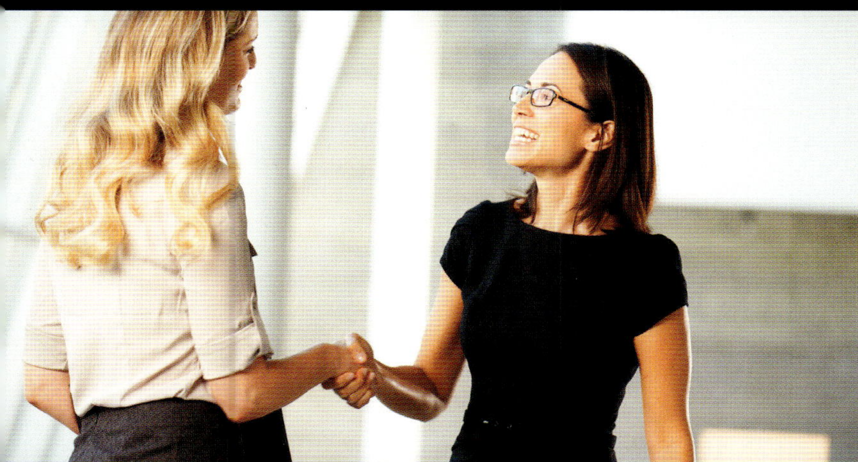

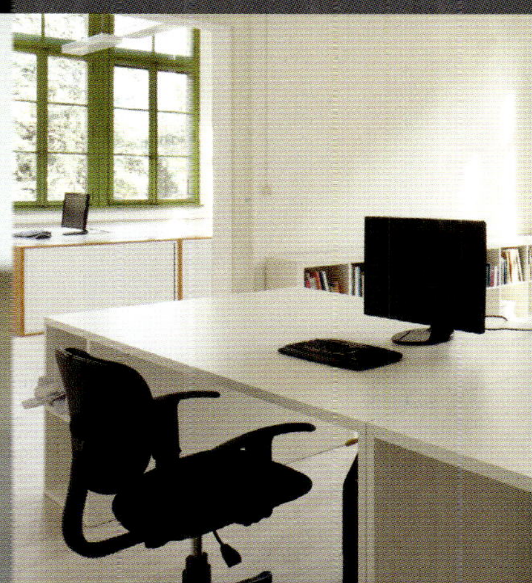

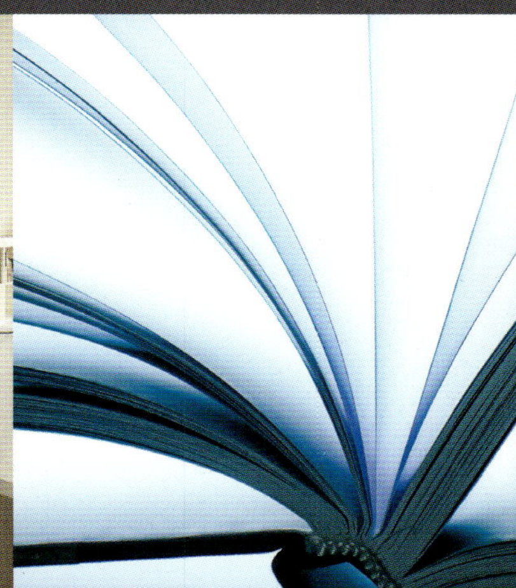

ABOVE: **COLD CALLS**
Make an appointment with the agency booker don't just show up on the off chance. You will not be taken seriously and this could be a move that will damage your future reputation.

ABOVE & ABOVE RIGHT: **DISPLAY YOUR WORK**
Agencies are geared up for digital when you are sending shots, but the majority of photographers still use printed books in agency meetings. It is beneficial to be prepared for both media.

# AGENCY TALK

**TO INCREASE YOUR CHANCES of success when approaching a modeling agency, first familiarize yourself with the industry lingo. Here is a glossary of some of the terms you might come across:**

BELOW: **SHOW OFF**
You don't need to go over the top to show that you know these industry terms when meeting with an agency, just be prepared and be yourself.

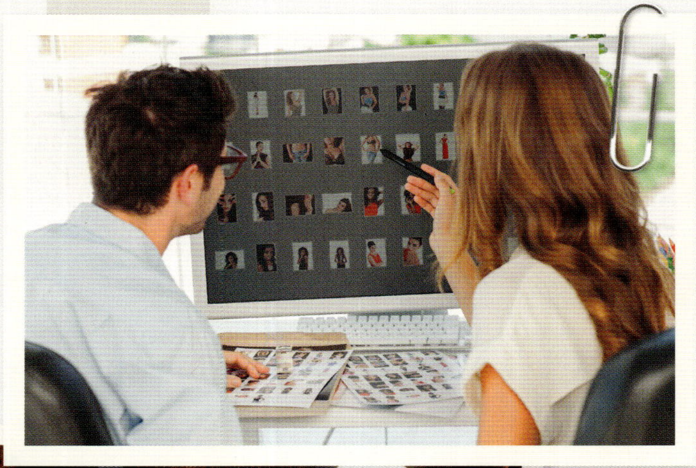

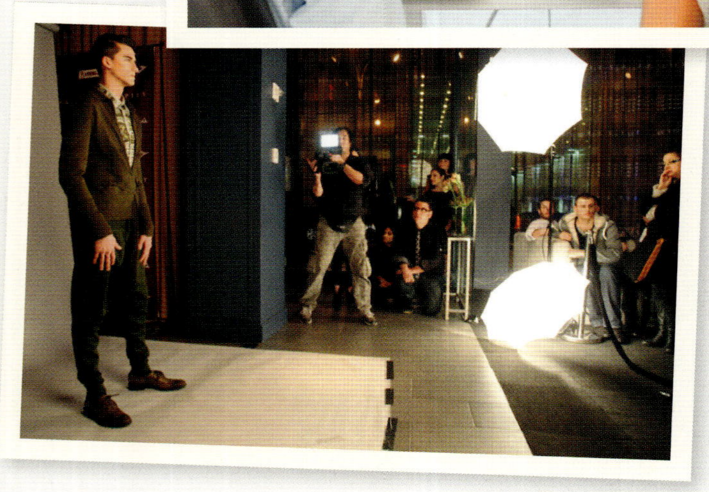

## GLOSSARY

**BOOK:** A model's portfolio of their work. Now applicable to electronic tablets too.

**BOOKED:** Confirmation that you have reserved the model for your shoot, on the date and time specified, and at an agreed rate.

**BOOKER:** A person who works for an agency through which you may hire models. These can section further into men and women's bookers, new faces, and so on.

**CALLBACK:** After the first casting you may feel the need to bring a smaller number of models back to narrow down your selection. Clients may be present.

**CALL TIME:** The time someone is due on set.

**COMMISSION:** A percentage of the model's fee that goes to the agency that represents them.

**COMPOSITE CARD** (aka Comp card or Z-card): A printed "business card" that includes photographs, measurements, and agency contact details for an individual model. One is left with each client a model visits.

**CONTACT SHEET:** Small proofs of the shoot, often used for agency approval.

**FITTING:** A session previous to the shoot where the model will try on wardrobe to ensure fit and allow specific outfits to be composed. Often paid by the hour if not included in the day rate.

**GO-SEE:** A model's appointment with a prospective client. Often when there is no particular job lined up, but for future reference.

**HAIR STYLIST:** The person in charge of styling and maintaining the model's hair throughout the shoot.

**HEADSHEET:** A poster displaying headshots and information about a model provided by the agency.

**HOLDING:** If you inquire about booking a model they may be placed "on hold" while other possible work in their schedule is arranged. This is not a confirmation: the model may be booked on a higher paying job. You can put multiple models on hold at any one time.

**MAKEUP ARTIST (MUA):** The person on set who will ensure the model is well groomed.

**NEW FACE:** Agencies often have a "new faces" board. These are less experienced, freshly scouted models that are often younger and with little or no portfolio. These are the faces that could be the next big thing!

**OPEN CALL:** A large-scale casting where the client will see a variety of models in the area.

**OPTION (FIRST AND SECOND):** Depending on how far in advance you are booking and how important your shoot is to the agency you will be given "options" on models until they confirm. If you have First option, you have priority, but if you have Second option that model could be booked on another shoot before yours. Bookers have a lot of influence over options so try and develop positive relationships with them.

**RATE:** Amount paid to model or photographer. Will vary depending on popularity and demand for model, as well as location and amount of clothing worn.

**RELEASE FORM:** A legal document signed by a model to agree to the release of the images in perpetuity or for a defined usage period. Agencies will often negotiate contracts and sign in place of the model.

**REQUEST:** A specific casting request to see a particular model. They will be notified it is a request and are more likely to show up because of it.

**STATS:** A model's measurements, hair and eye color, and so on.

**STYLIST:** The person on set in charge of providing or styling wardrobe and making sure the product is presented well on the model during the shoot.

**TEAR SHEET:** A copy of published work from a magazine included in a portfolio.

**TEST SHOOT:** An agreement to work on a mutually beneficial basis with no fees. The photographer produces images for the model's time. Also known as "time for print."

**UNION:** This refers to a model's status within the Actor's Guild. Not usually an issue for print work but if you are shooting video this could affect you so be sure to check the guidelines.

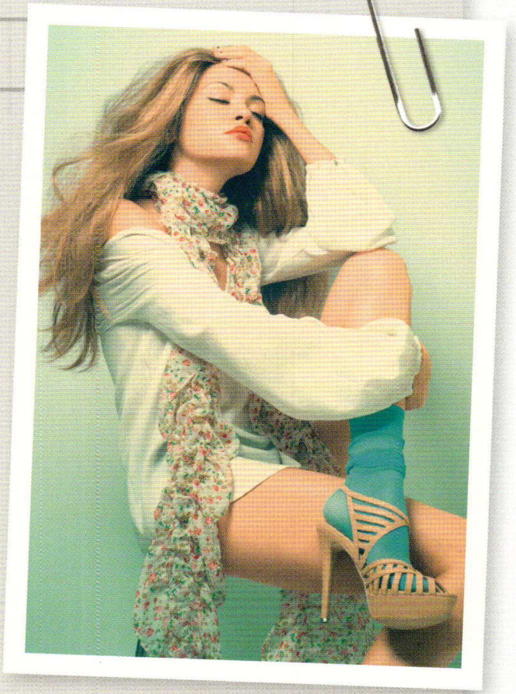

**USAGE:** According to time, distribution, and region, the amount a model is paid for usage on an image within a particular medium.

**VOUCHER:** Three-piece form with a model release on which the client notes the number of hours worked by the model. Used as a billing reference.

## BEHIND THE LENS WITH

# SCOTT NATHAN

**I WAS VERY FORTUNATE in the beginning of my career when it came to finding models. For many years before I was a photographer, my best friend was a modeling agent and I was living in Los Angeles. By the time I'd made the decision to turn pro I knew a lot of models as friends who were willing to lend a hand. When it came time to develop a relationship with the local agencies I just started smiling and dialing, getting to know them and constantly doing 'show and tells' via email and whenever possible in person. I made my share of mistakes. Still do. But as we bump into walls along the way, we begin to figure out how it all works.**

Many photographers worry about taking their portfolio to an agency, but I've always been a buyer (or occasional borrower) of talent, so I always felt that they were applying for the job, not me. A photographer looking to do tests should be able to make professional looking, commercial images, be they lifestyle, high fashion, or beauty. I don't think fine-art type work helps a modeling agent so much.

When I started out and shot for brands that didn't have budgets, I'd have models come to offices and we'd take Polaroids.

### BIOGRAPHY

Scott Nathan is an award-winning photographer and director based in Los Angeles and New York. In 2012 he was the recipient of the prestigious Professional Photographer of the Year award in the Fashion and Beauty Category by *Professional Photographer* magazine. He has quickly become one of the world's most sought after celebrity, beauty, fashion, and advertising photographers.

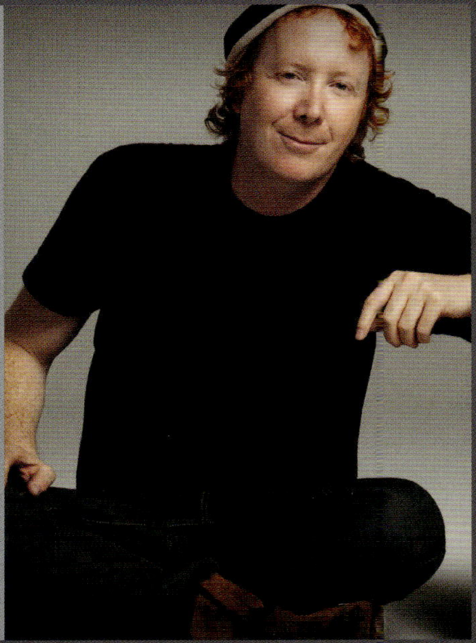

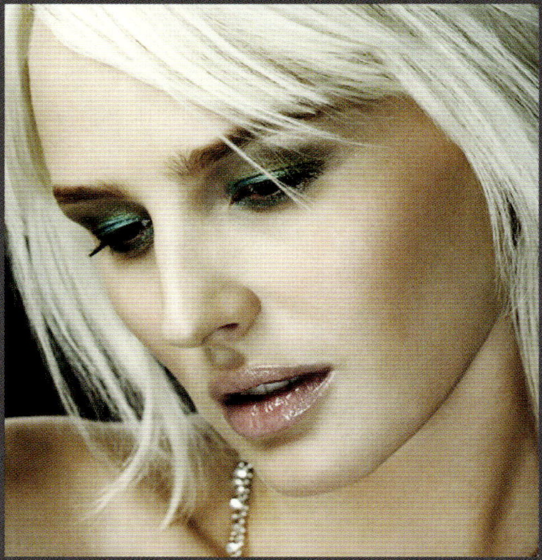

LEFT: **ADVERTISING BEAUTY**
Scott met Franki shooting for prestigious beauty campaign Urban Decay. From then on they have continued to shoot together whenever possible. Shooting with friends can be the best way for both photographer and model to grow as the environment is comfortable and forgiving.

RIGHT: **TESTING**
These shots were taken over a few hours in Malibu, California. Even by one of the most beautiful beaches in the world, some of our favorite shots were achieved in a nearby house being used for prep.

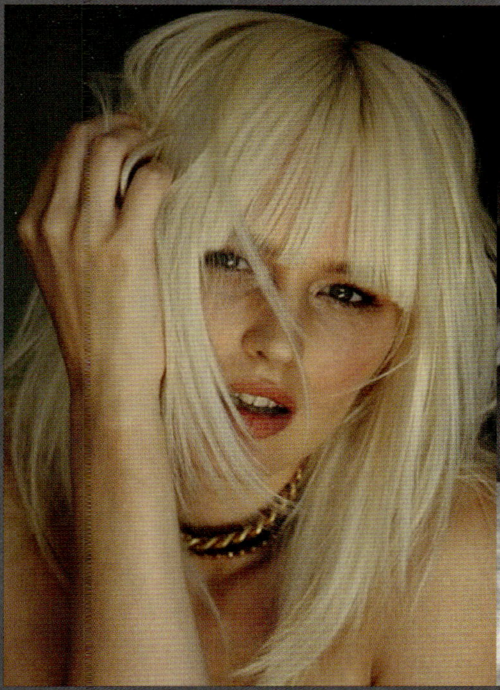

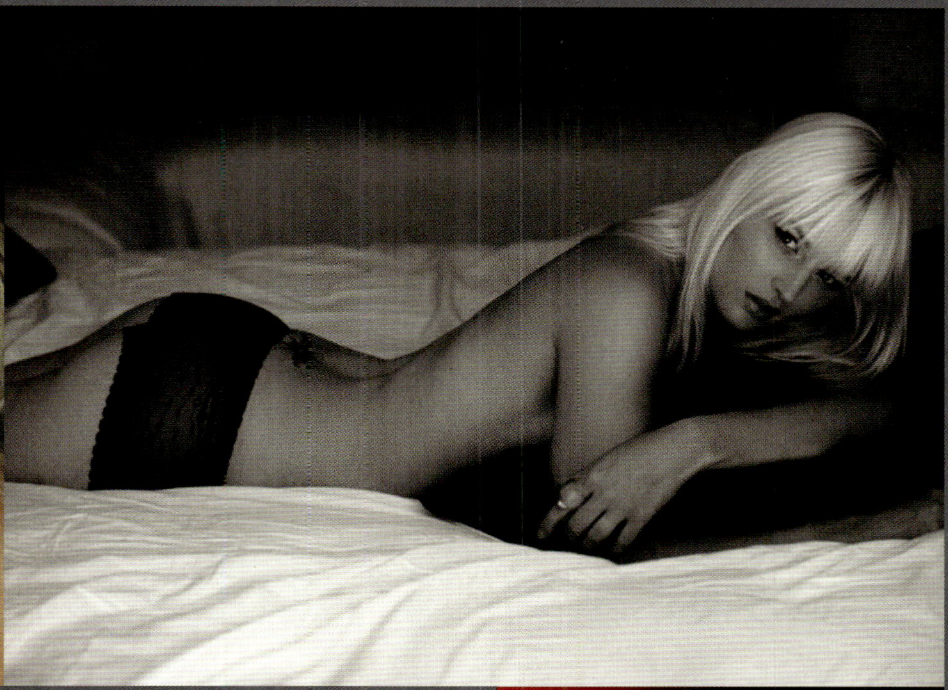

The trouble with that old system—at least for me—was that after 100–150 girls had come through I couldn't remember any of them! Now they have digital casting studios. A session runner puts all the talent on video, and I'll ask them questions just to get a feel for their personality and what it would be like to spend ten-hour days with them. As they're being recorded, they're uploading to a private web page in almost real time, so the client doesn't have to be in the room (or even the country) and we can make a well-informed decision about who best represents the brand.

A great model is a great actress of sorts. Genetics are important, but there are a lot of "perfect" girls out there. Personality is almost everything. You can have imperfect lighting and other imperfections, but if I don't have a well-formed relationship and a deep connection for that 1/125 of a second, I have nothing. No picture. During a casting I look for depth and the personality to convey what the product is. Sometimes it's inner joy and someone who's quick to laugh; sometimes it's the person that makes me fall in love with a stare; sometimes it's raw sexual energy. Different tools for different jobs.

Casting throughout my career, I've made just about every mistake a person could make and encourage everyone not to be afraid of making them. Falling down isn't failing. Staying down is. I feel great about most of the casting choices I've made. There were a couple of instances where I caved in too quickly to a client's wishes where I knew it wasn't right and it didn't work out as well as it could have. That said, I thankfully haven't lost a client because of it.

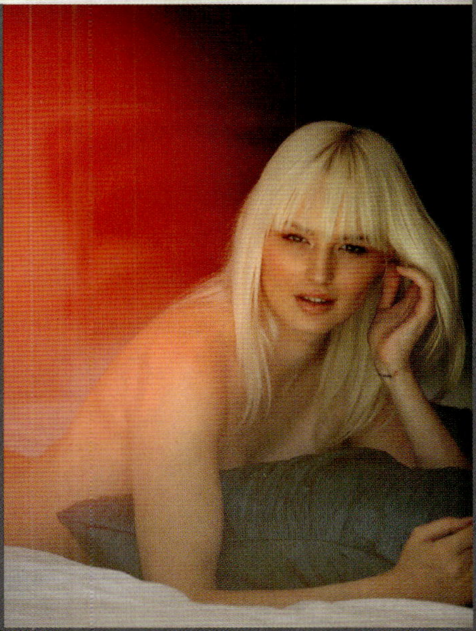

# 03

## THE BRIEF

**NEVER UNDERESTIMATE the importance of preparation when you are planning a photo shoot. You have to ensure the right people turn up at the right time and place, then hope the shoot goes off without a hitch. Even when you're fully prepared, unexpected things can happen. By creating separate briefs for yourself and the agency or freelance model, and then producing a detailed call sheet you can reduce the risk of problems developing later on. In this chapter we outline these briefs and talk in detail about the different types of modeling shoots you could produce, ending with valuable words from model Fo Porter.**

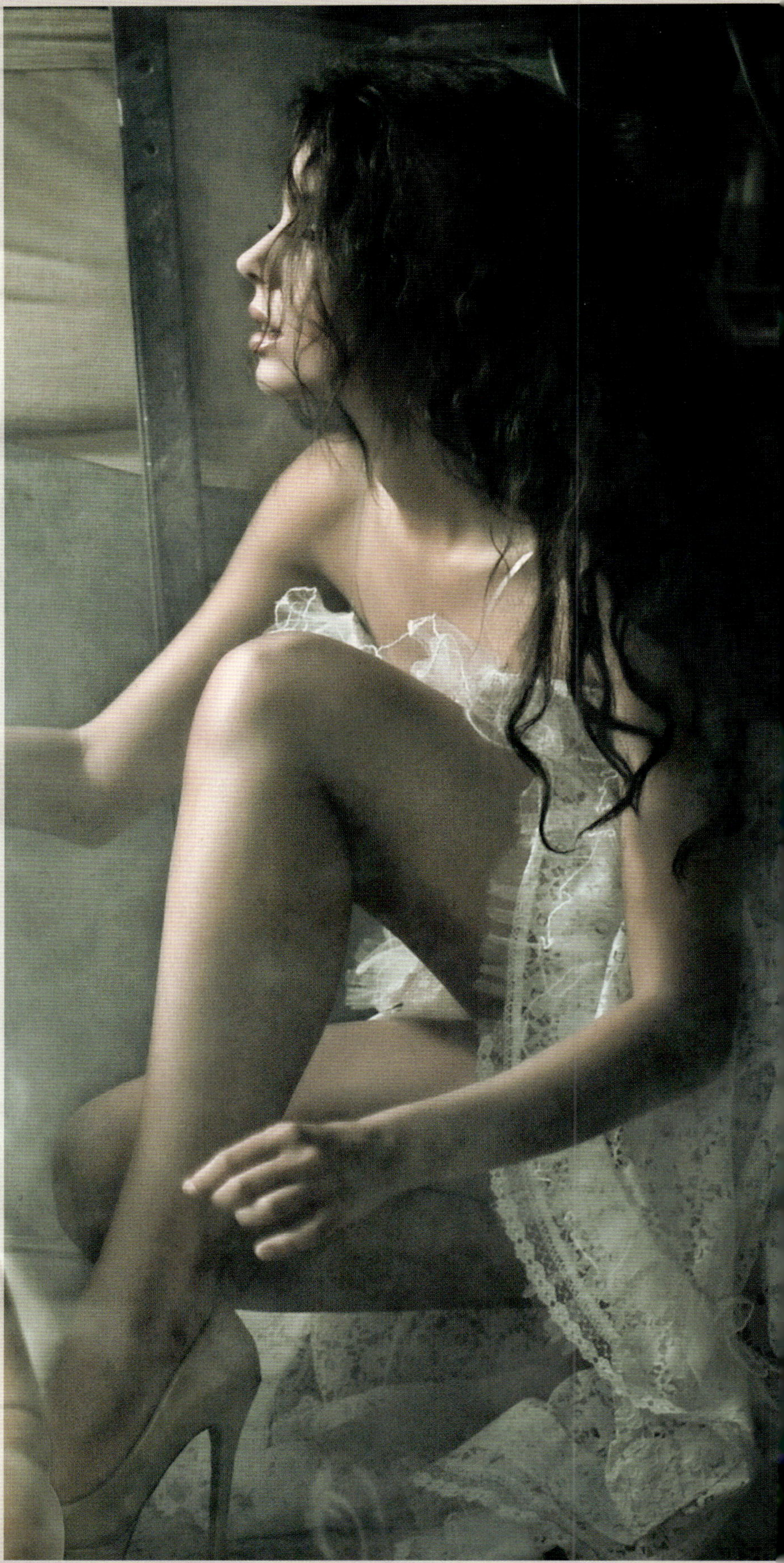

RIGHT: **KEEP IT SIMPLE**
You may never have written a brief before, don't let the idea intimidate you. It is a simple process to produce great shoots when you take the time to think things through.

# THE PROJECT BRIEF

**THE PROJECT BRIEF defines the purpose of a shoot, as well as the budget, target audience of the medium or product, branding/perception goals, technical specs, and shoot day particulars such as location ideas. Sometimes you have full control over a project, so have a free hand in creating the brief, but at other times clients, art directors, and PR people will influence it. If you are being paid for your services your initial brief must incorporate these people's wishes, including model choice, wardrobe that must be featured, the minimum number of shots required, and in what format. In addition, an overall description of the vibe and style that is put into words or visualized in a mood board can help when casting. Try also to write down what you are hoping to achieve. Ask yourself if the concept will challenge you, whether it will better your portfolio, or if it will increase your chances of booking future work.**

## CASTING BRIEF

Before a casting, review the project brief and list what you want: this will form a casting brief. Talk to bookers and send the casting brief to the agencies along with location, time frame, and contact details. If you want the models to dress a particular way for the casting, detail that here. This might be important if you need to see them in swimwear, or if a certain body part is the focal point. You need to work out what might be different about your shoot, if it involves a special skill, nudity of any kind, or a dangerous act. Then make sure you state these in the casting brief and reiterate the point at the casting itself. Some models may embellish their skills to book a job. I've seen this first hand with statements such as, "of course I can ride a horse," "no, I'm not afraid of snakes," and "I'm a fantastic swimmer," leading to disastrous results.

## THE CALL SHEET

Once everything is booked send out the call sheet to everyone concerned a few days before the job. Call sheets range in detail, but should confirm shoot information including locations, call times, contact details, parking or entry notes, a prospective lunch and finish time, plus on larger jobs, local hospital details and often a map. If the model is required to bring clothing or accessories that should be listed here. Again, keep it simple and informative so it can be used as a quick reference on the morning of the shoot.

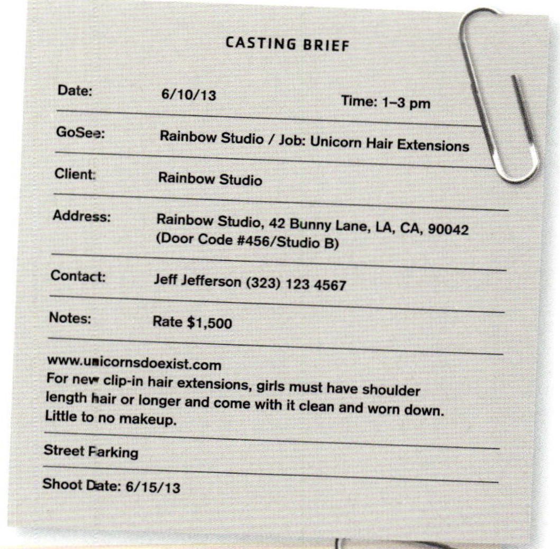

CASTING BRIEF

| | | |
|---|---|---|
| Date: | 6/10/13 | Time: 1–3 pm |
| GoSee: | Rainbow Studio / Job: Unicorn Hair Extensions | |
| Client: | Rainbow Studio | |
| Address: | Rainbow Studio, 42 Bunny Lane, LA, CA, 90042 (Door Code #456/Studio B) | |
| Contact: | Jeff Jefferson (323) 123 4567 | |
| Notes: | Rate $1,500 | |

www.unicornsdoexist.com
For new clip-in hair extensions, girls must have shoulder length hair or longer and come with it clean and worn down. Little to no makeup.

Street Parking

Shoot Date: 6/15/13

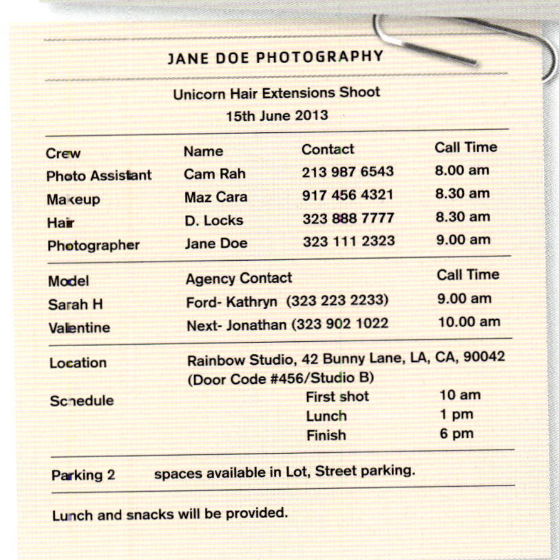

JANE DOE PHOTOGRAPHY

Unicorn Hair Extensions Shoot
15th June 2013

| Crew | Name | Contact | Call Time |
|---|---|---|---|
| Photo Assistant | Cam Rah | 213 987 6543 | 8.00 am |
| Makeup | Maz Cara | 917 456 4321 | 8.30 am |
| Hair | D. Locks | 323 888 7777 | 8.30 am |
| Photographer | Jane Doe | 323 111 2323 | 9.00 am |

| Model | Agency Contact | Call Time |
|---|---|---|
| Sarah H | Ford- Kathryn (323 223 2233) | 9.00 am |
| Valentine | Next- Jonathan (323 902 1022 | 10.00 am |

| | | | |
|---|---|---|---|
| Location | Rainbow Studio, 42 Bunny Lane, LA, CA, 90042 (Door Code #456/Studio B) | | |
| Schedule | | First shot | 10 am |
| | | Lunch | 1 pm |
| | | Finish | 6 pm |

Parking 2 spaces available in Lot, Street parking.

Lunch and snacks will be provided.

TOP: **CASTING BRIEF**
This is an example of what a model would typically receive from their booker before a casting. It includes important details such as time, location, and shoot dates.

ABOVE: **CALL SHEET**
A photographer should email out an accurate and up-to-date call sheet to all those involved in the shoot. It might look something like this.

# THE SHOOTING ENVIRONMENT

**WHEREVER YOU CHOOSE to take pictures, certain things are necessary to provide a comfortable and safe shooting environment. At the very least, water must be readily available, restrooms easily accessible, and the model must have privacy when changing. It is generally the photographer's responsibility to provide lunch and snacks on a test shoot so consider allergies and diet. Variety helps. Models are picky, so avoid only buying pizza or solely handing out quinoa-flavored kale. Allow time for breaks and be prepared, have contact details at the ready and have a contingency plan for an emergency situation. Coffee helps, especially first thing and after lunch.**

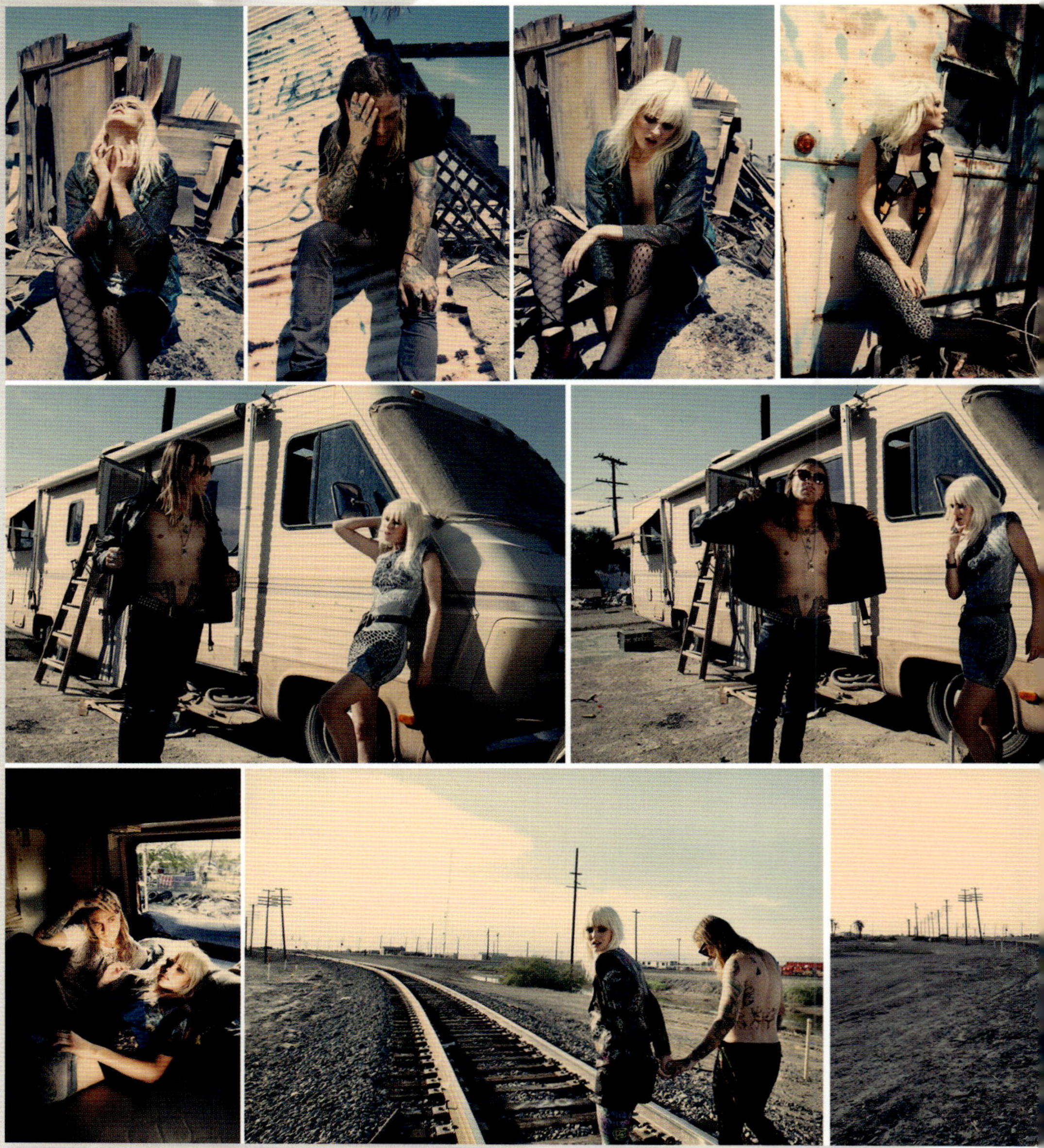

## A "HARD OUT" TIME

Having a "hard out" at a location means that everyone and all equipment has to be packed up and out at a specified time, not just the model after the final exposure. Leeway is unusual and can be costly.

## IN THE STUDIO

The great thing about shooting in a studio, whether at home or in a rented space is that it is a customized, contained environment where everything from equipment to kitchen utensils can be provided. This promotes a certain comfort level, a degree of familiarity for everyone concerned, and ultimately it makes a photo shoot easier to manage.

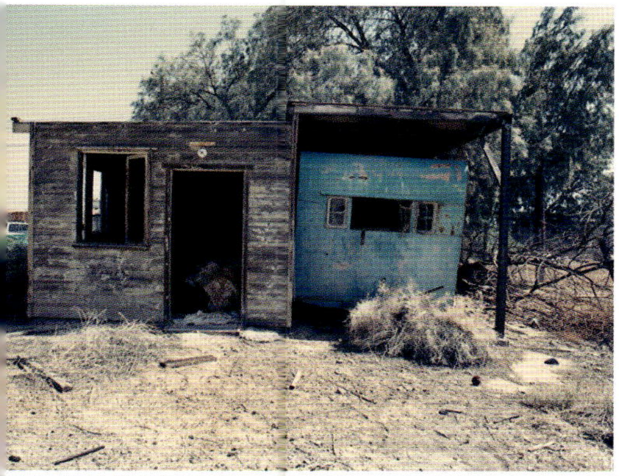

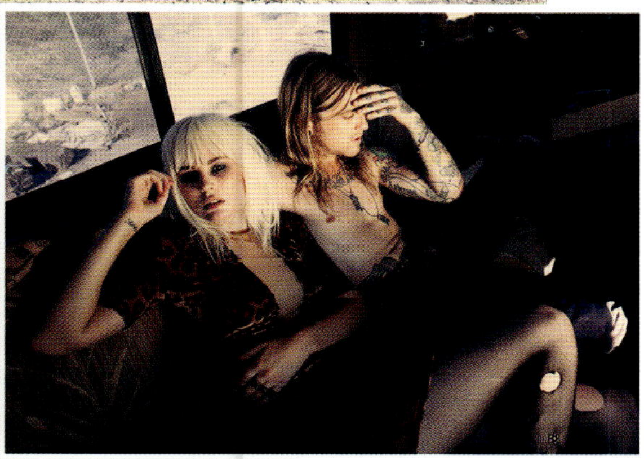

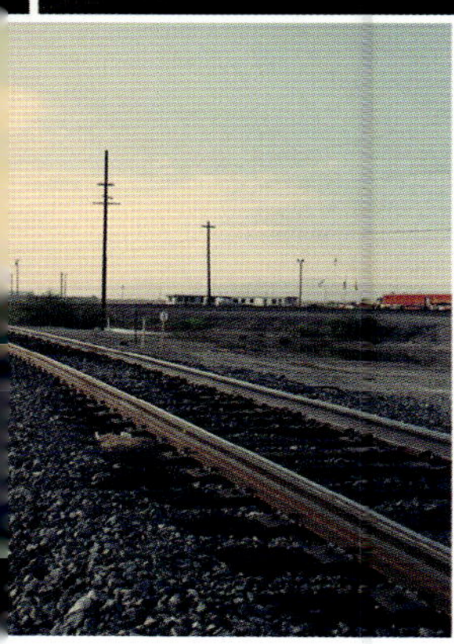

LEFT & ABOVE:
**FEELING HOT, HOT, HOT**
This shoot took place in 116 degree heat. It was imperative to stop for water breaks and to use fans to cool down in between every shot. My makeup ran, my hair matted, but it was worth it to work with a great team.

There will be areas for people to relax, mirrors and lighting for makeup, rails for clothing, and plug sockets for hair-styling tools, steamers, and cell phone chargers.

Although some photographers find studios restrictive, it's really about what you choose to do with the available space. Makeup and hair ideas are more expertly achievable indoors, when you're away from the hot sun and unexpected rain, and can create that windswept look with a handheld fan. Often there will be an on-site studio manager on hand to help out too, and it is a good idea to clarify with them whether you have a "hard out" time. If you have, then you must stick to it.

## ON LOCATION

If you decide to take a shoot on location there is more to consider than there is in a studio. Does the model have transportation, for example, and do you know exactly where you're going? Scout the location beforehand to save precious time on the day, highlight possible safety issues, and gauge how much equipment to bring. On bigger budget shoots it's someone's job to find locations and take care of any regulations involved, but you'll find information online if you're going to be doing this yourself.

Above all, check the rules. With indoor locations there could be issues with carpets, areas that are off limits, or furniture that cannot be moved to suit your needs, for example, while shooting outdoors may require a permit: the last thing you want is to have your shoot shut down, half finished because you haven't got the necessary paperwork. Make everyone aware of any rules in a polite manner.

Always take your team into account on location. Models are often shooting summer clothing in the winter and winter clothes in the summertime, so are permanently boiling hot or freezing cold—think sun screen and blankets. Makeup, hair, and wardrobe preparation takes time, space, and usually an electrical source. On smaller shoots, outside and without trailers, preparation often takes place at a separate location. Let everyone know before the shoot if you are traveling somewhere, as driving to locations often adds hours to a shoot and people appreciate knowing when they might get home.

After any shoot, clean up, but don't expect help from anyone else unless you have an assistant. Leave the space how you found it, as depending on how you act you could be refused back or you might score yourself a discount in the future.

### TIP PUMP UP THE VOLUME

Inside or out, music can be an important tool on a photo shoot. It can break the ice, set a mood, or simply pump up the energy on set during a quiet moment. Ask the model what music they like.

# TYPES OF SHOOT: EDITORIAL

**"FASHION" ENCOMPASSES a vast and diverse industry that involves multiple sectors. With technology in constant development and the strength of internet marketing growing, there has never been a higher demand for eye-catching, trend-focused, visual content. As a fashion photographer you can experiment with the area you prefer. Often you will end up working across more than one, adjusting your techniques to suit the individual project. A mixture of styles will add range to your portfolio and increase your odds of booking both creative and money jobs, allowing you to satisfy your artistic desires and pay your rent.**

## ON TREND

The editorial image captures trends through creative and artistic impression. The fashion capitals of editorial photography are recognized as New York, London, Paris, Milan, and Tokyo, where the majority of runway designers, agency-represented editorial models, and magazine houses are located. Fashion editorials are effectively "picture stories" that are spread over a number of pages in a magazine (usually with a title and running theme) that show the feel of the outfit in the way it was envisaged when it was designed.

With the development of online magazines there are now countless pages each month that need filling to showcase upcoming fashion trends. They are generally the lower paid jobs—if paid for at all—but they are good for building a reputation, and can provide you with published tear sheets for your portfolio that are more valuable than test shots.

The reason editorial work is popular with both photographers and models, even though it reaps the least financial reward, is the potential for freedom of expression. There are limitations and rules associated with the images you are required to produce for advertising and product shots, which can result in a stilted photograph that feels forced. However, when you are shooting editorial you get to loosen up and use your imagination. Clothing and accessories

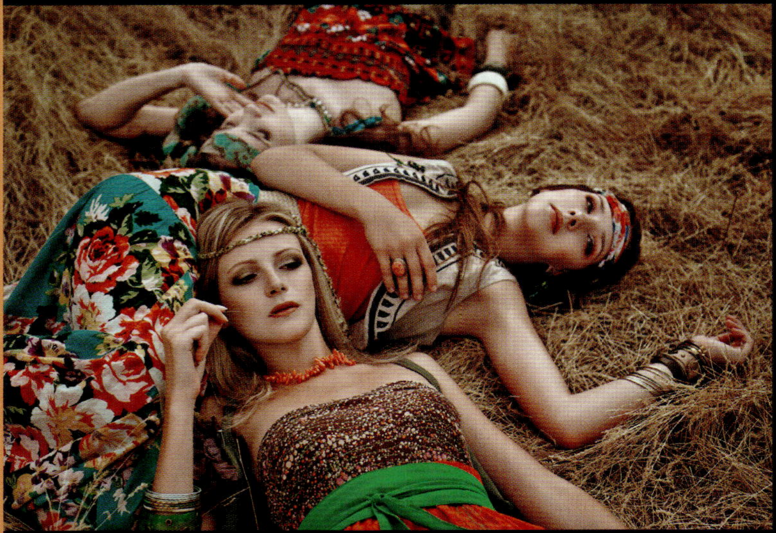

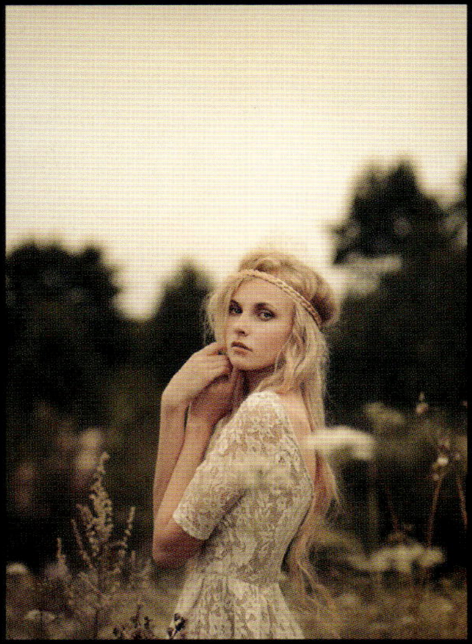

LEFT & FAR LEFT: **ON TREND**
Though specific styles might not be so obvious the editorial image captures trends through creative impression.

RIGHT:
**LET THE INSPIRATION FLOW**
There is no limit to where inspiration can spring from when you're brainstorming a great editorial shoot. Draw from your passions and fantasies.

FAR RIGHT: **MODEL LOOKS**
The aesthetic range of the editorial model varies much more widely than with commercial models. Editorial models often have a distinct or unconventional look.

### THINK OUTSIDE THE BOX

You don't have to break the bank to let your imagination run wild when shooting editorial. Stories can be told by a single expression and inspiration comes in many forms. You can set an entire editorial shoot around an apple box.

are credited and therefore do not need to be shown in full view at all times. Both you and the model have license to push boundaries and forget to worry about the perfect placement of a single ring or a brand logo.

A spontaneous energy is allowed to develop that can lead to legendary pictures. Research some of the greater collaborations between photographers and models with high fashion magazines. You will soon realize that once you have budget for editorial and access to the top styling teams and designers, you can work alongside set and prop designers to create a plethora of fantastical, new worlds. The sky has no limits.

Toward the start of your career you may have to be more financially aware, but that does not mean you have to restrict your vision. Editorials can be shot anywhere: against an expensive, custom studio backdrop or a simple white wall, with a linking storyline that can be concisely specified or incredibly vague. As long as you have an idea of what you want to achieve, you will be able to make the important decisions at speed on the day

## EDITORIAL MODELS

While it may seem that modeling is reserved for the beautiful, editorial shoots are where strange quirks are often celebrated: birth marks, gap teeth, scars, unique characteristics, and signature moves or androgynous features get noticed. Editorial models are often taller and slimmer, with a more distinct appearance than commercial models, and stereotypically they smile a lot less in pictures. However, if the model is talented and has range, then like the photographer they can be capable of shooting both (see *Types of Model* on page 50).

### TIP UP IN SMOKE

Never assume that a model will smoke for a shot. If it's vital to the shoot, address it when casting.

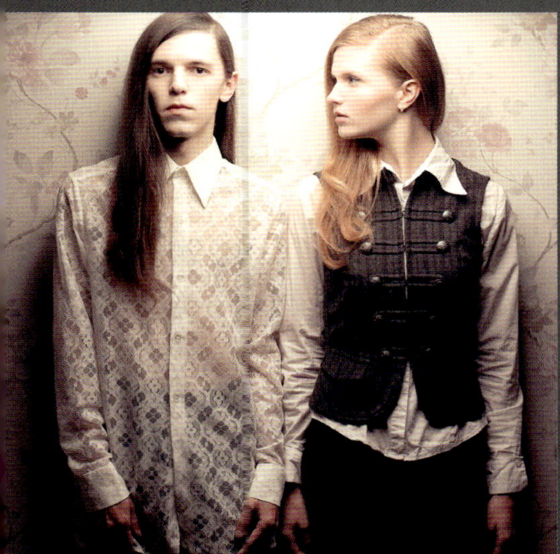

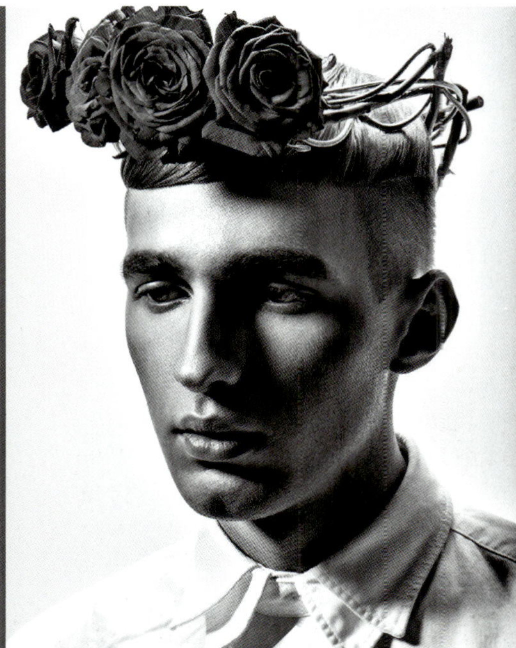

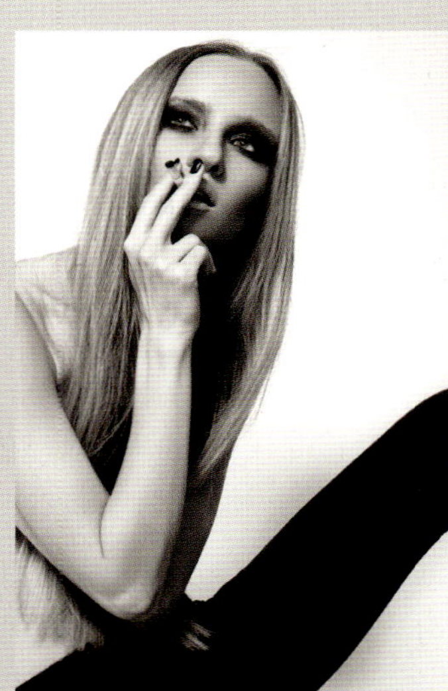

# TYPES OF SHOOT: EDITORIAL

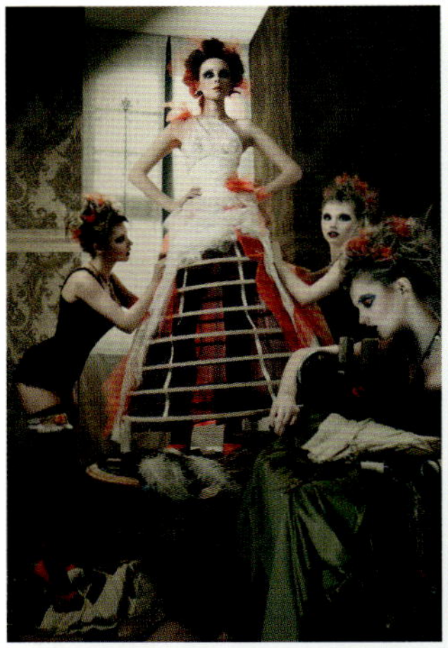

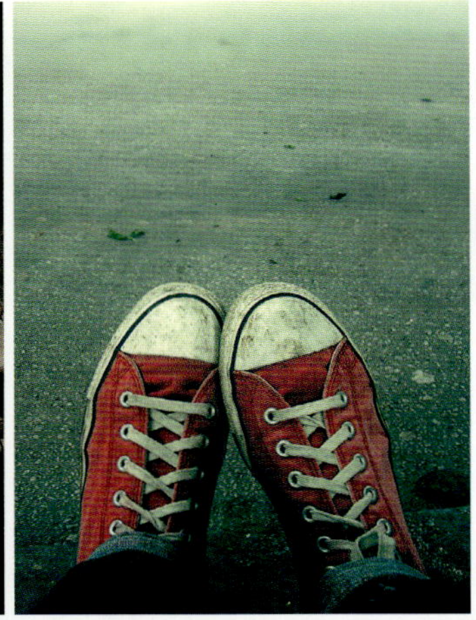

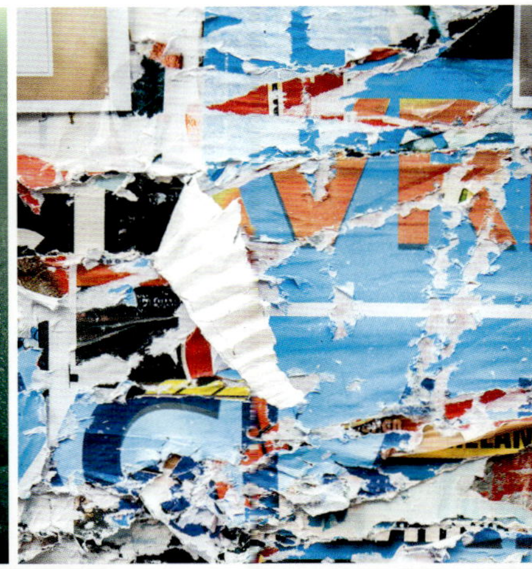

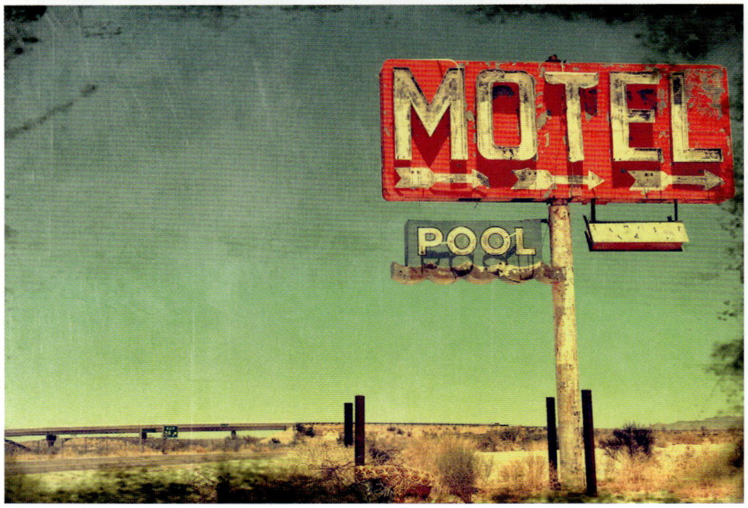


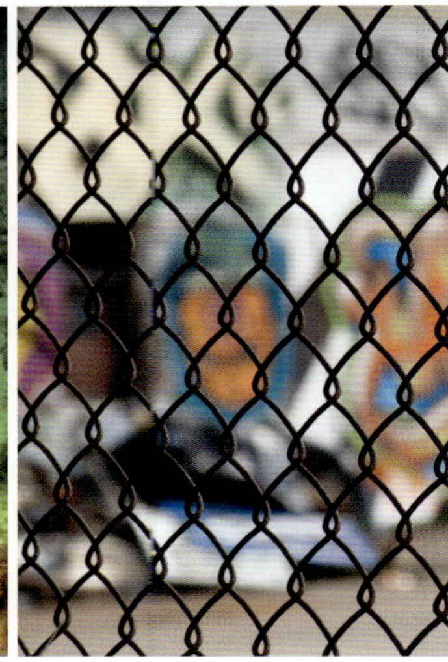

## EDITORIAL LOCATIONS

As mentioned, editorials can essentially be shot in any location. They conjure up images of "edgy" spaces, such as graffiti-soaked back streets and lonely train tracks, but there are no strict rules. On my first shoot I found myself draped over a gravestone, shooting 12 pages for a Swedish magazine in a dark, wet, London cemetery. However, since then I have shot editorial everywhere from empty warehouses, dive bars, and dark alleys to beach resorts, mansions belonging to millionaires, and Hollywood hotels.

Location decisions are inevitably made depending on budget and availability. Rental can be expensive and limited in more popular locations, but sometimes the use of a location can be traded for credit and exposure—the more famous the magazine, the higher your bartering power becomes. At other times you are going to have to plead with your friends to lend you their pool or Airstream, beach hut, or barn—any place that might create an interesting backdrop for the day. Another way to shoot on a smaller budget, depending on where you are located, is to explore outside the city, away from permits and prying eyes. For example, if you are based in Los Angeles you have the choice of the desert, the beach, snowy mountains, secluded natural hot springs, and vast empty salt plains that look like the surface of the moon.

The important point to remember is wherever you are shooting, be careful and aware of your surroundings. You may have to deal with extreme conditions, such as wind storms, intense heat, or altitude sickness. Be streetwise when shooting "street"—there is a reason larger jobs often hire security (I've even modeled with an armed guard in South Africa). Photo shoots and models create a spectacle, so if you are shooting in a

### TIP STEALTH MODE

It is possible to shoot guerrilla-style, without permits. Check the local rules, as certain cities allow you to shoot for free if you don't use a tripod, lights, or stands. Cameras can be handheld using natural light and you could maybe use white clothing as a make-shift reflector?

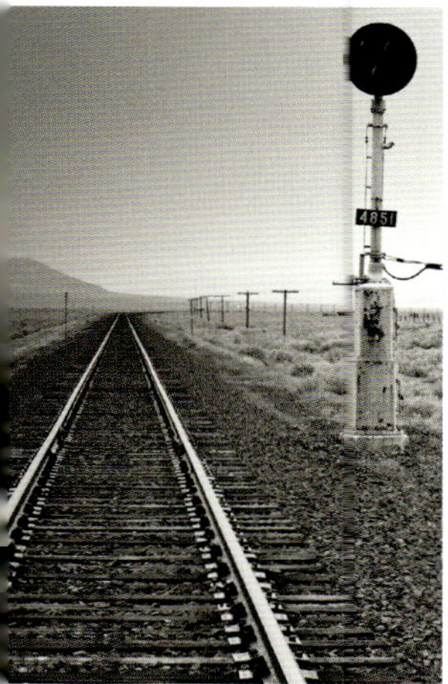

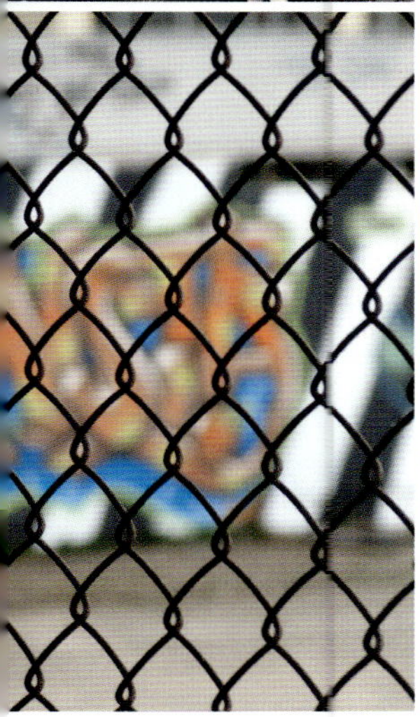
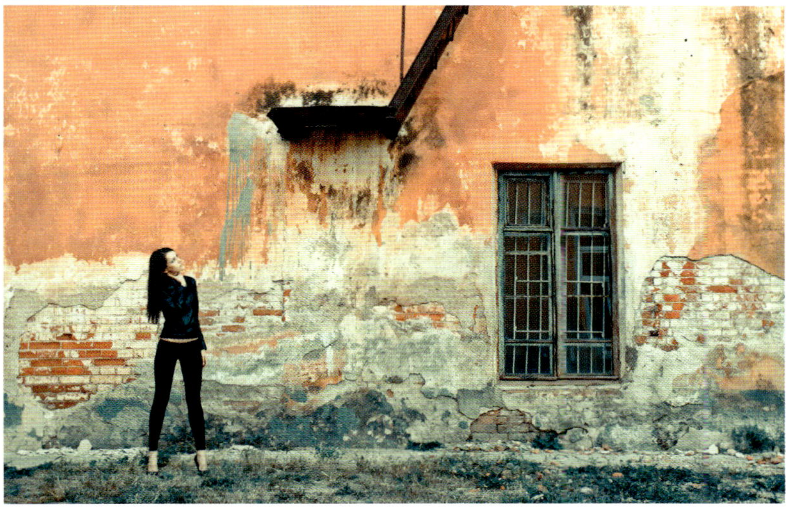

LEFT, BELOW & OPPOSITE:
**CREATIVE IMPRESSION**
With editorial work you really have the opportunity to explore a more creative path. You can use a wide range of locations to tell a part of the story. Look out for interesting shooting spots in your local area.

public place you must expect onlookers. Learn how to deal with these people politely, and remember that they are interested because it's fun to watch. If a stranger does becomes aggressive though, you must consider the safety of your model and team.

## EDITORIAL WORK

Certain kinds of job within the industry are more editorially based than others. The test shoot is most similar, but with an influx of magazines on the market there has been an increase in demand for "submissions." This means a photographer produces a shoot by themselves and then submits it to the magazine in the hope that it will be featured. Although the fear of rejection may deter you, if you put a little more effort into the wardrobe of your test shoots, you'll have nothing to lose as you will still have new images.

"Look books" are produced by fashion companies as miniature lifestyle catalogs that suit the brand and are often reproduced online. They are usually story- or theme-based and printed alongside still-life images of the products to allow the photography to have a more editorial feel. They are not highly paid, but it is paid work all the same.

The illustrious advertising "campaign" is one of the most sought after jobs in fashion photography. Though editorial-based it is a form of commercial print. With high budgets, the leading talent, and fewer shots, they focus more on storytelling within a single frame, while highlighting a product or lifestyle. These are images with enough impact to sell on sight—shots that can be reproduced internationally on billboards, in shop windows, and on bus stops, which is why these jobs can be so lucrative. The usage can be widespread and therefore satisfyingly profitable, and with photographers paid hundreds of thousands of dollars to shoot top-end campaigns it is definitely something worth aiming for.

### DRAWING A CROWD

When shooting in public you will undoubtedly attract attention. Therefore you need a model that can perform in front of a crowd without feeling self-conscious or getting distracted. You also need to learn to shoot confidently in front of other people as a photographer.

# TYPES OF SHOOT:
# COMMERCIAL

**THE COMMERCIAL ELEMENT of the fashion industry is vast and diverse, encompassing almost all work outside the editorial market. The majority of modeling agencies outside the fashion capitals, although unwilling to admit it, are commercially based. The term "commercial" refers to the promotion of various products over a variety of media. Requirements vary, depending on the client and brand image, but are often closer to real life and less stylized. Commercial print includes catalog modeling, in-store, mail order, and online, as well as beauty, lifestyle, and all fashion-based advertising.**

Commercial sets often depict scenes from everyday life, maintaining an image that the audience can relate to. With less story and more focus on showing the pieces correctly, they usually promote a relaxed, happy environment and models are captured mid-action, running, jumping, or laughing, rather than in the formal, stoic poses associated with high fashion. Often you will be asked to shoot group shots and couples, who must interact with one another without it feeling forced.

It is not unusual to need every detail of the cut, color, and fall of an outfit to be seen clearly in every image. There can be strict rules about what must be included and sometimes you will shoot the same outfit in ten different colors. The mass production of images can be frustrating, but a good photographer with a fun set will keep the energy up until the final click of the shutter.

Commercial jobs are usually well produced, with great locations and simple and direct project briefs. They pay well due to usages and widespread distribution, and most importantly they are normally well catered. Sometimes the hours are incredibly long and you can't imagine a day without a frighteningly early call time. But, then you remember you're shooting solidly for two weeks, for a great rate. That is a privileged position to be in as a fashion photographer: you might not receive the same recognition as an editorial photographer, but you can have a very attractive income and work steadily with longevity.

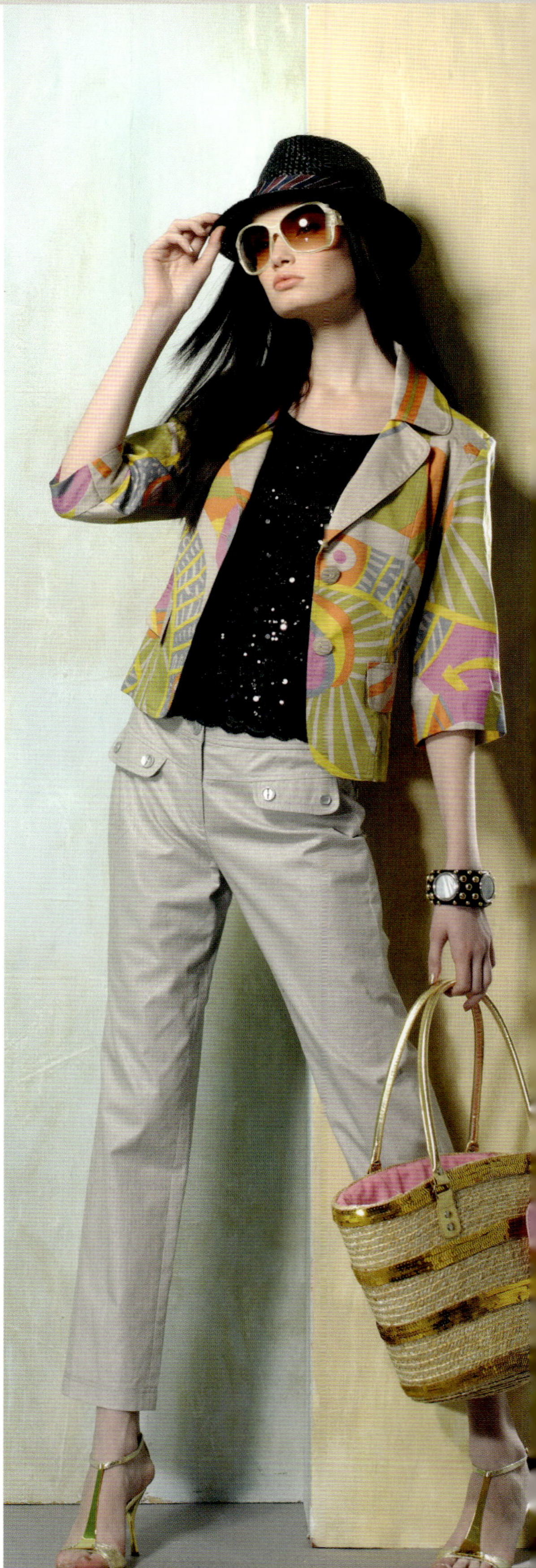

LEFT: **STRICT RULES**
Commercial jobs often include a large amount of product that has to be shot in a specific way. All the details of an outfit must be on display and visible to the prospective customer.

### SPECIAL CASES

Certain commercial clients require attractive specialists—professional athletes or yoga experts for a fitness catalog, for example. In these cases you need to be able to direct individuals with little to no modeling or industry experience.

## COMMERCIAL MODELS

Commercial models make up the majority of models worldwide and can be a much wider variety of heights and shapes than editorial models. Most child models are commercial models, and many industry observers consider male models to be commercially based. Age, body type, and overall looks are not as heavily regulated for commercial models. They can be shorter, heavier, or have "generic" looks. As with character actors, it is unusual for them to be recognized internationally. However, although the requirements are less rigorous, commercial models still often need to be attractive with great bodies, an outgoing personality, and an ability to act out a variety of roles.

A commercial model needs to be an idealized version of the client's target market, which can often include the general public. They need to be the "girl/guy next door" rather than the unattainable creatures that editorial models often appear to be. It helps if a commercial model is good at interacting with others, so watch for this when casting. They often have to recreate life-long friendships, dealing with instant parenthood, and fake marriage, becoming "24 hour families," as I like to call them.

## SMILEY FACE

As they usually shoot in happy scenarios, it helps if a commercial model has a fantastic smile.

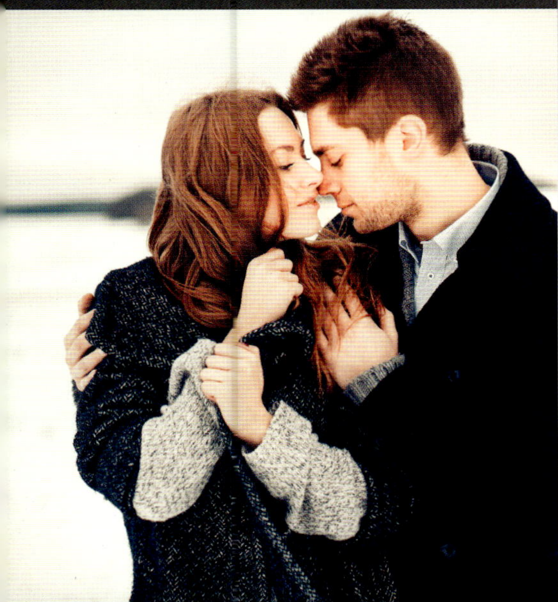

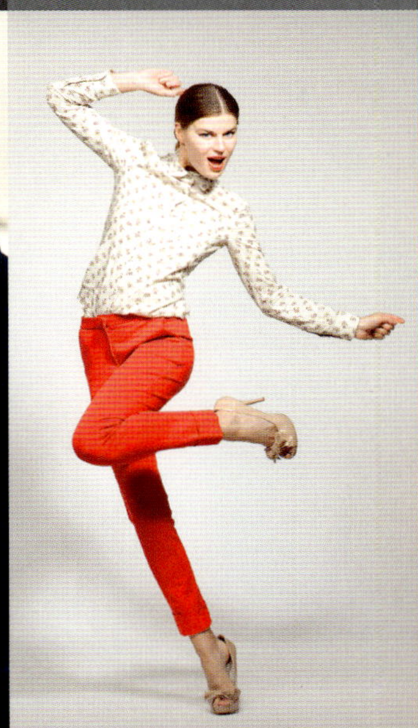

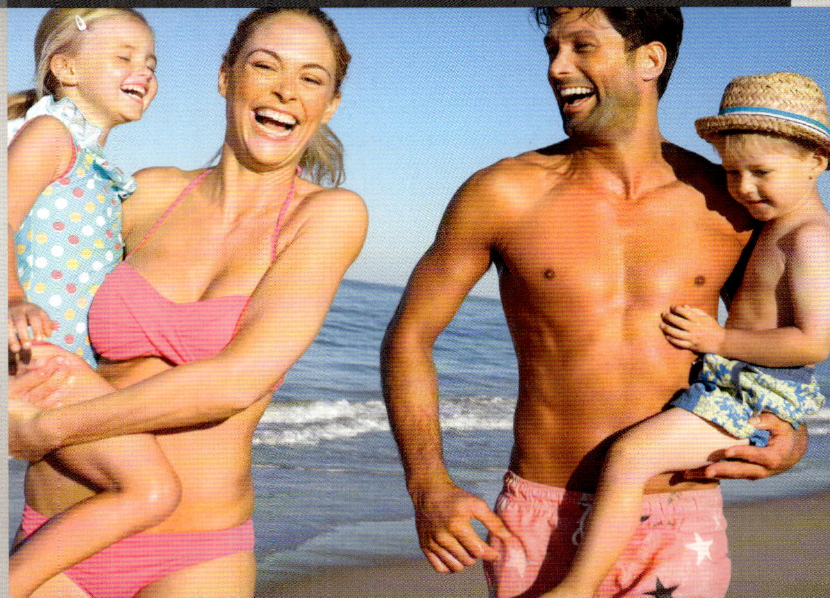

ABOVE: **LOVE AT FIRST SIGHT**
Commercial work involves trying to sell product directly from the page. Catalog customers buy on sight. The shots need to create a feeling the customer desires yet exhibit the clothes realistically.

ABOVE: **ACTION SHOTS**
Commercial shoots often require images where models appear happy and energetic. These can be achieved more easily if you encourage freedom of movement and fun.

ABOVE: **CREATING RELATIONSHIPS**
You will have to cast cleverly to create natural couples and families. Find models who are open and friendly rather than reserved and shy. They must be good at interacting with new people.

# TYPES OF SHOOT: COMMERCIAL

## COMMERCIAL LOCATIONS

Stereotypically, commercial jobs are shot in beautiful, exotic, locations where the sun always shines and everybody skips about merrily, laughing at how awesome everything is. In my experience, this is not a far stretch from reality. Of course, a vast amount of commercial work is shot in the studio (where the sun can also be made to shine permanently), but a lot of companies need to shoot on location, providing an example of what the customer could possibly look like on vacation, in the park, at work, or on their imaginary yacht, for example.

### TIP KEEPING UP THE PACE

On all commercial jobs you will need to work at a fast pace. Therefore you will benefit from booking a model who has experience and knows what they are doing—they should be able to move well and you must inspire one another.

RIGHT: **SUSTAINING MOMENTUM**
It can be hard for models and photographers on commercial jobs to keep their energy levels up all day. Try to pace yourself and don't let your models burn out after a few shots.

Catalog clients often have a vast amount of wardrobe to shoot. This can involve long trips away from home, intense shooting schedules with multiple models, and the stresses involved with working in close quarters with a team day in, day out. Be prepared to produce a large amount of images at the same location, so if you have a part in the decision-making process suggest a location that will provide diverse backdrops within short distances of each other. You will have a lot to cover and traveling between locations can cost you time. Styling teams will also have to work incredibly hard to transport the necessary rails of clothing.

Often, deals are made with hotels and vacation resorts to make production more simple, but wherever you are a commercial set needs a great vibe. There has to be a lot of energy in those pictures to make everyone stand out, and if you lose your momentum, so will the models.

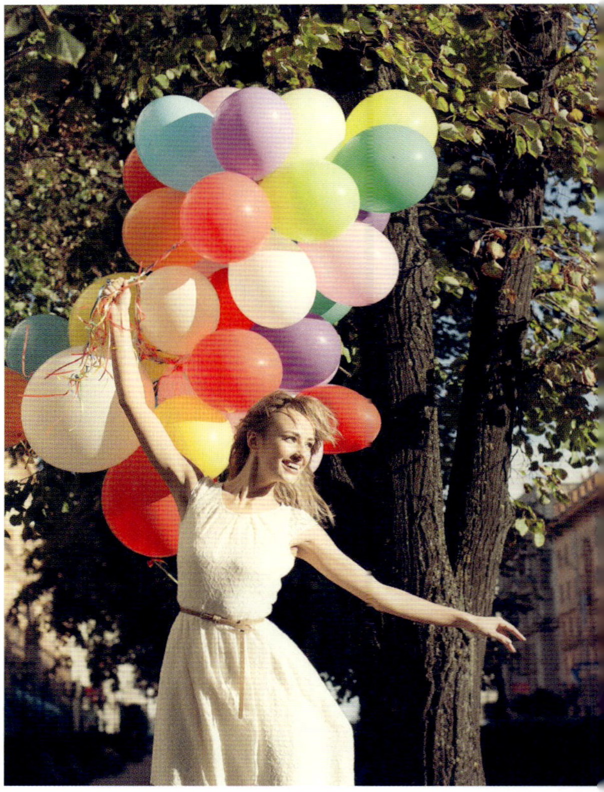

## COMMERCIAL WORK

As discussed previously, commercial work is varied and diverse, including many sub-categories of the industry. Catalogs are produced by all kinds of fashion companies, be it business-to-business, in-store, via direct marketing, online—the distribution outlets go on and on. This calls for copious amounts of branded content.

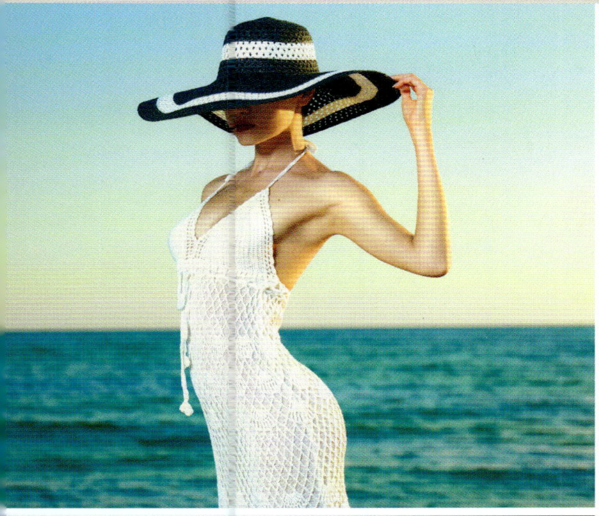

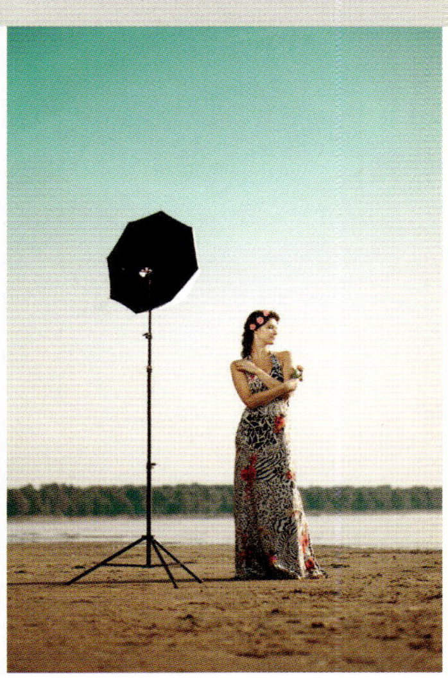

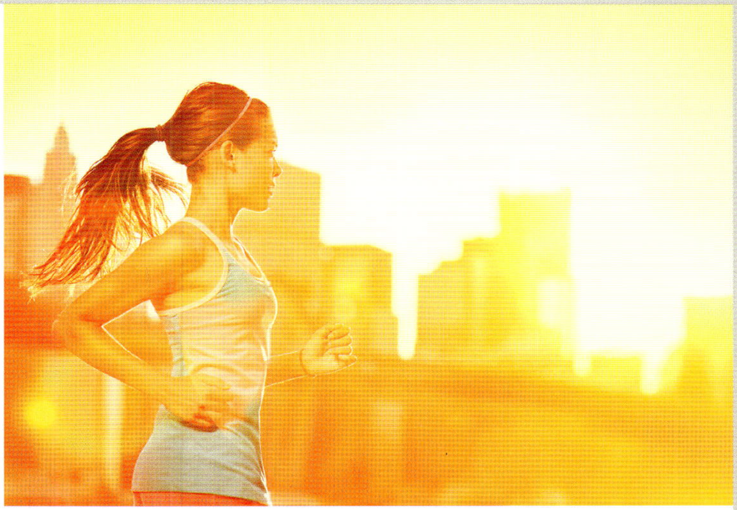

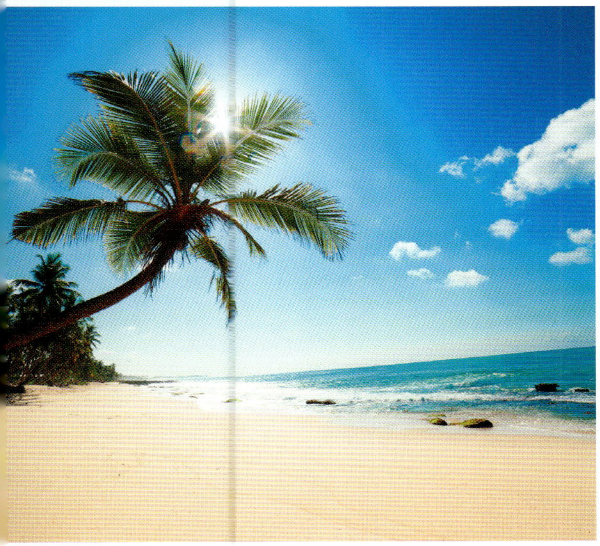

TOP LEFT & ABOVE: **STEADY WORK**
Catalog work can be low paid, especially at the beginning of your career, but can provide the experience to grow and regular work over a longer period.

LEFT: **LOCATION**
One of the perks of the job, commercial fashion photography involves travel. Though it is not all beaches and blue skies, your career could take you all over the world.

ABOVE: **LIFESTYLE**
Commercial jobs often entail combining model and landscape photography in one shot. Are you experienced with landscape or could practice enhance your fashion work?

### LET'S GET WET!

On all styles of shoot photographers can get excited and ask the model to "roll on the ground" or "jump in the water." But think before you direct something that might affect the clothes—if necessary, leave it to the last shot.

The development of e-commerce, or "e-comm," has provided hundreds of thousands of smaller fashion companies with an outlet to showcase their products online, in a gallery-style format. Certain discount and auction websites are shooting multiple fashion labels every day, every week, with no room for error. As a photographer these jobs can be low paid, but they provide regular work with room for promotion, which can be rare. However, these environments, where you work with the same people every day are at risk of becoming toxic—if you're not careful, these relationships can consume the workplace and a visiting model can feel excluded.

Lifestyle shoots can include fitness clients, vacation companies, and luxurious promotions of hotels and casinos. They all need models to make their product look good, but can incorporate shooting landscape simultaneously. Other niche areas of commercial work include working with corporate clients, bit-part models, and glamour photography such as swimsuit calendars and posters. Head shots and celebrity portraits can be a lucrative way of increasing your portfolio and learning to work with people as you are dealing with models and actors.

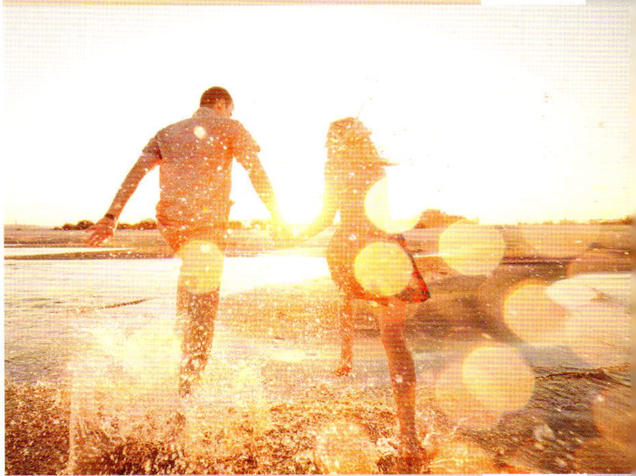

ABOVE: **THE LAST SHOT**
The last shot is sometimes referred to as the "Martini Shot," because the next shot you take will be out of a glass.

# IN FRONT OF THE CAMERA WITH
# FO PORTER

"I feel I lucked in when it came to becoming a model, as I was on a popular reality television show called *America's Next Top Model*. It was an exhilarating and overwhelming experience and after the show I was scouted by Nous Models (my current agency) and relocated to Los Angeles. Life hasn't been the same since—it was a true blessing!

My first shoot as a model in the real world was nerve-wracking. I really had no idea what I was doing. My booker said to me "This is a test shoot to start your comp card, but don't worry if you don't get any photos, think of it as a trial run." I shot for almost eight hours with an experienced photographer who was extremely particular and really worked me to the bone. When we received the pictures, my agency were floored—they loved them and to this day I have a shot from that session in my book. If you're working with a first-time model, I suggest taking into account their experience and talking them through the process. Be kind, but prepare them for what's next.

I prefer working on commercial and test shoots because honestly, what I'm good at is being really cheesy! With tests it's also so relaxed—most of the time you get a chance to really do what you want without the pressure of "a certain look" required by the client.

One of my favorite photographers is Nick Onken, who I shot with on an Adidas job when I first started out. Another is Cameron Davis—I remember when I first saw his work when he was in my home town of Albuquerque. Both are easy to work with and laid back. I love them because it's one thing to shoot quickly and directly just to be done with the shoot, but it's another to connect with the model, make them feel comfortable, and keep the energy up. Photographers need to talk to me like I'm human! Make me feel like I can really say or do anything for the camera and they're totally into it and have no limitations or judgments. Let me, do me, with no pressure. It really helps if you 'click' easily with people. One of my biggest pet peeves is when photographers over direct and just kill that vibe you go into a shoot with. That's one way to turn me off, so to speak.

I honestly don't think I've ever worked with a nightmare photographer—more often than not it is the shoot as a whole that makes me feel like I'm wasting my time. Basically when everyone involved is difficult to work with, nothing clicks or flows freely, and there is little organization or common courtesy for one another. That can be a nightmare. Really it's all about a photographer who wants a great shot and has an awesome, positive, attitude that makes me want to give them the best, so we can both go home feeling like we put in a good day's work."

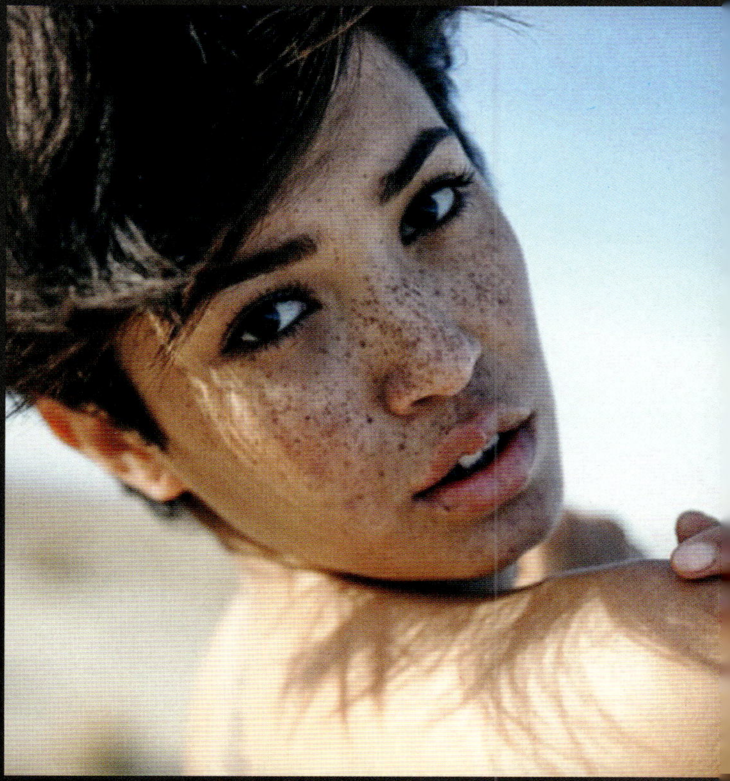

## BIOGRAPHY

Fo is a highly successful fashion model, specializing in commercial, beauty, and fitness work, with an extensive range of acclaimed, international clients. Currently based in Los Angeles, Fo regularly appears in advertising, magazine editorials, and catalog, working with some of the most talented and prominent photographers in the world.

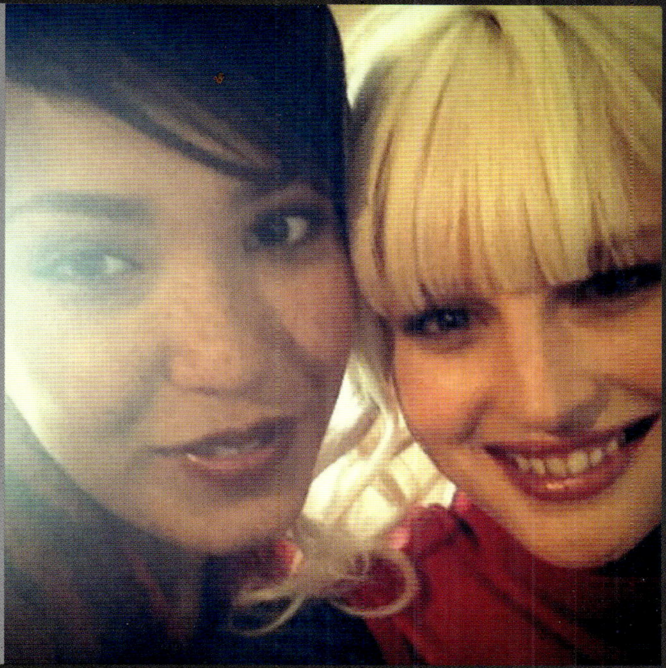

LEFT: **WORKING TOGETHER**
Fo and I have worked together on numerous occasions. I love her energy and contagious smile. It's important to find models that are naturally positive and fun to be around.

BELOW & OPPOSITE: **GO EXPLORING**
Finding new locations can be difficult if you are unable to travel or live in a small town, but hidden gems like this abandoned airfield can be just around the corner. Scout them out!

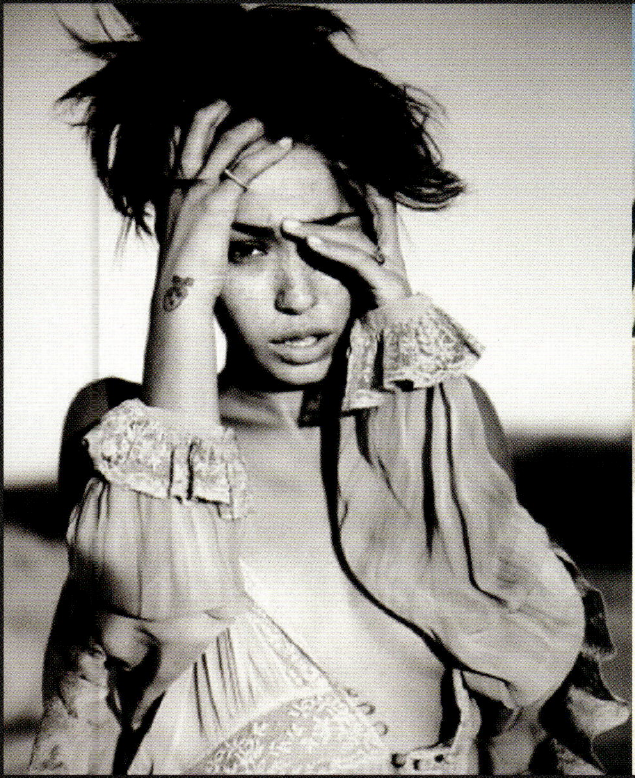

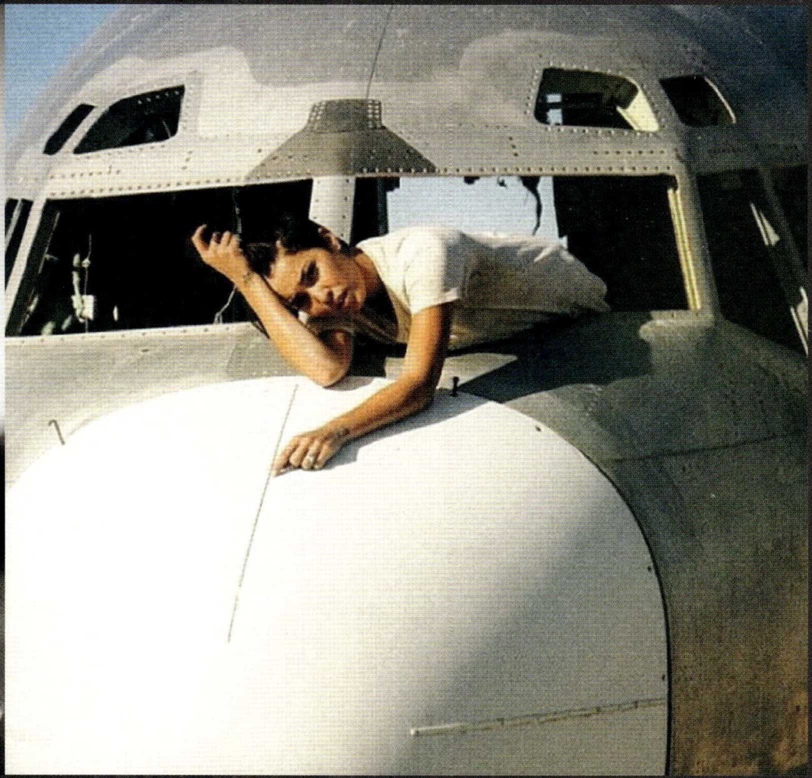

# 04

# EXPLAINING YOUR VISION

**AT THIS STAGE OF THE PROCESS you have booked your model and set up your shoot, so now it's time to get to work. In this chapter we discuss the importance of first impressions and how best to "break the ice" with a model to ensure susceptibility to your personal vision. Then we consider how to develop those relationships, adapt to and inspire the different types of model out there, and how to make them all feel more comfortable, resulting in the shoot day being more productive. We also focus on communication—both verbal and nonverbal—and the benefits of positivity over negativity, with insight from model Emma Meyer.**

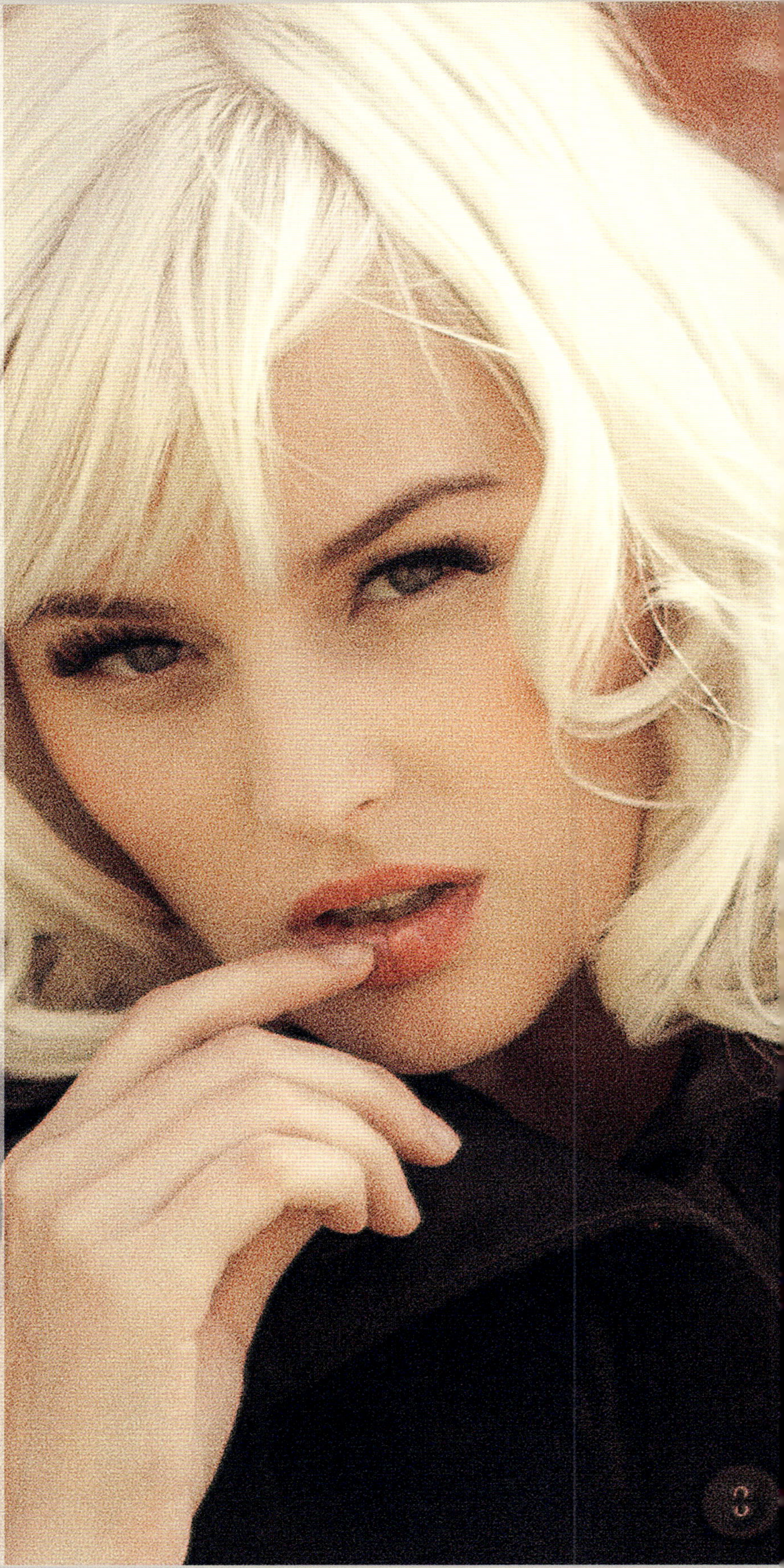

RIGHT: **MODEL CHAT**
When possible, talk to your model, don't be afraid to ask and answer questions. A better understanding of their character will help you explain your vision in a more effective way.

# BREAKING THE ICE

So, let's assume that there's a model in the room—now what do you do? Hopefully, through good casting you have some idea of their personality, but sometimes the person who came across well over five minutes behaves very differently on set. You have no idea what they are thinking, or what to say. They crack no smiles and react to your words as if you are speaking an alien dialect. Some people are just like that and will be tough to shoot—there's not much you can do about it apart from not book them again. However, some models just need you to break the ice in a way they can relate to.

The first few minutes when a model arrives can be critical. Models often appear looking lost, having never been to the location before. The model might look completely different to the images you were sent, so try not to act surprised or disappointed as it could affect their mood all day.

Greetings can also be a hurdle, especially if you are uncomfortable hugging strangers. If someone goes in for a certain kind of greeting, accommodate them, don't leave them hanging. Do your best to come across well in the beginning. Even if you are busy setting up when the model arrives take time to stop and introduce yourself. Make them feel welcome, not as though they are taking up space.

When they first get to the set, show the model the food and drink options, where the restrooms are, and the location layout. Now would be a good time to give them a short run down of the itinerary as well. Chat a little, but not about the shoot. Instead, find out some personal details you can refer back to later to avoid awkward silences. Don't be afraid to talk and ask questions. There is no need to be fake, even though it can be hard asking and answering the same questions repeatedly. Think outside the box. Try and find subjects that make a model's eyes light up—you might share common interests outside the industry.

## SPEED TALKING

If you have no chance to talk to your model before you start shooting you must explain what you want more quickly. Name the emotions you're aiming for, any poses you had in mind, and discuss the crop so they know where to focus. Concentrate on each individual shot rather than the overall vision.

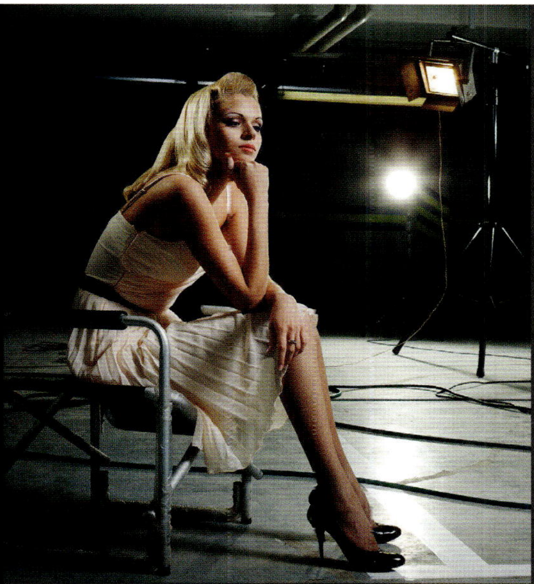

LEFT: **LOOKING FOR A REACTION**
When it comes to explaining your vision, only you know the level of thought put in. You know whether you will use a flowery, descriptive, approach where your images portray deeper meaning, or if you prefer to point and shoot, find your inspiration in the moment, and connect the shots as you go. There are no rights or wrongs, but try to let the model know and watch how they react. Some models love character profiling, thriving from directing notes and treating it more like an acting role. Others might check their phone when you are discussing your all-important vision, preferring to hit their mark and let loose, giving out a range of emotions all at once. Try not to get offended either way—allow yourself and your concepts to be flexible enough to work with all types of models.

# BUILDING A RELATIONSHIP

**YOU HAVE VERY LITTLE TIME to forge a relationship with a model, so you have to connect quickly. Praise their past work, show interest in their morning, figure out if you have mutual friends in the industry, or ask if they had fun on a particular shoot from their portfolio. People need to feel naturally at ease around you as you may be going to ask them to break the boundaries of social etiquette in close and emotionally intense situations. Make an effort to relate to your model and hold actual conversations. Some photographers treat these as throwaway relationships and ignore their models altogether, but while it's true that you rarely see the people you shoot with more than once, this can create a clinical atmosphere.**

Everyone is busy and has a lot going on outside the shoot, but sitting on your phone all day and refusing to speak to anyone at lunch will affect morale. Interacting with people should be one of the main reasons you shoot fashion. Take the time to engage, to listen, and to enjoy the experience—your model will feel more comfortable.

Models are going to be concentrating on you from the moment they meet you, attempting to figure out what kind of photographer you are, your likes and dislikes. They might be nervous, especially if you have any sort of reputation, so the sooner they know you are a happy and easy person to work with, the better. Many models are worrying from the second they arrive about their performance and your reaction to it, and are in desperate search of affirmation. They want to impress you, so let them, and let them know when you are impressed.

Try to put across quickly who you are, what you love, and where your boundaries lie, but listen to your models at the same time and watch their body language. By all means

*I have less experienced models take a walk with me. I'll explain the importance of blocking out all the extraneous chatter—all the people and distractions. Pay attention to them—if you want a horse to run well, you need to nurture it properly. Be complimentary. Get them water whether they ask for it or not. Inquire about dietary restrictions before you order catering. Details are everything in photography.*

**SCOTT NATHAN,** *photographer*

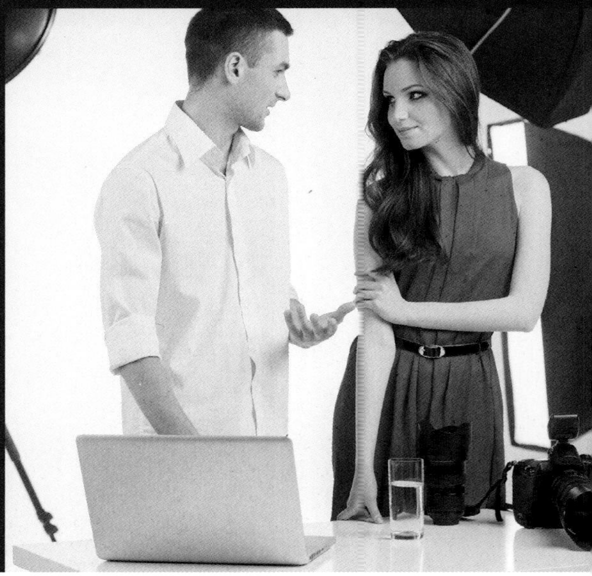

crack jokes—dirty ones even—but be aware of people's insecurities, beliefs, and cultural differences. Don't offend someone in the first five minutes because you are trying to come across as funny and hip.

Before you begin each shot, talk for a short while with the model to calm them down and re-establish that one-on-one relationship. Reassure them that they are doing a great job and explain exactly what you are looking for from the next scenario. Constant communication while shooting will let the model know what you want and help them adapt to your individual style. This is particularly important near the beginning of a shoot.

Keep checking on your model throughout the day. Ask how they are doing and if they need a break, are hungry, or thirsty. Keep an eye on their comfort levels, because basic manners and a little consideration can go a long way. Models are not always treated well and most of them can appreciate the small things. A model is not your meat puppet, so avoid talking about them like they are not in the room. Don't objectify models, acknowledge their presence when you are talking about how they look with another person. And never criticize a model's appearance to their face.

At the very least keep all communication with them light, positive, and professional. Assess quickly how receptive a model is and how quick they are to put forward ideas and opinions, or whether they are more reserved or seem disinterested in what you are saying. Maybe it's because they believe they cannot relate to you, or maybe they just appear that way because they are petrified of angering the "almighty photographer" that they must impress so their agency doesn't fire them. Either way, prove them wrong or let them know you are not a scary force to be reckoned with and they can relax around you without worrying about reprimand.

## RELAX

Both model and photographer should be comfortable when shooting. Monitor how you are feeling, whether you are relaxed, and if there is anything you can do to change that if you are not. The mood you are projecting will affect the shoot as a whole and has a huge impact on your relationship with a model.

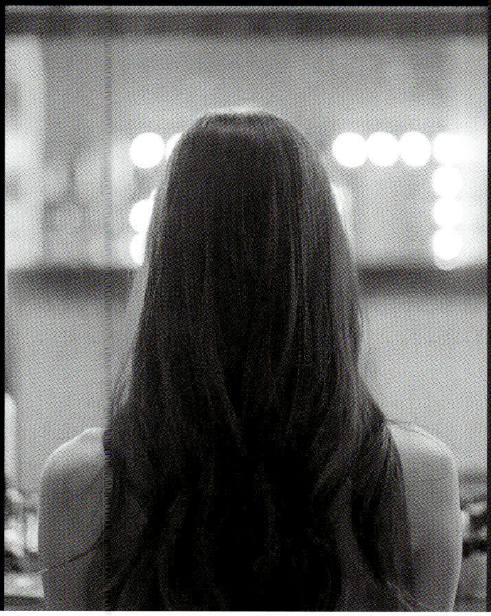

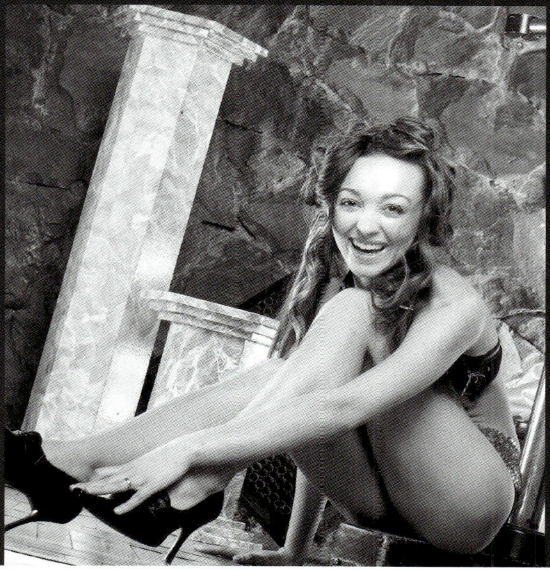

FAR LEFT: **TIME TO TALK**
If you can connect with your model, working together will be a breeze. Engage and talk about subjects other than the shoot itself.

CENTER: **ARE YOU OKAY?**
Check at regular intervals that your model is comfortable. Ask if they need a break, or a drink of water. Kindness is appreciated.

LEFT: **GET INVOLVED**
Try not to let your model feel excluded. Involve them in conversations and allow them the space to communicate with you. An ignored model can start to get extremely insecure.

# TYPES OF MODEL

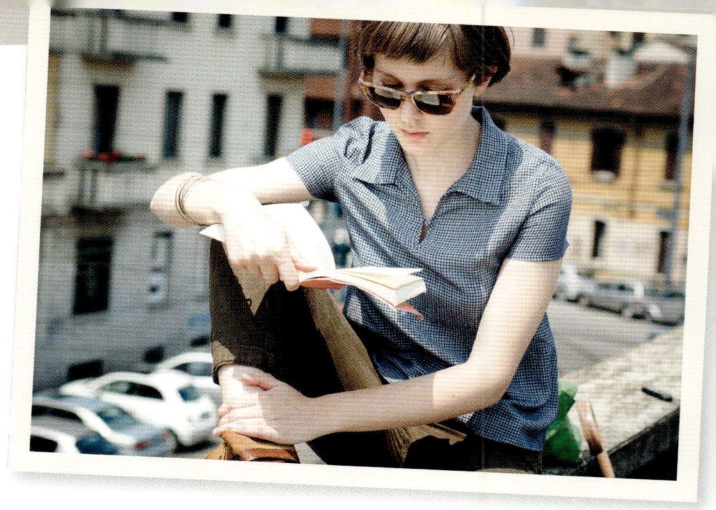

NOT ALL MODELS CAN BE LABELED strictly as "commercial" or "editorial" —in fact, it's hard to put labels on models in general as they are scouted all over the world with vastly different backgrounds, contrasting cultural beliefs, and all manner of baggage. There are no specific requirements for becoming a model other than physical appearance. There are no qualifications necessary, no education —if their face and body look a certain way, they're in. That is not to say that the stereotype of the "dumb model" is true, though, as there are models with PhDs who run their own, successful companies. What it does mean is that there are all sorts of models, so there cannot be any regimented categorization. You are going to meet all kinds of personality types and will have to learn to adapt to individual temperaments and thought processes to get ahead.

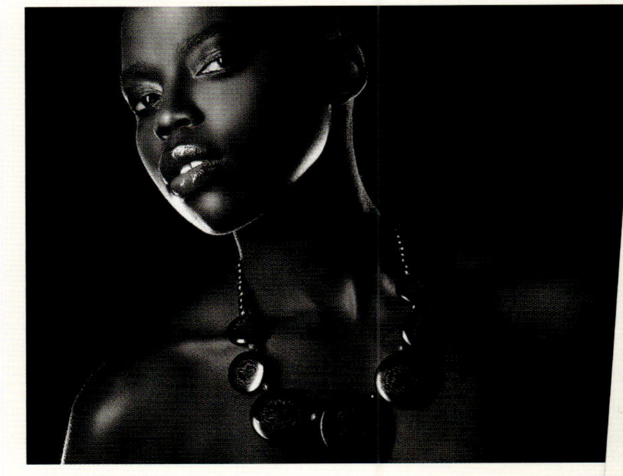

> *Female models, for the most part, aren't what you think they are. Despite looking like grown sexy women, many are very young, innocent, and often from small towns. They sit in waiting rooms everyday with others with thicker hair, bluer eyes, clearer skin, and longer legs. Great models usually weren't the best looking girl in high school, they were tall, awkward geeks. Be sensitive to this. Be nice. Kind words cost nothing.*
>
> **SCOTT NATHAN,** *photographer*

Certain personality traits however, do pop up more often than others. For a start, there are the extroverts and the introverts. You may automatically think that all models must be wild exhibitionists, but you would be wrong. Yes, there are models who will sing and dance to be the center of attention at all times, but there are those who are shy, reserved, and unspeaking, usually with a book covering their face between shots.

ABOVE & RIGHT: **TYPECASTING**
Models are scouted all over the world, with different cultural backgrounds, beliefs, and lifestyles. There ages vary, as do their personalities. There truly is no typecasting.

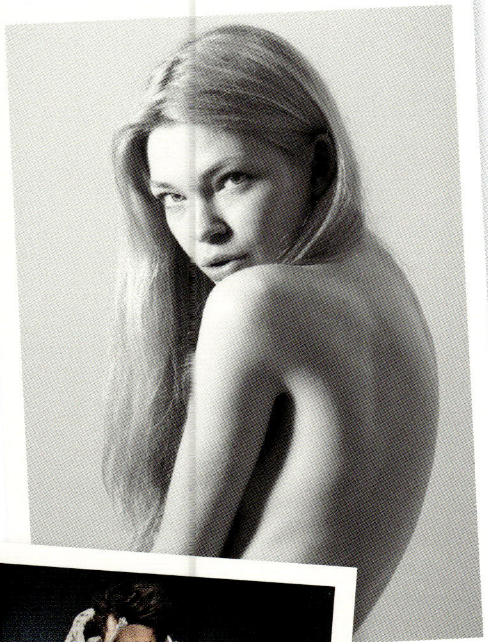

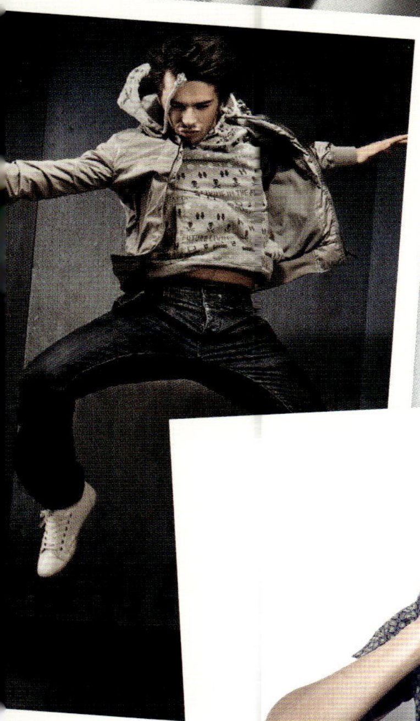

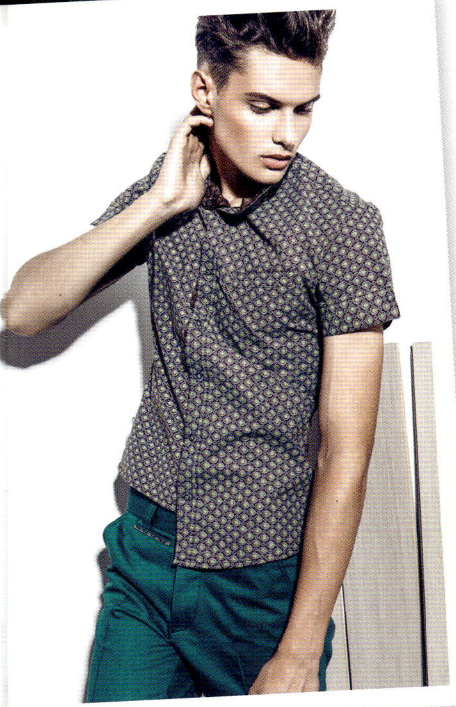

You need to find ways to connect with people and it's not always going to be easy. There are girly girls and tomboys, guys who scream "Jock," but have never played sports, and skinny, beautiful, boys who have no idea how to let out their feminine sides. There are models that try too hard and others that don't try hard enough. There are immature older models and 15-year-olds who seem wiser than you could ever be. There are models that think they know more about photography than you do, that make you want to scream and rip your hair out, and those that are overly flirtatious, who understand their power with the goods to back it up. There are divas and complainers who believe their good looks and modeling contracts mean they never have to lift a finger and that the world—and fashion shoots in particular—revolve around them. I promise you, though, there are also friendly, down-to-earth, hard-working models who never whine and moan, but get on with their job professionally, with honed talent.

What seems to differentiate many models is how they view the industry as a whole and whether modeling is a job or a lifestyle for them. There are hardcore models who become obsessed with the fashion industry, who will test your knowledge and talk solely about the shoots they have worked on and their next booking. Others refuse to call themselves models altogether, deeming it a hobby or a part-time financial stepping stone to some bigger, "real" career.

It can be understandable, as there is stigma attached to being a model. How someone deals with being told they are an "airhead" or they don't have a "proper" job is as important as how they handle being told they are attractive and "special." Humble or egotistical, there is a part of every model that is relying on you to lead by example on set.

Try not to judge a model too quickly, especially if they are in the makeup chair or early in the morning. Give them time to warm up, to get used to the space, to drink coffee, or to relate to someone on your team. Be prepared for anything and everything. Don't make assumptions, even if a disheveled wreck arrives that morning and barely speaks to you. In a few hours they could be a completely different person.

### THE SELF-CONSCIOUS MODEL

It's important to look out for models who lack confidence. They might pull constantly at their outfits trying to hide certain areas and find it harder to relax. Watch them when the camera is held up first though: some people literally transform in front of your eyes when they know it's time to work.

# ADAPT & INSPIRE

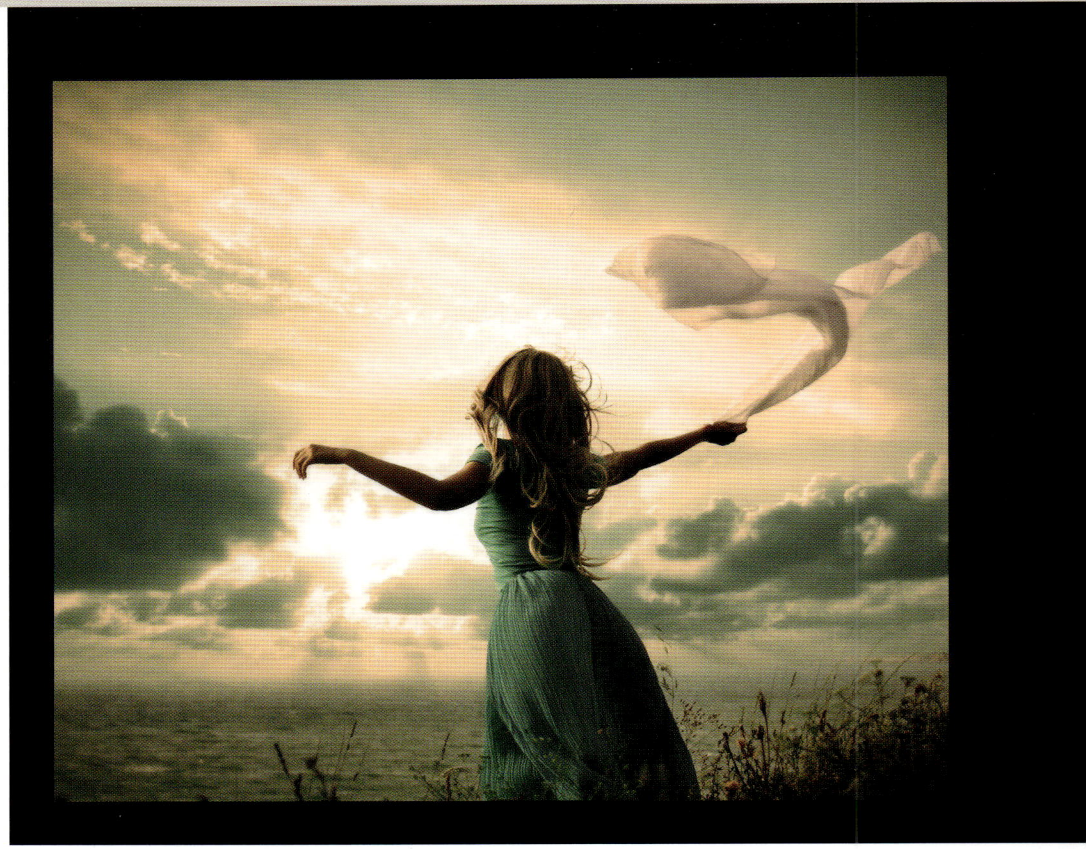

**WHEN SHOOTING TOGETHER, the movements and moments between you and your model can resemble a form of dance. At times it will feel like you are performing a mesmerizing ballet, attuned to one another's every breath and step, mirroring each other's movements. If they burst out in a moment of unbridled spontaneity you would be right there to catch it. At other times it will feel like you are barn dancing, blindfolded, in clogs. Everything seems awkward and clunky, the timing is all off, you click, and they blink. The pair of you are not connecting on any level and it shows on camera.**

### CHANGE IT UP

Over long working days emotions will fluctuate, including yours. You need to slow down at times, on and in between shoots, and work out just how inspired you are feeling and how you can change things up to feel more creatively fulfilled.

If this starts to happen, take the lead. Some models move fast, whipping between poses, flailing their arms, sticking out their tongue, raging through all kinds of expressions. Sometimes they can move too fast, so you must either reign them in or let them loose, depending on your preferred style of shooting. Other models move frustratingly slowly, or not at all. You have to describe individual movements, "Move your hand here. Look there. Now at me." It can be a lengthy, disjointed, and frustrating way of shooting. However, some photographers actually prefer it this way.

Both model and photographer need to learn to adapt quickly to one another. If you have a distinctive style of photographing people, it might not work for everyone. You might not wish to change your methods, but to enjoy working with all the different kinds of models out there you are going to have to learn to compromise and find a balance. In a way you are in a position of authority, but you should aim to be as flexible as possible. Work on your leadership skills.

Inspiring someone can be a daunting task, it can be as simple as well articulated direction, a great song, or a compliment at a moment of crisis, but it can be difficult to work out what makes a model tick and motivates them to work harder. It is not just first thing in the morning either—both you, your model, and your team will need sparks of inspiration throughout the day. People get bored and tired, plus each new shot usually requires a different emotion. A storyline, character, or description of a feeling can help when starting to shoot. You could also relate to a model's loves or hates to inspire an

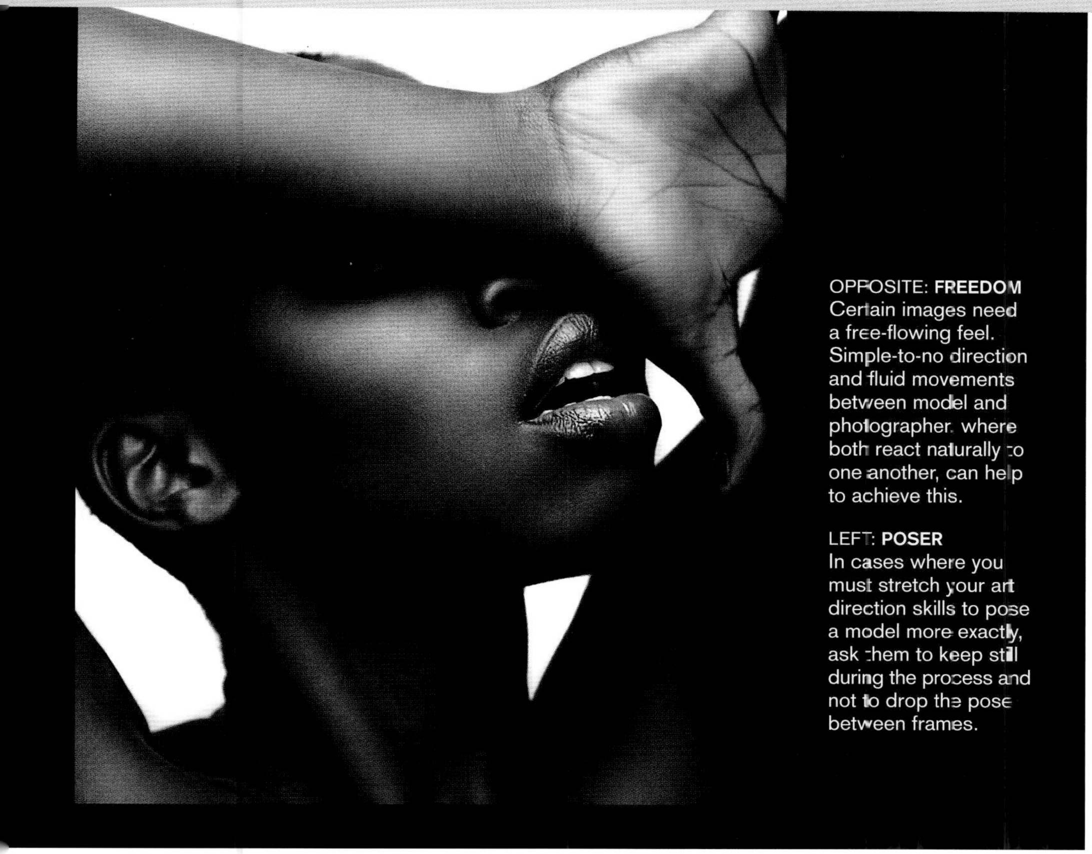

OPPOSITE: **FREEDOM**
Certain images need a free-flowing feel. Simple-to-no direction and fluid movements between model and photographer, where both react naturally to one another, can help to achieve this.

LEFT: **POSER**
In cases where you must stretch your art direction skills to pose a model more exactly, ask them to keep still during the process and not to drop the pose between frames.

### TIP NATURAL MOVEMENTS

Observe how a model moves; whether they are jittery, overexcited, and jumping about all over the room, or more peaceful and graceful, with delicate movements. Work with their innate energy, rather than against it, and it will make your job easier.

expression. If they ride horses, ask them how they feel when they're cantering, encourage them to use their imaginations to envisage the feeling at that moment.

Try to keep everyone upbeat in other ways. Talk about how great the pictures look and where they could end up. Ask opinions, involve people, anything you can do to challenge someone constructively. Be enthusiastic and compliment good work. Let the model know how great they look in their outfit. Highlight their unique points. It might seem overindulgent, but you should spoil your model on shoot day to make them comfortable and content.

Models often get pigeonholed by their agencies and are not made to feel special, so allow them the space and freedom to be creative, don't point out mistakes or pick up on faults, and applaud talent and individuality. You have the ability to influence someone's career and every model remembers the photographer that changed how they saw themselves, or their job. Give them a verbal "mojo" injection. Tell the model why you cast them and let them know what you believed they could bring to the shoot. This will boost their confidence and you will get better pictures as a result. If they consequently start to over perform, guide them politely. Models will be pleased you had faith in them and want to prove you right and make you proud. Be conscious of this, and try not to get angry with a model because they can't give you exactly what you want. Good models want to deliver more than is expected of them and can deflate quickly.

You can also inspire people by being passionate, excited, and enjoying your job. People respond well to positivity, especially on set, whereas misery brings people down. This job relies on confidence on both sides of the camera and artists are sensitive souls, who are serious about what they do. If you appear depressed, everyone will start to question and blame themselves. Even when things are going badly, try not to let it phase you, keep on trucking. Sometimes the last shot of the day steals the show. Nearing the end of the shoot, discuss how many shots are left so the model can pace themselves—you need energy levels up all day.

# MAINTAINING THE CONNECTION

**IF BOTH YOU AND YOUR MODEL can cut out all the peripheral distractions on set you can localize your concentration and bond through a powerful "one-on-one" connection. You might witness a model lose themselves completely in a moment, capturing pure emotion as it pours out of them at your beck and call. However, maintaining this connection is not always easy. In reality all kinds of mundane anomalies can stop you shooting. Every few seconds the flash won't fire, the clothing will shift to reveal an underskirt, or an individual hair may move slightly to cover an eye. The model might have lipstick on their teeth, or need to sneeze, or adjust themselves. The client may not like how a prop is styled, or the stylist may realize the model isn't wearing an important item. Constant interruptions disturb your flow.**

This is why flexibility is so important, so look out for models who have the ability to deal with these situations without letting it affect their performance. Some will be able to switch their emotions on and off easily, joking with you one moment then returning to their original position the next, while others will block everything out and hold their pose and expression as still as statues. Both are good models to work with as they tend to be able to handle the innumerable distractions on a photo shoot with greater ease.

There are always going to be random spectators, whether it's the caretaker creeping through the back of the studio or a crowd of nosy onlookers out in public. A model might find themselves attracted to your assistant, or to you, losing sight of the concept while they try to flirt unashamedly. They could be very uncomfortable in a restrictive outfit

*"Never minimize the contribution from makeup artists and hair stylists. Some photographers want a bare face. They'll yell 'Don't touch her, leave her alone,' when even light makeup could enhance the image. Consult with us beforehand, and on set, conveying your direction clearly. Don't just get up in my face and say 'no, no, no,' every time I move a strand of hair, especially when you have no idea what you want."*

**TYLER COLTON,** *hair and makeup artist*

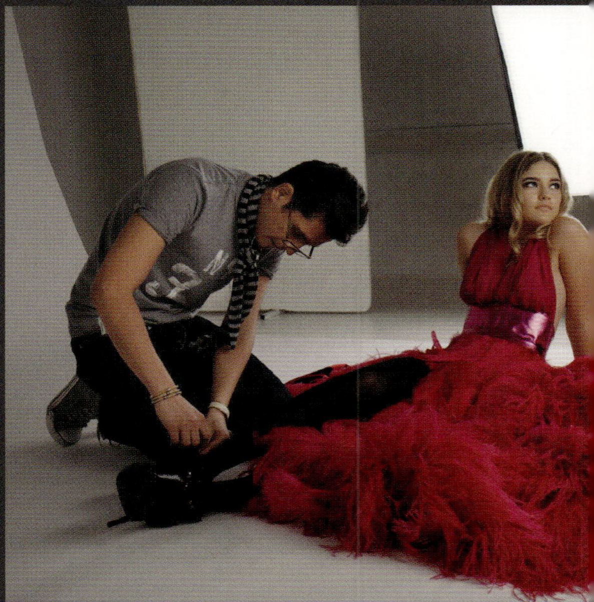

or their shoe might be so tight it's gnawing a blister on their heel. All the time a model is worrying about looking fat or wondering when lunch is coming they are not giving you their full attention and connecting with you.

This can be especially hard in group situations, where there might be singing, in-jokes and giggles when you need serious, somber faces. Keep models in check. Nudge and remind them that they are working and you need them to concentrate. If you are shooting singles, take models away from the group so you have a chance to focus without being watched or heckled. In general it can help to keep things simple. That doesn't mean the concept as a whole cannot be meaningful or deep, but break down each shot as an individual part of the story to make it more accessible to a model and quicker to grasp. Hopefully they will then be able to fall in and out of character or achieve the look you are going for, even when stopping and starting.

It is inevitable that technical and styling problems will crop up when shooting, and the larger the production and the more people involved, the greater the opportunity is for things to go wrong. It can be hard to find a balance when you are trying to shoot and team members constantly want to jump in and adjust seemingly minor details, but you have to let them do their jobs and trust they know that specific detail would have affected the image dramatically, or, let them know that you need some space and they can sit back for a while. It is best for you to give your team sufficient time, light, and space to work at the beginning of the shoot, to allow them to prepare a model properly and therefore decrease the need for touch-ups later on.

It is all about constant communication and organization. If you provide them with the correct information about whether it will be extremely hot, or windy, they can style the model to best suit the conditions. This will reduce interruptions to your shot flow, allow you to take a model off by themselves and give you the best chance of rekindling that connection each time you start to shoot. Give your team the time to do their job, but if they are stepping in too much don't berate them in front of their peers. You are going to be directing everyone, not just the model, and it helps if everyone understands that you need space to do your job too.

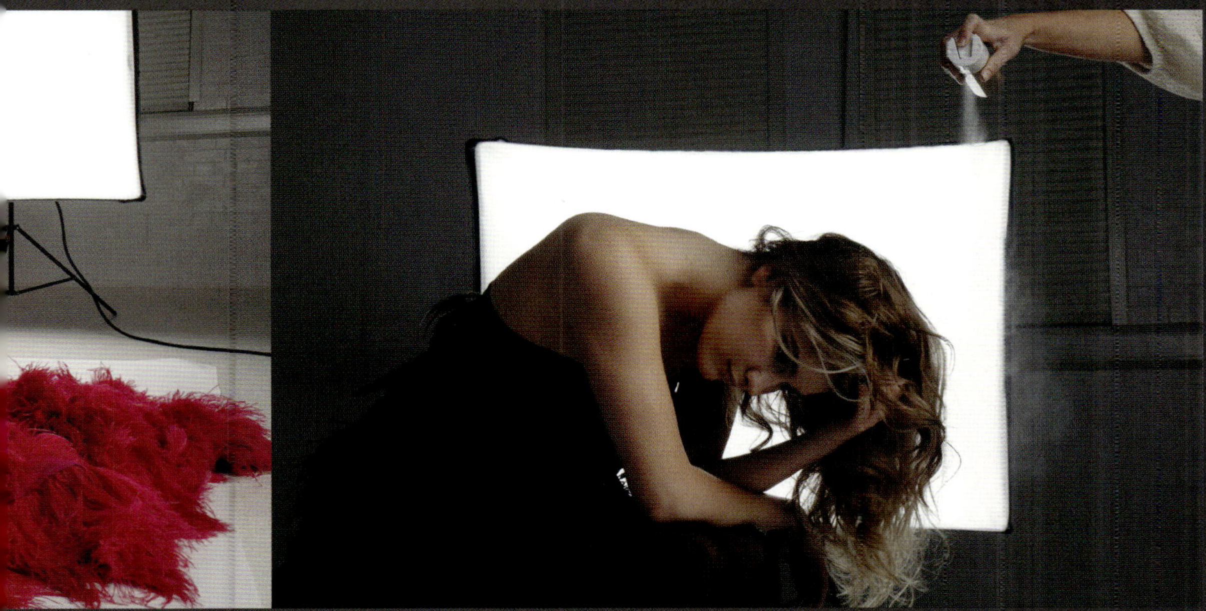

FAR LEFT: **STYLING TIPS**
Stylists will want to adjust clothing once a model has been positioned correctly for the shot. Let them hide labels and button sleeves before you start shooting. Take this time to talk with your model.

LEFT: **STEPPING IN**
Hair stylists and makeup artists can sometimes seem to be obsessing over the slightest detail. Their reputation is at stake too and perfectionism comes with the territory. Let them know if you prefer not to be interrupted.

# COMMUNICATION: VERBAL

**AS A PHOTOGRAPHER, everyone on set will scrutinize your behavior as they try and assess how happy you are, how confident you look, and whether you are secretly mad at them. Positive communication is essential in all your interactions when shooting, but especially when posing your model and asking them to express emotion.**

The most effective way of managing any behavior is through the application of "positive reinforcement." This is particularly important when directing an inexperienced or younger model. Learning anything new requires immediate and continuous reinforcement to become inherent. Actions followed by positive reinforcement are more likely to be strengthened and repeated. Your praise inspires them to work harder, but should be selective and specific, and try not to sound condescending or patronizing.

Always use positive directions. "No, no, no, no, no," is not effective communication when posing a model—tell them what to do, rather than what not to do. If you shout at a rambunctious male model, "Don't jump off that wall!" it's quite obvious what he will do. People just don't like the word "don't." They are by nature rebellious. "Don't" statements also fail to identify what it is you would rather have the model do. Be clear and constructive. As a photographer you hold a position of power, models will look up to you, seeking advice and affirmation. What you tell them, they will absorb completely. Try to boost confidence rather than destroy it.

Your positive verbal interactions should not be limited to directing models, try being positive in every interaction you have with every person you meet—maybe just on shoot days to start with—and try to be positive yourself. There will be some rough times as a freelance photographer and you need to learn to look on the bright side.

You can have all the creative ideas in the world, great technical know-how, a fantastic location, brilliant team, top-notch cameras and lenses, brilliant light, amazing clothes, and a stunning model styled to perfection, but when it really matters, when the shutter is fired and the shot taken it's down to the interaction between the photographer and the model. The model has to know what the photographer wants, and the photographer needs to know how to effectively communicate that. That

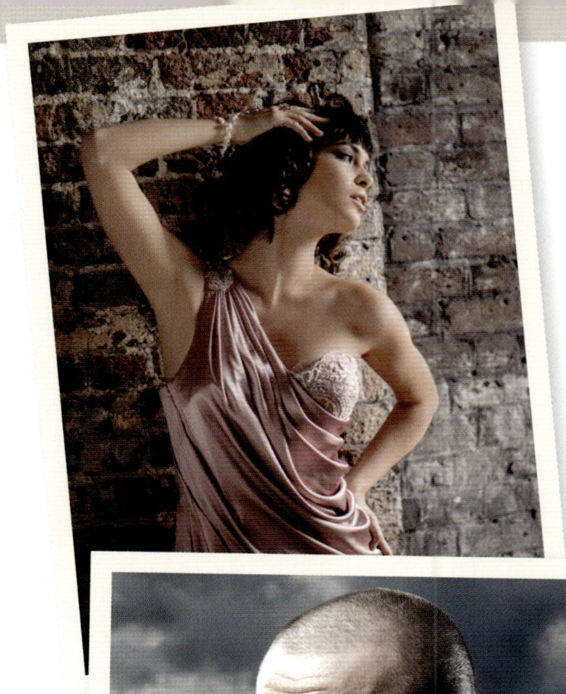

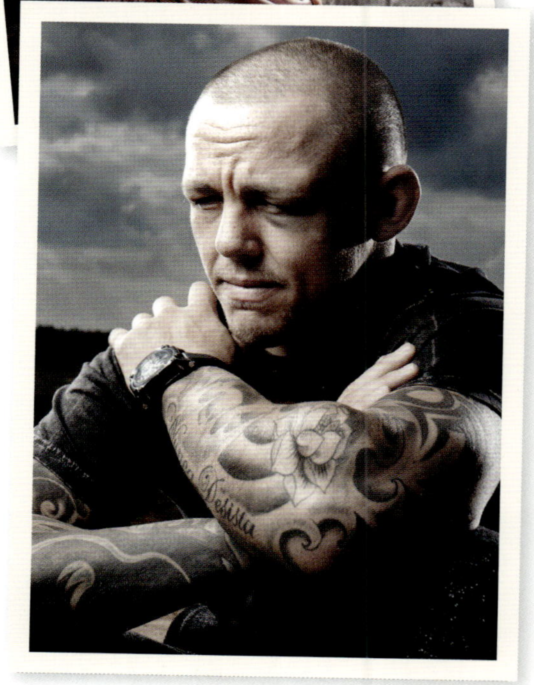

TOP: **EXPERIENCE HELPS!**
This experienced, international model was instantly at home on set, wearing fantastic clothes, and she came up with her own ideas. It's important to let the shoot evolve, trying out ideas from the model—even if the photographer doesn't think they will work. Often they can be the best shots.

ABOVE: **CAPTURING THE MOOD**
A top MMA fighter, still bruised and swollen after losing a fight the day before a shoot, was in pensive mood. There was no point trying to cajole him into a lighter, more fun photo.

OPPOSITE TOP: **FEELING COMFORTABLE**
A male model, on his very first shoot, being shot by a male photographer can be an unusual pairing. But it's still about making the subject comfortable to get the best out of them.

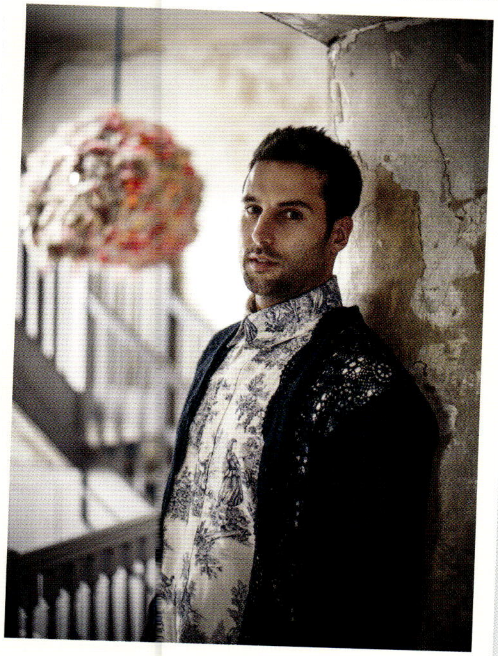

means working on one-to-one communication and not constantly fiddling with lights, camera settings, or worse still, looking at the camera's LCD screen or laptop screen after every shot and cursing!

Even the most highly paid and experienced supermodel is a real human being, with an innate desire to please and get it right. If a photographer is constantly looking at the images and being obviously negative about them, it's not a great way of coaxing a great performance from the model. That's especially true of a younger or less experienced sitter. You may be upset at the lighting, location, or clothing, but the model will just be faced with a barrage of negativity. Self-doubt can creep in, or the model will shut off and simply "go through the motions" for fear of getting it wrong. Either way, it's not ideal and tears on set are not unheard of. And that's a fine way of getting a terrible reputation as a bossy or uncaring photographer with clients, models, or anybody else involved in the industry.

Everyone likes to be communicated with in different ways. Some people are very visual, meaning they like to see examples or sketches of ideas. Some are auditory, where a list of spoken or written commands can be most effective as getting over an idea. Others are kinesthetic, which is much more about how you feel. Lots of people are a mixture of all three.

Some people talk at 100mph, others very slowly. Your natural way of communicating could be to bark out a list of things to do at a vast rate. If you do that to a model who is a very slowly-spoken, considered, touchy-feely person, then you'll be off to a bad start. It's about trying to quickly understand how a person likes to be communicated with, and modifying your communication style accordingly.

Of course, the gender, age, and experience of the model and photographer are key points in effective communication. A female photographer who is an ex-model would have much more empathy with a young up-and-coming female model and could probably get away with a level of informality really quickly. A male photographer of more mature years would not communicate in exactly the same way, but the goal would be the same—to get the model to relax and understand the vision, and pull together to make it all happen.

## CLOSE THE SET!

For some photographers, the one-on-one bond with the model is the key to the whole shoot and everything is done to ensure it's right. This could involve assistants setting up lighting and camera equipment before the shoot while the photographer spends all his or her time with the subject, getting to know them, building up a level of trust, and creating a shared vision for the shoot.

On bigger shoots it is not uncommon for an army of people to be on set, from first and second assistants, to hair and makeup, clothes and set stylists, an art director, the client, digital technicians, and even caterers. All of these people will be watching what's going on, so it's no surprise that when it actually comes to taking the shots, some photographers will close the set and make everyone apart from the most essential people get out. That way, the model isn't distracted, can understand fully what the photographer wants, and is more likely to give their best performance for the camera.

# COMMUNICATION: BODY LANGUAGE

**OUR NONVERBAL COMMUNICATION exhibits far more about how we truly feel than we could possibly articulate through words. Verbal and nonverbal messages can contradict one other and it can be more obvious than you think, so you might have to improve on your nonverbal communication skills. This can be challenging, as you might not concentrate regularly on what you do with your arms and legs when you talk to people. Body language is reflexive in nature, automatically matching up to what our minds are thinking at that time, but it is possible to train yourself to overcome any negative body habits.**

Nonverbal communication can include body language such as posture (how you stand, sit, and hold yourself); gestures (hand movements, points, and nods); expressions (affirming smiles, disapproving glares, or tired, blank stares); eye contact (which can be hugely important); and, depending on the situation, appropriate touching (high fives, hugs, and pats on the back).

You also communicate a tremendous amount about yourself by the way you dress, through your style and your hair—remember this is the fashion industry and people tend to judge!

The most important time on set can be first introductions. If necessary make the first move—be welcoming, sincere, and try to give off a positive attitude for the day ahead. It is important to appeared relaxed, confident, and in control. Keep your shoulders back and own your space—sitting or standing with your legs slightly apart can portray self-assurance. Keep your head up, be approachable, and be in the moment.

Positive nonverbal communication includes universally accepted signs such as smiles, nods, winks, "thumbs up," and the "OK" finger position.

When interacting with others, give confirmation that you are listening. Laugh with people (even if a joke isn't that funny, be polite) as you would appreciate the same in return. To show interest you may naturally lean toward someone, to appear relaxed you might lean back slightly, but watch out for appearing creepy or arrogant at the same time.

### TIP FEEL SOMETHING

It is said that if you smile more in life you end up feeling happier. If you sit up straight you feel energized and in control. If you slow down and appreciate the small things, you will feel calmer. Maybe your behavior can affect your feelings?

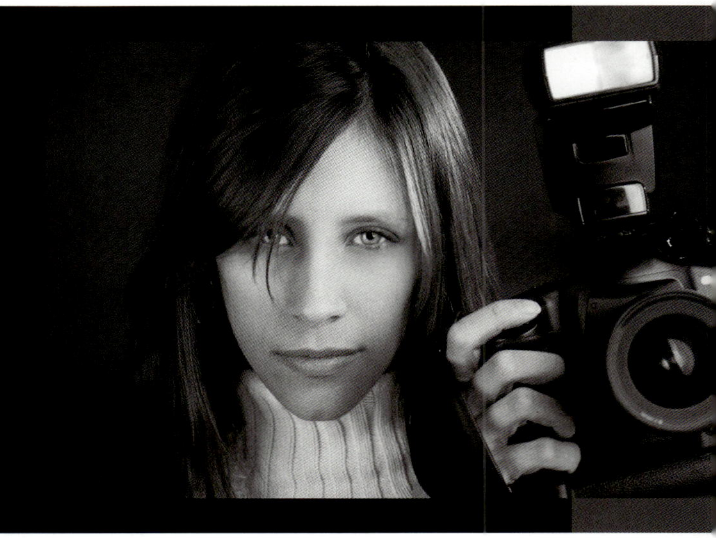

RIGHT: **HAND GESTURES**
Using your hands is a good way to get simple directions across quickly. They are also useful when your model is a long distance away from you. Avoid getting overly complicated though.

Behavior you might think is natural may come across as negative to others. Try to refrain from crossing your arms and legs too much, it can make you appear guarded and harder to approach for models. Standing too close to people can freak them out, so be aware of personal space, although most models are used to people invading theirs! Eye contact is positive and can create a connection, but it can be difficult for some people to maintain. Work on this, if you break it often it can make you seem insecure, distracted, and disinterested. But be careful not to stare longer than is socially acceptable.

If you touch your face mid conversation it can indicate nerves and is associated with deception, while stroking the chin can convey judgment. Fidgeting with your collar can also be unsettling to others, and if you scratch your head a client might think you are doubting yourself or the shot. Try to keep track of your gestures and any nervous ticks you develop. You might shift your body weight repeatedly or unconsciously "finger drum" when you're tense. If you can start to notice your body habits you can change them for the better.

## LANGUAGE BARRIERS

No matter where you are shooting, you will probably work with a model who speaks a different language, or very little of your own. Sign language and nonverbal methods might be your only way to communicate throughout the shoot so your hand gestures and facial expressions will be extremely important.

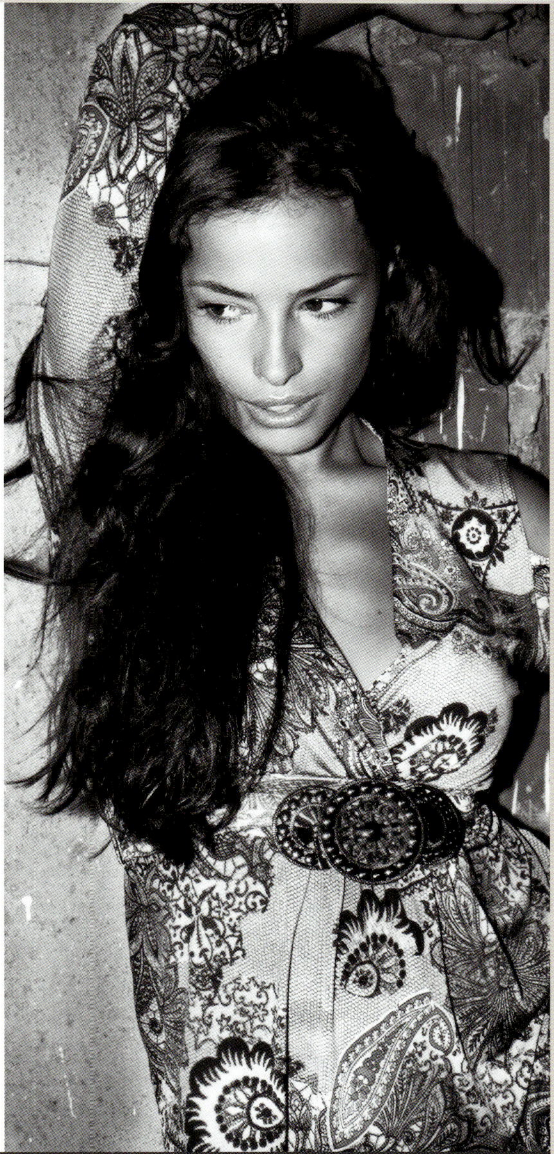

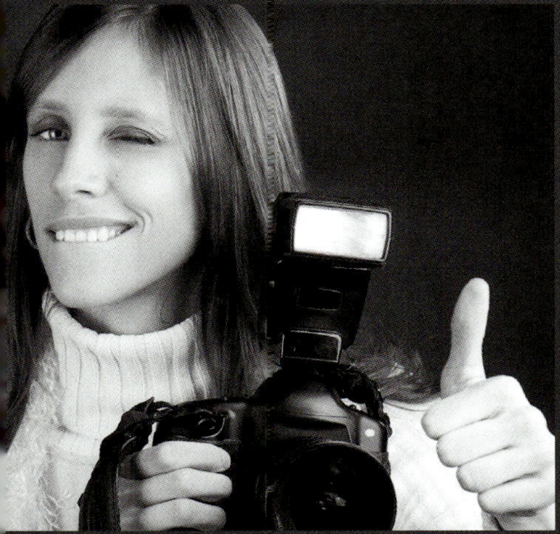

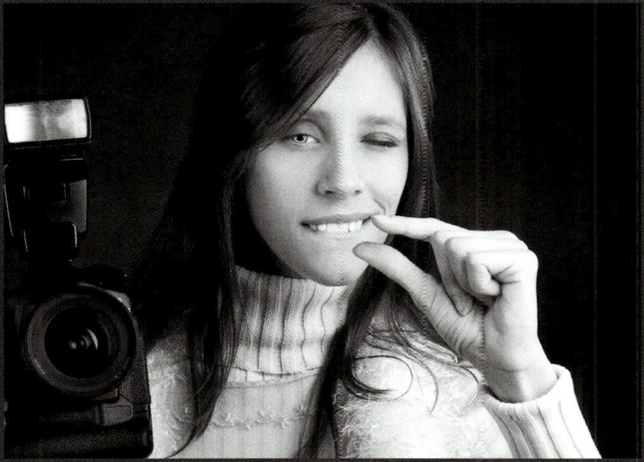

ABOVE: **P.M.A.**
Adopting a positive mental attitude can affect your body language as well as your mind. If you physically relax and reduce your stress levels it will affect you inside and out.

## IN FRONT OF THE CAMERA WITH
# EMMA MEYER

"Although I got into modeling in a very unexciting manner (it's hard to make 'I submitted Polaroids to an agency and they signed me' sound compelling!), the process of finding my footing in the industry has been a bit more interesting. On my first shoot I was still in such shock from (in my opinion at the time) successfully duping an agency into signing me that I consequently forgot to ask questions about how to actually model.

Fortunately, the photographer was a total lifesaver. When, 15 minutes in, I ran out of the Kate Moss knock-off poses I was poorly re-enacting from memory he gave me this advice: 'Don't stop moving, ever! If you keep moving, even if it is ridiculous, even if it feels weird, you're still giving me something to work with instead of nothing at all. You shouldn't be afraid of taking a bad picture—even *Vogue* throws out hundreds of images for each "good one." It's inevitable that some things wont work, but if you don't put yourself out there then we won't get the shot and we both end up just wasting time.' I think of that conversation every day that I'm on set.

Obviously the aforementioned conversation doesn't apply to every on-set ice-breaking situation, but it's important to realize that it can be hard for a model to stomach that you, the photographer, has complete control over the final product, especially if there is no trust. If you can create an environment where a model can feel safe, empowered, and creative, then there will be no ice to break. That, and being yourself always helps. Unless you're a jerk, in which case pretend to be someone nice.

Directing a model can also be a bit tricky. Personally, I think direction can be super helpful, especially if it comes from a constructive place. A phrase like 'don't do that' isn't nearly as helpful as 'I like that, but try...' Have some empathy and take into consideration that many elements may be at play in making a model appear uncomfortable. They can be stuck with ill-fitting shoes, heavy makeup, unruly hair, constrictive garments, or all of the above. Sometimes they may just need 30 seconds to acknowledge to themselves that they are doing a crap job, get over it, and move on.

I can't speak for everyone, but when I have felt most inspired on a job it has always been a result of being treated like a team member with equal importance. Being appreciated (dare I say 'celebrated') for my specific talents and personality instead of being treated like an inter-changeable clothes hanger is also a bonus. Thankfully I haven't worked with any nightmare photographers, but I've certainly worked some weird ones. In those situations I just try to remember that everyone has their own creative process and their own way of working. As long as the photographer is respectful and hard working—a basic understanding of how a clock works is always nice too—I'm happy to work with them."

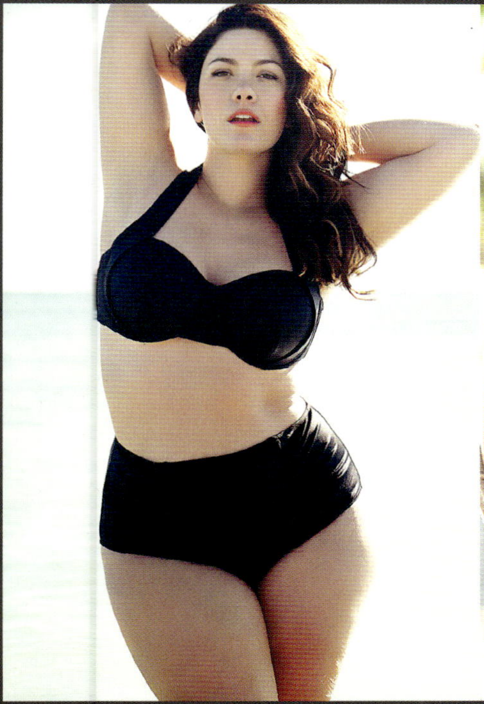

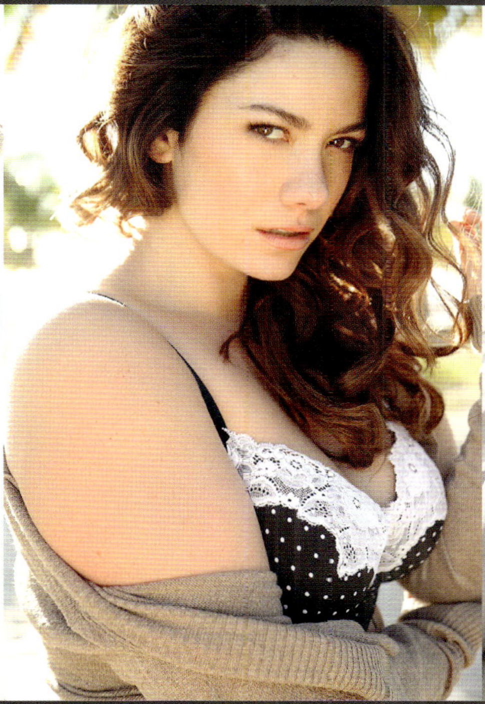

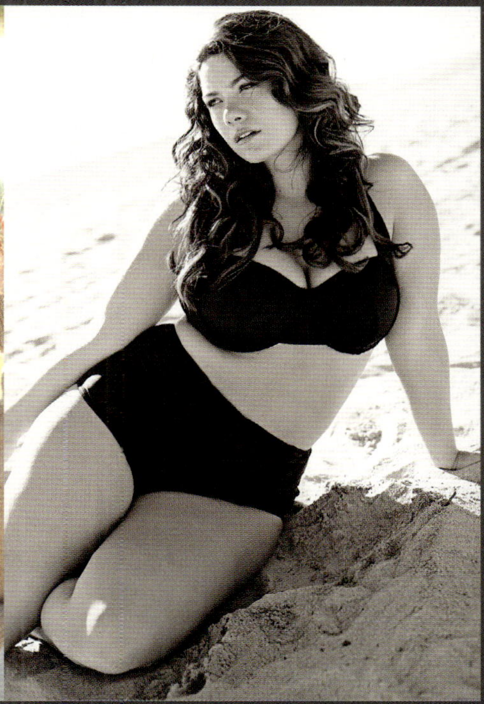

## BIOGRAPHY

Based in Chicago, Emma Meyer has modeled for Lane Bryant, Old Navy (where she met Franki), Nordstrom, and Lord & Taylor, to name-drop a few. She spends a great deal of her free time plotting new travel adventures, counting down the minutes until the next *Walking Dead* episode, and reminding herself how lucky she is to have such a rad (sometimes insane) job. She likes wine, but prefers beer and hopes to one day figure out how to make a living from watching online videos of corgis and cats.

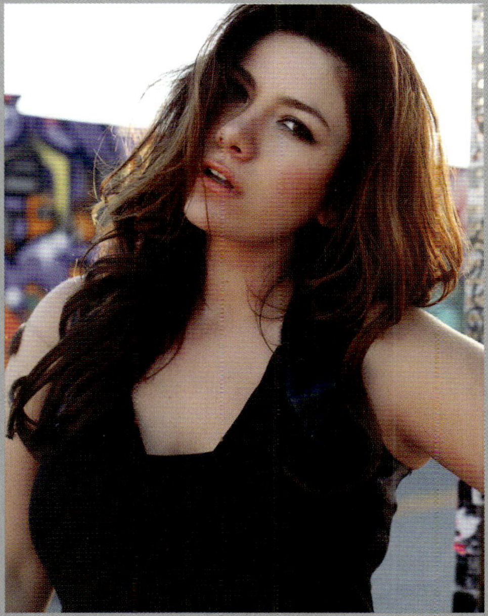

ABOVE: **TEAM, WORK IT!** Photography is all about creative collaboration. As Emma explains, it's about treating everybody equally and with respect. When models feel comfortable and inspired, that's when the magic happens.

# 05

# POSING

**IN THIS CHAPTER we focus on successfully directing your models through a series of poses to ensure you produce a variety of natural-looking shots every time you pick up your camera. Working from their heads down to their toes, advice is given on how to inspire a model of any ability to find poses and angles that best suit their outfit, body shape, and the image you are trying to achieve. We finish with an interview with prolific fashion photographer Nat Sin, concentrating on his experiences posing professional models across America.**

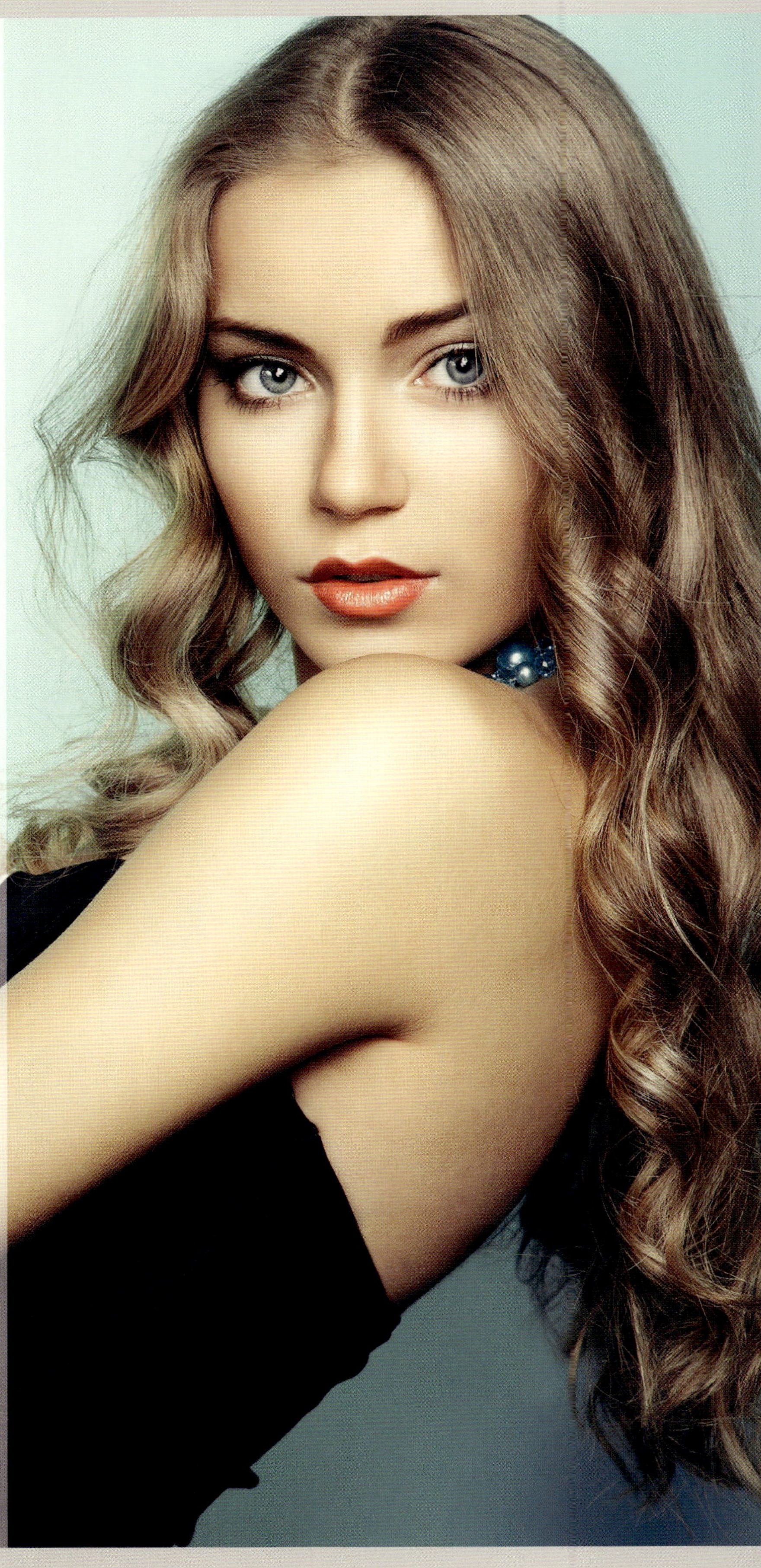

RIGHT: **HOLD IT**
The way a person holds their body can greatly affect their appearance. Good posing is easily underestimated and the majority of models improve as they gain experience.

# POSING FROM HEAD TO TOE

**THERE ARE SEEMINGLY endless ways in which the human body can hold a pose (some more flexible than others) and you will discover more every day if you shoot often and do your research. When you are directing a model, make sure that you consider what kind of shoot you are producing: high fashion editorials often require more angular and dramatic poses, from dead straight limbs to wild and statuesque shapes.**

A less experienced model may find it hard to relax and let their bodies tell a story, constantly reverting back to the same few catalog poses they were taught at "modeling school." You will have to work hard with these models, coaxing them into each and every position, relying on your own knowledge to get the best shot. Commercial photography may seem easier as the images tend to be casual and relaxed, but at times it can be harder to capture naturally happy pictures.

It is only when you work with an exceptional model that you really understand the difference between a confident professional and a nervous, self conscious, new face. It can take years for a model to become fully aware of what is actually happening on set, why they need to face a certain direction or angle their body a particular way due to the technical implications of lighting, or the affects of a specific lens.

Models who have been in the business a long time, who you may have booked off a strong portfolio, could have needed serious and detailed direction in the past and may require the same throughout their careers.

Not all models—even those with agency representation—are naturally aware of what looks good on camera, and some might struggle to pose on their own.

It is difficult to constantly keep your body moving through attractive poses that highlight clothing in the most effective way. It requires skill, energy, and talent on the model's part—your job as a fashion photographer is to spot the ones who possess these traits.

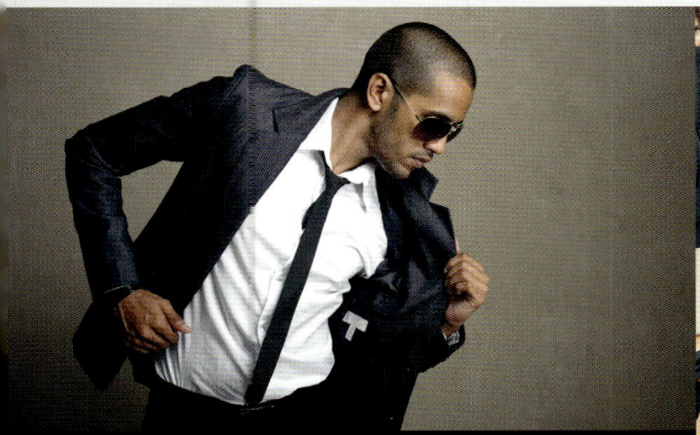

ABOVE: **THROWING SHAPES**
A number of models who pose well have a background in dance. They understand fluidity and form. Modeling can require a combination of the arts.

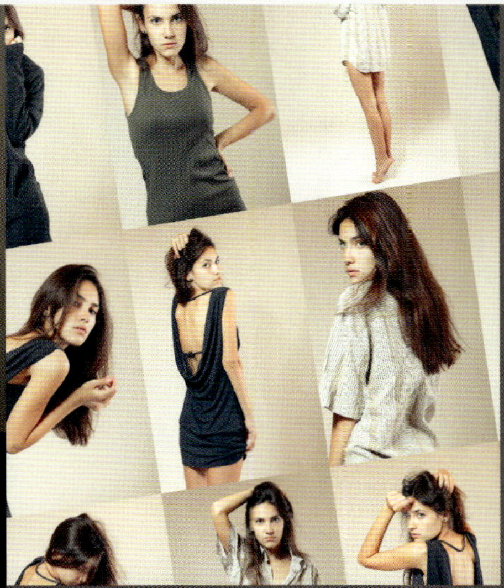

### TIP REVIEW TO IMPROVE

When shooting, take the time to stop and look at what you have got. It might feel like you're on a roll, but checking every once in a while can save you time in the long run. Let the model see the pictures as well and discuss where they could improve with a positive tone.

# FULL-BODY POSES

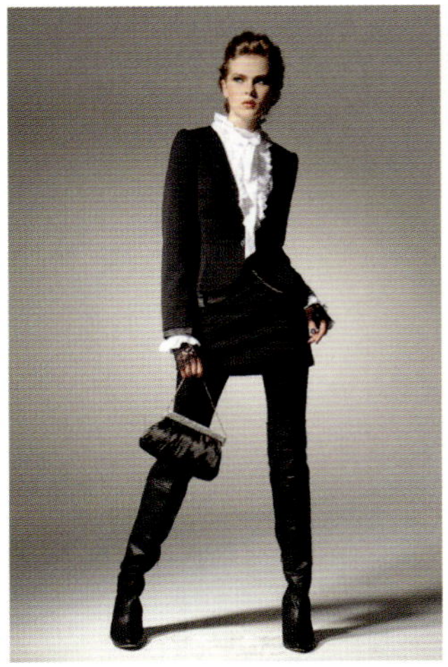

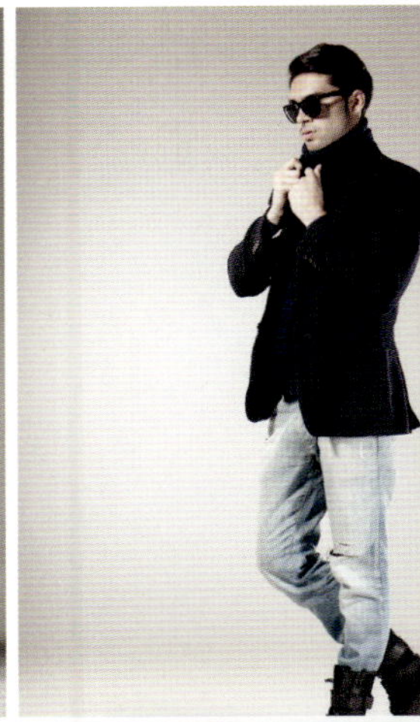

ABOVE & RIGHT: **FLOOR 'EM**
There are even more posing possibilities on the floor if you shoot from above. Always look for new and interesting angles, especially for your editorial portfolio.

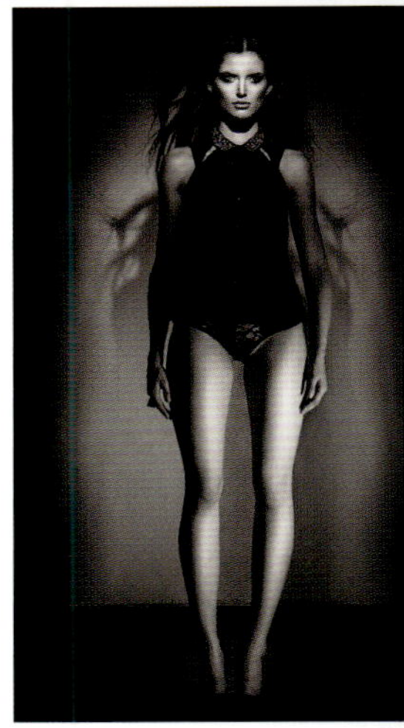

**IN A PERFECT WORLD A MODEL arrives in front of your camera, coiffed impeccably, and on your word immediately begins to pose themselves. They move gracefully within the frame, holding shapes long enough for you to shoot, but not so long that they feel forced, and they work each individual part of their body, pivoting from hip and shoulder, listening attentively for your approval or adjustments.**

In reality there will be times when you come face to face with a model who believes their only job is to stand in front of you and look grumpy. You are going to need to help them understand that there is more to modeling than pouting and get them to loosen up if you want interesting and marketable shots.

As always, breathing is important. Some models unknowingly hold their breath while being photographed, which can affect their posture and overall expression. You want your models to be relaxed, so if necessary get them to take some deep breaths and stretch out their muscles.

Adapt the model to the amount of movement you require. They need to be aware of all their limbs and joints and how changing their position even slightly can affect a shot dramatically. Sit them down with their legs crossed, stand them up with hands on hips, and make them kneel down with one foot stuck out to the side—then show them the results. In each scenario ask them to move and find a few poses themselves within your frame.

### TIP THE SHAKES

If a person holds a pose for a long amount of time the pressure of supporting their own weight can cause a body part to shake uncontrollably. Watch for this, as it means the model is uncomfortable and it may show in their facial expressions. Give them a few minutes to relax out of the pose.

If they seem unaware that bringing an arm or leg too close to the camera can morph its size, then let them know—most models tend to lean away from the camera instinctively when it is much more flattering to lean toward it. Explain what works, which angles are flattering, and what looks great—at this point they need constant information and affirmation. Use experiences like these to experiment with angles yourself. Try shooting from lower or higher than you would normally. Stay creative at all times.

The body can bend, so get your model to bend theirs. Arching their back, dropping a shoulder, bowing a knee, anything to break up the artificial look of a symmetric, straight pose. Direct the model to do something different with each side of their body. Balance their weight unevenly, tilt their hips

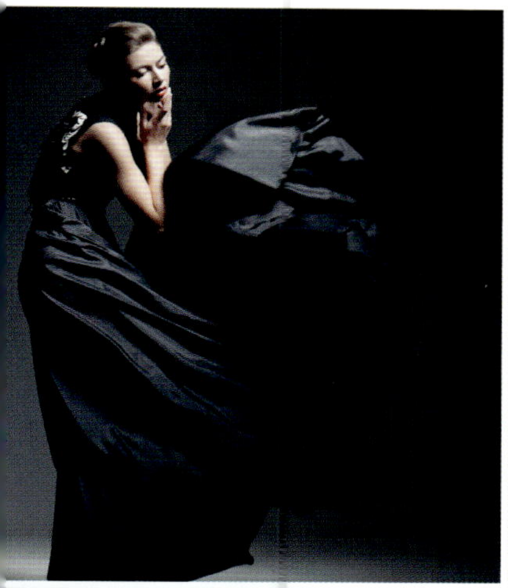

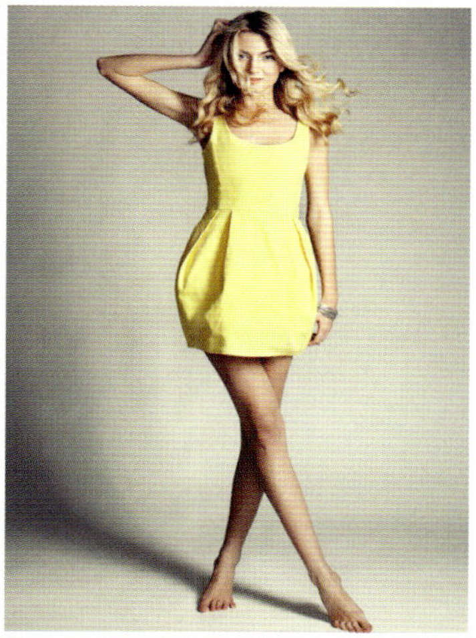

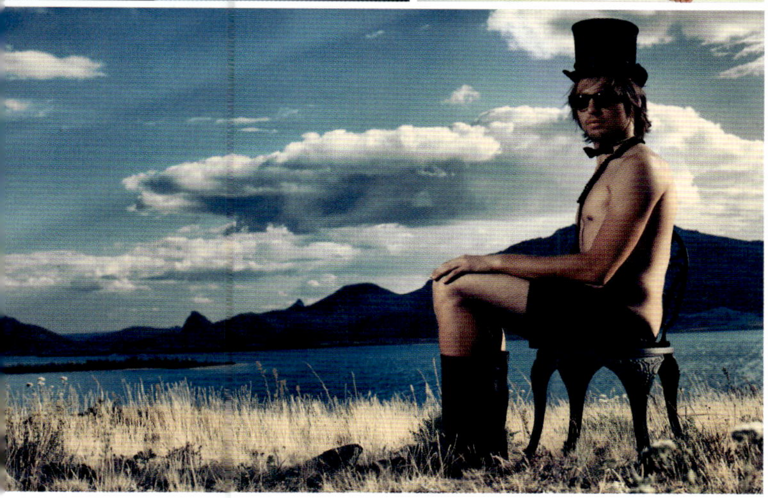

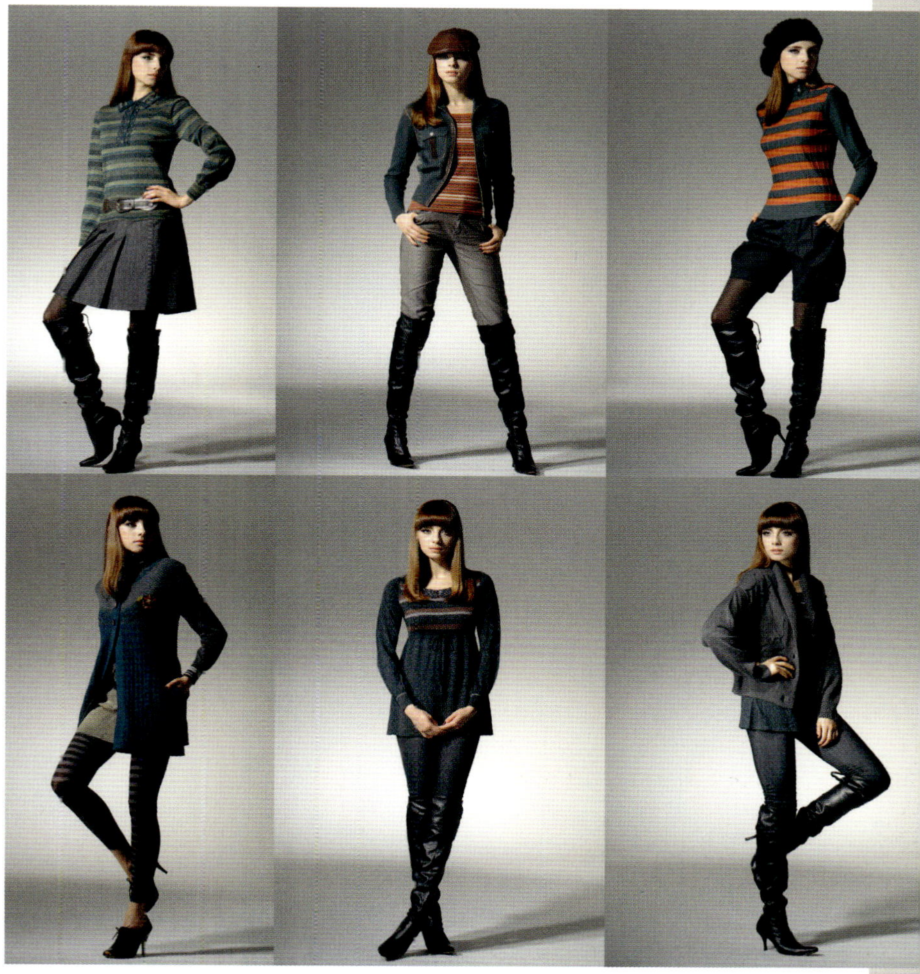

away from their chest, or in opposing directions. If they bend one arm get them to keep the other straight. Get them to slouch a little, or a lot depending on what is flattering, to push out their rump, to lean, or hunch over if that fits the concept.

Poses are a strong tool for portraying emotions and creating characters. Use stereotypes, break them, and experiment with strong, iconic imagery. If you are still struggling with a model point out specific poses on a mood board—sometimes it can be hard to explain what you want with words, so find an example they can copy. If all else fails, do it yourself. Physically show them what you want, no matter how silly you might look. If nothing else, these moments often lighten the mood.

ABOVE RIGHT: **E-COMM**
Working in e-comm you may photograph hundreds of outfits a day. To reduce repeats make sure you research similar websites and remember some simple key poses.

## STRETCH IT OUT

Alert your models to the importance of stretching. Certain poses can be very difficult to hold and wearing heels all day can strain a girl's calf muscle. Many models exercise, but not all are used to the intensity of a long shoot day. Stretching beforehand can reduce the risk of injury.

# HEAD, NECK, & SHOULDERS

## HEAD

Even though we're starting at the top, it can help to leave posing the model's head and face until the last minute, after you've finished positioning the body. Models take up an expression, then are forced to look down to check their feet, zip a jacket, or fix a cuff-link. Their original head pose will have changed three times and is very easily forgotten.

When someone truly relaxes, their head naturally leans to one side. Models often forget there are head positions other than straight on to camera, so ask them to tilt to either side, working the hair if possible. They can also tilt up and down, go profile, or pivot to look toward the floor or off into the distance.

In general, the model's eyes should follow their nose but if they keep their gaze on your lens when the angles are not too dramatic it can provide you with a variety of expressions. A three-quarter pose can slim down a wide face or thick jaw line, for example, while a larger nose is best shot straight on and from a slightly lower angle. Learn which angles flatter different face shapes and which can hide common problem areas.

### CHIN UP

Explain to an unaware model that the direction the light source is facing is important and can cause their facial features to cast shadows, distorting their appearance. If the light is top heavy, for example, tell the model to keep their chin up to prevent the brow bone from darkening the eye area.

Appreciate beautiful jawlines and cheekbones and learn how to highlight them. You can even experiment yourself in the bathroom mirror—no one has to know!

## NECK

The model's neck can make or break an image. It is generally advisable for a model to elongate their neck at all times, rather than drawing the chin down and shortening its appearance (this can give even the slimmest person a double chin). Tell your model to stretch out their neck, but let them know if they go too far and you are looking up their nose.

Another neck issue can be creasing. No matter what size or age a model is, the moment they have to turn to look at you, their skin has to fold and crease. It can be difficult to erase this in post production, so either ask the model to turn their upper body toward you, or move yourself more to their side than behind them so they are not forced to strain to see your camera.

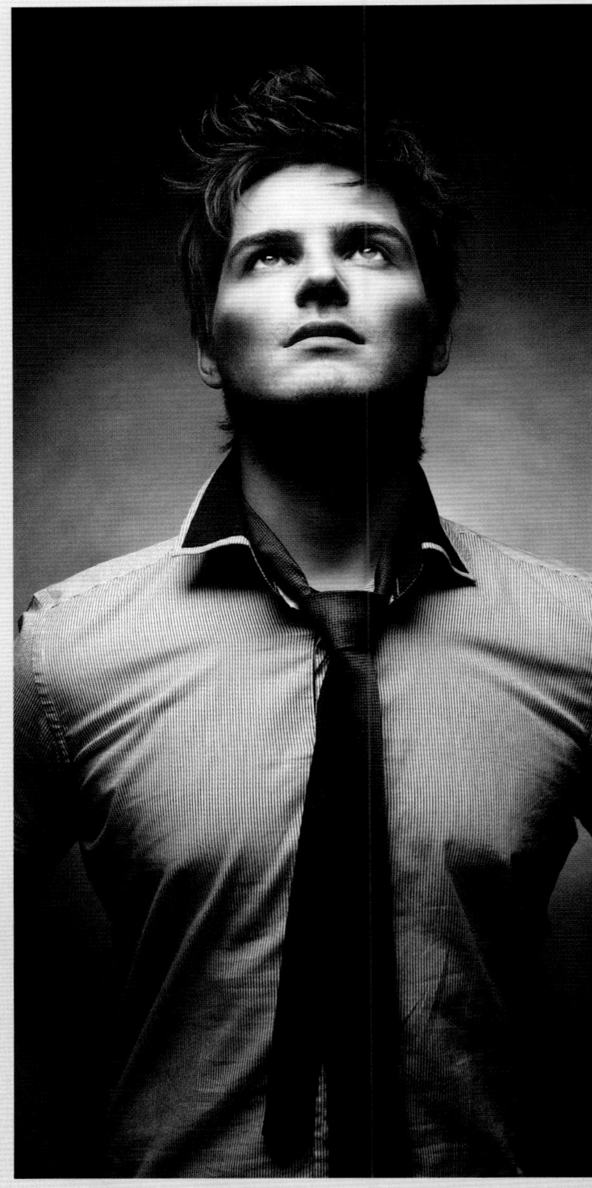

## SHOULDER

You should always be aiming to shoot your models in the most flattering pose possible, varying angles for a slimming effect. Shooting the shoulders straight on highlights the widest part of the body, which can appear out of proportion and at times and uncomplimentary. Instead, angle the model's body to the camera to lead the viewer into the shot and toward the face. In doing this, the width of the shoulders will seem smaller and can help flatter a difficult outfit. Experiment in increments all the way from front-on to profile to see the effect in action.

If a standing model angles their body and puts their weight on their back foot, the back shoulder will naturally dip lower. This pose looks more relaxed and can feel more comfortable for a nervous model. If the shoulders are high and tight this can be a sign of tension, so they might need to shake it out or relax back into a pose.

Conversely, slouched shoulders can convey "attitude," but if they slump too far forward or back it can have unflattering results.

BELOW & OPPOSITE: **EYE CONTACT**
Both parties can forget that the model does not have to stare into the lens for every shot. Sometimes you will need them straight into camera but at times you will need to remind your model that they can look elsewhere.

### TIP MASK IT

The beauty of stills photography is that all manner of problems can be covered up and the viewer is none the wiser. Use long hair to hide neck folds, shadows to contour rounder faces, halter-neck tops on broad shoulders—whatever it takes to get the shot.

BELOW: **TEAM WORK**
A wide range of makeup and styling tricks are at your disposal when creating the perfect fashion shot. Learn from your team.

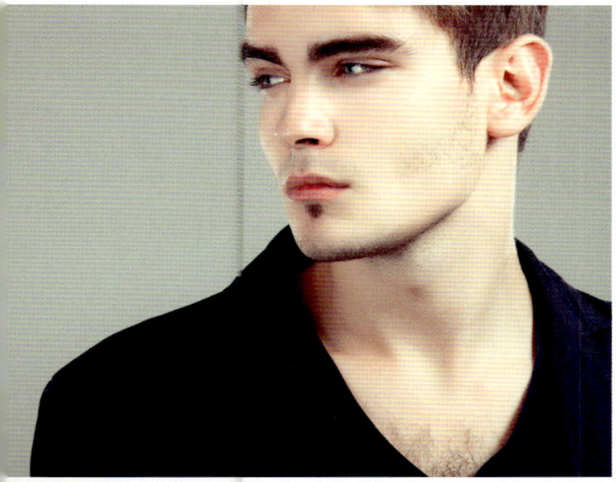
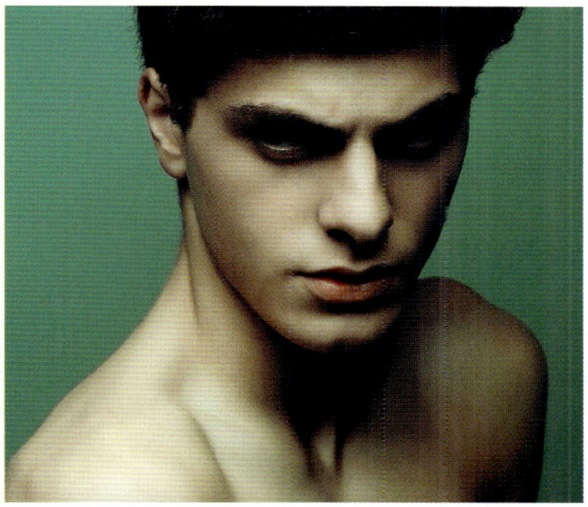
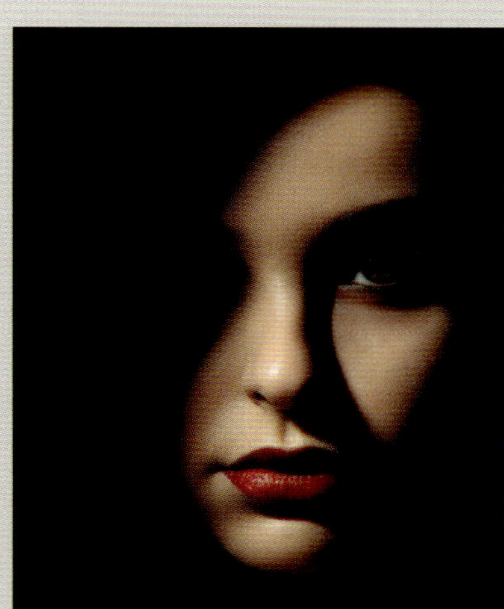
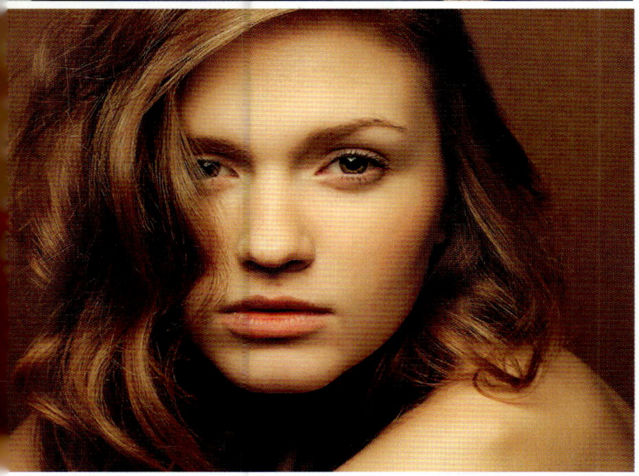
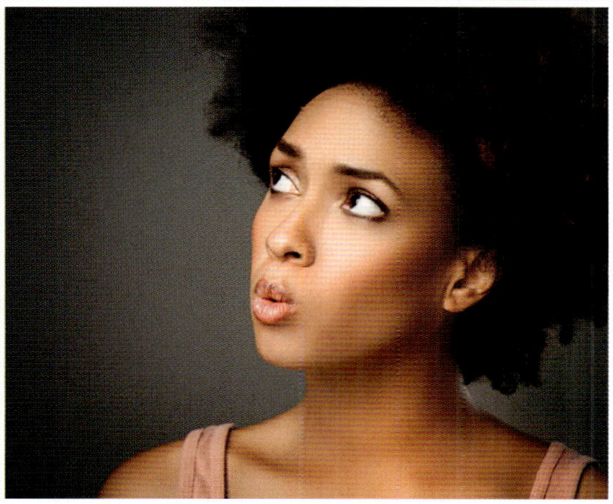
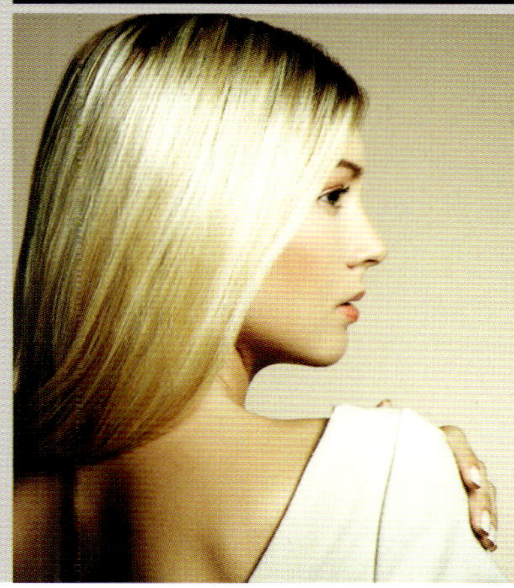

# ARMS, HANDS, & FINGERS

### ARMS

The arms offer endless possibilities in their range of motion, but not every pose works with every model in every outfit. When creating a pose, start with the upper arms and consider triangular forms. The arms and elbows can create diagonals with strict lines. It is generally favored for models to position each arm at a different level with elbows out, away from the body.

As a guide, arms should not point toward the camera, as this may shorten their perceived length. Nor should they be held tightly against the chest, closing visible gaps, as this flattens the arms and widens the appearance of the torso. Putting pressure on the soft upper part of the arms can also create an unflattering bulge at the point of contact, but don't tell a model it makes them "look fat." Instead, tell them to bring their elbows out slightly to create spaces, even when their arms are folded. When posed appropriately arms can hide any problem areas a model may have on the day and can be used to lead the viewer's gaze to a particular area or product.

### HANDS

If you watch anything when you're shooting, make it the hands. Don't fire off an entire set only to realize the model looks like they have severe writer's cramp. You can tell a lot about a person from their hands and that applies in fashion photography too. The hand pose can effect the overall mood and focal point of an image, portraying warmth and elegance or anger and trepidation. If hands are hidden from view it can appear abnormal, as if the shot unfinished or the pose is closed off.

Hands can also obscure the face or important product details if placed incorrectly. Avoid shooting hands straight on to the camera to prevent

**TIP CROP SHOT**

Think about how you will be cropping your shot when a model uses their arms. If necessary ask them to keep them tighter into the frame. If you do need to crop an arm out of a shot, crop between joints (wrist, elbow, and shoulder), not at them or across them—if you do then a limb can look as if it is amputated, rather than cropped, which isn't ideal.

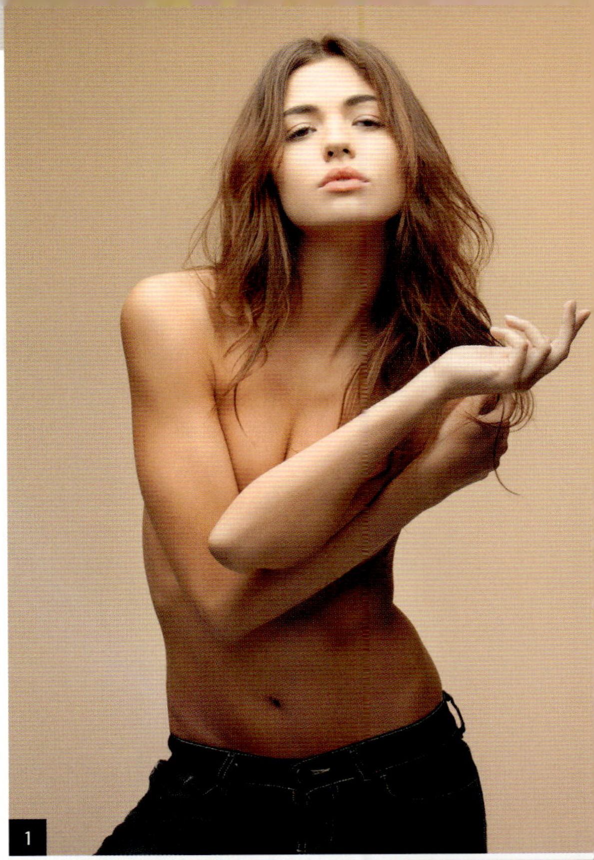

1

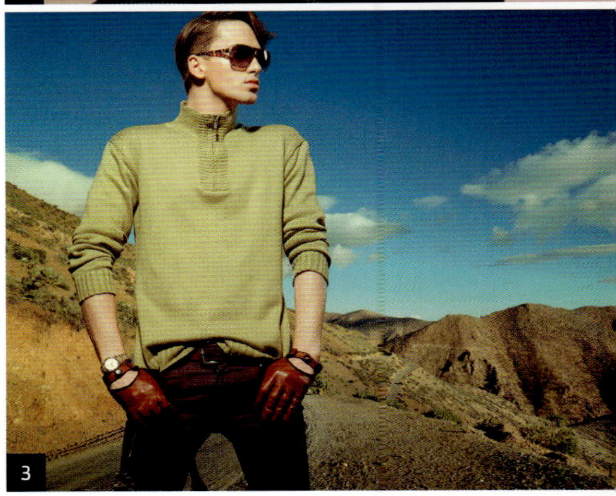

3

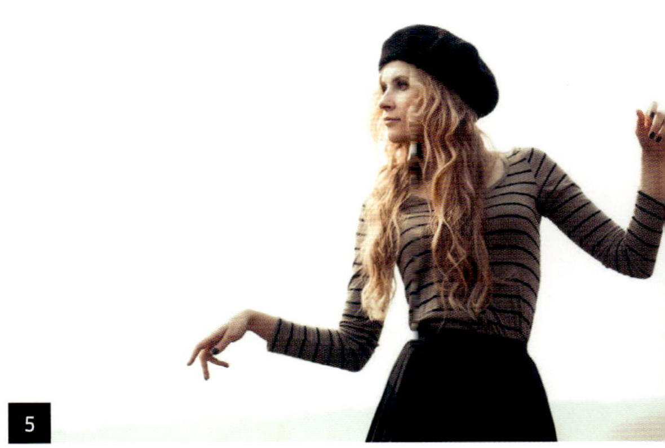

5

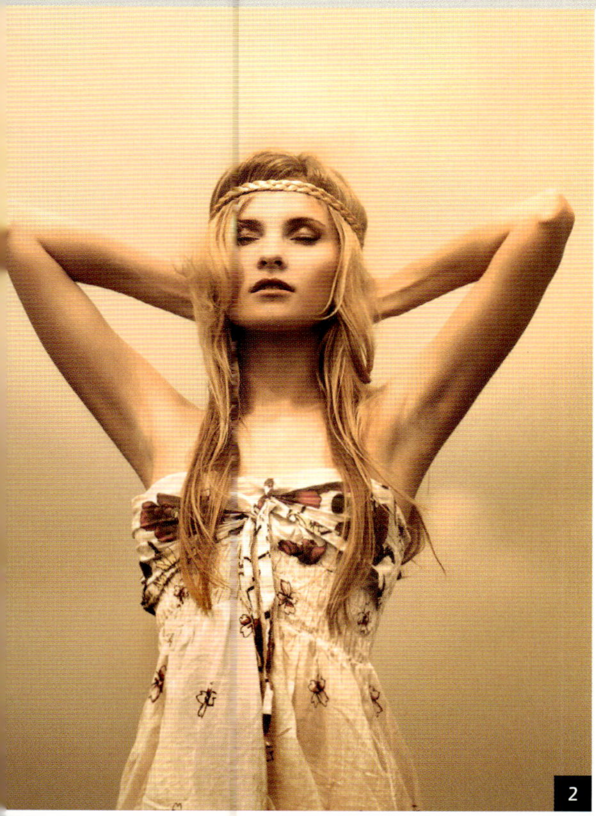

2

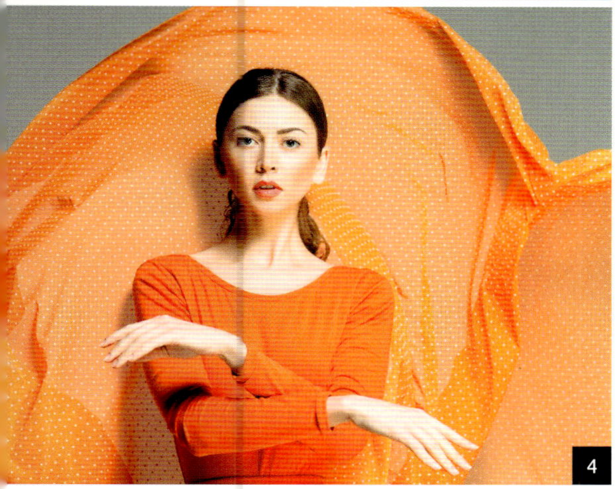

4

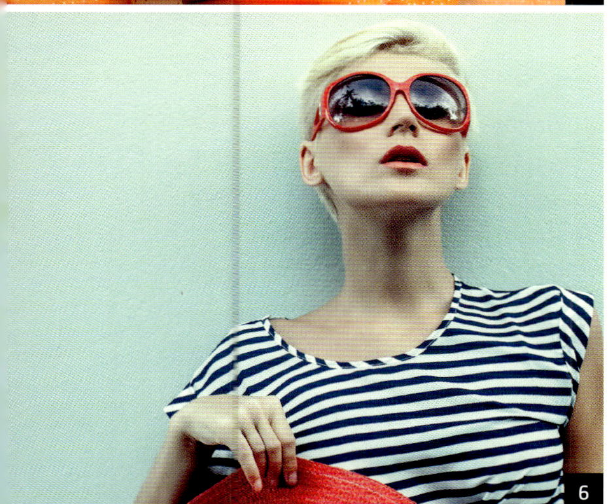

6

1, 2: **ARMS' LENGTH**
Models can use their arms in a variety of ways, they can stretch them out behind their head in a relaxed manner or enclose themselves in a secretive way. Use poses to reveal expression.

3, 4: **HAND HOLDING**
The way a model's hands are held can strongly affect an image overall. If they cannot stop fidgeting or appear awkward, suggest they put their hands in their pockets.

5, 6: **PINKY FINGER**
Watch those pinkies! Little fingers often creep out to an unnatural angle during shooting. It can appear delicate, but it can also detract the viewer's attention.

## DISTORTION

Ideally, a model's hands should be on the same plane as the face. You might have to explain the principles of "planes" (frontal and horizontal), but essentially, if the hands are closer to the camera than the face, the hands have a tendency to appear larger and distorted, especially if you are using a wide-angle lens.

them from appearing distorted. Instead direct the model to hold them at an angle so you can see the edge of the hand as a continuation of the lines of their arms. Note that if a model shows too much of the back of the hands it can resemble a fist.

You should also be wary of gestures that are too obvious, but know that a simple bend in the wrist, a hand held to a forehead, or placed inside another's jacket can be extremely powerful. If a model is sat with weight on their hands check the direction the wrists are facing looks natural in relation to the body. If necessary get them to shift their weight to their hips so the hands are able to rest gently rather than buckle under pressure.

### FINGERS

The placement of the fingers can be critical: they can be useful for drawing the eye to an area, but extremely distracting if you don't pay attention. Models may not realize they are pointing or clenching, splaying or gripping their fingers. Watch out for curled fingers that make a fist, or rigid digits that resemble "the claw." You might have to remind a model to relax their fingers multiple times.

For a female model, delicate hands that are gently outstretched with slight separation between each finger appear graceful. Men's fingers tend to curl inward, promoting strength, but be careful if you don't want them to appear aggressive. Any time a model places their fingers or thumbs inside their pockets make sure it looks natural, they don't appear to have lost any, and they're not throwing accidental gang signs.

# LEGS & FEET

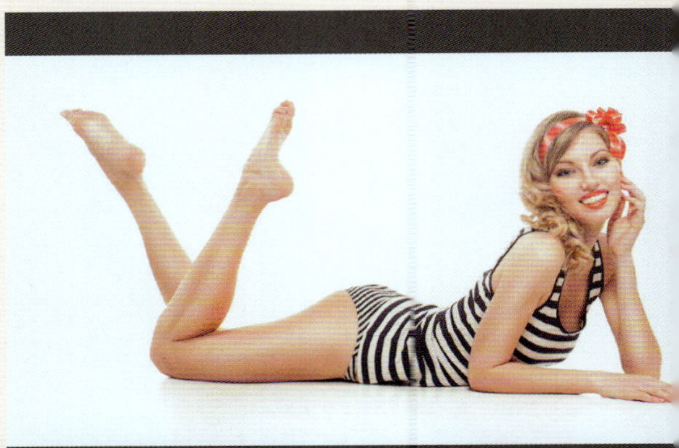

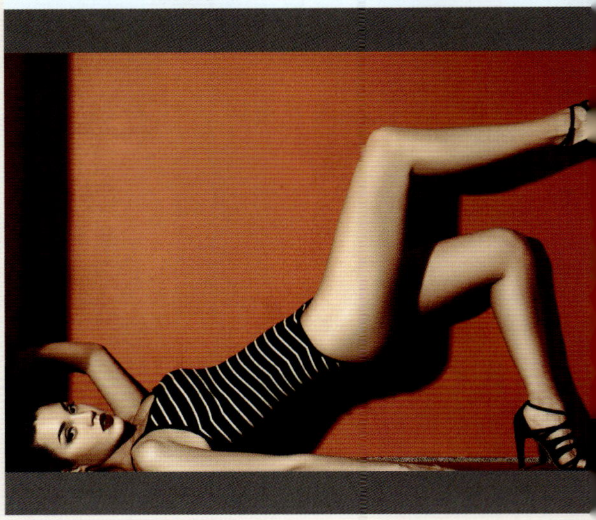

**A MODEL'S LEGS pose numerous "problem areas." From cellulite to thigh gaps (or a lack there of) and saggy bottoms to chubby ankles, legs can be a source of contention for both model and photographer. Not only will you be dealing with your subject's industry imposed self-esteem issues, but it can be technically hard to shoot flattering leg shots.**

Even long and slender pins can look squat depending on the pose, weight distribution, lighting, angle of shot, wardrobe—the list goes on. Many models are unaware of this, and some forget their legs completely when posing. It sounds strange, but they are often concentrating above the neck. Others have an unimaginative and limited repertoire of clichéd leg positions. You should be scouting for models who are naturally creative, but who put thought into their movements.

In most cases, posing the feet should come first. For full body standing shots it can help to start with the model's back foot pointing away from the camera at just under 90 degrees, and the front foot pointing toward you. This naturally turns the body slightly for a slimmer, more attractive stance. If they relax one leg, watch how the knee and ankle naturally bend, pushing the hip bone up and out. This can make the model look and feel more relaxed. From this starting position watch how the model moves—if they change their legs between shots, bend their knees, and rotate their ankles to offer you more options.

### LEARN TO TELL THE TIME

Think of a model's feet as the hands of a clock. Use their supporting foot as an imaginary hour hand, and the non-supporting foot as the minute hand, and the line toward the camera as twelve o'clock. Practice yourself in the mirror from the model's perspective. Remember times to call out after you have explained the principle on set.

If the model forgets to give you separation between the legs, remind them of the importance of gaps to allow definition. If they are regularly standing square on to camera this causes a widening effect, so explain that you need to see the side of the foot—if they lift one foot up slightly and point it outward it can make the legs looks longer. Explain their options, such as crossing their legs over, tip toeing, knocking their knees, duck feet, clicking their heels, and so on.

Guide them simultaneously—models have a tendency to underestimate the dramatic effect that small movements can have and overcompensate. For example, if they stand against a wall and place a foot nonchalantly up behind them, they might feel cool but their knee morphs in size and their leg disappears. Check to see

LEFT: **BOTTOMS UP**
Avoid shooting the bottoms of shoes. If sat on the floor, the model may have to be very flexible to get their shoes horizontal and it can be even harder in tight jeans.

BELOW LEFT:
**HEELS VS FLATS**
Heels are a girl's best friend, arching the back and pushing the buttocks skyward. Flats can be harder to shoot effectively.

RIGHT: **DIRTY PAWS**
Watch out when doing cutesy poses with a model's feet turned up if they have been walking on the dusty studio floor. The bottoms of feet are commonly overlooked.

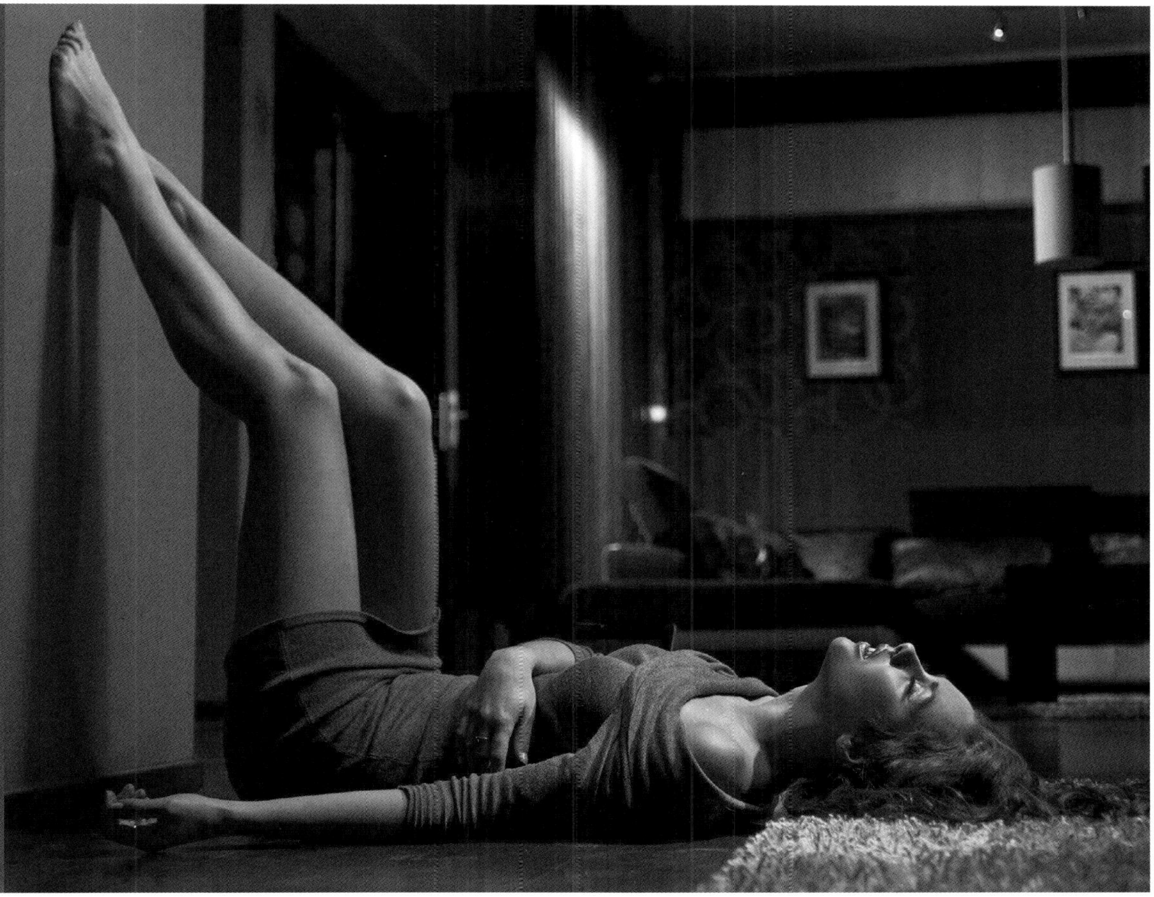

if the model's weight is evenly distributed, or if one foot is the supporting base foot, and note the direction the torso is facing in relation to the legs and the resultant effects.

Models should sit on the edges of chairs and walls, balancing and leaning rather than slumping back. Muscles should be kept tight and though it might feel unnatural, they must arch and bend where necessary to avoid their legs squeezing together or against a surface. For female models the crossing of the legs can be elegant and graceful or clumsy and unforgiving if posed and shot incorrectly. Crossed at the knee or ankle both should generally be shot from the side rather than face on. Spreading the legs apart into a wider stance is common for male models and can be used well with girls, but avoid the "crotch shot" unless trying to make a statement.

### TIP TOE BE SURE

Toes are as important as fingers and should generally be pointed rather than splayed. Watch out for toes creeping over the edges of open shoes. If shooting a shoe story, cast, and advise pedicures beforehand—many top models have terrible, blistered feet from wearing multiple pairs of ill-fitting shoes.

# "DON'T POSE! DO NOTHING!"

**AN INFLUX OF FASHION COMPANIES are calling for more lifestyle-orientated images, which are supposedly easier to relate to, as if these pictures are a window into an individual's life and the photographer is almost non-existent in the viewer's mind.**

These photographs can be set up to flow organically, or posed very specifically to look "unposed." There really are no hard and fast rules, and some shots that are supposed to be natural can end up looking stilted, while posed shots can fall apart and lead to beautiful, natural-looking mistakes. It can be unpredictable, but that's what makes it fun. When you are shooting, try and describe the amount and the style of posing the job requires before you start, so it doesn't lead to problems later on.

As a model, when you are stood stock still, not moving a muscle and a photographer shakes their head at you and says "don't pose, do nothing," it can be extremely confusing and frustrating. The model—in their head—is saying, "I'm not doing anything, so how can I be posing? Now I think about it, everything is a pose!"

This can cause the model visible consternation. They start to forget where their hands normally go, as if they have never used them before in real life. They forget how they stand naturally, and how it feels to put one foot in front of the other. The more they think about *not* posing, the more posed and contrived everything seems, and their limbs are suddenly awkward and

> *Positive reinforcement is key. I am very clear about what I like. I also try to be as clear and concise when I'm directing. There's no vagueness in my words. For example, instead of saying 'relax,' I'll say 'let's roll out your left shoulder and loosen up your elbow a little. I can see a little tension on your left side right now.' In fact, words like 'relax' are forbidden in my books when I have a camera in my hands: it's totally overused and such a condescending word that I think it freezes up communication.*
>
> **VIVIEN KILLILEA,** *photographer*

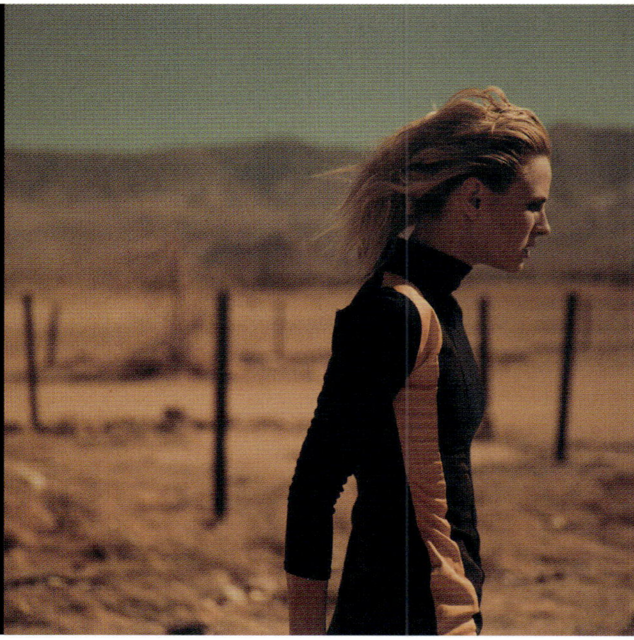

stiff. They end up doing the opposite to what you want! The same goes when you tell someone to "just relax"—this is exactly what you don't want to hear mid panic attack! Pointing out the obvious is unproductive and can cause embarrassment, further antagonizing the issue.

What you want is for the model to act "real" in an imaginary scenario of your choice so that the photographed moments appear spontaneous, as if you are not even there, and the audience truly believes it could be a part of their reality—that beautiful girl really is floating away holding those balloons, or wading through a fountain to meet her true love, or trekking through a forest after base jumping that cliff in the background.

When authenticity is lost it can reflect badly on a brand's image, so explain this to the model. Suggest that they try and ignore you, that they don't look directly into camera, and they move freely without stopping to hold a pose. If they immediately put their hand on their hip and stare down the lens, tell them again that they need to drop their arm and maybe daydream a little. Describe the behavior you want, tell them to avoid the poses they would see in catalogs or when shopping online. Let them know they can freestyle and loosen up, but remember this can be hard for some and may take time.

Models work with different photographers every day. On Monday they could have to act like a mannequin, holding specific poses for great lengths of time, being directed like a remote controlled puppet. Tuesday they might have to stage dive and mosh with a bunch of strangers, or stand alone in a studio and pretend to be the last leaf of corn, blowing in the wind, in a lonely field. Not everyone can readjust quickly.

Models are not mind readers, either—only you inherently know what you want and how you want it done. If you are adamant something must be achieved in a particular way, let the relevant people know in a polite manner. Communicate. When shooting, be as concise or as descriptive as you like, but talk to your model. Don't expect them to know everything and don't judge too quickly. It can be demoralizing for someone to hear they are doing something wrong. It is mean, emotionally damaging, and unnecessary in this format. It's not always about what the model can't do, or what they have to offer, it's about what you can create together, and what you can teach one other.

LEFT: **TIME & SPACE**
For a more voyeuristic approach allow the model time and space to relax. For this shot the photographer designated beforehand a wide area I could move around without stepping out of frame, then let me start walking and gave very little direction throughout.

RIGHT: **CASTING TIP**
If you want a less posed image, when casting, keep an eye out for models who constantly shoot catalog and e-commerce. They can find it more difficult to let loose

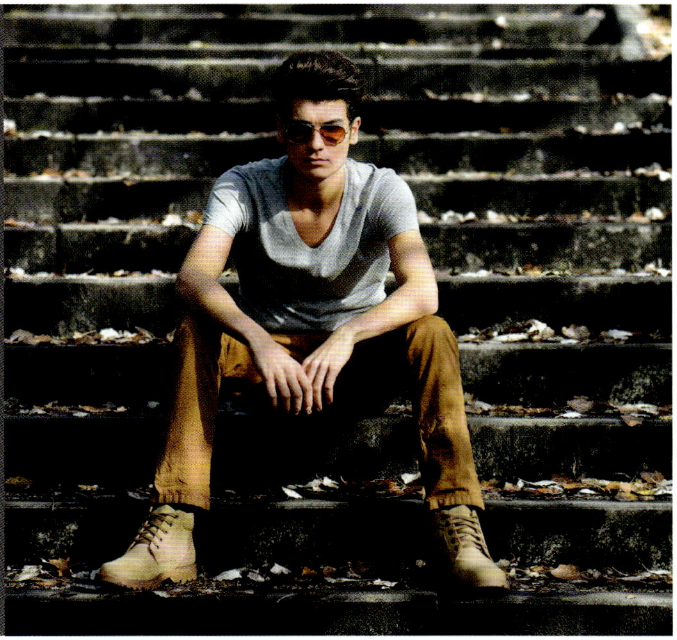

**"GO WILD, GO CRAZY"**

At a casting early in my modeling career an intimidating photographer told to shake my body, to "go wild, go crazy." I threw my arms and legs about until he suddenly yelled "Stop!" and held up his camera. Instinctively I took on a fashion pose. He was angry. He'd wanted me to fall on the floor, to crumple without worrying about how I looked. It was a harsh but important lesson to learn.

# BEHIND THE LENS WITH
# NAT SIN

When I started out I had the fortune of working as a photo assistant for two seasoned lifestyle and catalog photographers. I learned a lot valuable things on set just from observing them working, like how to speak to models and give directions on set. So when the time came for my own freelance practice, I had a good sense of where to start.

Walking poses are always flattering because they convey strength and energy. It's an easy pose for models to start with, and it kicks off the shoot on a strong note. Full length shots can definitely be more challenging, as everything about the model, from head to toe, has to be just right for the shot to come together. When reviewing shots with clients, I often hear them say things like, 'Oh this would be the winning shot, if only...'

It's rare that a model refuses to move, but often they don't move in the right way and with the right vibe. I usually bring tear sheets of poses and facial expressions to communicate with models during hair and makeup. This way, they see photo examples instead of having to interpret my verbal instructions. Since we're all visual people, it takes the guess work out of it—a picture's worth a thousand words, you know?

Also, playing the right music for the style of poses is key, as it creates an atmosphere. When I shoot 'look books' and for online it can mean photographing dozens of looks in one day, which can affect everyone on set, especially the models. I always give props to the model as they pose, and playing good upbeat music is a must. In this situation my advice is to avoid overshooting—give your models a specific shot count for each look so they can pace the variety of poses.

Two common problems occur when posing. The first is shortening the neck. It's essential for models to elongate the neck at all times, but an inexperienced model often doesn't realize this and poses with her shoulder covering her neck. The second problem is when a model poses with one leg in front of the other on a front facing pose. On camera, this makes the model look ike she has only one leg. I call this pose 'The Flamingo.'

I have a couple of tips for an aspiring photographer to learn about posing models. One is to spend time looking at the works of iconic fashion photographers, from the statuesque work of Herb Ritts to the spontaneous energy of Ellen Von Unwerth. Second, take a formal class or workshop on fashion photography. Many classes give valuable instruction on poses and how to communicate. Lastly, watch reality TV shows like *Top Model*. Sure, they're produced for entertainment and drama, but the photo shoot and critiques can be good lessons for both models and photographers.

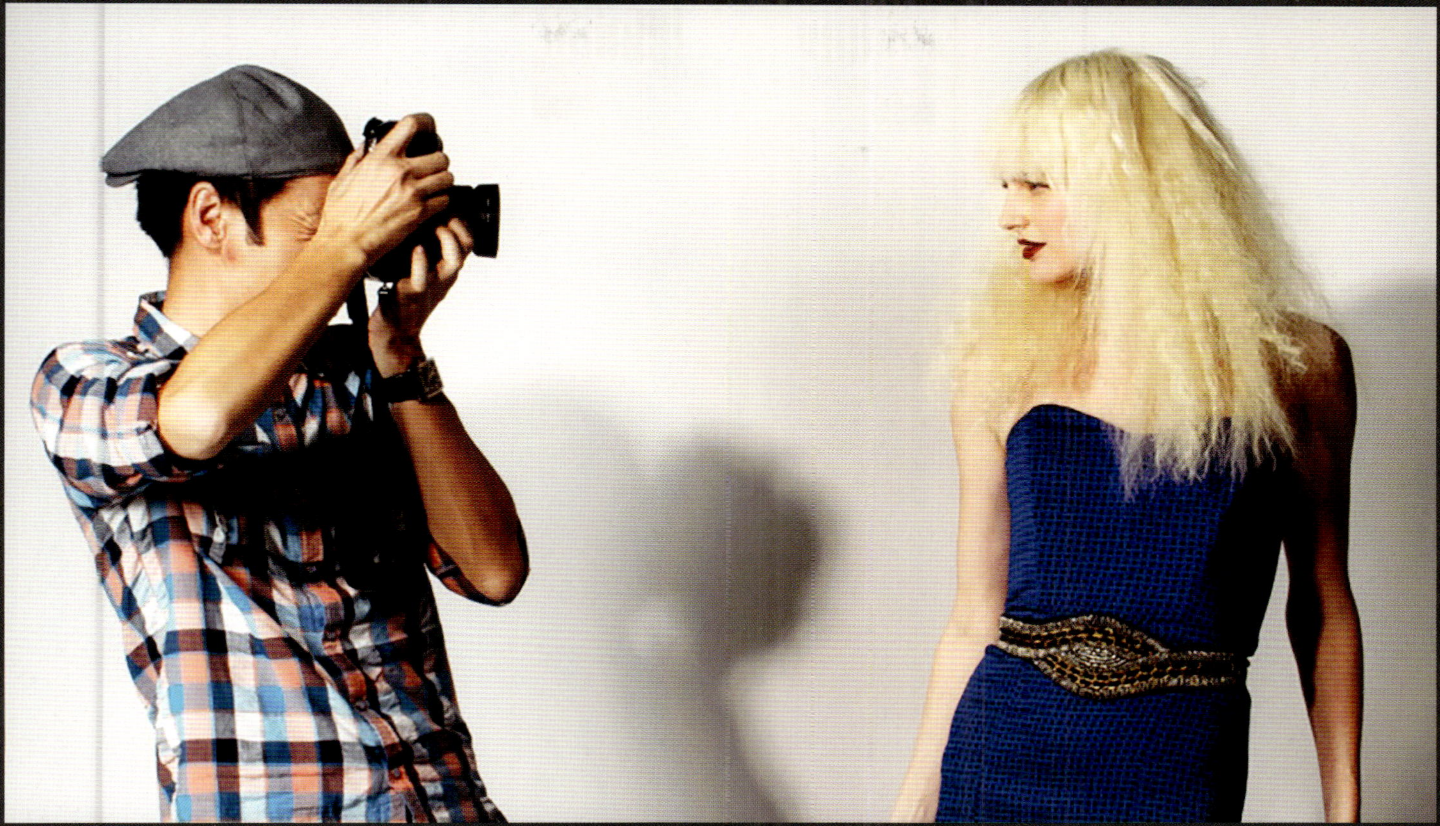

ABOVE: **WORKING TOGETHER** Nat and Franki have worked together shooting brand "Look Books." These require numerous looks throughout the day and a quick shot rate. Both photographer and model need to be able to use their skills at speed to achieve results the client will approve.

## BIO

Nat Sin is a freelance photographer based in Los Angeles, whose photos consistently show an easy relationship between himself and his subjects. Nat engages his subjects to let down their guards and tell a good visual story. When shooting, Nat's perspective conveys a sense of place and a facet of character, and his individual perspective allows him to capture candid authenticity in his subjects.

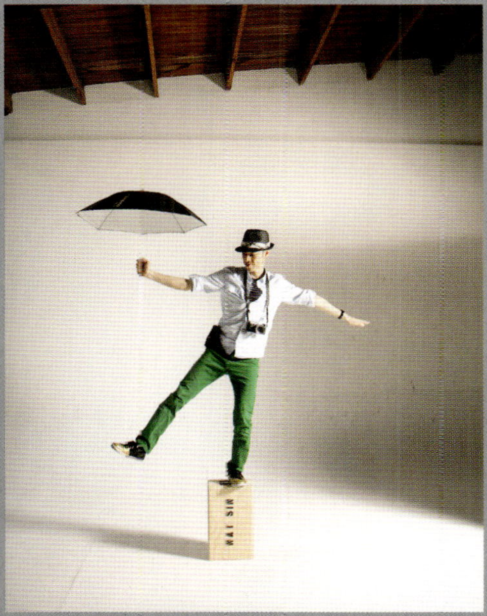

# 06

# SHOOTING BEAUTY

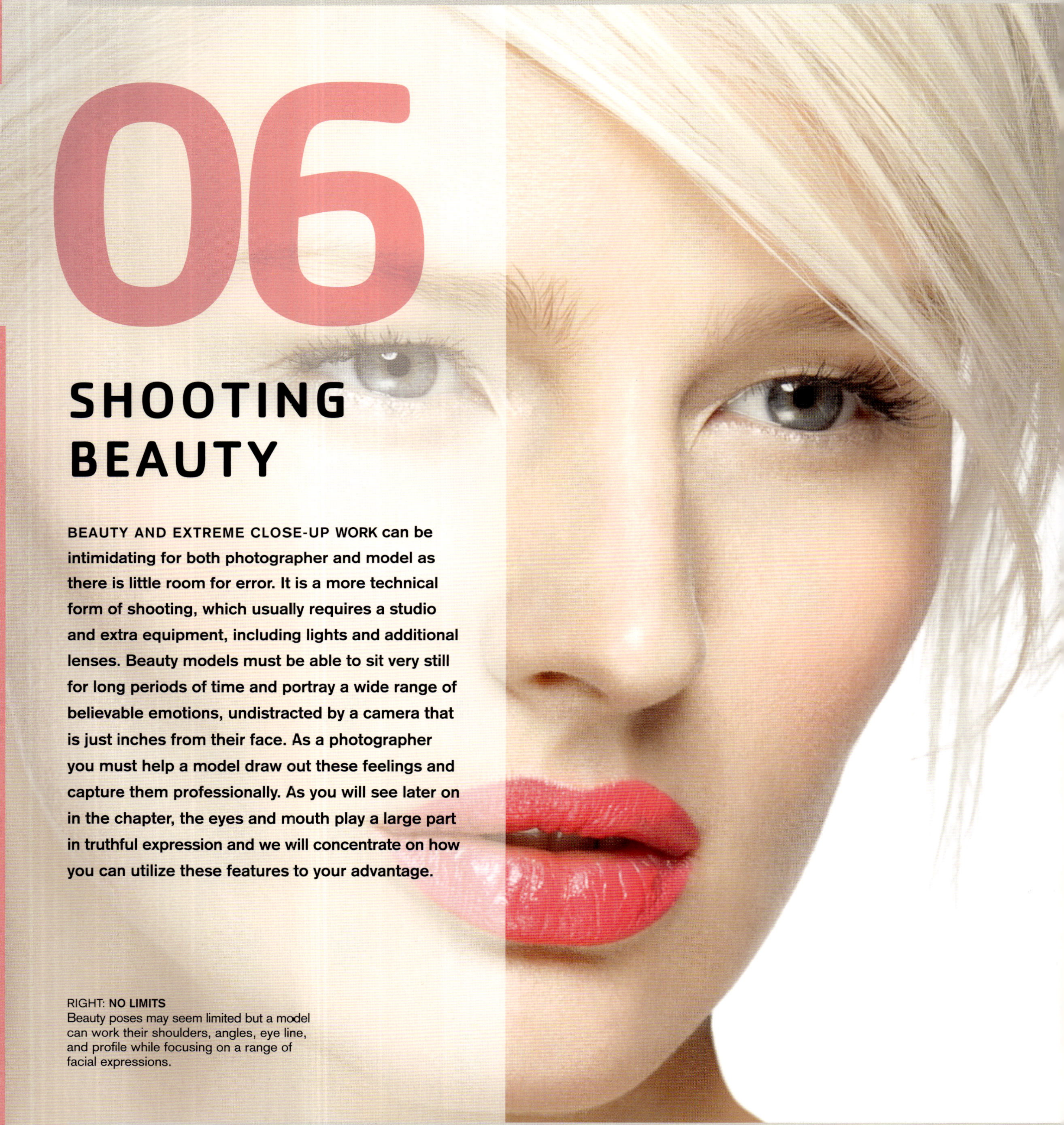

**BEAUTY AND EXTREME CLOSE-UP WORK can be intimidating for both photographer and model as there is little room for error. It is a more technical form of shooting, which usually requires a studio and extra equipment, including lights and additional lenses. Beauty models must be able to sit very still for long periods of time and portray a wide range of believable emotions, undistracted by a camera that is just inches from their face. As a photographer you must help a model draw out these feelings and capture them professionally. As you will see later on in the chapter, the eyes and mouth play a large part in truthful expression and we will concentrate on how you can utilize these features to your advantage.**

RIGHT: **NO LIMITS**
Beauty poses may seem limited but a model can work their shoulders, angles, eye line, and profile while focusing on a range of facial expressions.

# WHEN THE FOCUS IS ON THE FACE

**BEAUTY SHOOTS CAN BE INTENSE. In general you will be working with meticulous cosmetic clients and paying acute attention to detail: there is a lot of pressure, everyone is working under hot lights, and one slight movement could ruin everything. When the focus is on the face, there is only so much you can do other than rely on your model, so make sure to cast well. Even experienced fashion models may be new to beauty work and it is an entirely different form of modeling to editorial or commercial. I have seen girls who have worked well for years sent home from beauty sets because they couldn't handle the stresses involved.**

The set environment should be relaxed and if possible encourage your models to get rest the night before and drink plenty of water for healthier looking skin. Talk to your model when they arrive, explain how much they are going to be able to move, whether there is a side they favor, and the types of expression you are looking for. This gives them the time to prepare mentally while they are sat in the makeup chair.

As with all modeling there are certain rules that apply to beauty models in terms of measurements and symmetry, such as the size of the eyelid to display eye shadow, or how their jaw line lies, but personality plays an equally important part. It is imperative the model has a great face from a variety of angles when stock still, but it takes character to portray real emotion within a still frame. The style of shoot will determine the kinds of expressions you are looking for, ranging from the universally recognized, stylized advertising poses to goofy, off the wall antics. Select models appropriately to make your job easier.

Once you are set up for a shot it will help if you shoot quickly and efficiently, as you don't want your model to get tired. Let them know when they can relax because you are focusing or re-lighting so they don't hold an expression unnecessarily. With all beauty work you want your model to really connect with the camera, to look directly into the lens.

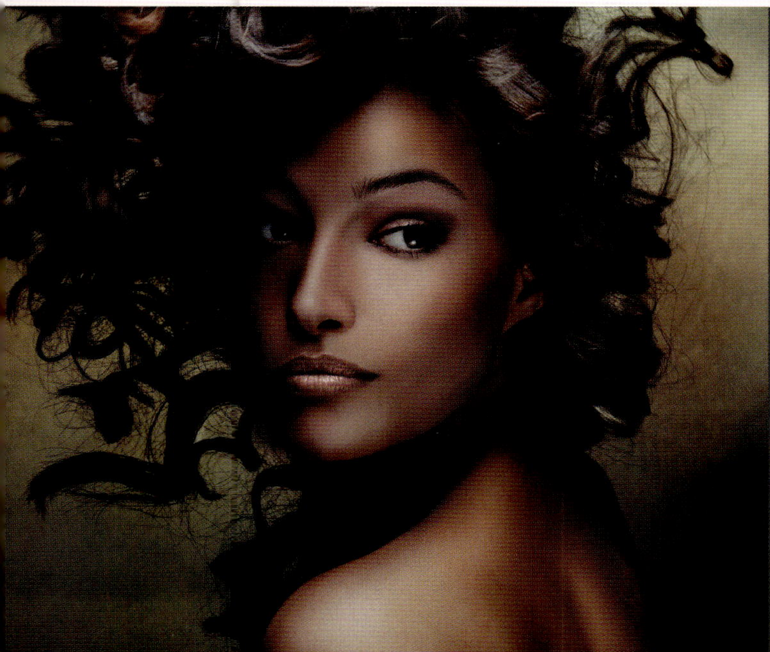

LEFT: **UP TOP**
For beauty work models are usually required to have their shoulders uncovered, so ask them to bring a strapless top or "boob tube" to set to avoid any issues.

RIGHT: **HAIR BACK**
If not the main focus, hair is often tied back away from the face to avoid distracting the audience from the model's makeup.

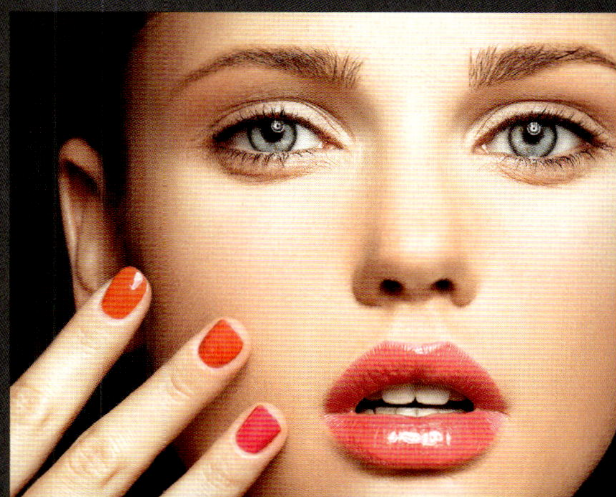

# EXPRESSION:
# REVEALING THE TRUTH

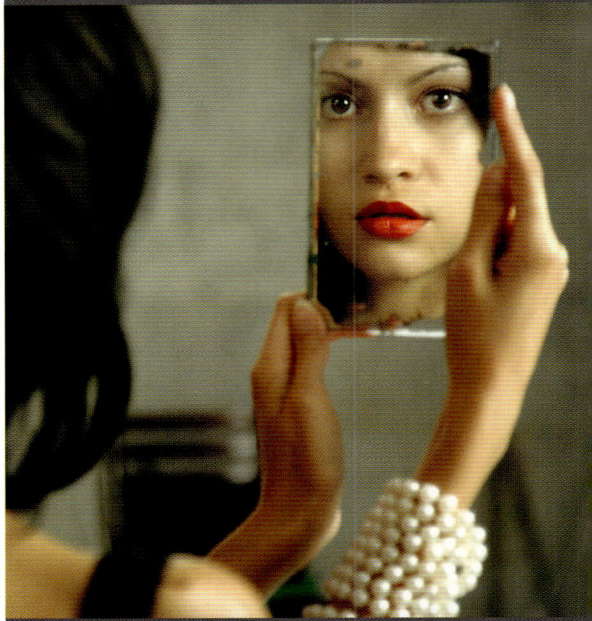

ABOVE: **TELL ME THE TRUTH**
Asking people to express their true feelings on camera can make them feel exposed and vulnerable. Create a comfortable shooting environment that promotes respect.

**TRUTHFUL EXPRESSIONS can be intensely powerful. Whether a model is physically reacting to stimuli or is able to create a true feeling within imaginary circumstances, the result is captivating to the audience because they believe in it. If you are selling something, you want that person to buy into it, even if "it" is only a concept. It is much harder to convey emotion in a photograph than in a movie, so to provoke a reaction in the viewer you need to inspire real pleasure, sadness, or anger in your model.**

Some models will arrive on set and just let loose. You will find yourself fighting to keep up as they flip between personalities in seconds. Other models will be more introverted and quiet, less ready to burst open with their innermost feelings. Those who are younger, or naturally timid may find it harder to express themselves at first.

The majority of models I know were bullied at school because no matter what they looked like, it was different to the other children. This can lead to issues with low self-esteem and a lack of confidence, so you may find them very closed off, even though they spend their days having their picture taken. If you encounter this, attempt to break down those walls a little. Try and make them understand they can access their private selves without being embarrassed or judged. Models can mistakenly believe their outer shell is enough to produce great fashion and beauty shots, but there is much more to it than being a beautiful, empty vessel.

The amount of acting involved with good modeling should not be underestimated—even formal poses

### TIP JUST DO IT

If you want your model to portray anger, actually make them scream out loud. Some models will just hold their mouths open silently and pretend to look like they're shouting. Get them to really do it—it might scare the model if they rarely release their emotions, but it's good to break boundaries.

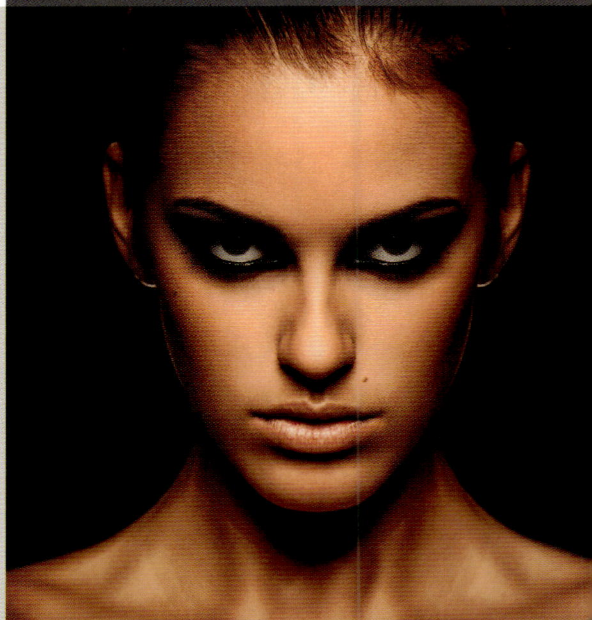

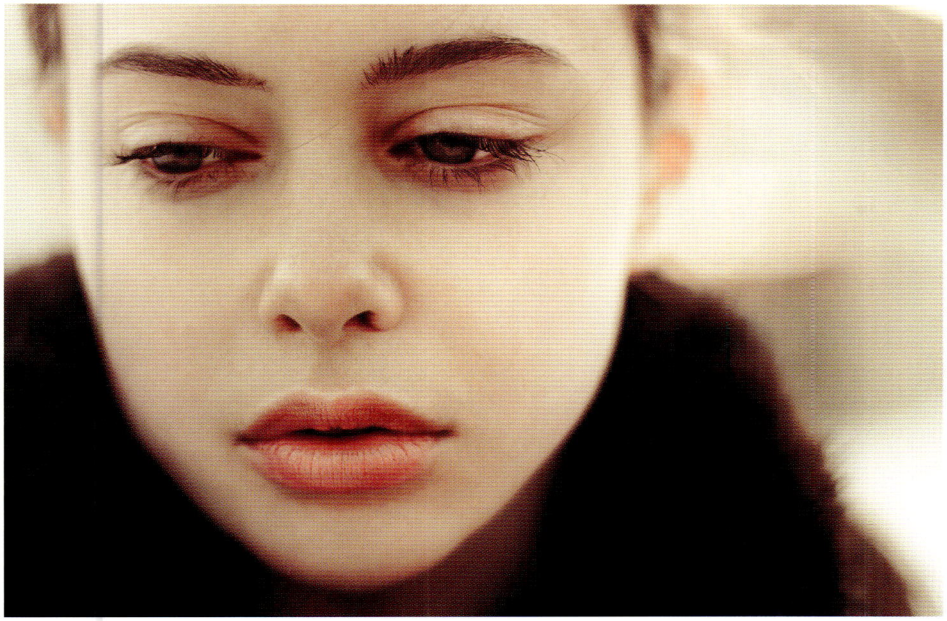

ABOVE: **INNER TRUTHS**
When shooting, if you ask a model what they are thinking and they reply, "nothing," remind them modeling is similar to acting and requires accessing your private self's thoughts and feelings even without speaking.

## PUMP IT UP

Even if you are only shooting close-ups, allow a model to move freely while they work, if possible. It is less restrictive and feels more real. Wearing high heels can make a girl feel sexy and empowered, so let them wear them even if you are only shooting their face.

> *Photographers deal in things which are continually vanishing, and when they have vanished there is no contrivance on earth which can make them come back again.*
>
> **HENRI CARTIER-BRESSON,** *photographer*

require a strong expression, if only from behind the eyes. You want your model to be thinking about something, feeling, dreaming, or pretending to be somebody in their mind. This is why directing on your part is so important—only you can choose how much or how little you tell the model about your vision. You can describe in detail the storyline of the character they should play, how they are feeling at that point in time, and what their motivations are, or it can be more simple, such as describing the emotion you are going for in one or two words. Models really appreciate a passionate photographer who knows what they want, and giving them a definitive brief will save you both time.

To get a shot to ring true ask your models to think about things that affect them. If you want them to act excited or sad, for example, then get them to think about something that makes them feel that emotion. They don't have to say what it is, but they should actually "think" it.

The best moments are usually unposed and unpredicted; when someone speaks to the side and the model turns, a loud noise startles them, a dog barks, an alarm goes off, or they overhear a crew joke and crack up, for example. Play with these natural instincts, because if you can get your model to relax and feel comfortable it will loosen their inhibitions, boost their confidence, and allow you to see sides of them other photographers may have failed to capture.

# IT'S ALL ABOUT THE EYES

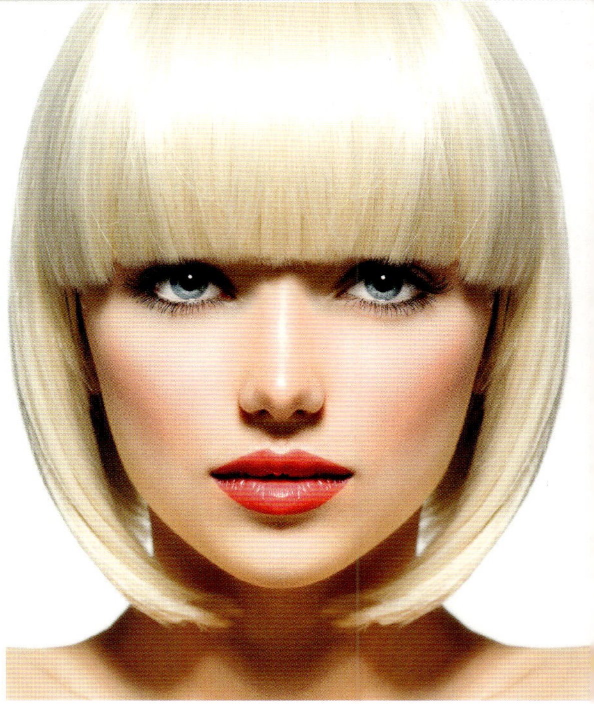

**OUR EYES ARE ONE of our most powerful and revealing features. Eye contact can be heart-stopping, and regardless of whether you believe our eyes are the mirror to our soul or our minds, or not, there is no denying they say a tremendous amount about how we truly feel. In fashion photography, where words are unavailable, a model's eyes can be an important tool in the storytelling process, whether they are smiling or crying.**

The most important advice I ever received was on my first beauty shoot. I was working with photographer Iain Crawford. About half way into the first shot he told me I had "dead eyes" that weren't focusing on anything and to actually, "look into the camera." He taught me about interacting with the lens as if it was a person.

This advice changed my career. Before then I had never understood truly connecting with the camera, playing to it as if it was a member of the target market, or that focusing and un-focusing my eyes had such a visible effect. Make sure your models understand this. Explain the importance of having real thoughts in their head. If they are staring blankly into space ask them to focus on something, whether it's a nearby lightstand or the camera lens itself. This will remove the empty or glazed look that models often get when they're sleepy or bored.

Models can have all kinds of issues with their eyes. Some models have a very low shot ratio because their eyes are always closed. Timing their blinking can be difficult and may need specific direction. Having makeup applied can lead to tearing, as can wind machines and any kind of dust or water, so have your team standing by. Models can develop pulses in their eyelids or nervous twitches, and in these situations you have to give them time and let them relax back into the shoot.

When you start concentrating on a model's eyes you will come to realize the importance of a talented makeup artist. The application of eyeliners, shades, mascaras, and false lashes with diamantes and glitter can have all kinds of dramatic effects. Models can arrive hungover with puffy, tired, eyes with dark circles, red veins, and dilated pupils, so you may need help to get the best possible images, especially as too much retouching can ruin a good beauty shot.

Very minimal movements of the eyes can have a dramatic effect. Looking in different directions from different angles, working the neck and head—side to side and up and down—can have an impact, as can closing the eyes, then slowly opening them.

> *Beauty is how you feel inside, and it reflects in your eyes. It is not something physical.*
>
> **SOPHIA LOREN,** *actress*

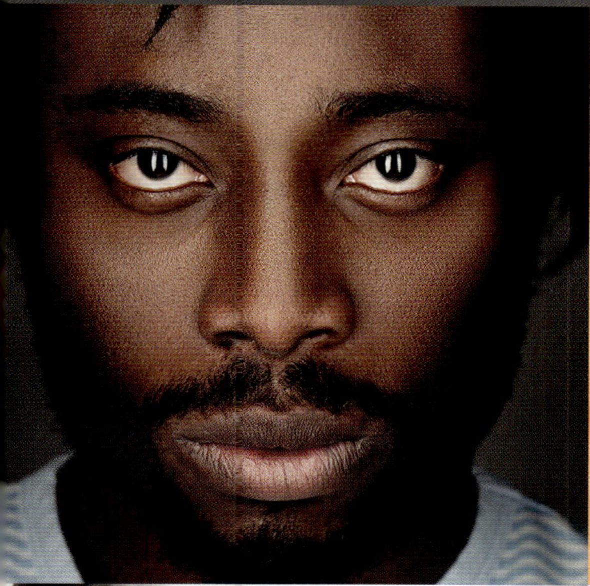

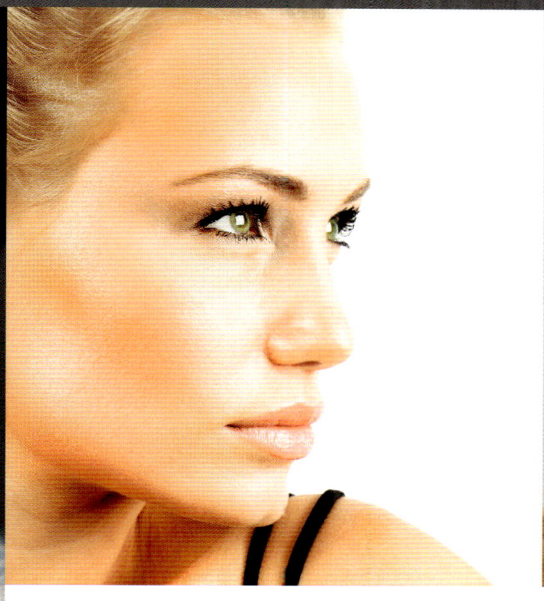

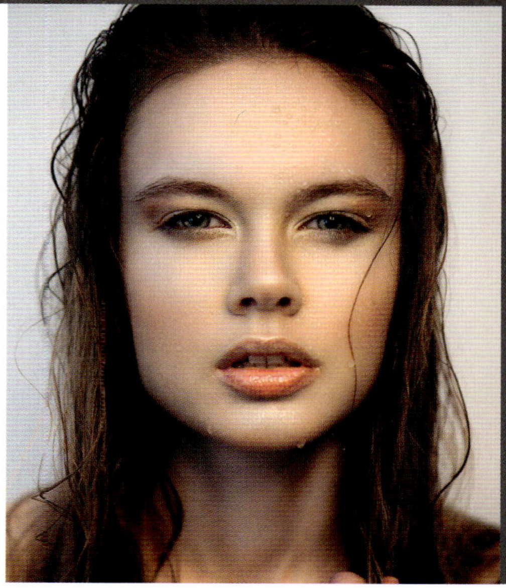

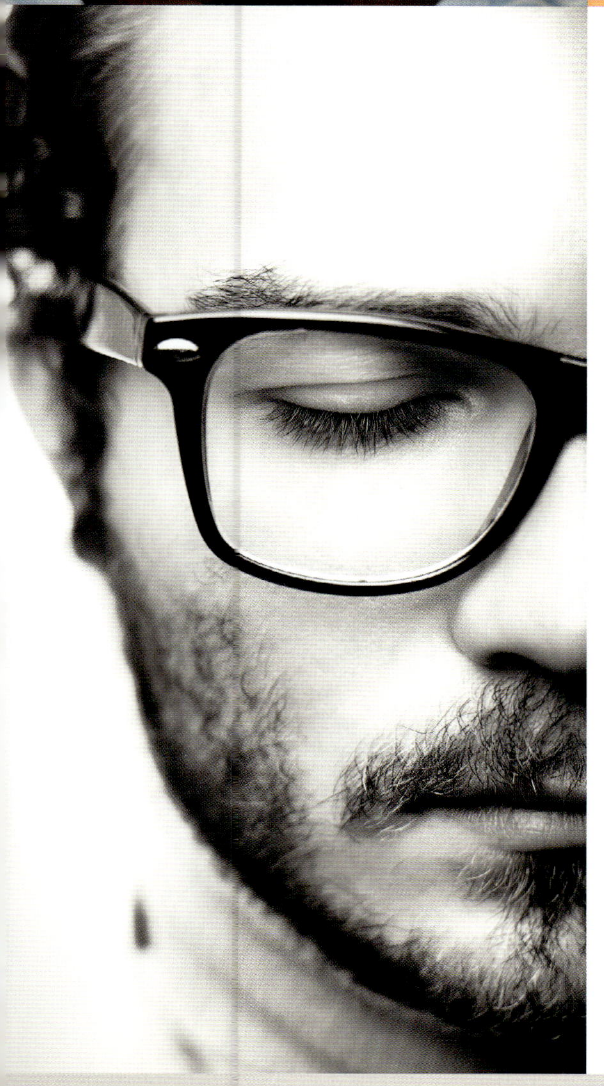

OPPOSITE & ABOVE LEFT: **FOCUS!**
If a model appears to have "dead eyes" it may be because their sight or mind is unfocused. Ask them to focus the eyes on something and think real thoughts.

ABOVE CENTER: **INTO CAMERA**
Not all beauty has to be shot with eyes into the camera to have a dramatic effect. Experimenting with angles can reveal the best way to display makeup and highlight eye color.

TOP RIGHT: **SQUINTING**
Bright light, especially if reflected off water or a white wall can cause squinting. Models with sensitive eyes can struggle on location and in studio.

LEFT: **CREATE A SPECTACLE**
Eyeglasses can look great, but watch out for reflections—often on set they will remove the lenses. Some faces don't work with glasses, so try frames on your models when casting.

## TIP SQUINTY EYED

Bright lights and sunlight affect people's eyes, and blue eyes are more sensitive than others. Techniques for avoiding problems include having the model shutting their eyes while you count to three and focus the shot, then making your exposure when they open their eyes. Remember, water and white walls all reflect harsh light that might cause your model to squint.

Softening and hardening, widening or squinting, furrowing a brow, raising an eyebrow or giving a cheeky wink—experiment when directing your models, but watch for the whites of eyes and unnaturally creased foreheads affecting the shot.

Remember, not all shots need to be "into camera" for eyes to have an effect, and the range of emotions a human can display is mind-boggling. Try to invoke true reactions or feelings so the image comes across as powerful and the viewer can relate to it.

# SMILE FOR THE CAMERA

**EVERYBODY KNOWS SOMEONE who has a smile that lights up a room, but while a genuine, warm smile is a gift, a faked smile that has been held too long is obvious from a mile away. If you are shooting commercial work for cosmetic campaigns—especially lipstick, glosses and stains—you will often need a model with a great smile that lasts all day long.**

It is stereotypically true that some models hate to smile, as they believe it is against the rules in high fashion, but not every shot requires a moody pout. If you know you're going in a happier direction make sure that you, your team, and the shooting environment are as positive and light as possible. Your personality and behavior as a photographer will affect how easily you can make a model laugh—if they are worried that you are unhappy they won't be able to relax. I am not suggesting you wander around with an enormous grin on your face all day, but smiles are famously contagious.

There are many types of smile, with all kinds of connotations for you and your model to play with. There's flirty, embarrassed, and "know-it-all"; smiles

## COMMERCIAL VERSUS EDITORIAL

Smiles are often associated with commercial work, rather than editorial. Don't limit yourself by thinking all smiles have to be cheesy grins and shy away from shooting them. Use the smile and the wide range of emotions it can display.

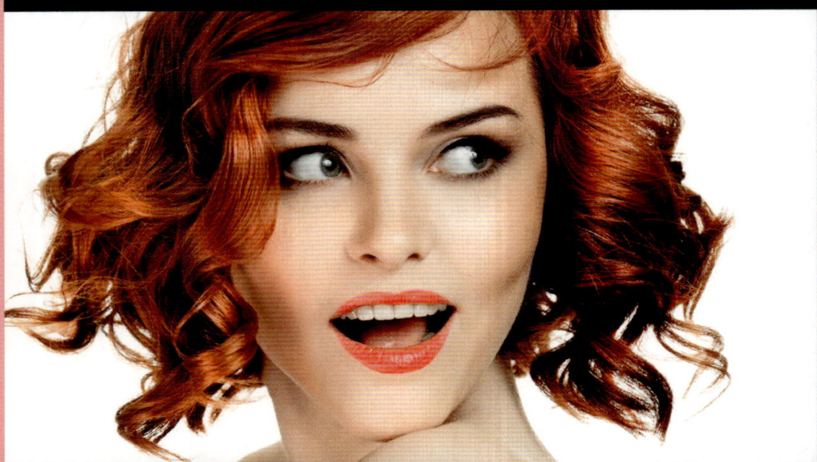

ABOVE: **SURPRISES**
One of the best ways to get a real smile out of someone is to shock them. Banter, tell jokes, or ask the model to pull a funny face then shoot their reaction afterwards.

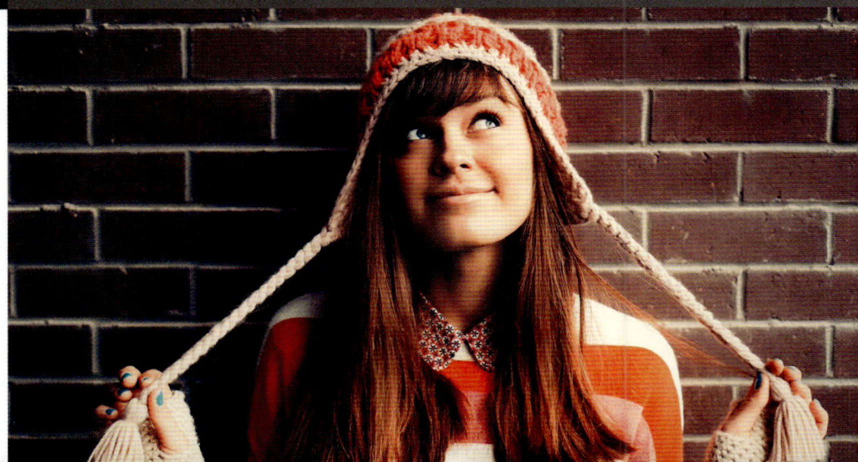

ABOVE: **THINK BACK**
It's hard to know what makes someone happy, especially if you've only known them a few minutes. If necessary ask models to think back to amusing moments in the recent past and shoot as their face changes.

that say "I'm in love," or sexy, seductive, confident smirks that say "I'm the boss," with a mischievous undertone. Smiles can range from satisfied and proud, to smug and pompous, with wide-open mouths or tight lips. Watch out, though, because a smile can easily turn into a grimace if the face freezes up and it loses its connection with the eyes. Keep everything natural and if you are looking for a spontaneous reaction, don't make the model hold an expression for too long.

It is common practice in castings for models to be asked to show a small, closed mouth smile, a big smile with teeth showing, and a big smile with no teeth showing. Watch out for lip shape and size, noting fun quirks such as dimples, gapped teeth, or a tongue piercing. It is not unusual for a person to dislike their smile, especially on camera, as a smile or laugh can make you appear younger, older, or goofier than normal, depending on the individual. This mentality can be awkward on a beauty shoot where a model should be confident at all times with a well-practiced repertoire of expressions, ranging in size.

It's great if you can find a model with a similar sense of humor so you can set each other off. A happy shooting environment will only lead to happier models and happier pictures. Smiles are usually easier to spark when you have multiple models on set—group shots and doubles can often lead to laughter and even giggle fits when the models work well with one another. Unfortunately some models refuse to smile. No matter what, and there will be times when you have to rethink a shot to suit your model's natural expression.

It can be hard to keep smiling over a long shoot day, especially if it is cold or the model is hungry. Do your best to keep the energy up. If they are struggling late in the day, ask your model to start thinking back to embarrassing moments or family vacations. Funny thoughts can have a great effect on the face. Making someone smile is the best feeling.

**TIP SMILE!**

Don't forget to smile. It might seem twee, but if you smile it can help with networking. Smiling might not fit your style, but in overwhelming situations a smile can save you a lot of words and put those around you at ease in an instant.

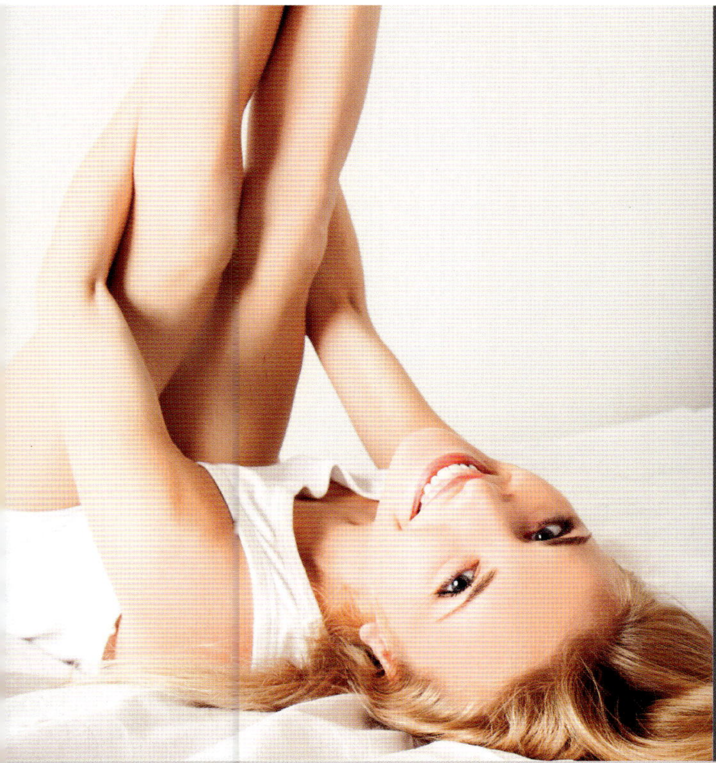

LEFT: **NATURALLY HAPPY**
Some people have a more positive attitude than others and seem naturally happier. The amount someone smiles during a casting can be a good representation of how much they will smile on set.

RIGHT: **BEHIND THE SCENE**
Establishing a good rapport with a model off set is a good way to ensure an easier shooting experience, especially if you need to make them laugh. Try making friends beforehand.

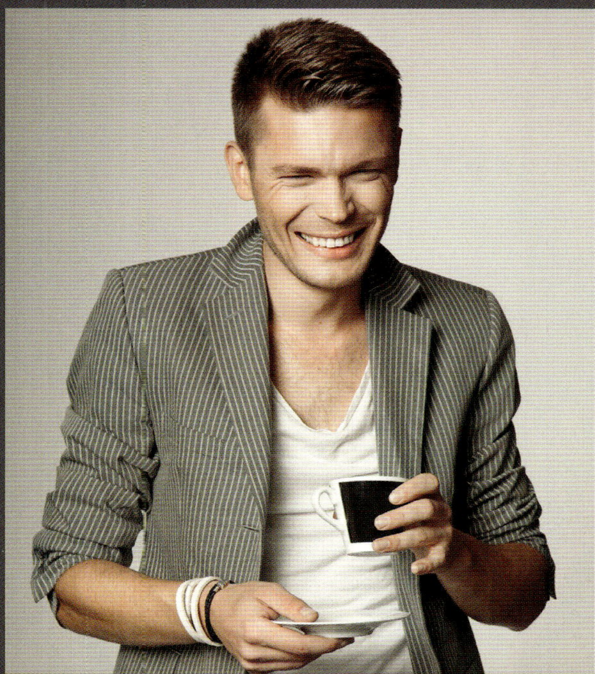

# HAIR & MAKEUP

**AS A BUDDING PHOTOGRAPHER you may know very little about styling hair and the latest trends in eye shadow. Working with professionals will of course help you to learn the basics, as will researching fashion magazines, talking to your own hairdresser, and watching online video tutorials.**

However, you should never need to touch a model's face. If you are just starting out you can ask them to bring products, but don't expect expert results. Models are programmed to arrive at a shoot with a bare face and clean hair, so many are inexperienced when it comes to applying their own makeup. If your artist suddenly cancels it can help for you to keep a few styling aids handy: hairspray, pomade, a few hair-bands, clips, and maybe a small makeup kit. It's unhygienic to share cosmetics such as mascara without disposable wands, but eyeshadow, concealer, blush, and lip balm can all be useful in an emergency situation.

### IF YOU EXTEND IT, YOU PAY FOR IT

The wide range of wigs and hair extensions available can transform any model, allowing you to change their look dramatically.

Remember, these products are extremely expensive, though, and you cannot count on your hair stylist to foot the bill. If you or a client asks for extensions, make sure you budget accordingly.

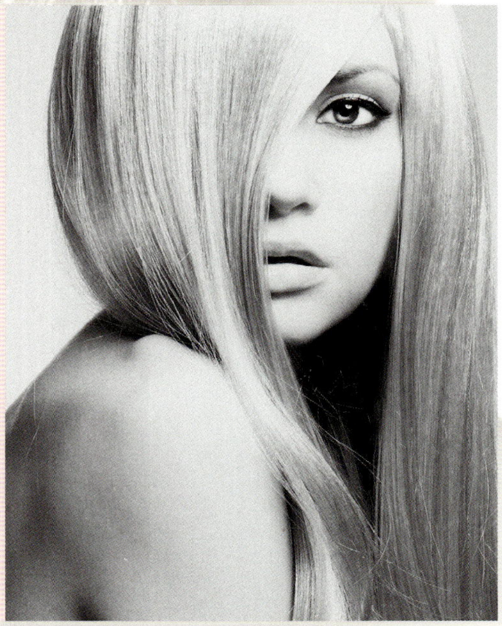

### HAIR

A model's hair can be in a statement in itself. The styles possible expand every day with the creative imaginations of hair stylists around the world, but in basic terms there are "up dos," "down dos," and "half up, half down dos," all of which are affected by a model's hair length, type, and texture.

Certain styles are much more complicated than others, which might not always be obvious. Anything sculpted, heavily curled, or shaped will need attention throughout the day, but even simple, "beachy waves" can cause a hairstylist grief if the hair drops quickly. Remember, models change clothes multiple times, and pulling a tight top over their head can instantly ruin hours of work. If a model arrives in tight clothing they should consider putting on a robe before being made up.

With all styling it is important to think about your location. Although you want the hair to suit the surroundings and your vision, you have to be practical: if you want super-straight hair with blunt, perfect bangs, shoot in a studio not on a windy beach. If your hairstylist has to leave early, make sure the model's hair is manageable for you both. Keep it simple, rather than trying to maintain a beautiful but fragile art piece, and remember that models naturally like to touch their hair and can unknowingly pick apart an intricate design.

Men's grooming might seem simpler, but it can be just as complicated. Male models can have long hair, but even with short hair it takes diligence to keep it looking fresh throughout a shoot.

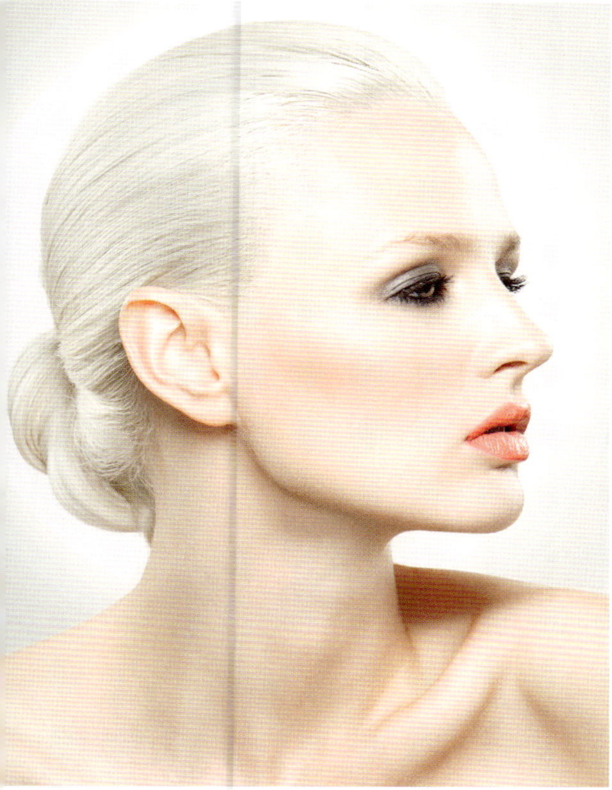

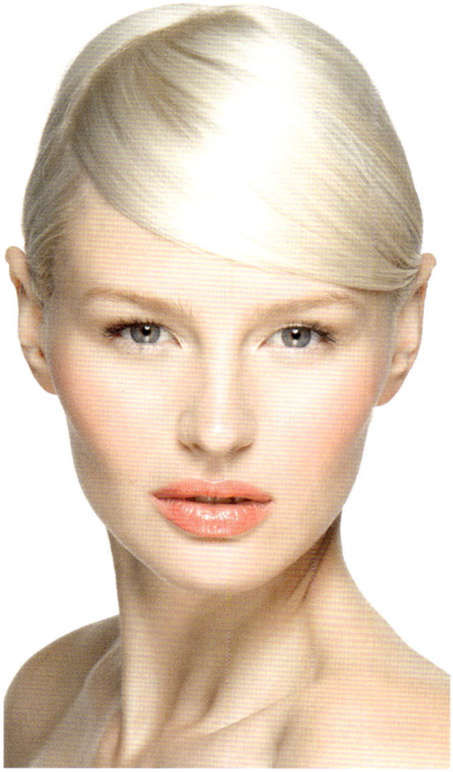

**TIP**
**PRE-PRODUCTION**
Not every hair or makeup artist is competent in the techniques required to produce all looks, or to work with models of every skin tone and hair type. Make sure you consult with your team beforehand to ensure everyone will be comfortable on the day, and if necessary, change your team to suit the model and the shoot.

FAR LEFT **PULL FOCUS**
When shooting beauty it can help, especially if your artist is stronger with make-up, to literally scrape the hair back from the face completely. Simple, effective and highlights the make-up.

LEFT: **NATURAL LOOK**
Photographers often underestimate the time it takes for a make-up artist to achieve a "natural look." It requires base coverage and detailed color work. Try not to rush art.

Never underestimate how hard it can be to get a model looking their best and keeping them that way over a long, sweaty day.

## MAKEUP

A talented MUA can morph a model to fit the image in your head, so appreciate their importance even when you want a light, natural look. There is a huge difference between a tired, slightly hungover model without makeup and a fresh-faced model with a balanced smooth complexion and imitation color in their cheeks. Find an artist local to you who you feel comfortable enough to talk to about "looks." Show them tear sheets of your favorite images and ask them how difficult they would be to recreate. Research "smoky eyes," "cat eyes," "contouring," and any other makeup terms you might have heard, but don't truly understand and look up their visual definitions.

As with hair, suit the makeup to the location in a practical way. Extreme heat will melt heavy foundations and cause the model's lips to perspire, so stay away from bright lipsticks that need constant touch ups. A lot of photographers are inexperienced when it comes to makeup, but most decisions can be made using a bit of common sense.

If you don't have access to an MUA, cast a model with good skin. If they are confident doing their own makeup let them start off with their go-to look and adjust from there. Yet with or without an MUA you should be regularly checking how the makeup looks on camera. It can read differently for many reasons, whether it's the lighting, colored gels and backgrounds, or even the reflection of an item of clothing. If your model looks blown out it might be time to make their features more defined.

# 07

# LIGHTING

**TO CREATE GREAT IMAGES of people it's essential that lighting becomes second nature to a photographer. From studio flash and continuous lighting indoors to using flash or reflectors outdoors, understanding how best to use lighting is a key skill. Any potential fashion photographer needs to understand how, why, and when to modify the light to get the best effect, be it highlighting garments for a commercial shoot, achieving an edgy editorial look, a classic beauty shot, or a summery portrait.**

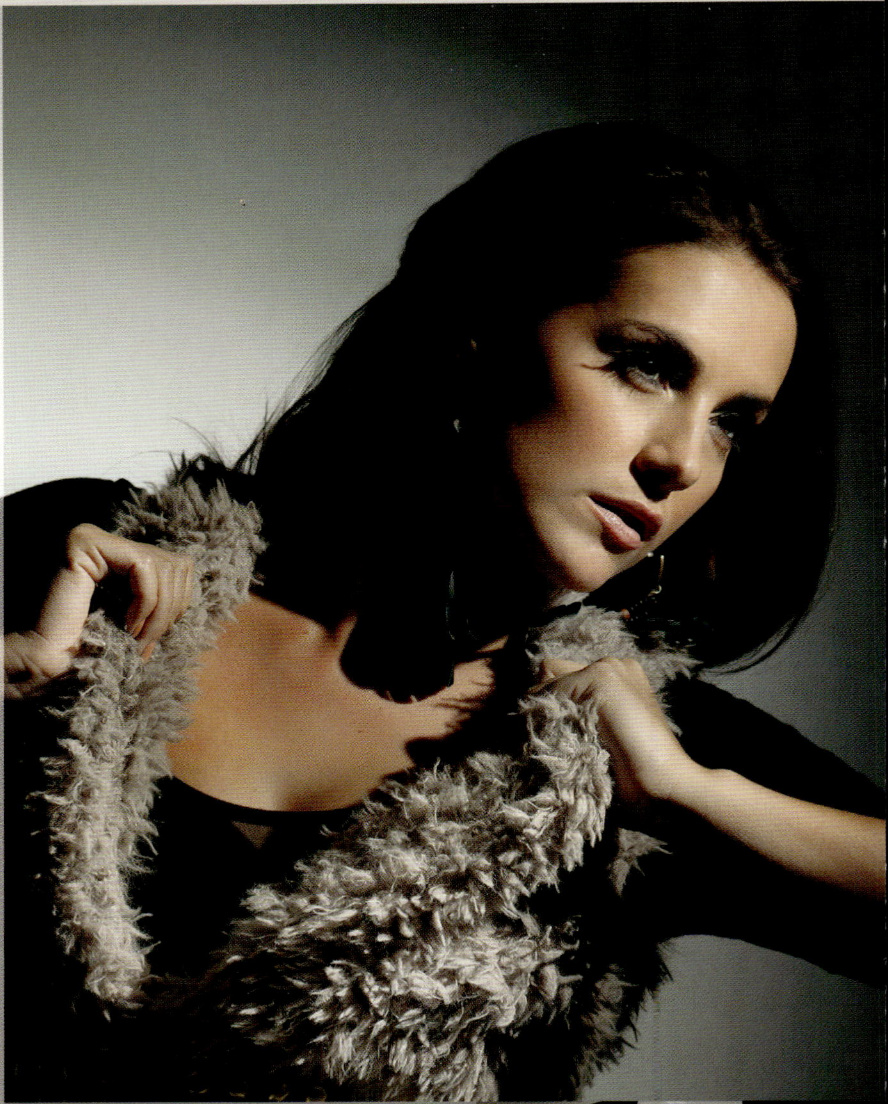

RIGHT: **HARD LIGHTING**
Hard lighting gives harsh shadows but these can be used for very dramatic results, like this shot of our model up close to the wall of the studio. The flash head was fitted with a narrow snoot so it produced a relatively hard-edged, defined circle of light. This was used to give a spotlight effect, with the shadow cast by the model an important part of the composition.

The model was asked to face toward the light source, which was around eight feet away and a couple of feet higher than her eye line. This ensured her face was well lit, rather than being half in shadow as it would have been if she was facing the camera.

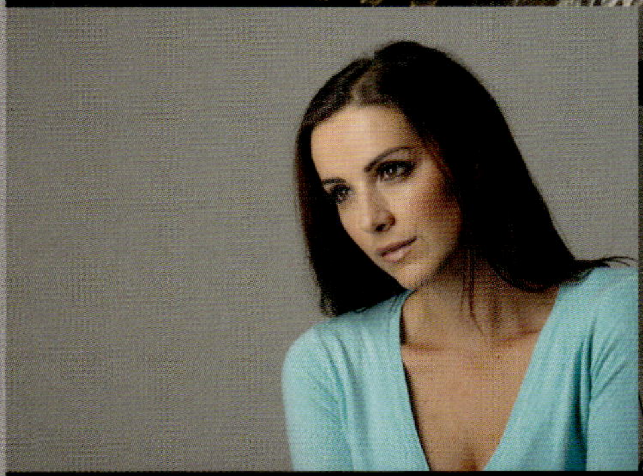
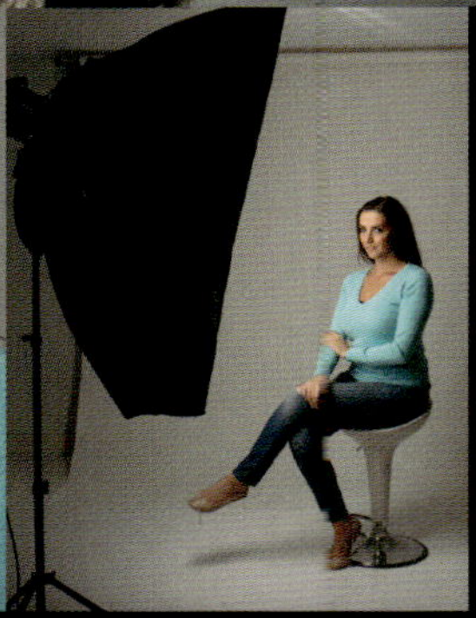

ABOVE: **LARGE SOFTBOX**
The first shot shows a relatively large softbox that is around six feet away from the model, who in turn is roughly six feet from the white paper background. The light is soft and flattering, producing large catchlights in the eyes and a light gray background tone.

# INTRODUCTION TO LIGHTING TECHNIQUES

**LIGHT HAS MANY PROPERTIES that a photographer should consider, such as its intensity, color temperature, evenness, and contrast. But two of the most important properties that can transform your photos are the direction and the quality of the light. The direction of light may seem like an obvious property, but is one that can be overlooked when a novice photographer is under pressure. Many amateur photographers tend to use light that comes from the same direction as the camera—keeping the sun over your shoulder, or using the flash on top of the camera. This gives flat results. Having the direction of the light off the axis of the camera creates shadows, which is how our brain recognizes an object is three-dimensional. The further the light source moves around the sides and back of your subject, the more dramatic the results, but you have to watch out for too many shadows appearing on your model's face.**

The "quality" of light refers to how hard or soft it is. Hard light typically comes from small and/or distant light sources and gives very hard, defined shadows with lots of contrast. Hard light can create a really dramatic effect if used well, but it can produce unflattering results on all but the most flawless complexions. By using a larger light source and some diffusion, the light becomes more flattering. An ideal place to understand lighting is in a studio. All the shots here were taken using just one light source in a white studio with a white paper background, yet they show very different results.

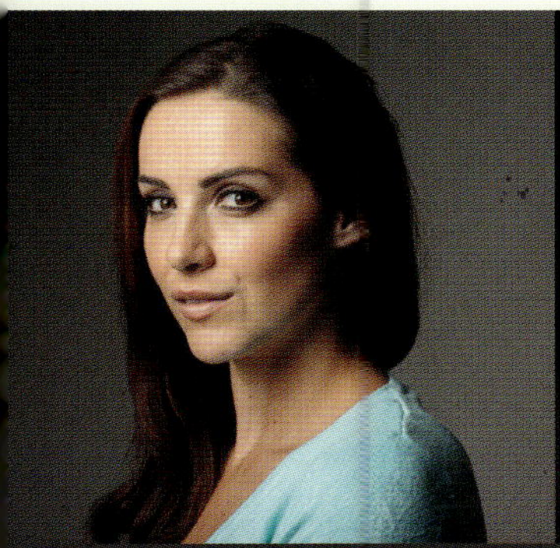

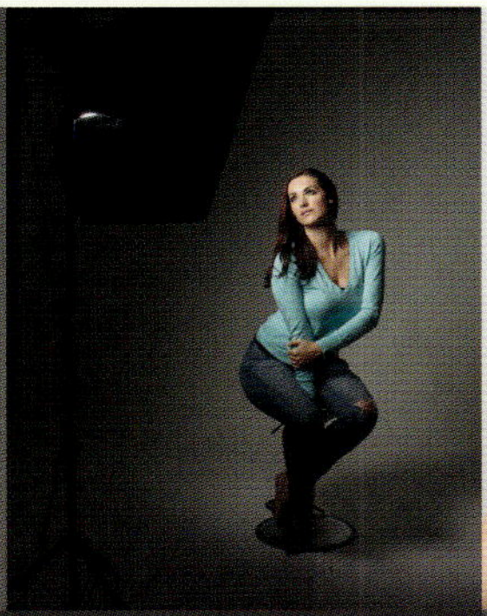

ABOVE: **SMALL SOFTBOX**
If we change to a smaller softbox from roughly the same distance, the light becomes marginally harder. When the softbox is fitted with a fabric honeycomb grid, the light retains most of its softness on the subject, but is channeled away from the background, which appears much darker.

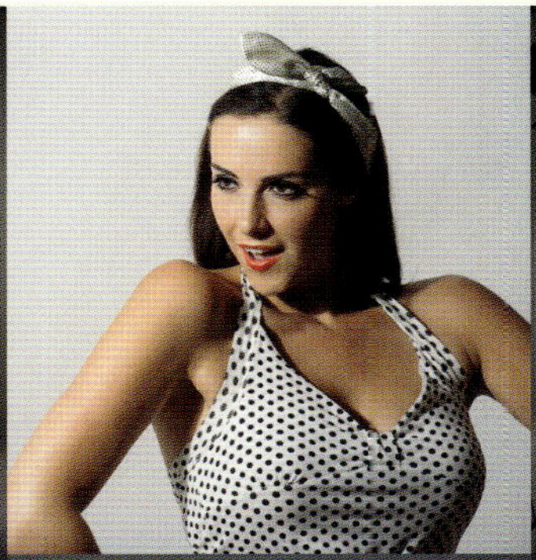

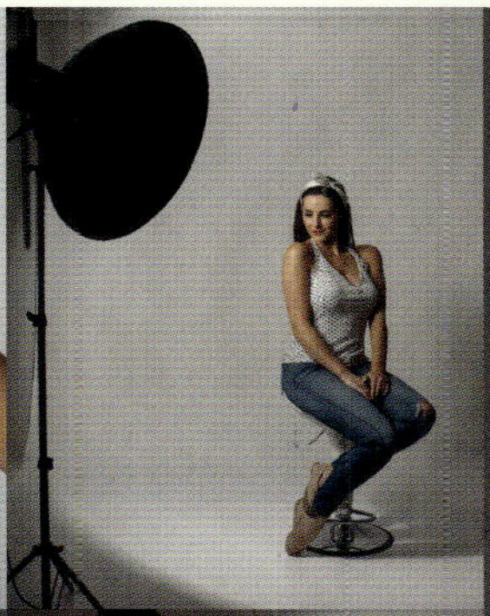

LEFT: **ADDING A BEAUTY DISH**
If we change the softbox for a silver-lined beauty dish, the light is more crisply defined and has a harder quality. It also floods the background with light. In the pullback shot it's easy to see the fall-off at the edge of the light beam is relatively well defined.

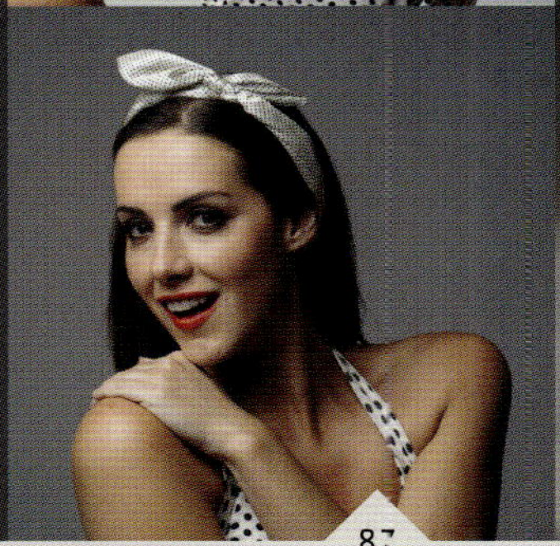

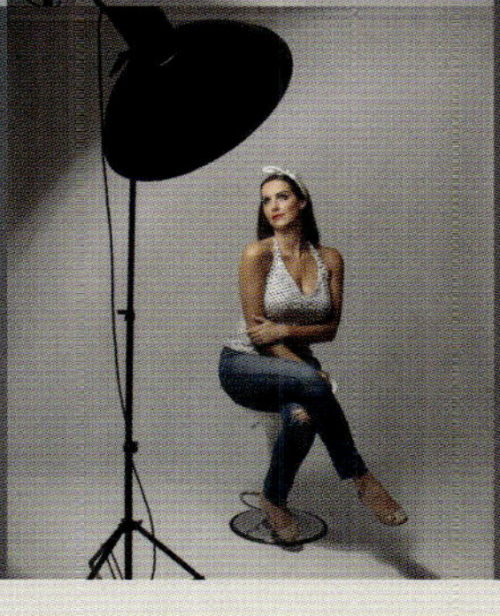

BELOW LEFT:
**ELEVATING THE BEAUTY DISH**
Moving the beauty dish much closer to the subject and moving it slightly higher means the quality of the light is softer on the model's face. Because it's much closer to the model, the fall-off of light intensity is more pronounced and the background appears much darker. Fitting a honeycomb grid to the dish channels the light away from the background even more, resulting in it turning almost black.

# STUDIO

**SOONER OR LATER, any photographer shooting models will have to take photos inside a studio, so it's worth learning how to get the best out of a controlled, studio environment. Of course, every studio is slightly different, and physical aspects such as its size, the color of the walls, and the height of the ceiling can all affect how your lighting works.**

A studio flash head is basically a powerful flash. Typically, the only thing you can change on the flash is its power output, although some very expensive units will allow you to alter the flash duration as well. The light itself is modified by whatever you fit to the front of the flash head: softboxes, grids, barn doors, snoots, and beauty dishes are just some of the accessories you can use in a studio setting to alter the light output in various ways. The flashes are triggered either by a sync cable that plugs into your camera or, more typically, by a remote control unit that sits on the camera's hotshoe. For many shots, it's best to start with a single light—sometimes called your main light or key light. Then, add other lights to either reduce contrast (as a fill light) or to highlight other areas.

## BUTTERFLY LIGHTING

Starting with just a white-lined beauty dish and the model close to the white wall of the studio, this portrait is an easy one to take. Positioning the flash on a boom directly in front of the model's face and above the camera produces a telltale shadow under the nose, which is said to resemble a butterfly. As a result, this is often called "butterfly lighting" and is used a lot for beauty work. You can tell how close the model is to the background as you can see the shadow of her shoulder right behind her.

For a less contrasty or beauty shot, a fill light or reflector could be introduced to lessen the darkness of the shadows under her chin, for example. Notice the difference in feel between these two shots: it is much more than just the model's expression. The shot without the reflector has an editorial vibe, while the shot with the reflector has a lighter, more commercial feel.

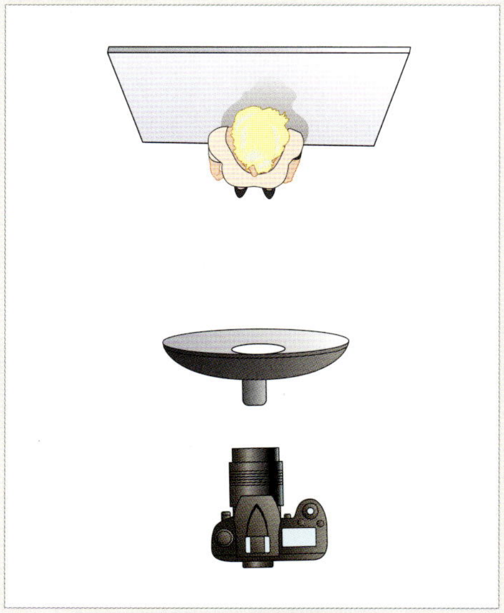

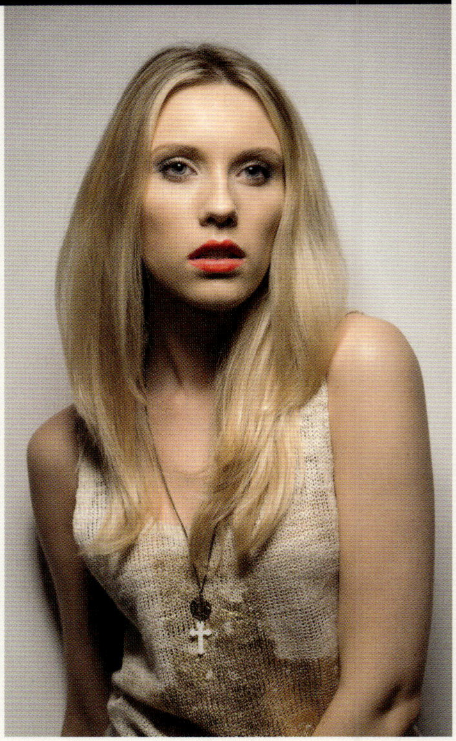

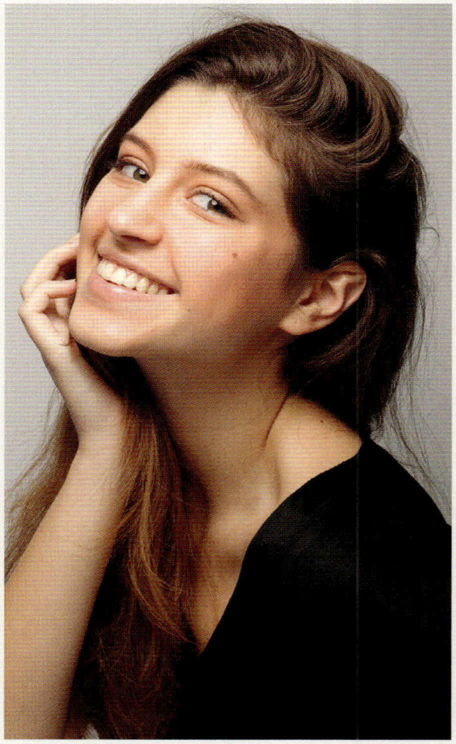

## USING MORE THAN ONE LIGHT

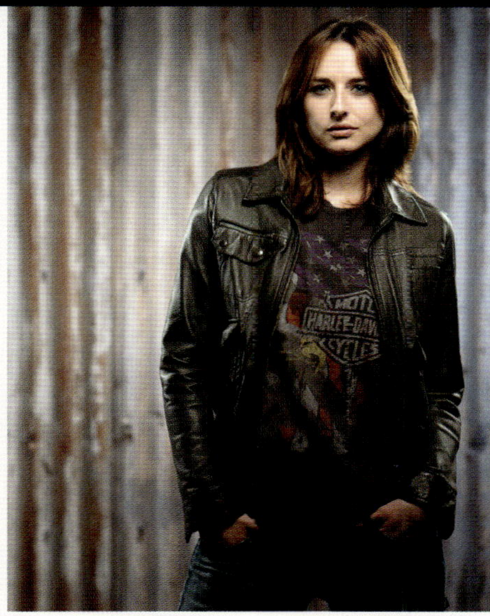

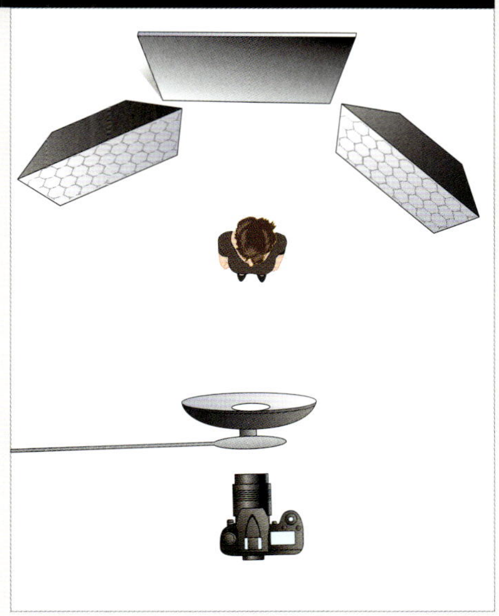

When you have more than one light at your disposal you can really use them creatively to highlight certain parts of the images, such as a hair light or a rim light to separate the subject from the background.

When you have a subject in dark clothing against a darker background, you really need to do something to make the subject stand out. For this shot of a model in a leather jacket against a background of corrugated metal, it was important the shot remained moody, but the model didn't disappear. In fact, the background isn't really steel, but a printed photographic background designed especially for the job.

The main light on the model is a white-lined beauty dish held on a boom arm directly in front of the model, but slightly overhead. This lights up the face well, leaving some dark shadows under the nose and chin that suit the image. The fall-off of light means the subject gets darker the further down the frame you move, but this is OK—it's her face and jacket we're interested in.

To light her hair and separate her from the background, two rear, three quarter rim lights were added. These were fitted with softboxes and honeycomb grids to stop the light spilling everywhere.

## USING A SINGLE FLASH HEAD

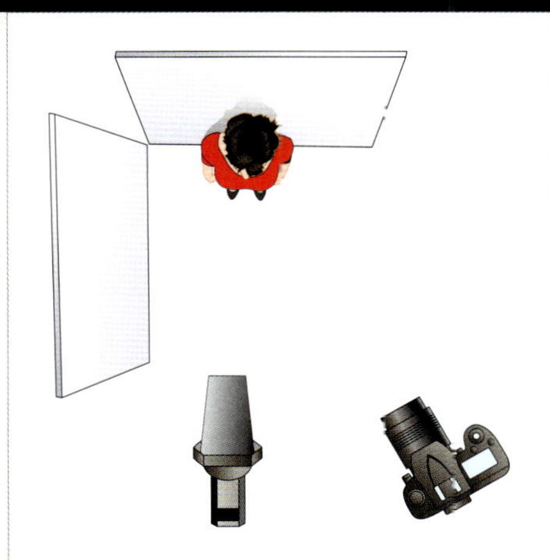

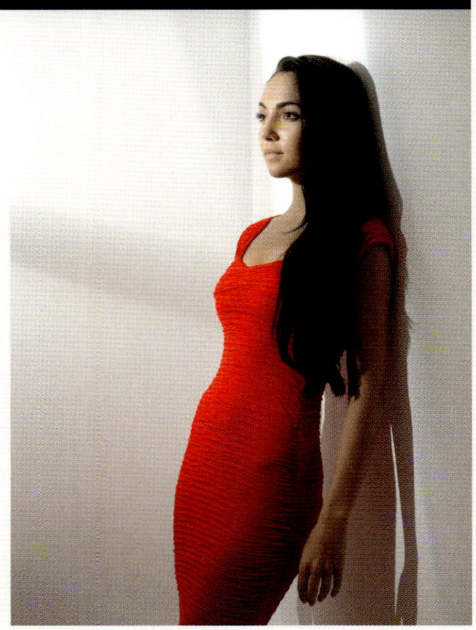

This shot of a model leaning against the white wall in the corner of the studio gives the impression that light could be streaming in through a window, complete with the shadows of the window frame itself. In fact, this is a closed studio with no open windows at all.

The shot was lit with a single flash head, which was shone through a projector device fitted with a "gobo." A gobo (also sometimes called a cookie) is a metal disc that has a shape laser cut into it—this one had the shape of a window, but lots of others are available. By adjusting the projector unit, the "window" can either be brought into sharp focus, or appear much less defined, as here.

# LOCATIONS: INTERIOR

**THE MAJORITY OF FASHION shots are done on location rather than in a studio. Working on location means you can give context to the image—everything from beautiful stately homes for couture fashion to gritty, decayed cityscapes for something more urban, with countless options in between.**

When you are working inside buildings, the first consideration is the quality and brightness of the ambient light. This could be wonderfully soft, with diffuse daylight streaming in through a north-facing window, or it could be so dark you can hardly see your hand in front of your face. It could be lit with the false orange of tungsten lighting or candles, or illuminated by the scourge of all photographers, fluorescent lights, which flicker and can record as anything from green to magenta.

Often, the lighting can be a mix of some daylight, some tungsten, and some fluorescent—a nightmare for photography! In these cases, it is often better to turn off the artificial interior lighting and just use the daylight with a reflector, if you can. Alternatively you can introduce your own lighting—often flash—to lift the light levels in the room or provide the main lighting.

Sometimes you'll want to balance your flash output with the ambient light coming in, perhaps using it to reduce contrast from large windows. Other times, if the ambient light is too low, you may wish to use your own lighting to recreate a daylight-type scene or make a wholly unnatural one for dramatic effect. Each situation is different.

On setting your shot up you have to ascertain whether the ambient light is to be used in the shot. If it's just too low, you'll either end up using a high ISO (which could ruin image quality) or a combination of a wide aperture and very slow shutter speed to let the light register. A wide aperture means the depth of field may be too shallow, while a slow shutter speed may mean that you need to use a tripod, and your subject has to stay as still as possible during the shoot. That's often not ideal for fashion, and is impossible if your model wants to move around. In cases like this it is often better to light the scene using your own lights, potentially replicating the light patterns from outside. Putting flash heads outside windows or hung high from a boom to replicate ceiling lights is relatively common.

## CREATING A PENCIL-BEAM SPOTLIGHT

Sometimes there just isn't enough ambient light to register without a ridiculously long exposure time, so the best option is to create your own lighting. That is precisely what was done here in this shot of a model on an old staircase. The subject was lit by a single flash—in this case a Nikon SB800 Speedlight—fitted with a honeycomb grid to turn the light into a pencil-beam spotlight.

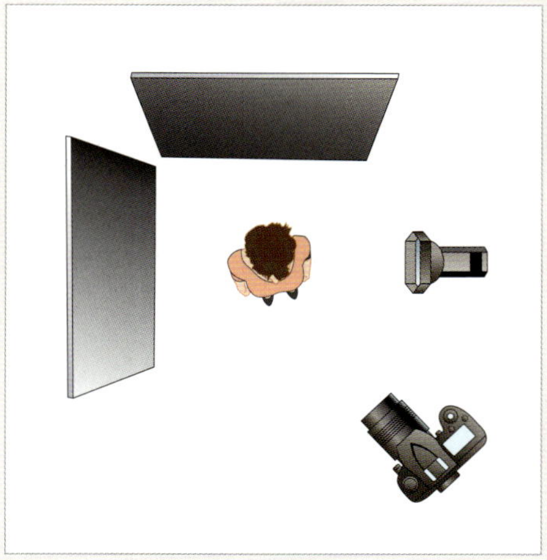

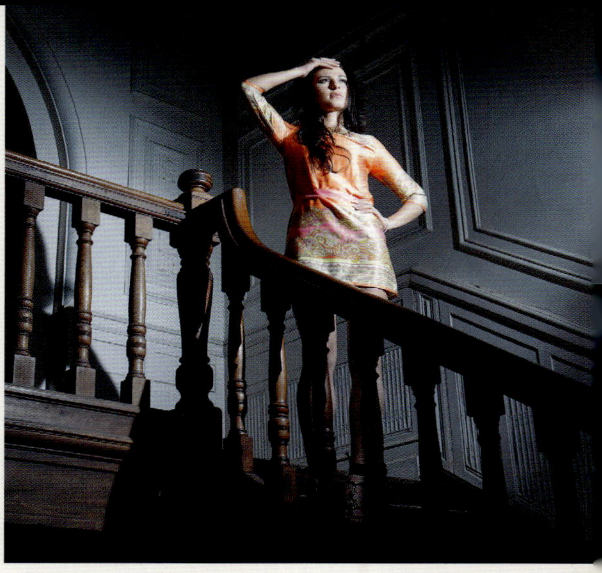

This was set to the right of the frame, high up and out of the shot. The beam of light was used to pick out the subject and then vignette out toward the left edge of the frame. If you look closely you can see the pattern of light coming out of the flash on the wall to the left of the model.

## ONE SINGLE FLASH, TWO DIFFERENT RESULTS

This shot of the girl leaning on the piano was taken in a room using a single flash. The shot predominantly used the soft natural light flowing in through the large windows. Using a 50mm prime lens, an exposure of 1/160 sec at ƒ/2.2, and ISO 200 meant the shot could be handheld successfully without compromising too much on quality. The model could also lean on the piano so she wouldn't be moving too much.

As the contrast from the windows was quite high, a fill light was used. This was a flash with a beauty dish, which was to the far right of the scene, aimed toward the subject. This subtly filled in the shadows to make the shot appear as though the lighting was 100% natural.

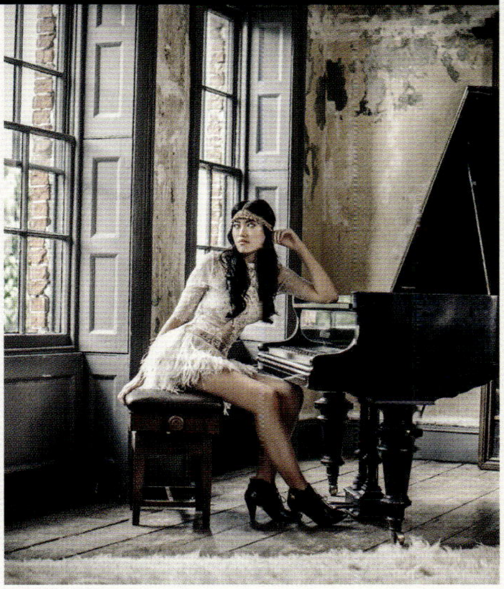

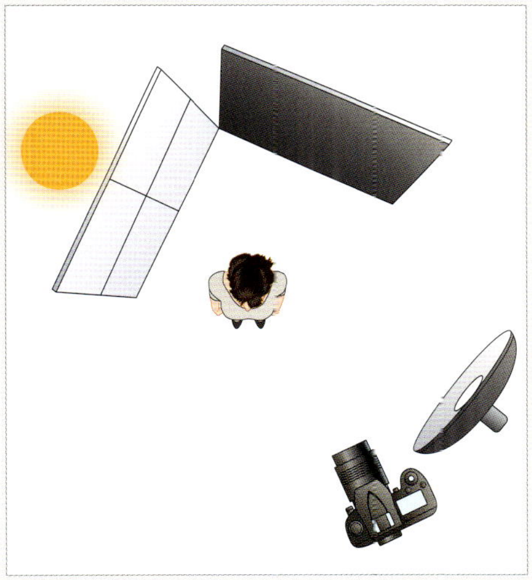

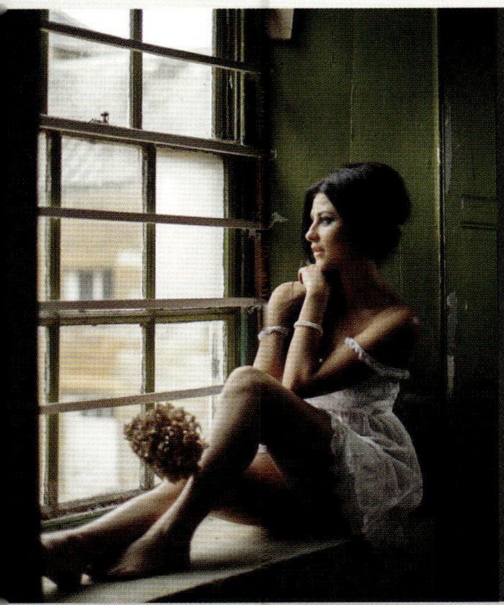

This shot of a girl leaning up against a window was lit almost entirely using ambient light, complete with dark shadows on the unlit side of her face and body. Using any light on the shadow side just looked too unnatural.

However, a small flash fitted with a honeycomb grid was used to put a pool of light on the green wall behind her, to prevent her hair from disappearing into the darkness. It's a subtle use of a flash.

## USING NATURAL DAYLIGHT

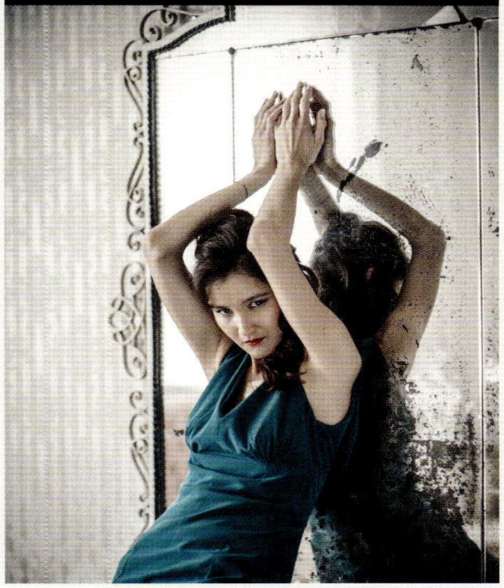

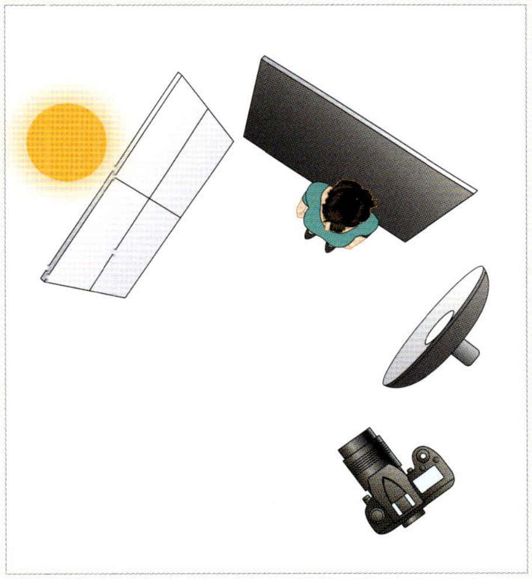

Light coming in from a window at the right of the model was the key light on this shot. By taking an ambient exposure reading, the camera was set to ISO 500 at 1/160 sec, with an aperture of ƒ/1.8 on an 85mm lens. However, the side of the model's face nearest the camera was in shadow, so a flash in a beauty dish was used at the right of the camera. Its power output was adjusted until it filled in the shadows on the model's face to give a more even look to the skin.

# LOCATIONS: EXTERIOR

**WHEN YOU WANT TO MIX artificial light with natural light outdoors on location, you are faced with a similar problem to shooting indoors—striking the right balance between the ambient light and your own flashes. The difference, however, is that it's often the power of your flashes that becomes the limiting factor in choosing your exposure.**

Indoors, the light levels are often low, leaving you with the option of boosting the ISO or setting a slow shutter speed, but outdoors the ambient light is usually much brighter. For your flashes to have any effect, they need to be relatively powerful, especially if it's a sunny day—with a maximum sync speed of around 1/250 sec on most DSLRs you can't just use a faster shutter speed. Although some cameras offer a "high speed" flash sync using dedicated flash units, this comes at the cost of cutting lots of power from your flashes.

If you are using studio lights outdoors, perhaps powered by battery generators, then you can use special radio triggers that allow you to adjust the flash sync timing to allow you to use higher shutter speeds, but that's a pretty advanced technique and one that requires an investment in equipment and time to learn to use it all properly.

Shooting outdoors usually means using battery-powered flashes, rather than studio lighting that requires mains power. Small "speedlights" can come into play, especially when modified through umbrellas or softboxes. There is also a whole new range of battery-powered, studio-style flashes such as Elinchrom's Ranger Quadras, which combine portability with the option to use studio-style light modifiers such as beauty dishes and large softboxes. Of course, any large light modifier used outdoors is easily blown away, so some sandbags or assistants willing to hold onto the kit can be essential accessories!

## USING FLASH WITH AN UMBRELLA

The most common outdoor lighting technique is to use flash to fill in the shadows created by harsh sunlight. On a bright day, with the sun high in the sky, you will either have your subject squinting into the sun (which is never ideal) or have them turned so the sun acts like a huge backlight. This can give a very pleasing rim light or hair light effect, but it will leave the face in shadow. Using a flash with a softbox or umbrella outdoors will allow you to light up the face with beautiful, soft light.

In this shot a single Nikon Speedlight at the right of the camera was fired through a large white umbrella. A wide aperture setting (ƒ/2.8) was needed to get the yellow flowers in the foreground and background out of focus, but because it was so bright and the shutter speed limited to the flash sync speed of 1/250 sec a neutral density filter needed to be used.

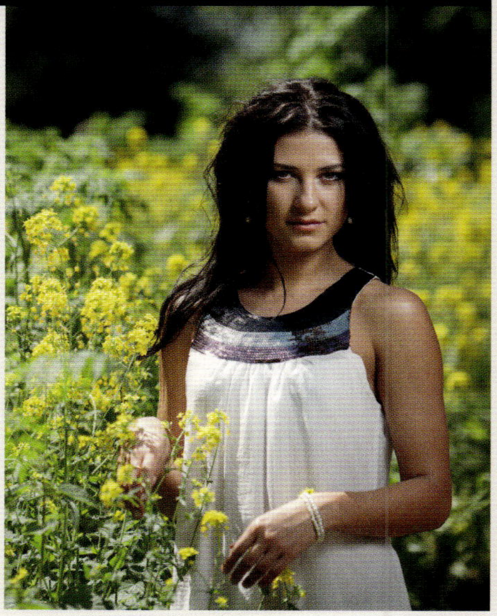

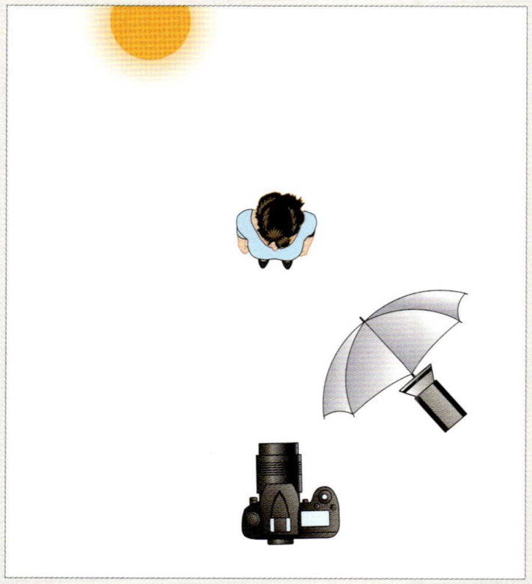

## AVOIDING DIRECT SUNLIGHT

If you have to shoot outdoors in the height of summer on a bright day, one technique is to find some shade for your model and use that. In this shot, the model reclined on the trunk of a large tree, out of the glare of the direct sun. However, the light was very green in color as it was filtering through the green leaves of the tree and reflecting off the green grass. Green-tinged light is not flattering to skin, so a speedlight was shone through a white translucent umbrella, just out of frame to the left. The model was moved until a small patch of clear sunlight hit the top of her head, which highlighted her hair.

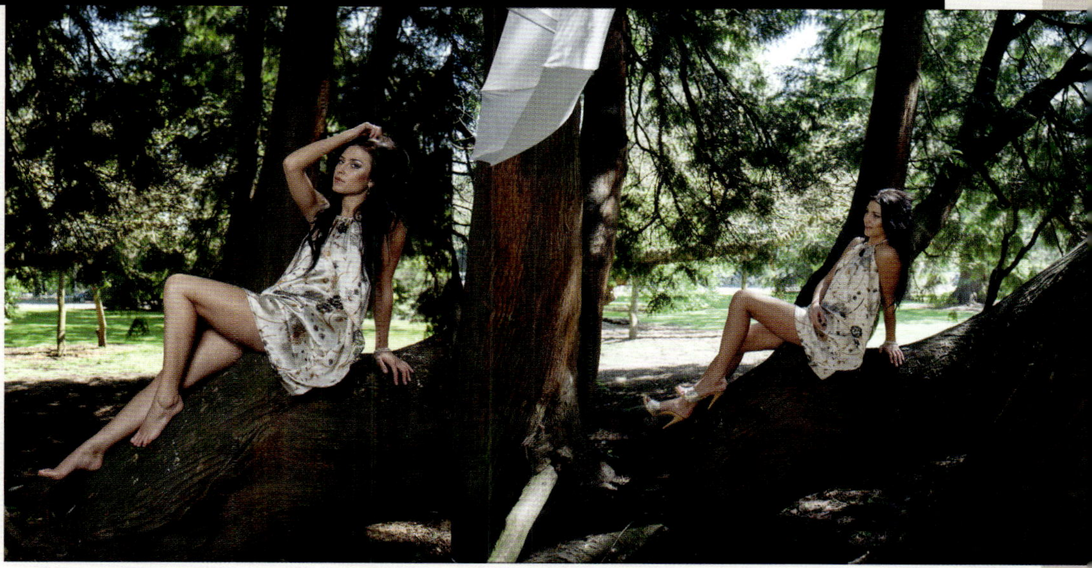

## USING FLASH AND REFLECTORS

A mixture of flash and reflectors is a great combination when used outdoors, as in this shot. The garden was in shade, despite it being a bright day, but a patch of sunlight was clearly visible on the right side of the garden. To take advantage of this, an assistant stood on a chair and used a silver/gold reflector to bounce the light onto the models.

This reflected light formed the key light, casting distinct shadows on the sides of their noses and legs—although it looks like a flash was used as the main light, it was the reflector doing all the hard work.

The flash that was used was fitted into a small softbox at the left of the frame. This acted as a fill light to reduce the contrast of the light being bounced back from the reflector.

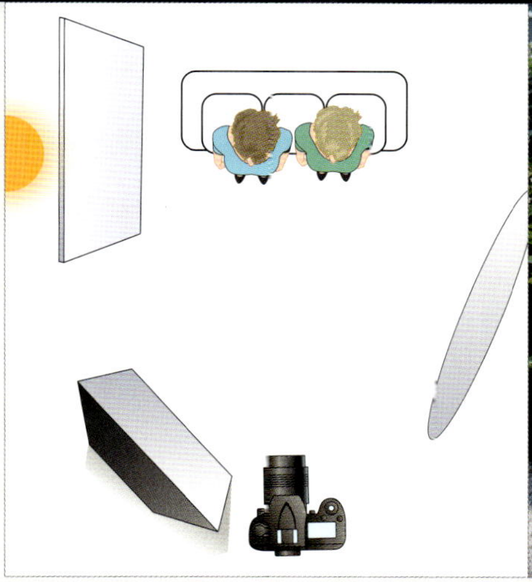

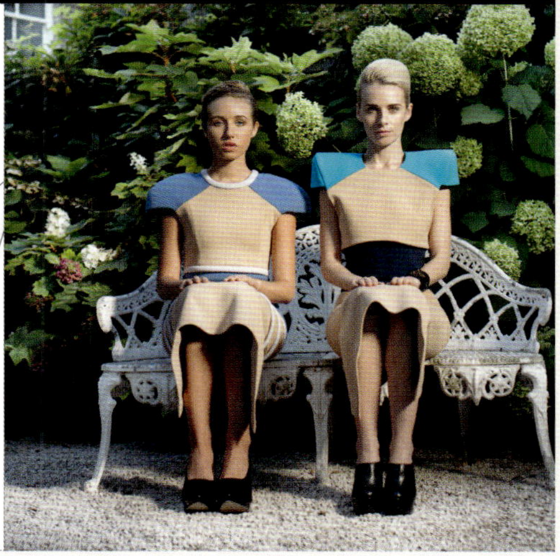

### TIP CONSERVING BATTERY POWER

Using flash outdoors can seriously eat into your battery power. Separate plug-in power packs are available for most flash units, giving them far longer battery life and faster recycling times.

# CONTINUOUS LIGHTING

**FASHION PHOTOGRAPHY has a long history of using continuous lighting rather than flash: the majority of early fashion work was done under hot, predominantly tungsten, studio lights. They were warm in color temperature and very hot to touch, causing makeup to run and models to faint in the sweltering heat of a confined studio. That's partly why flash became popular—with its instant output of light over a very short time models didn't have to squint into bright lights any more. Flash can also be far more powerful than continuous lights and as it is much shorter in duration it freezes action far better, whether that's the twirl of a dress or the flick of hair.**

However, one huge advantage of continuous lighting is that you can see exactly what you are getting before you push the shutter release. There's no guesswork or approximation, as there can be with flash, and you can use all of your camera's automatic modes, if you like, or stick to manual.

A second benefit is that some continuous light sources have focusing Fresnel elements in them, meaning that the light beam can be adjusted between a hard "flood" of light or a more focused pool of light (which is actually softer). Of course, the output can also be modified using softboxes, umbrellas, or, more commonly, scrims, but there really isn't the range of accessories that there are for flash. However, for photographers shooting video, as well as still images, continuous lighting is a necessity.

Modern continuous lights typically come in three different types: tungsten, HMI, and LED. Tungsten lights are the cheapest, but they get very hot and have a very warm color temperature: they can be gelled blue to match daylight, but this reduces their intensity. HMI lights are more modern and more expensive, but have the added benefit of being daylight balanced. However, many can't be turned off and on again instantly—they have to cool down and warm up, unless they are the more expensive "hot re-strike" versions. Finally, LEDs are gaining ground as they can sometimes be adjusted for color temperature, and they run cool. They aren't quite as powerful yet, though.

The biggest issue with all continuous lights is power. There are only so many lights you can run off a domestic mains electricity system before fuses start to blow, and even then the light output is a fraction of that of flash. More often than not, you'll be increasing the ISO, using fast lenses with the aperture almost wide open, and using on a tripod to help counter slow shutter speed. For that reason continuous lighting is relatively useless outdoors unless it's used in deep shade or later during the evening, but for certain indoor jobs it can be ideal.

### CLASSIC PORTRAITS

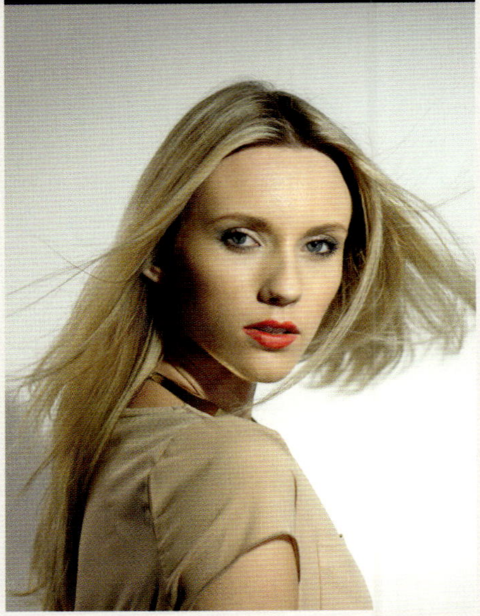

A Lupolux LED light with focusing fresnel lens is ideal for capturing classic portraits in a studio. With the light beam set to a more focused spot, the light quality can be soft enough for Hollywood-style portraits and with the light within four feet of the model, an exposure of 1/250 sec at ƒ/2.5 and ISO 200 was possible. This was fast enough for me to be able to handhold the camera, but slow enough so that the hair (blown by a wind machine) registered as blurry.

## HMI LIGHTING

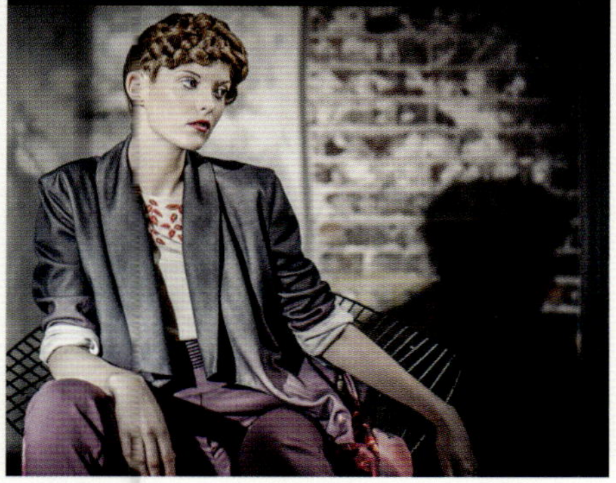

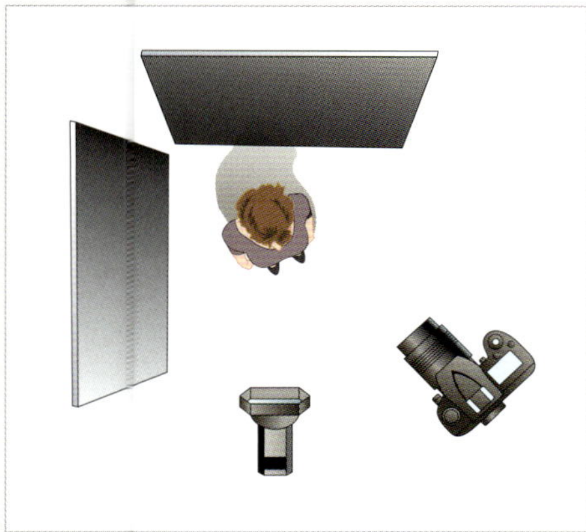

A bare HMI light set to spot was used to illuminate this model in an old building. With the light high and to the left of the camera, the model's shadow on the wall becomes an interesting part of the composition.

## GETTING THE MOST FROM TUNGSTEN

The warmth of the orange tungsten light was combined with some daylight in this gloriously golden shoot in a room with a copper-colored feature wall. By using two tungsten lights inside gridded softboxes (one either side of the camera lens), a shadowless light has been created that envelops the model and spills onto the background wall in the tight headshot.

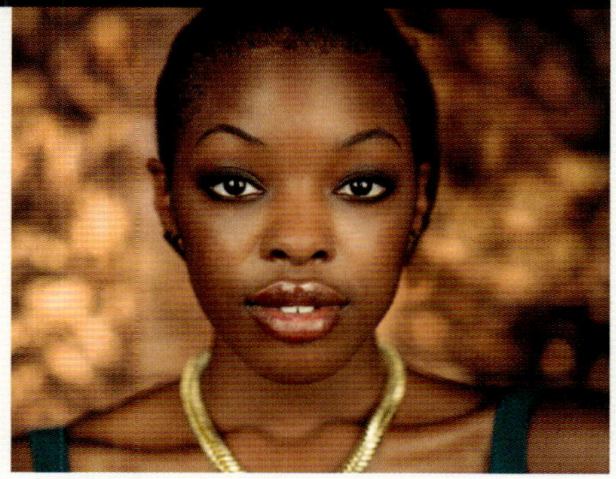

Moving the model to the other side of the room, closer to the natural window light and much further from the tungsten lights meant that the light levels were lower.

The pair of lights were aimed at the back of the model, to give a warm orange glow that matched the color of room set.

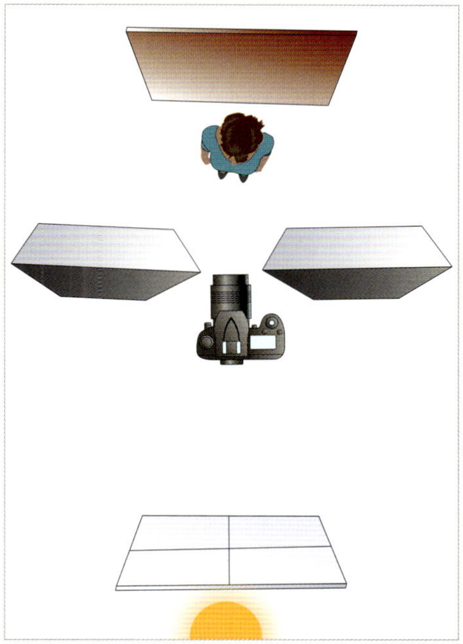

## CREATING EVEN LIGHTING

A tungsten light inside a softbox provided the key light on this model, and a lovely even light on the face. Behind her, to the left of the frame, a small window lets in some natural daylight. With the camera's white balance set to tungsten to match the main light, the small daylight rim light renders slightly blue.

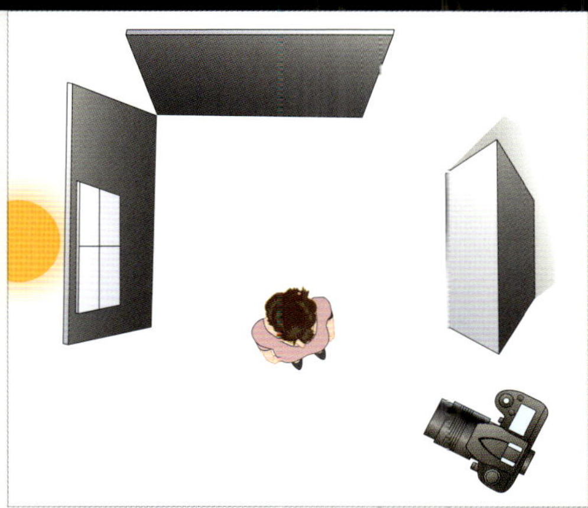

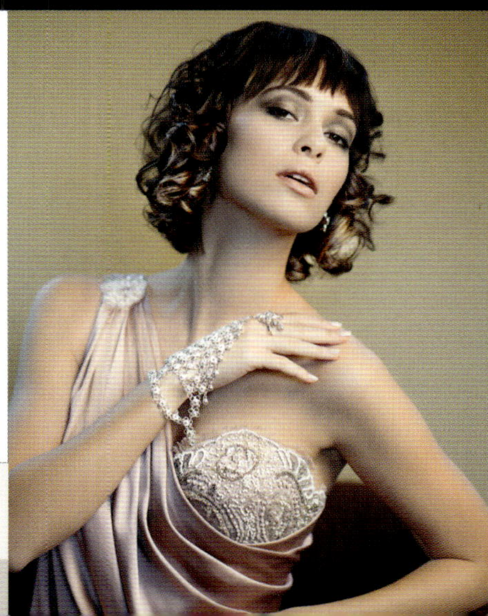

# NATURAL LIGHT

**FOR MANY PHOTOGRAPHERS, ambient, or "natural" light is the best light you can get, especially as it's free! That's not to say there is wonderful, glorious light all the time—sometimes it's low and warm, and other times diffused by clouds, which may or may not give you the look you are aiming for.**

Knowing how the quality, intensity, direction, and color of light changes throughout the day is key if you plan on using daylight alone for your shoot. Overhead, midday summer sun can be a nightmare, as it's harsh and creates lots of shadows. Early morning, pre-dawn light can be soft, but also very blue in color and relatively low in intensity. Evening sunshine can be very directional, but sometimes a little too warm.

Many photographers use Google Maps, weather checks, and various apps to work out where the sun will be at the time of a scheduled shoot. If you are prepared, you can come armed to modify the light to your own tastes and requirements. As with continuous lighting, when you use natural light and reflectors what you see is what you get.

## USING SHADE

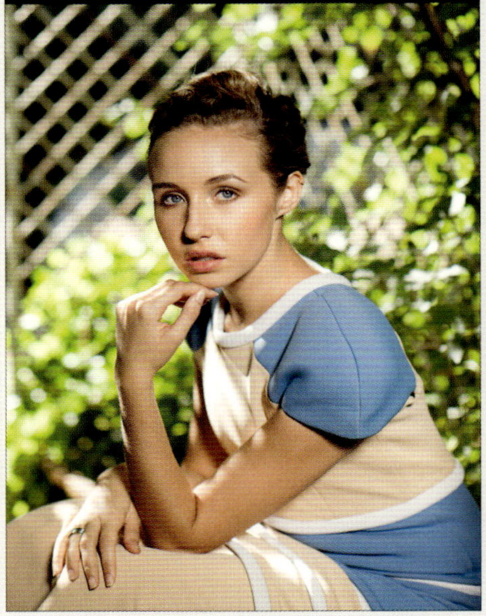

The bright sunshine in the garden of a large house was too harsh for flattering photos so our model was moved under the shade of a plant-lined arbor. The light flooded in from beyond the arbor, producing a natural backlight, but the subject's face was in shade. A silver reflector, aimed from outside the arbor, back in toward the model, provided a strong key light that makes it appear almost as if flash has been used.

## EARLY EVENING LIGHT

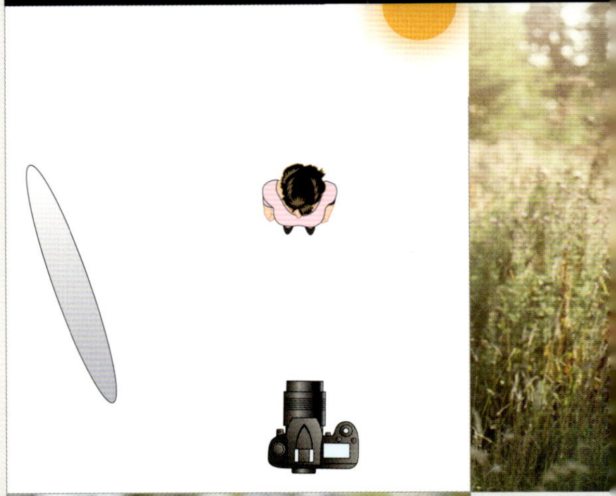

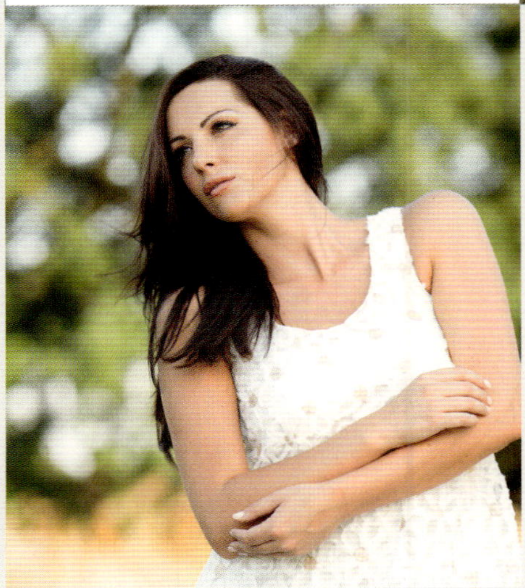

A shoot on what turned out to be the hottest day of the year was scheduled for early evening, to avoid the overhead sun. Instead, there was lovely low, warm sunlight, which is ideal for backlighting not only your subject but also any plants and trees.

For this shot of a model on the edge of a wild meadow, the sun was behind the subject and shaded partly by the leaves of the big tree. There is some flare in the shot, which is a result of shooting directly into the sun, but that adds to the summery atmosphere.

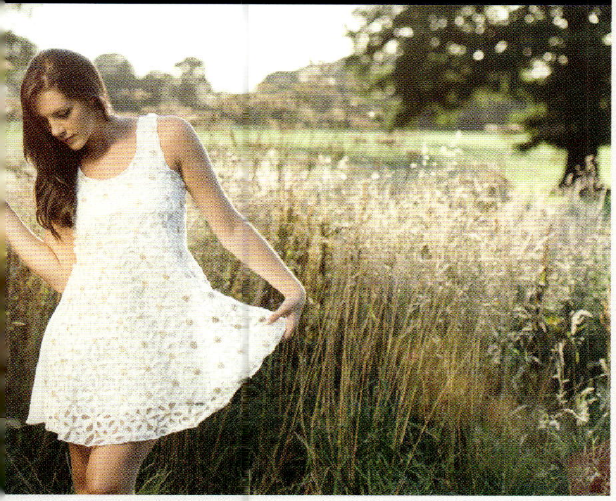

Of course, with the light behind her the model's face was in shade. One option was to expose for the face, allowing the background and her hair to "blow out" due to overexposure, but this also loses edge detail in the white sundress. Instead, a silver/gold reflector was used at the left of the camera. This was held high and aimed so that the reflected light hit the subject from above, producing a more natural-looking shadow. Many photographers use reflectors too low, which can give an under-lit "horror" look if you're not careful.

By turning the model around and shooting in the opposite direction, the low sunlight was directly on her face, which was unflattering and quite painful. This time, a large translucent diffuser panel was held up so that the sunlight was diffuse by the time it hit the model's face. This gives a lovely, soft flattering light, and by exposing for the model's face—which is essentially in the shadow of the diffuser panel—the distant trees in the background appeared even lighter. So, two different looking shots from one location.

## CATCHLIGHTS

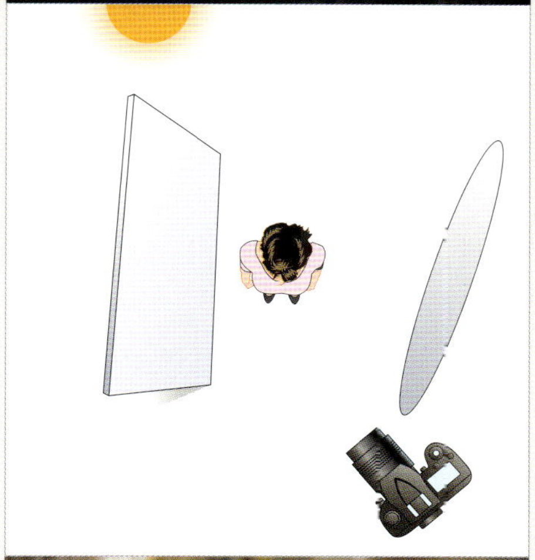

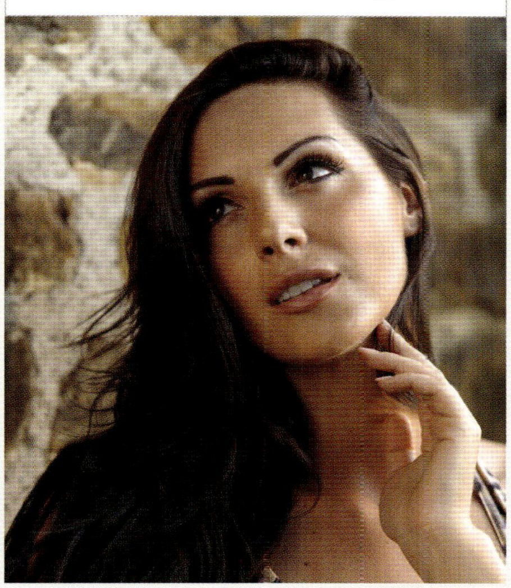

If the sun really is too bright, an alternative is to find some shade. In this case, an old wall at the side of a disused abbey made an ideal shady spot to photograph our subject, complete with light wrapping around her face from the edge of the wall. In cases like this, moving your subject just a few feet can have a significant effect on the light falling on them. The only thing missing was some catchlights in the eyes, so a large silver reflector was used to bounce a little bit of light back in to the face and give some nice catchlights.

## USING NATURAL LIGHT INDOORS

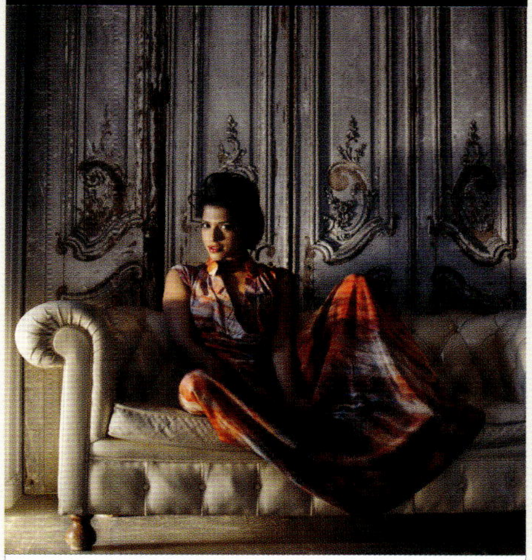

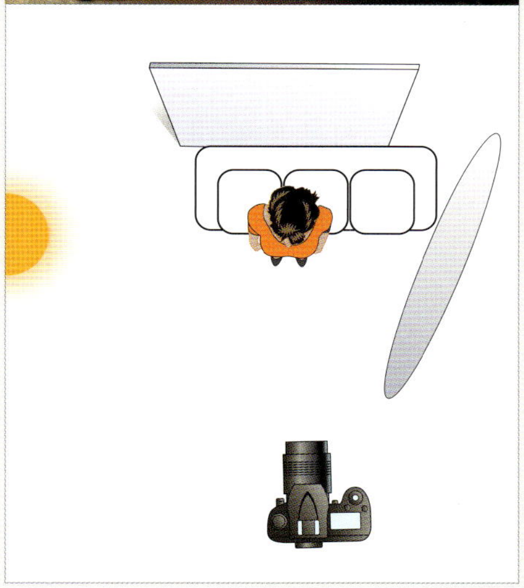

Just because your model is indoors doesn't mean you can't get away with natural lighting and a reflector. A huge front door let light flood into this amazing house and onto the model, who was reclining on the sofa in front of an old carved wooden panel. Of course, the contrast was very high, but a reflector placed just out of shot bounced enough light back into the darkest areas to retain some detail, without making the shot look unnatural.

# 08

# RELAX THE SITUATION

**IF YOU ARE FEELING UNCOMFORTABLE or embarrassed, one of the worst things someone can say to you is "just relax!" As a photographer it can be hard to avoid using the phrase when a model freezes, but in this chapter we take a look at the reasons why they might feel uneasy and how best to calm an individual down. We talk about how certain direction can allow you to capture those "in between" moments that add a realness to an image rather than forced, specific poses, and examine the rise of the digital era and it's affect on the relationship between model and photographer. Finally, focusing on ways of reducing stress wherever possible, we discuss how to choose your team members wisely and to prepare for a smooth shoot on location and at night.**

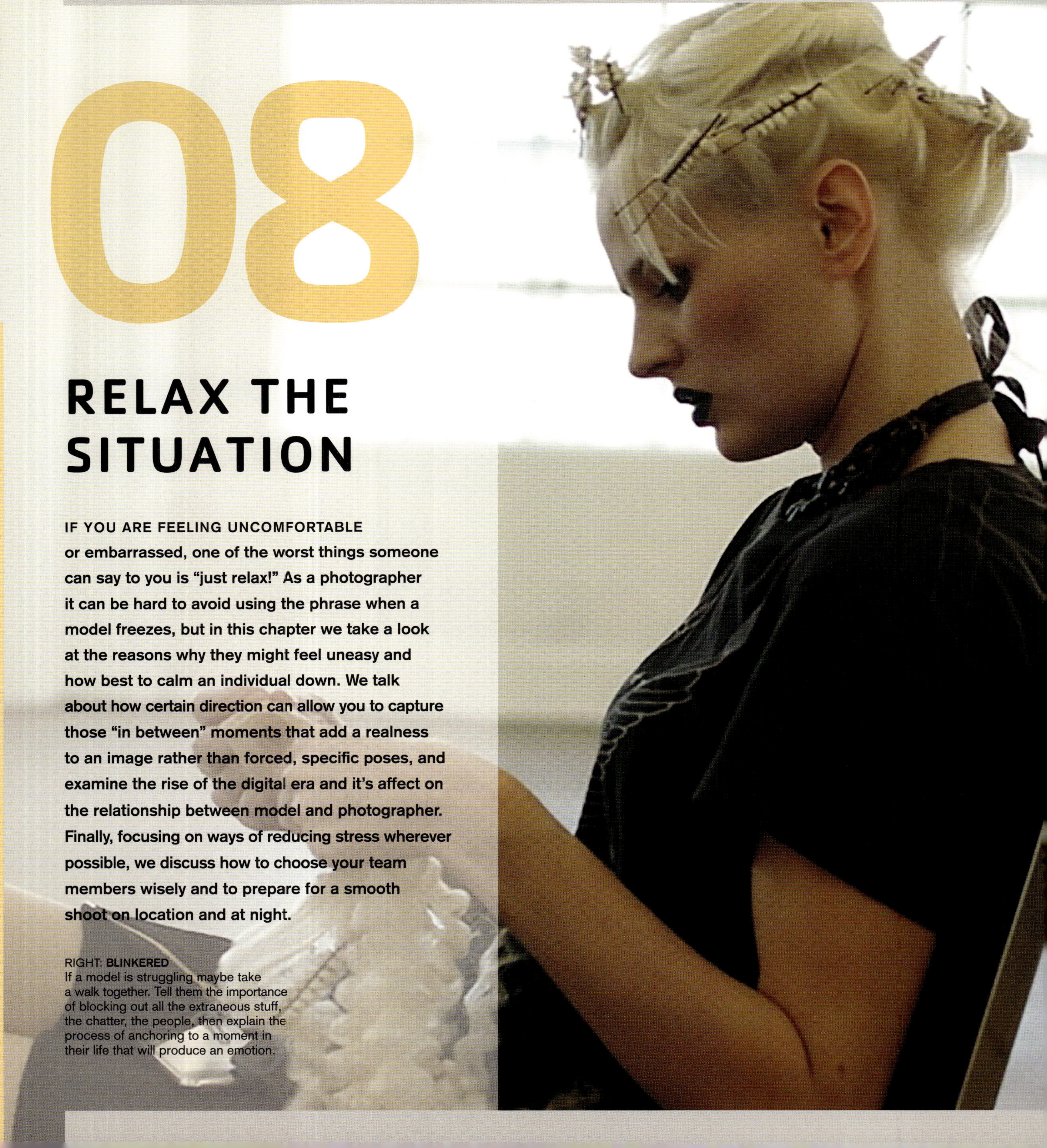

RIGHT: **BLINKERED**
If a model is struggling maybe take a walk together. Tell them the importance of blocking out all the extraneous stuff, the chatter, the people, then explain the process of anchoring to a moment in their life that will produce an emotion.

# EASING ANXIETY

**YOU ALWAYS WANT YOUR MODELS to be comfortable when you photograph them, but how quickly and easily they relax can depend on their level of experience, personality, the individual shoot environment, and even the side of the bed they got out on. The first hour or so of a shoot is a critical time for establishing connections and models who have worked less, are younger, or are excessively self-aware may need more attention and direction than others. However, there are many factors throughout a day that can affect a person and at any point, any shoot can turn.**

The unfortunate truth is that when a model feels awkward or scared, it shows on camera. Often their movements will become restricted as their shoulders get high and tight, shortening the neck and leaving the arms and hands stiff and rigid. Faces contort as jaws clench, eyes flash wild, and teeth grit. It is not easy to take great pictures in this situation and at this point you need to change things up. Take a moment to decide whether you can solve the issue with a few kind words or whether you need to separate the model from the current environment to snap them out of it.

Remember, models have a lot going on in their space, with up to three or four people at a time constantly pulling at them, poking them with brushes, preening, plucking, and tweaking. It can be hard to "let go" when the focus is so intense and a camera is inches away. They may appear to ooze confidence and sexuality, but models are just as insecure—if not more so—than everybody else.

They are often worrying about things you've never even considered. For example, maybe in the first shot a girl is wearing pants and is comfortable and easy to work with. Then the stylist, who made a remark about how the fit was off, puts the girl in a skirt. While you're busy posing her, the model is worrying about how her legs look. It applies to male models too, especially if they are expected to remove their clothing. No matter how many years a model has worked in the industry they can never be expected to be 100 percent comfortable all the time.

RIGHT: **ONE ON ONE**
Sometimes it's important to get one on one to relax a model, reduce the number of spectators, and make the shooting space your own. Get the model to physically shake off any pent up energy. Let them know they are free to make mistakes. Compliment, explain, and speak positively between shots.

FAR RIGHT: **OVERKILL**
Be careful not to over direct, frustrating and restricting the model. Don't over complicate poses, or force them to recreate a mood board picture exactly. It will make the model self-conscious, and maybe ruin something you could have shot in five frames if you'd just let them do their thing.

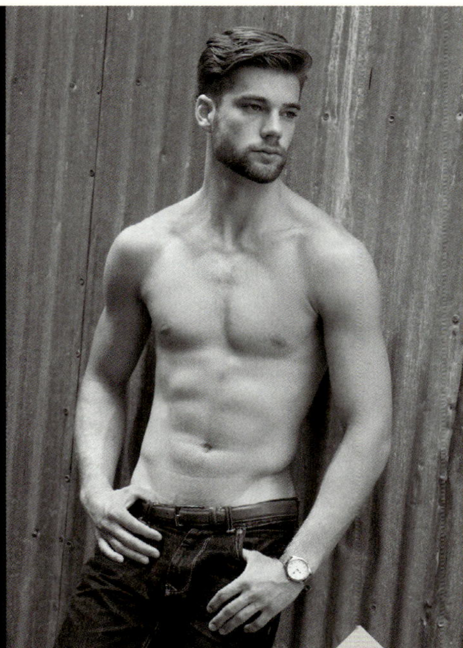

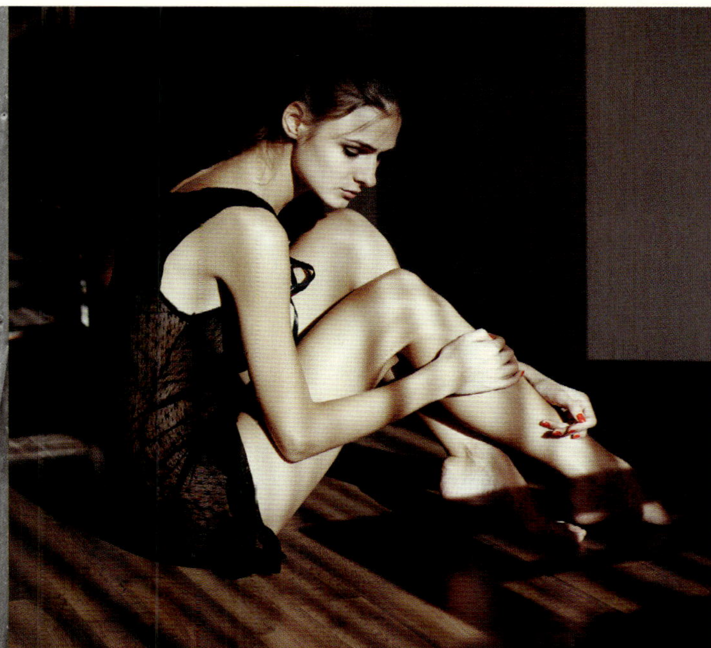

# THE "IN BETWEEN" SHOT

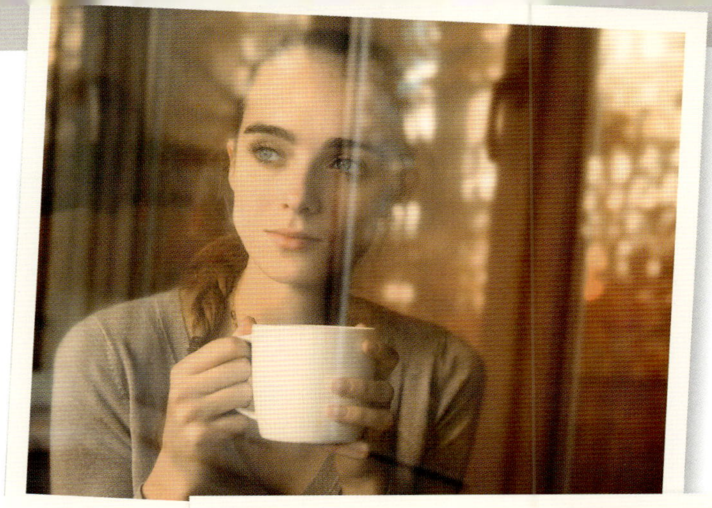

**MODELS ARE OFTEN REQUIRED to sit or stand very still, in traditional poses, with minimal movement between shots. These images can be easier to direct, light, and shoot quickly, but there are times when these formal set-ups lack energy and life. Though technically more difficult, capturing movement and moments—often mid action—can lead to more exciting and dynamic pictures that appear spontaneous and impulsive because they truly were.**

You can catch an "in between" shot in the moments when a model is naturally unaware of the camera. This could be during a movement, or the seconds before or after an action is performed. It can even occur between shots, when the model believes they have finished shooting and relaxes slightly. You have to watch out for these instances, which can be big and wild, or small and intimate, but are over in a flash and hard to recreate. You must shoot quickly and be ready for anything—it's a well-known fact that models give you their best work when you're not holding your camera.

As we discussed in *Expression: Revealing the Truth* (see page 78) it's about highlighting the model's natural behavior and expressions, only this time with their body as well. If something about a shot isn't working, never be afraid to change things up and ask the model to step out of their comfort zone a little. Just make sure you capture their reaction.

Depending on the style of shoot there may be certain rules concerning how much of the outfit you need to see, but even unprintable shots will be great for your personal portfolio. Be open and willing to let someone else inspire you with his or her actions—every model brings something new and fresh, so use it!

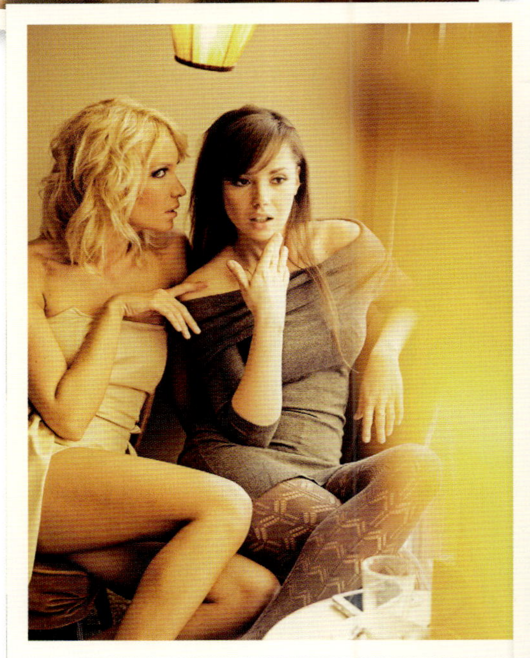

### SURPRISE!

If you have a great relationship with a model it can be fun to surprise them from time to time. On the final shot get a crew member to spray them with water, or whisper to another model to push them in a pool. Think outside the box for the best reaction shots, but be ready to click!

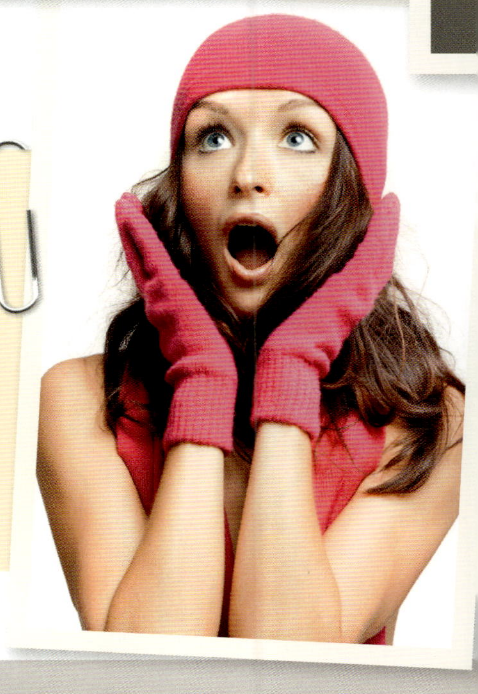

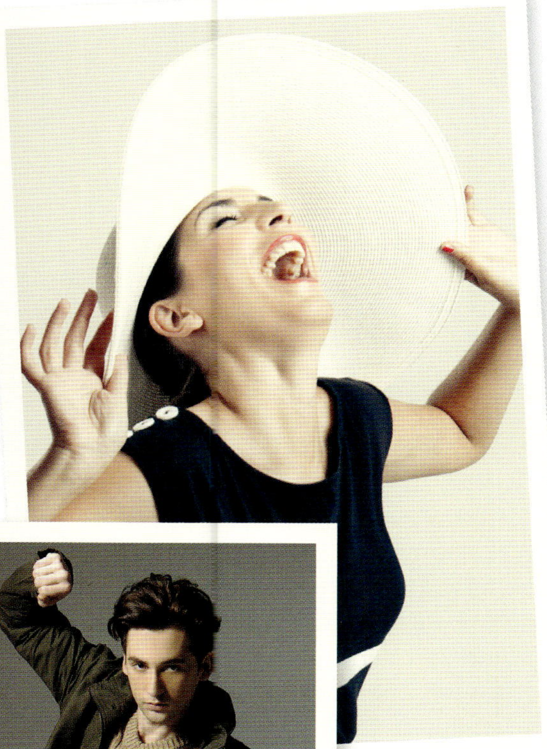

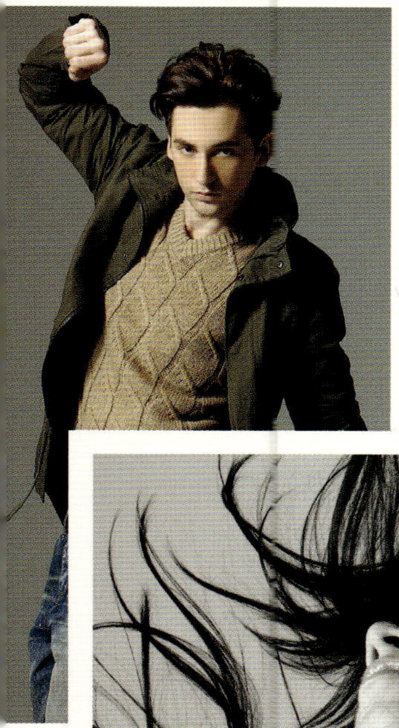

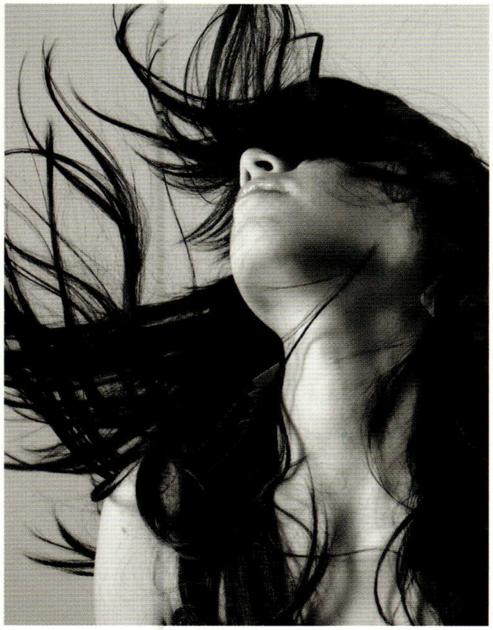

## ACTING OUT

A shooting environment that promotes experimentation without judgment will lead to better "in between" shots. If you are looking for a little inspiration when directing movement try asking your model to perform some of the following actions:

**WALKING:** Even a single step can be effective, but also try working with different speeds and stride lengths.

**RUNNING:** Make sure the outfit allows for lots of movement and watch out for high heels!

**SPINNING/TWIRLING:** It's hard to catch a clear face shot, but good for lifestyle images.

**SHAKE IT OUT:** Make your model go crazy—to fling their arms and legs about and shake their head all over.

**JUMPING:** Can be beautiful if controlled well with timing. Change up the direction and eye line, and maybe add a trampoline for fun.

**BALANCING:** Just asking a model to stand on one leg can lead to hilarious results.

**DANCING:** Be kind and have music playing! Never joke about someone's dance moves—let them feel free to look silly.

**TALKING/LAUGHING:** A good model has a great fake laugh, but getting models to talk or whisper—especially in a two shot—can produce very natural-looking results.

**PROP INTERACTION:** If there's a bicycle, ask the model if they can ride it. Sometimes props can be seen as cliché, but they can also add a lot to a picture.

**FIX SHOE:** Will the model bend down or lift their leg? People respond differently even to what seem like simple requests.

**WORK THE HAIR:** Let your model swoop it, whip it, ruffle it, whatever works.

**LOOK DOWN:** Sometimes a model will check their footing and you'll realize how perfect the shot is when they look down. Use their natural instincts.

LEFT & OPPOSITE: **BREATHE LIFE**
True moments of expression and feeling whether posed or unpredicted can breathe life into a still frame. Human emotion can be powerful and the range is limitless. Whether quiet or loud, small or big, these are the images that tell a story.

# THE DIGITAL REVOLUTION

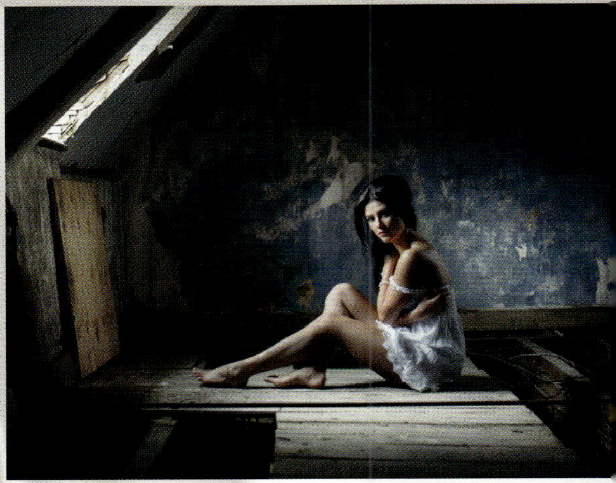

**TO SAY THAT DIGITAL CAMERAS have revolutionized photography is a huge understatement. Of course, there have been cost implications—digital cameras that lose their value overnight versus the steep price of getting film processed and its availability—but the biggest change has been the ability to see what you have taken instantly, and shoot more pictures.**

Some may disagree, but fundamentally this means the "old world" of cameras, chemicals, and films has been democratized and thrown wide open—for good and bad. The good is that photographers can see their results instantly. As a consequence, it's easier to experiment: you can take far more shots, and take more risks with tech-niques as you are not wasting expensive film. Seeing the results straight away means more photographers can experiment with super-shallow depth of field, for example, or complicated lighting set-ups and know they've nailed the shot before leaving the set. Of course, this can lead to people using the "spray and pray" method, where some shooters blast through thousands of images to see if they can get a decent one!

The film versus digital debate has raged for years, but in recent times the arguments have changed. Initially, it was all about quality. Cameras had only a few megapixels, offering far less resolution than comparable film cameras. They had small sensors, so the depth of field of lenses was far greater than before, making the shallow depth of field look harder to achieve. They were also poor at high ISO setting, and very expensive to buy, with hideously priced memory cards as well. Plus, of course, you needed a memory-hungry computer to process the files, and some expensive software—a whole new learning curve for many photographers.

But over the years, technology caught up. Pixel ratings rocketed, sensors got bigger, storage media got cheaper, and the computer skills are now taken for granted. It has also become far easier to get your work seen internationally via the internet, and also to look for models and other creatives.

Working with the newest batch of cameras is far easier than with film cameras or the earliest breed of digital SLRs. Compared to a film camera, especially when shooting on transparency film, the ability to gauge exposure and white balance using the LCD screen and histogram is a real godsend, especially when you mix in the potentially unpredictable results of flash or other artificial lighting. Compared to the early digital cameras, the LCD screens are now far bigger and have a greater resolution, while many cameras can also shoot "tethered" to a laptop or other computer. This means the camera is connected to a large computer screen via a long cable and the image is displayed almost instantaneously on the big screen, using software such as Capture One or Adobe Lightroom. Combined with clever tools such as highlight warnings and focus mask warnings, a photographer can instantly see if a shot is sharp and correctly exposed. So too can the client, art director, or the model.

It also means the files are stored on the computer hard drive, either in addition to or instead of being saved to the memory card. Some software can also send the images automatically to a tablet computer via WiFi so someone else can watch what's going on, while some cameras can accept WiFi-enabled memory cards so the images are beamed wirelessly to a computer. However, all of these images need to be kept safe, which means "backing up." Many photographers have a RAID system where an instant backup of every shot taken is stored separately,

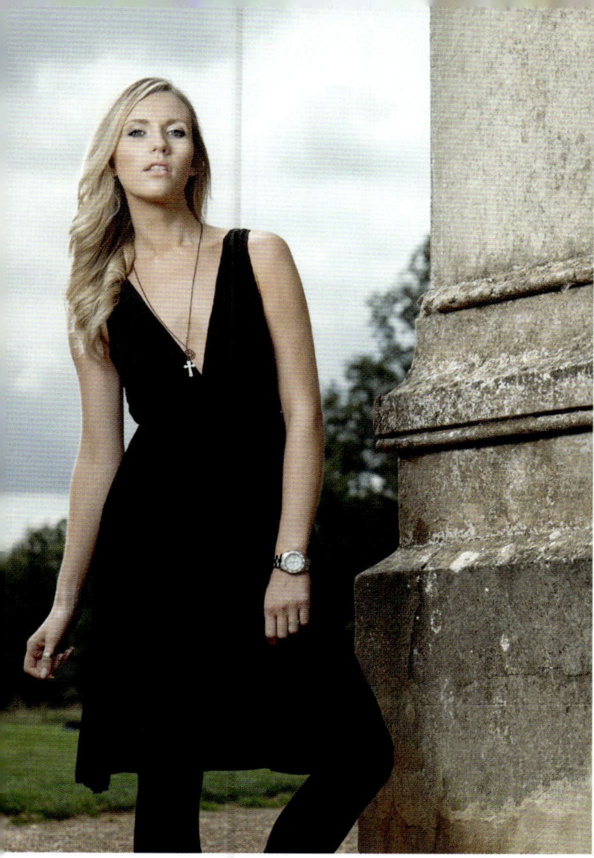

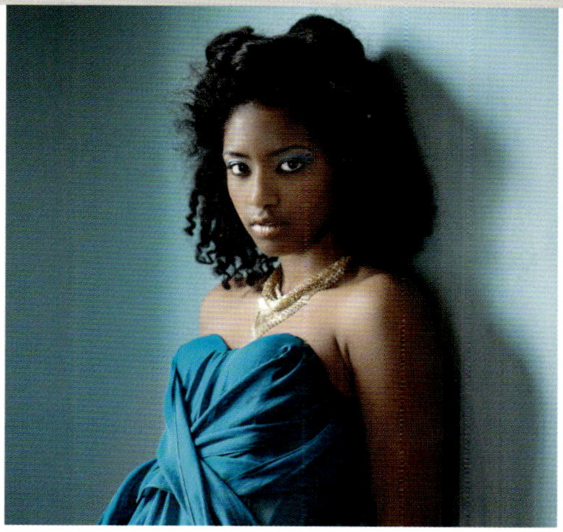

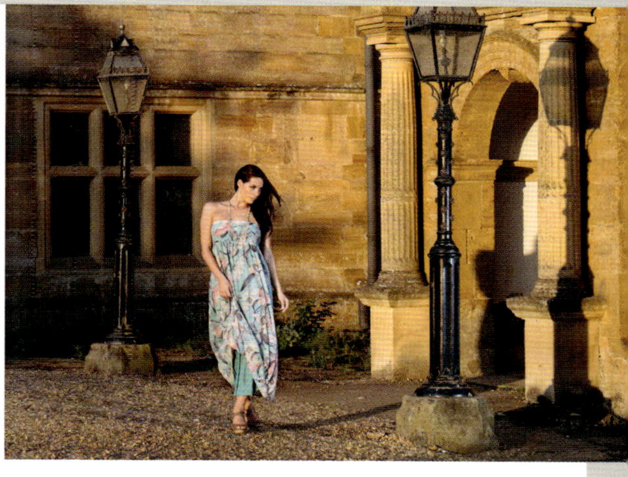

ABOVE OPPOSITE: **MIXING LOW LIGHT**
Mixing the low light of a disused interior with a splash of flash on the back wall to bring out the blue color would have been a nightmare using a film camera. With a modern digital camera, setting the ISO to 640 allowed an exposure of 1/160 sec *f*/1.8. The sharpness and exposure could be checked instantly on the LCD screen.

ABOVE: **SOFT WINDOW LIGHT**
Soft window light meant using an aperture of *f*/1.8 to get this natural looking shot. A digital camera meant the focus could be checked easily on the screen.

ABOVE LEFT: **MIXING DAYLIGHT**
Mixing daylight with flash outdoors would have been an exercise in tricky light metering on a film camera, but with digital you can ensure the exposure is right.

ABOVE RIGHT: **WARM EVENING SUN**
Warm evening sun and a little bit of fill-in light from a hidden flash unit would have played havoc with the color on film, but with a digital image it's easy to correct during post-production.

on a second hard drive. If you are on location, all of this kit needs power, so a generator or huge batteries are required to make it all work, plus some sort of weatherproofing!

On film, some cameras only got ten or 12 shots to a roll—or even a single shot in the case of large-format sheet film. Typically, 35mm film was used in 36-exposure rolls, but each roll of film was expensive, as was the cost of processing. Film had to be bought in batches with matching serial numbers and stored in a fridge if it was to be consistent, and as the resulting transparencies are originals there is no backup unless each one is scanned and stored on a computer (and retouched to get rid of dust specks and the like).

However, film is not totally dead and many purists believe it has a different look and feel to digital files. Some argue that clever digital post-processing means you can get very close to the film "look" with a digital image, but others say there really is no substitute, and are starting to use film again—complete with the associated costs and hassle of getting it scanned.

## TO SHOW OR NOT?

With digital cameras, everyone knows a shot can be reviewed instantly on the back of the camera or on a separate screen. Some models like to be shown shots so they can see what's working and what's not—and to give themselves some confidence. However, some photographers see it as a huge intrusion into the shoot, ruining the "flow."

International fashion photographer Perou is leading the way in refusing to shoot with his camera tethered to a screen. "Or else the art director will take over the shoot and want to look at and critique every photo," he says. Instead, Perou uses his digital medium format Hasselblad in a similar way to a film camera: he records the images to the memory card inside the camera and hardly ever looks at the LCD screen during the shoot.

# CHOOSING THE RIGHT TEAM

**VARIOUS FACTORS, such as budget, availability, and client will affect your decisions when choosing a team for a project, but when you have control over who you invite to set it is important to remember that your choices can have a dramatic effect. You are not the only person who will interact with your model on set and they could have met any number of crew members before you even arrive.**

To guarantee yourself the best chance of working with a happy, relaxed model, you need to find compassionate, respectful people that are understanding of other people's needs. Allow for a certain amount of eccentricity, but avoid rudeness and aim to book individuals who can immediately put a stranger at ease. Within minutes of meeting your model they are going to be in their personal space, touching their face, and adjusting their underclothes. At no point do you want to have to stop a shoot because a model feels uncomfortable with a member of your team. In a litigious society you need to be able to trust the people you

> *A wonderful way for an emerging photographer to find a stylist to partner with is to research stylists' assistants. Generally, previous or current assistants of major stylists are hungry to pair up. Photographers should look for stylists whose general aesthetic and taste they admire. Photographic sensibility is a language and it should be shared—some people love edgy, boundary pushing photography, while others prefer romanticism and softness.*
>
> **NATALIE TOREN,** *stylist*

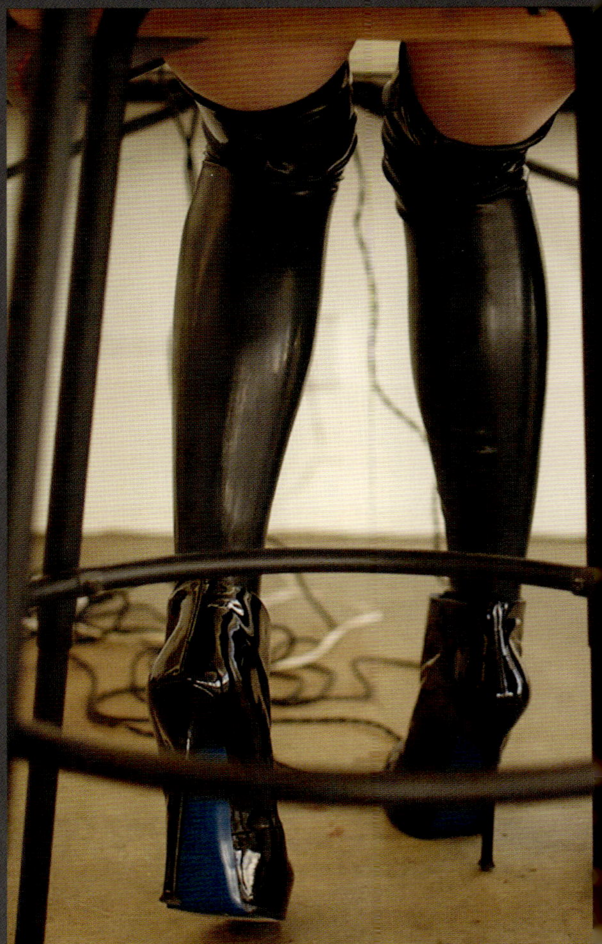

RIGHT: **BEHIND THE SCENES**
Nowadays no one has the time, or the budget to deal with demanding personalities amongst the team. Photographers should chose an artist to suit the individual job and remember that they will be spending long hours together during prep when making booking decisions.

employ. Contacting a talent agency is a great way of ensuring a level of professionalism and also to tap into emerging artists, as agencies are looking to build their younger talent's book, just like models.

Photographer decisions on who to employ behind the scenes vary greatly depending on the individual. Think about the male to female ratio on set, for example. Some photographers prefer all-female teams as it can create a nurturing environment and a maternal figure can be useful in emotional situations. Young teenage girls might also feel more intimidated taking their clothes off in front of a group of burly, older men, but you will need help moving equipment and holding bounce boards. Every job is different, which is why you want to provide a good balance, with a team who embrace the atmosphere you are trying to create. Those who are happy in their work will always bring a more positive energy to set.

One of the most significant decisions you will make as a photographer is who to hire as your assistant. There will be many personal factors in your decision, but try to bypass those who are in the industry just to meet good-looking people. They need to be 100 percent professional at all times and know when to be quiet. An assistant needs to be hardworking and capable of operating in an environment where beautiful girls are taking their clothes off—a great assistant can make a model feel comfortable and attractive without coming across as creepy.

Finding a team and sticking to it can allow for a shorthand language to develop, resulting in better quality work and a streamlined set day. You will come to rely on your team more than you can imagine. In general, find people you like: it makes everything easier, more fun, and you could end up working with your best friends every day.

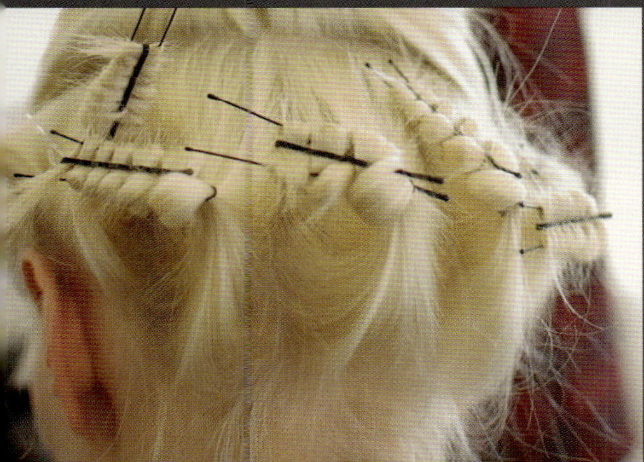

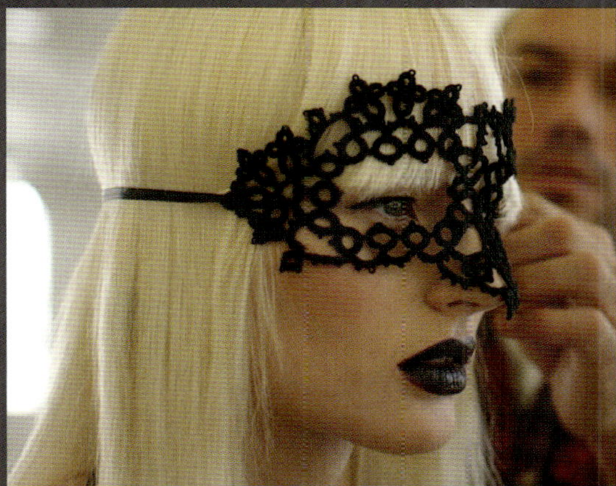

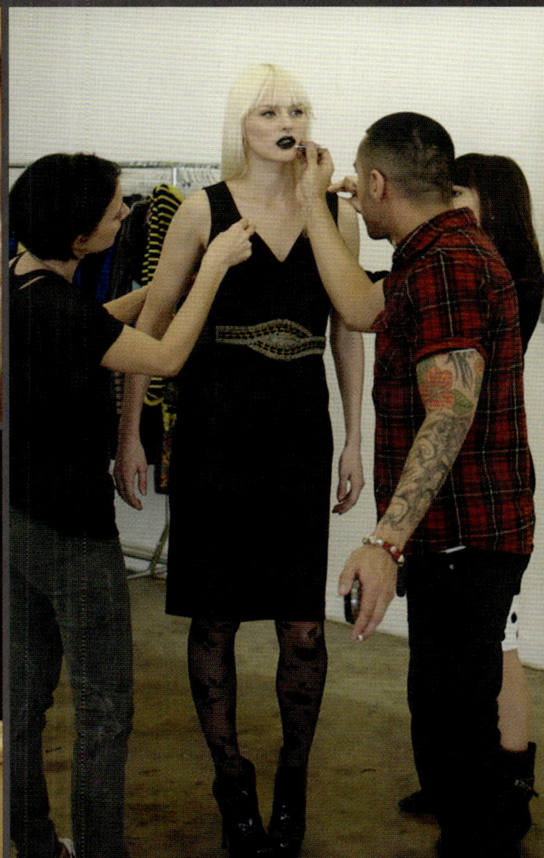

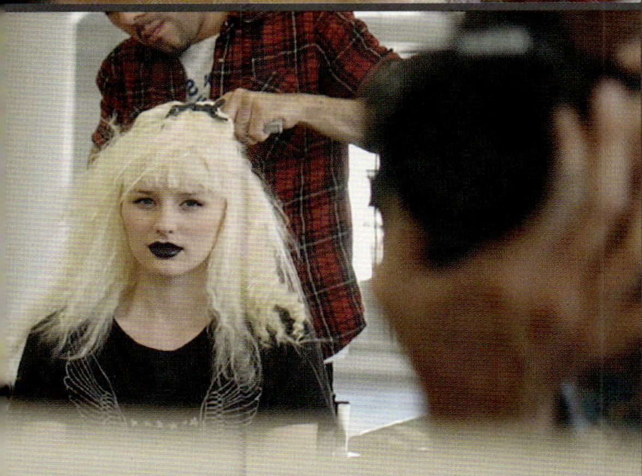

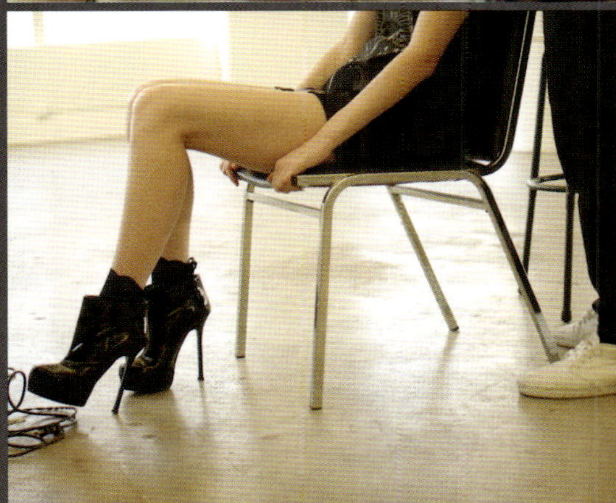

# ON LOCATION

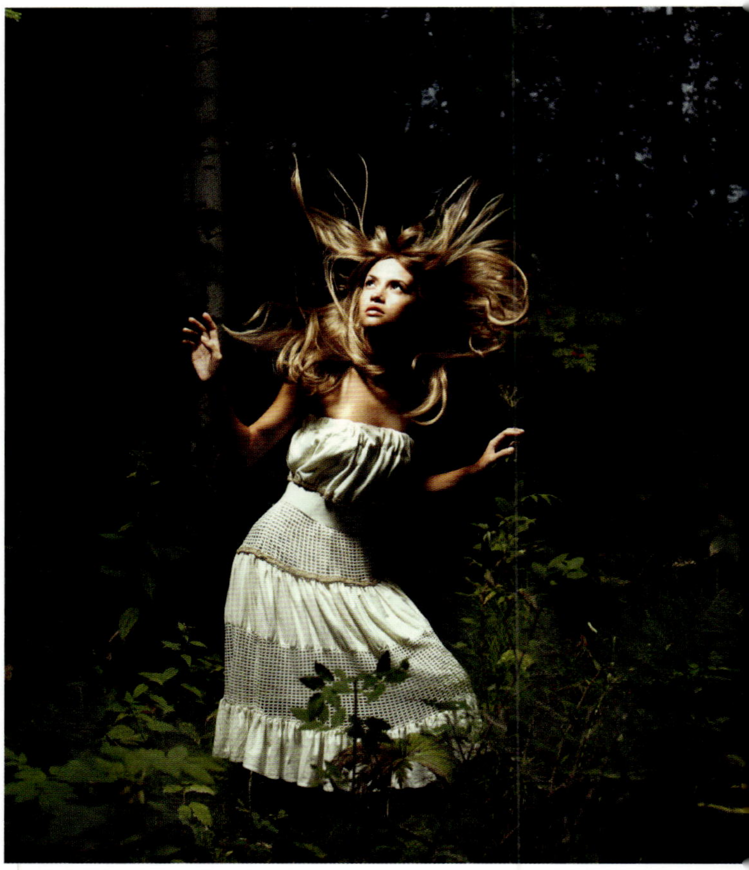

RIGHT: **PANIC ATTACK**
More people than you realize suffer from anxiety and panic attacks. Even those who may appear confident on the outside can be agonizing internally. Attacks can be frightening and disarming so be prepared.

**TAKING A PHOTOGRAPHIC SHOOT on location—whether it's just for a day or for a week-long trip—can add to the usual stresses experienced on a working set. Traveling is rarely hassle-free. There may be passports and work visas to consider, and grouping together strangers who are operating outside their comfort zones means that location shoots can turn ugly, fast. As always, the key is preparation and organization. If you are planning a location shoot you must take into account all foreseeable emergencies: medical, emotional, and technological.**

Accidents can happen at any time. If you are driving, you should have a plan if you were to break down. Be sure to check your cover and insurance policies and keep your license up to date. If a model drives themselves, you must trust that they will arrive on time and be able to keep up between separate locations. Models can disappear for hours during a shoot when they drive off, get lost, and realize there is no cell phone signal.

The more isolated your location, the more careful you must be, as it is much harder to deal with medical issues such as allergic reactions, bug bites, falls, and asthma attacks. For innumerable reasons people can feel unsafe or uncomfortable and start to panic. Get to know the signs, talk to the individual calmly, distract them, tell them to breathe deeply, and if possible make them laugh. Take a walk with them and try not to rush someone in this situation—it's all about getting them to physically relax.

Your equipment is also prone to accidents. It can be dropped or stood on, lenses can break, cables snap, bulbs blow, and tripods get forgotten, There is no knowing what might happen so be prepared for anything and have backup options whenever possible. It pays to be flexible. Don't let things affect you so much that you get worked up and lash out. Sometimes it feels like

### BE PREPARED

It is imperative that you are aware of the nearest town and hospital to your location—it only takes a few seconds to look it up on the internet and you don't want to be unprepared if something goes wrong. You could also consider enrolling in a first aid course.

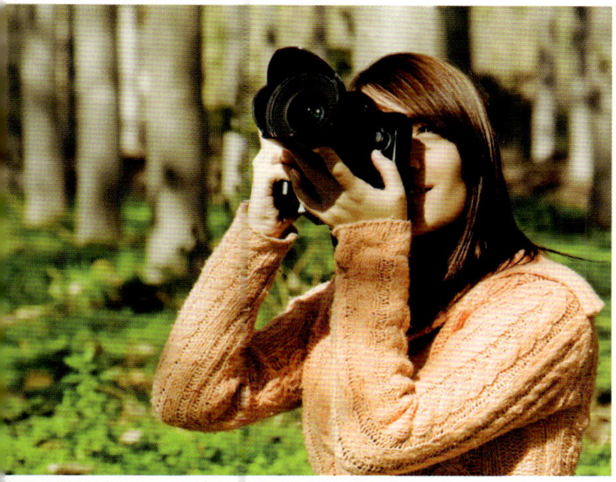

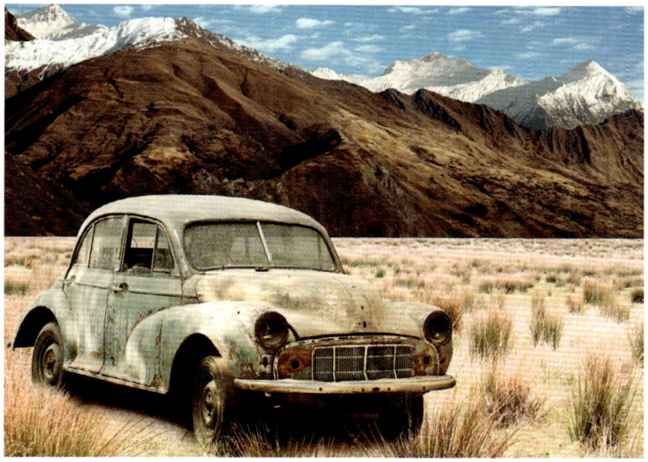

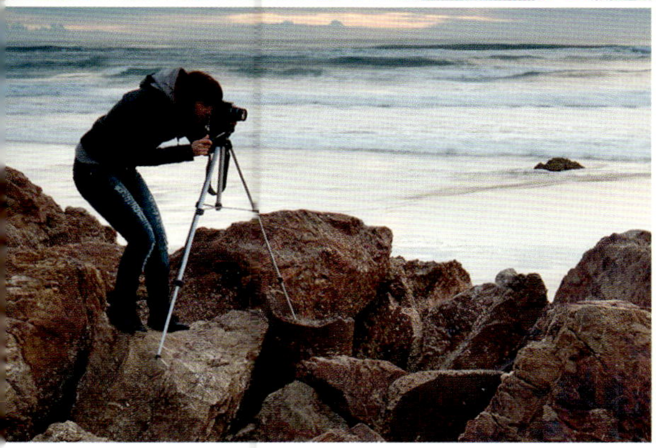

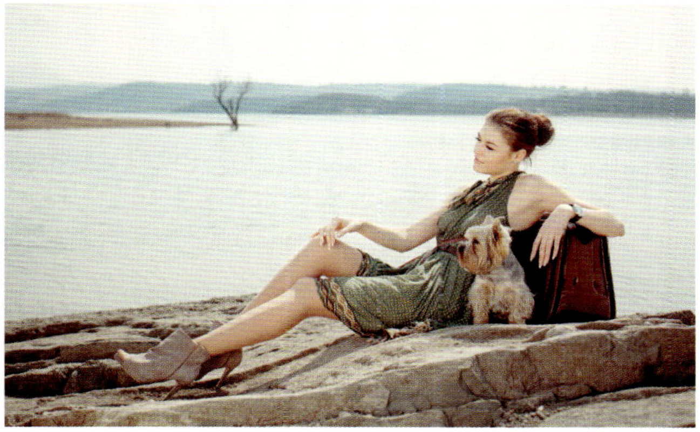

FAR LEFT & BELOW CENTER: **TECHNICAL ISSUES**
If your equipment is rented, make sure you have the rental company's phone number to hand in case of emergency. Maybe you can't work a piece of the equipment, or something is missing. Program important numbers into your cell.

LEFT: **ISOLATED AREAS**
Have you been to the location before? Do you know you are shooting in an area that is safe? Before you head out into the wilderness with no experience, think about the basics.

LEFT: **ACCIDENTS HAPPEN**
More often than not the clothing and shoes the model are expected to wear do not suit the terrain. Be careful when girls are in high heels or if the ground is uneven, especially when near water or busy roads.

everything (and everyone) is working against you, but often those are the days when you get the best pictures.

When staying overnight, book suitable accommodation. It might save you money, but no one likes to share a room. If there's no other option, never mix males and females in the same room. Be polite and ask if anyone has preferences or issues beforehand. You can't expect everyone to get along and although it is one thing to be professional on set, it can be hard to maintain that demeanor after hours.

It is generally polite to ask your team to dinner, but don't be offended if someone refuses—everyone is different and has all manner of personal problems going on. People like to celebrate on a shoot, and can go a little wild away from home. Have fun, go for drinks (it's important to keep moral up as a leader), but be aware of drinking ages and limits, and early call times. Models and team members have been known to bring illegal items such as drugs on longer shoots. Deal with this in whatever manner you see fit, but never allow it to endanger anyone else or affect the shoot in a negative manner. You cannot be expected to control consenting adults, but keep your eyes open.

### TIP EASY ACCESS

Think about whether there will be internet access and a phone signal where you are going. Let everyone know if you are going off the grid—people can get antsy when they can't communicate with the outside world. Check your phone battery and take chargers—if you can, you should aim to be contactable at all times.

# NIGHT SHOOTS

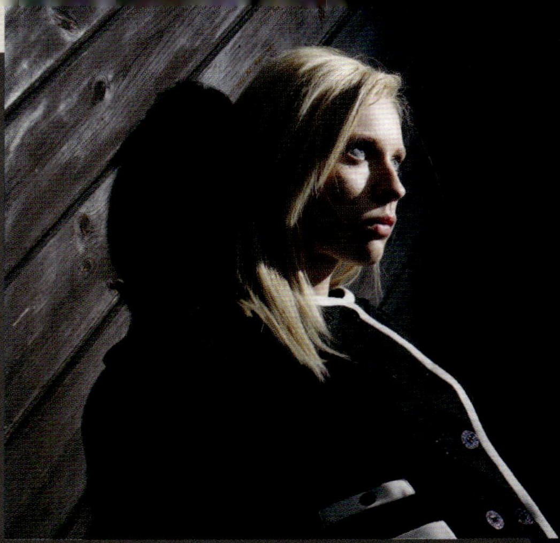

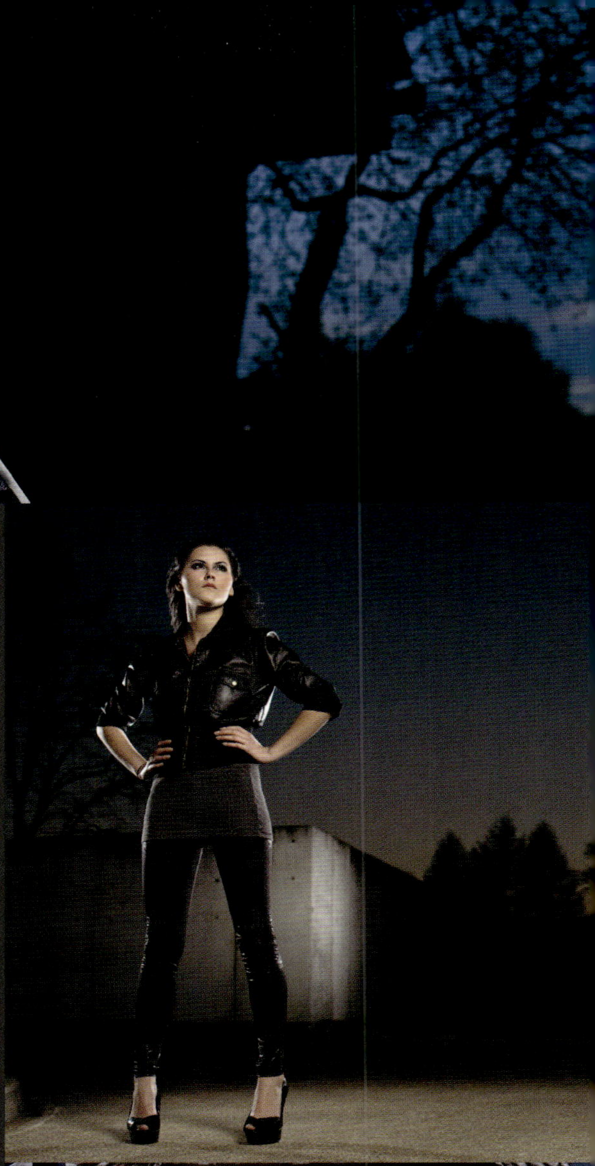

**THERE CAN BE SOMETHING very special about shooting models at night. Nighttime can be a metaphor for moodiness or atmosphere, and can suit a glamorous dress or a grungier, more "urban" look. With the absence of lots of daylight, the shot takes on a whole new look: twilight skies can be exposed so they go a moody blue, twinkling artificial lights can give a real atmospheric effect, and you can even use everything from street lights to flash to light up a scene for dramatic effect.**

But there are lots of challenges involved with night shoots that you also have to consider, from the actual photography side to the logistics of the shoot which, of course, has to involve an element of making sure everything is safe. There is nothing that attracts unwanted attention as much as lots of expensive photo equipment and attractive models—it can be like a beacon attracting the undesirables of society.

No photograph is ever worth risking the safety of a person for, so always be aware of where you are shooting and perhaps take along extra helpers to keep a watchful eye. Make sure someone knows where you are going and make sure you have cell phones that work well. Cities can be just as dangerous as the wilderness at night, and both have their own risks. Whether it's criminals or the risk of frostbite, heatstroke, to getting lost, you should be overly prepared. Take warm clothes if it's likely to get cold, plus drinks and some food, and remain vigilant at all times.

The logistics of a nighttime shoot mean you may need some power for light to illuminate the set and the surrounding working area. If it's near a power source,

TOP: **HOTSHOE FUN**
A small hotshoe flash fitted with a grid was enough to provide the pool of light on this model at twilight.

ABOVE RIGHT: **USING FLASH**
Four flashes were used to light this scene. Two were used to create a rim light around the girl from either side, while a third was fitted with a softbox and used as the main light. A fourth flash put a splash of light on the wall behind the model.

RIGHT: **CREATING DRAMA**
Three small hotshoe flashes were used to light this dramatic scene. The first was just out of shot to the left, to light the model's face and body. A second, fired by a radio trigger, was behind the bush the girl is sitting in front of, aimed back toward the camera. A third flash was aimed at the roof of the building to stop it being totally dark.

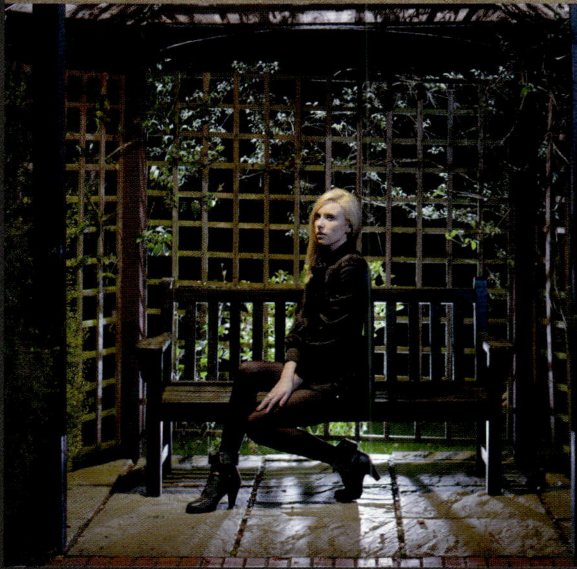

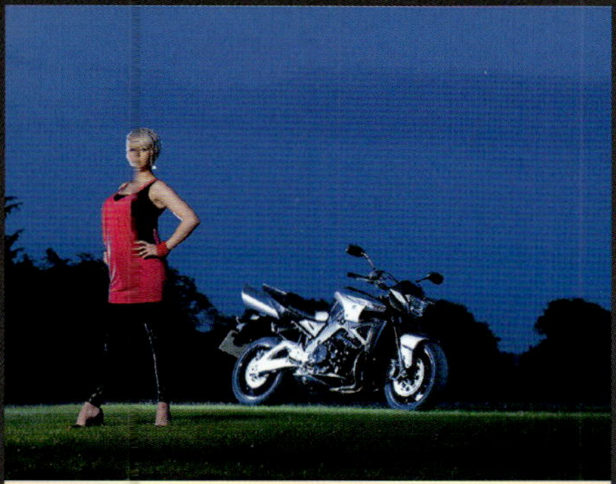

## GELS TO MAKE BLUES SING!

To make a blue twilight sky really vibrant, set your camera's white balance to tungsten. This will make the sky turn a strong blue color, as in this shot of a model near the motorcycle. The model and the motorcycle were then lit with small hotshoe flashes used off camera. One was pointed directly at the bike, one at the rear of the girl to rim-light her legs, and one from the left of camera, fitted with an umbrella to make the light softer. All three flashes were fitted with orange "CTO" warming gels, to give them a tungsten color temperature to match the white balance of the camera. As a result, anything lit by the flashes recorded as its "normal" color, but the sky turned and intense blue.

this isn't a problem, but you may have to take a generator or battery power packs so that models, assistants, and anyone else on set can actually see what they are doing.

A head torch may seem like overkill, but any photographer who has lost a small item of kit on the ground (or even in the depths of a camera bag) will know they can be an invaluable aid. Also, if the set itself is dark, cameras may struggle to snap into focus. An assistant with a torch to shine on the subject can be a great aid while your camera's focus system locks on.

Of course, the biggest issue when shooting at night is the lack of ambient light! If you shoot at twilight, before the sky has turned completely black, then it's often far better. At his time of day the sky will still register with some blue in it, rather than just going inky black. However, for any ambient light to register you are going to have to either increase your camera's ISO sensitivity—which can lead to noisy images—or slow your shutter speed right down. This means you will more than likely end up with your camera on a tripod and your model will not be able to move too much. You'll also probably end up using your fastest lenses almost wide open, which not only has a small impact on the lens' sharpness, but means the depth of field can be very narrow.

At night or twilight, streetlights or lights from shops can register well and you can use them to illuminate your scene. However, these lights will have varying color temperatures, so it's best not to rely on them as a main light in fashion work as they can affect skin tones and the color of garments.

Artificial continuous lights such as tungsten, LEDs, or HMIs can be used successfully at night, as their relatively low power becomes less of an issue. You will still end up increasing the ISO and using quite low shutter speeds, though, so a better solution is to use flash. This freezes motion, has a relatively consistent color temperature, and you can stick to lower ISO settings for better quality. Smaller hotshoe flashes are ideal at night, as you don't need huge amounts of power, but if you do have larger battery powered flash units they will offer a modeling light facility, which makes it much easier to see the results you will be getting.

Using flash at night is similar to using it in a studio. You can choose a reasonably wide range of working aperture and then adjust the power of the flash until the exposure is right. With the camera on a tripod, you can slow down the shutter speed until just the right amount of ambient light is registering, too. This is often referred to as "dragging the shutter." Be aware that using very slow speeds means there's a risk of a ghost image around the subject if they move slightly, though, and the color is also more likely to be affected by artificial lights as more ambient light registers.

# 09

# MAINTAINING CONTROL

**PHOTOGRAPHIC SETS RANGE IN SIZE dramatically. Whether you are alone with a model or there are 50 people whispering in your ear and stepping into frame while you shoot, it is important you remain the "master of ceremonies." This chapter focuses on the managerial role the photographer must play in a variety of scenarios involving working sets and shooting more than one model at a time. We take a look at how some of the greats have run the show and discuss the pitfalls of working in the illustrious "fashion industry," which is rife with oversized egos and attention seekers. All kinds of magic and mayhem can happen on set and you have to try to contain that energy, manipulating it as necessary to create the perfect image.**

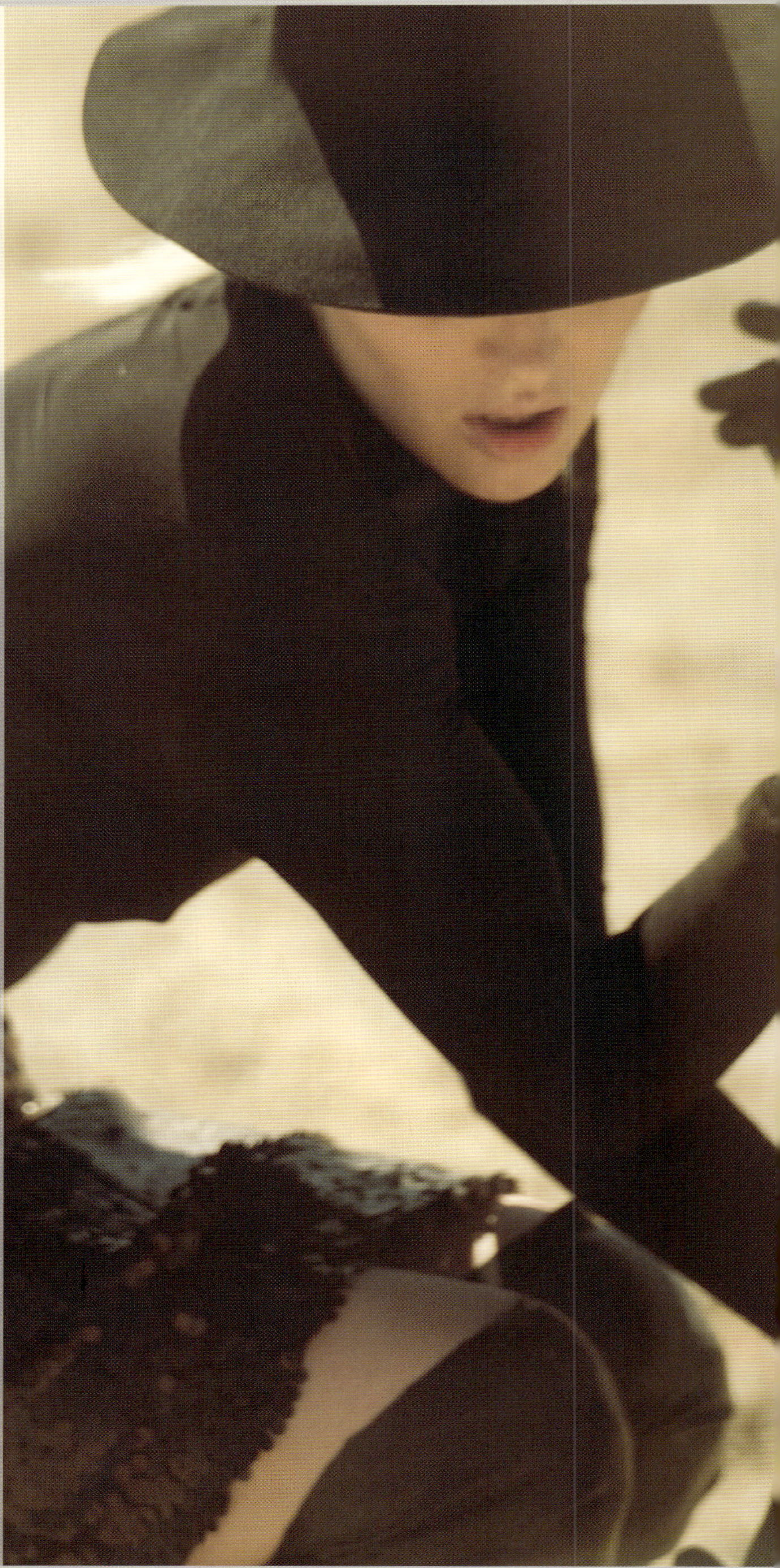

RIGHT: **POINT OF CONTACT**
Try not to let external influences affect your connection with a model. You should be the welcoming beacon they seek in times of conflict or confusion. It can be disappointing when after an hour on set no one has a clue who the photographer is. Make it obvious who is in charge.

# TAKE THE LEAD

**PHOTOSHOOTS ARE GENERALLY positive and fun environments, but the industry breeds competitiveness and insecurity. Attitudes can vary and although it's not unusual for everyone you meet to be friendly and down-to-earth on set, on the majority of larger shoots there's always one person that can't help but annoy everybody. Maybe it's a loud-mouthed model, or maybe the substitute hair stylist you had to book last minute has a wicked mean streak. Though you may often have the luxury of a producer to act as a middle man in these situations, at times you are going to have to deal directly with conflicting personalities.**

You are the metaphorical captain of the shoot. You will reap the benefits from its success and sink with it in failure. You must honor the welfare of your crew and learn what hits their buttons or how to react if they are having a bad day. It is a balancing act in a world of sensitive artists, but you need all of them ship-shape if you are to voyage further. Try to create a working environment of mutual respect, weeding out the trouble makers and drama starters. If any model or member of crew is emotionally affected by something, talk to them, be a good leader. Be aware of body language, as people often say one thing but mean another. A lot of trash talk goes on behind backs on set, so keep a mental track of who is bonding with whom and if anyone isn't getting along, especially on long trips. You should never stand for abuse of any sort, ever. It should be dealt with immediately and followed up with the respective agencies and authorities.

One of most common problems on set is time management. Photographers frequently underestimate the amount of time elements of the shoot will take, spending hours on the first two shots, then having to rush the last six because they're chasing light. Keep on top of things. This is why I stress the importance of understanding everyone's jobs. You'll learn when you have to cut a location because realistically it's too far away from base camp, or when you can feasibly rush the prep team to make the shot. Remember, even if a hairstyle or makeup look appears simple on a mood board, it does not mean it can be achieved in minutes. If in doubt, ask, and work out beforehand how much time it will take to get the look you want. If you want to change styles throughout, allow the time for it!

RIGHT: **HAVE FUN WITH IT**
If you make sure that the people on your set know what they are doing and are happy doing it, you will provide the perfect environment for creative energy to shine. Accept the responsibility of leadership with pride and people will be desperate to jump aboard with you.

FAR RIGHT: **ARGUMENTS**
It can be frustrating when team members or models don't get along. It can affect everybody's mood. Sometimes talking it out is important, sometimes keeping your head down works best. Unfortunately you must learn from experience.

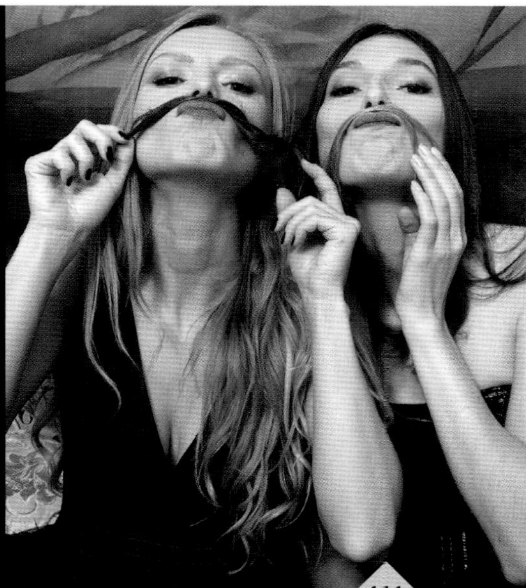

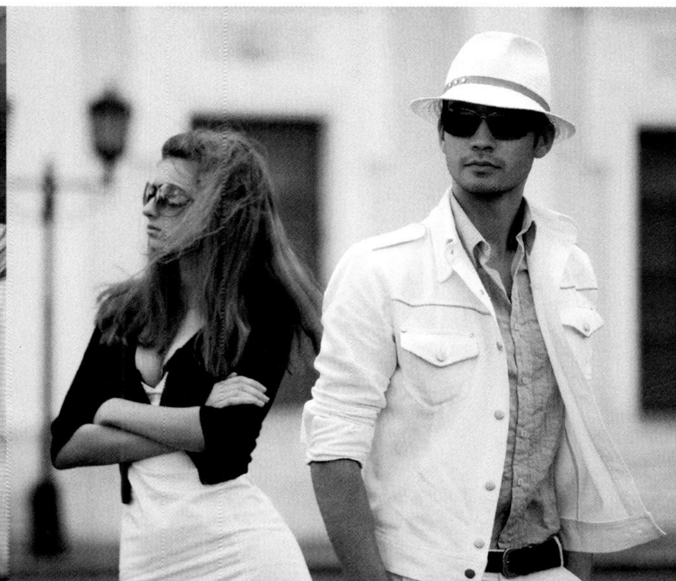

# PHOTOGRAPHERS GONE WILD!

**IT IS NO SECRET that a number of photographers get into the business because of the over-the-top stereotypes associated with fashion—wildly dressed photographers sipping champagne and writhing around in front of glamorous beauties yelling, "Give me more Baby, more, that's it ooze at me...now you're a tiger, ROAR for me Baby!" There are people that believe working in fashion is all parties, exotic locations, award ceremonies, and being asked to take portraits of celebrities and royalty. These are the people that truly think taking pictures for a living is an easy job that leads to automatic riches and magnetism.**

Be realistic. You are not going to get anywhere if you think this is going to be easy. Yes, you will have fun, but the truth is the industry is evolving and the opportunities to become famous with outrageous demands and an unlimited budget are becoming less and less.

Famous photographers of the past paint a rose-tinted, starry-eyed picture of shooting fashion and only a handful of photographers shooting today can follow in their footsteps. The internet and the mass call for content means everything has to be produced faster, cheaper and with less frivolity.

Decadent and wondrous shoots still exist, but they are fewer and further between: everything today is more efficient and litigious.

There are more opportunities to become photographers, more courses, more cameras, and that means more competition. If you get obnoxious or cocky, there'll be a nice guy behind you waiting to fill your place. As a modern photographer you have to realize that you are not the only one who is good at what they do and important on set. Without you everything wouldn't just fall apart. Nowadays it's likely your stylist or makeup artist is a part-time photographer and could finish the job.

> *There are no rules and regulations for perfect composition. If there were we would be able to put all the information into a computer and would come out with a masterpiece. We know that's impossible. You have to compose by the seat of your pants.*
>
> **ARNOLD NEWMAN,** *photographer*

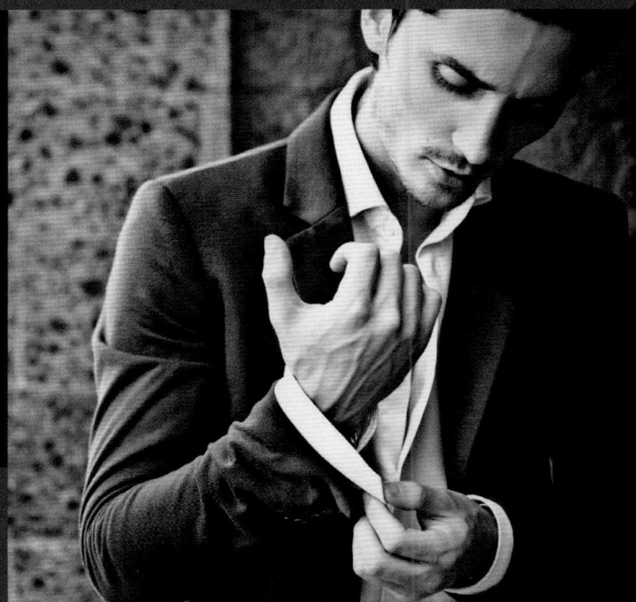

Raise your game in a different way. It can take one job to ruin a reputation and they are hard to shift.

Don't become that nightmare photographer that nobody wants to work with. It is important you are able to connect with and relate to your models, and you can't complain about shooting a "diva" if you are one yourself. It will sometimes seem like the bad guys are winning, booking jobs you deserve, but as soon as you start to become negative or cynical you will cut yourself off from innumerable jobs. It is a case of the tortoise and the hare

Make your style your own and embrace your individuality—it may sound like a cliché, but it's the truth. Shoot what makes you happy and try to learn to embrace collaboration. Use whatever it is inside you that makes you want to become a photographer to discover how you work best, so you can be productive but still have fun.

> *It is more important to click with people than to click the shutter.*
>
> **ALFRED EISENSTAEDT,** *photographer*

It is imperative you keep dreaming, I have had experiences on fashion shoots that I like to believe are reminiscent of the Sixties—some things that happen on set, stay on set. However, to get to that position takes hard work, determination, and honor in face of continuous rejection.

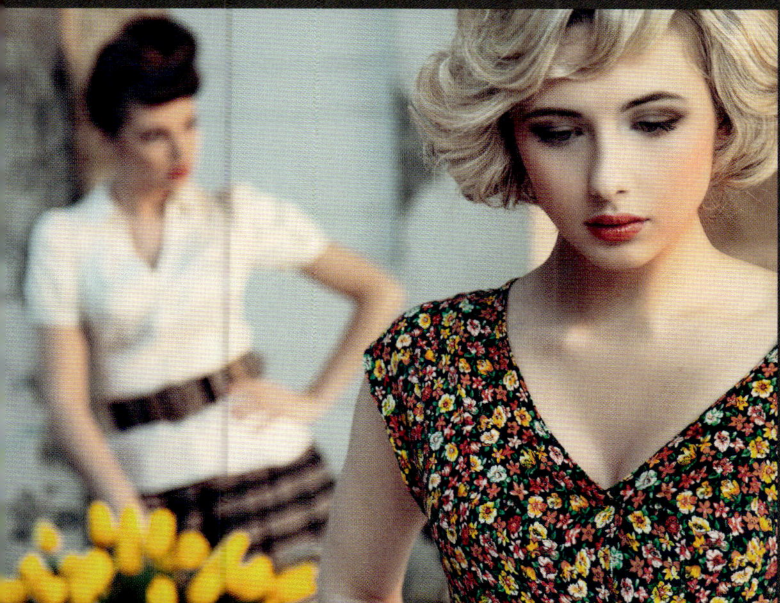

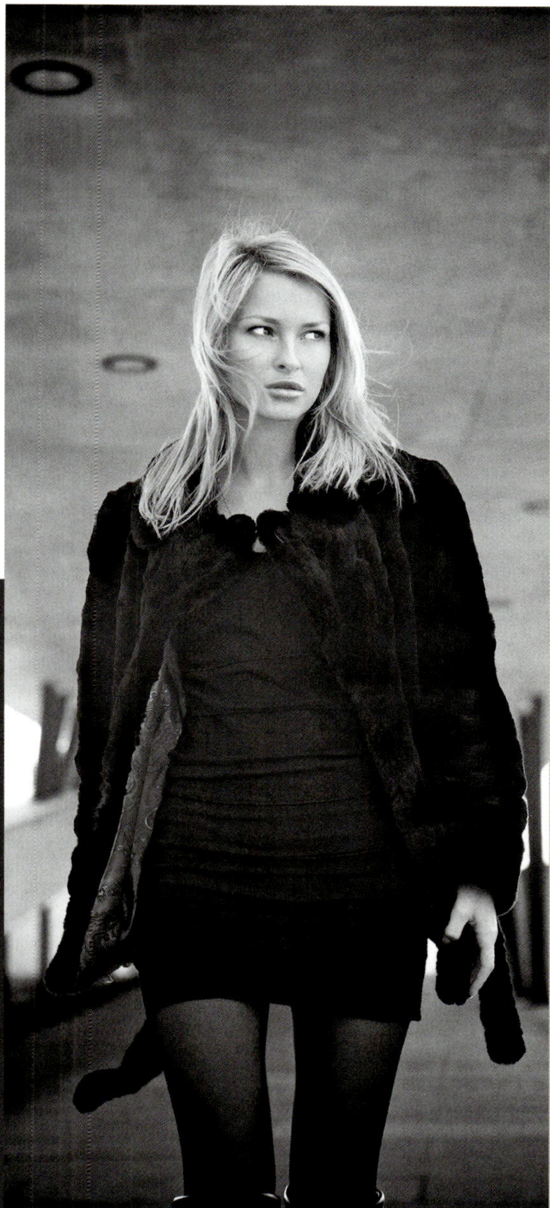

OPPOSITE, LEFT & RIGHT:
**UP THE STAKES**
As a fashion photographer you must create constantly and learn to produce high-quality, stand-out images at speed. You must be able to compose on a whim yet remain a receptive and kind person. It is important to aim to continuously up your game and excel in your field.

# WORKING WITH DIVAS

If you spend any length of time working in the fashion industry you will inevitably come across an unsavory character or two. You are not going to like every person you shoot and not every day will run smoothly with mutual co-operation and equal effort on all parts. It might surprise you how someone that seems so sweet at a casting can turn into "model-zilla" on set. However, no one in fashion—photographers included—should develop the dangerous mentality of believing they are irreplaceable. I have seen models sent home and photographers lose huge contracts on the spot. Beware of divas, and of becoming one!

The word "diva" is generally associated with women, and suggests a drama queen or self-involved individual, but believe me, there are plenty of male models that fit the bill as well! Thankfully, against stereotype, the vast majority of models you work with will be intelligent, charming, and respectful toward everyone they meet.

There will be a time when you find yourself in the company of a compulsive complainer, though, and all you seem to hear is "I'm cold," "I'm hungry," "My feet hurt, these shoes are too tight," "I have somewhere I need to be at five, can we hurry this up." Or it will be an obnoxious personality who butts heads with people for fun because they enjoy getting a rise out of others. It can drive everyone on set nuts, but you have to remember to breathe and complete the shoot in the most effective way possible.

No one wants to spend 12 hours with a diva, but there are those with difficult personalities that work consistently because they are irrefutably good at what they do. Depending on your influence over casting choices, you will have to learn to grin and bear it at times. If a model is producing the shots when necessary, their behavior behind the scenes may have to be forgiven. If it is a well known fact that a particular model is hard to work with, try to book them for individual shoots rather than group work, or with models of the same sex with whom they may feel they are competing.

If someone is behaving like a diva, remember they might be acting out to cover up personal insecurities. Give them the benefit of the doubt. Try to talk to them and get them to loosen up—maybe they're just having a really bad week. Crack jokes, and see if they have a sense of humor at all. Find a point on which to relate with

### TIP: YOU WANT ME TO DO WHAT?

There will be times when a model will refuse to do something you ask. Handle the situation with grace and stay professional, and remember it when they cast for you again.

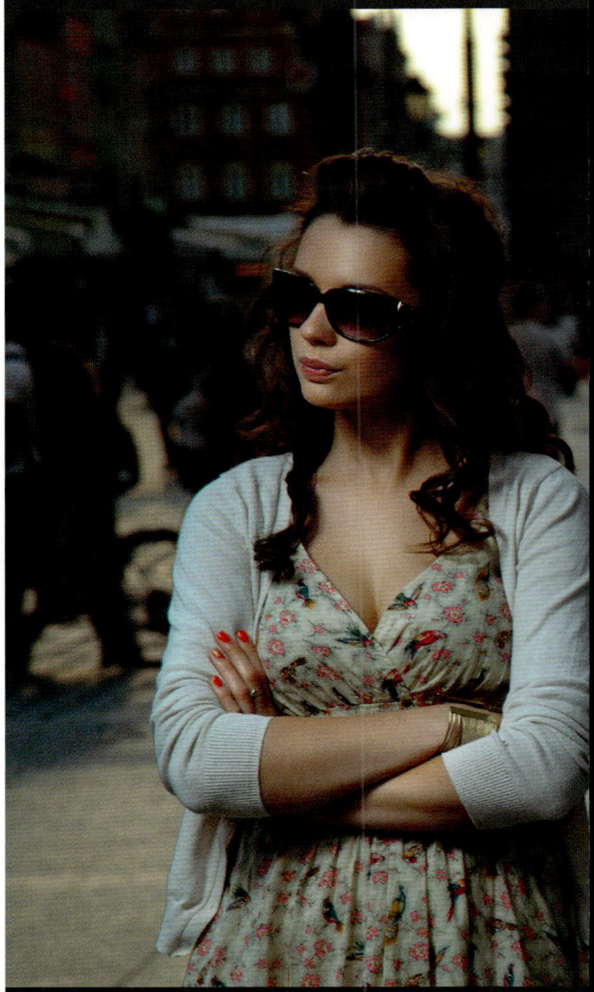

> *The biggest thing I look for in a model is good energy and a great personality that can get along with everyone. And I mean really get along with everyone, not just when the camera is pointed at them, but the entire day. At my casting calls we'll even get four or five models in a room together and just wait to see how they interact with each other.*
>
> **SAM ENZ,** *art director*

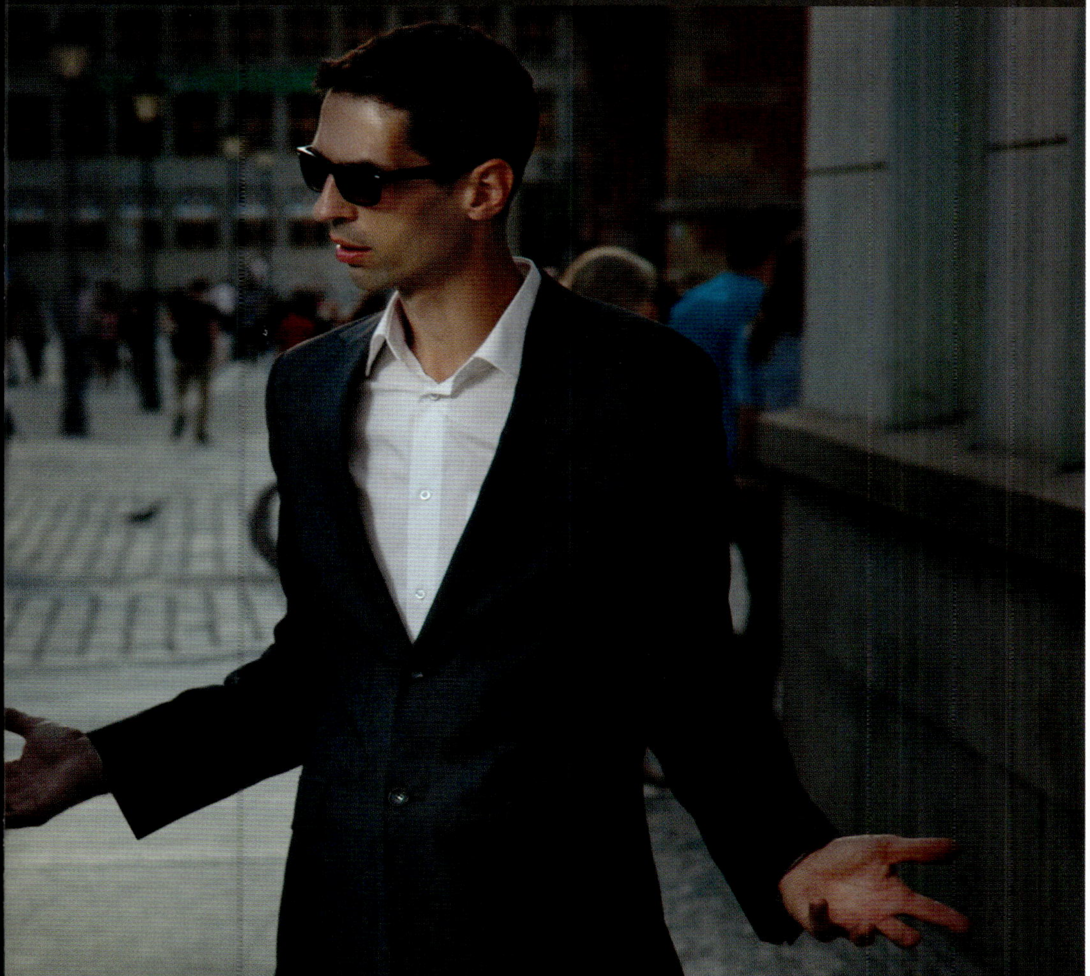

### WHEN IT'S OK TO ACT LIKE A DIVA

A model's image is their career, so if an accident happens when styling, such as a burn from a hot curling iron or if hair is cut accidentally, don't berate them for being upset. Try to calm the matter, and remember that legal action has been taken in the past for loss of earnings...

them, whether it's music, their home town, or something else. If someone is downright rude or truly affecting your shoot, then ask them to take a few minutes—don't overreact and bring yourself down. If it continues then it might be worth giving their agent a ring.

You will experience all sorts of people on set, with all kinds of personalities. There will most likely be tears at some point, the odd temper tantrum—I've even witnessed screaming. No matter what happens, as the photographer you must maintain control at all times and ensure the focus remains on getting the shots you need.

LEFT: **PERSONALITY CLASH**
When shooting you may find that your models are offish towards one another. Most will work through their differences, but at times you may need to interject. Try to lighten the mood but remind them they are working on a professional set.

# DIRECTING GROUPS

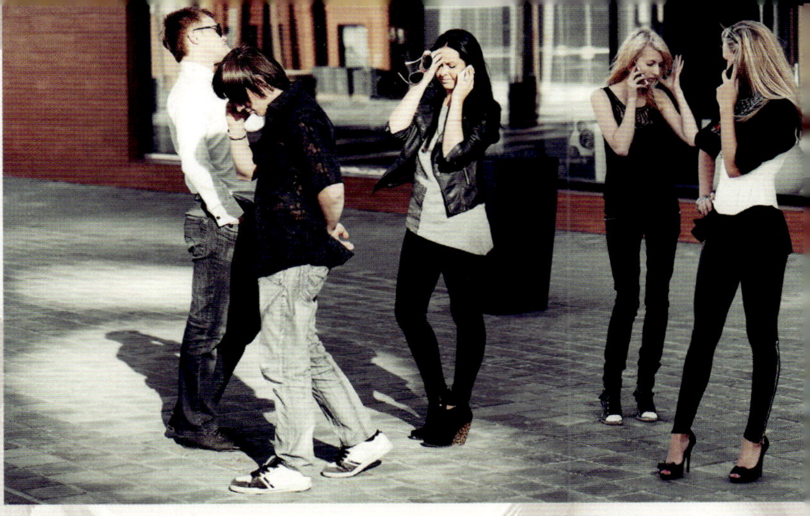

ABOVE: **CALLING IT OFF**
You are going to have to learn to put up with cell phones on set—models are physically attached to them. However, on large sets it's not unusual for phones to be banned completely, especially when there is a risk of images appearing prematurely on social networking websites.

I'm not sure if there is an official collective noun for a group of models; a "tantrum" of models, perhaps? A "pout"? Either way, when they gang up on you, directing them successfully can be as hard as herding cats, blindfolded. If no one is paying attention things can get messy, and shots start to suffer. Therefore you must take firm control in a group situation and work hard to maintain the atmosphere you require, whether it's a full blown party scene or a formally arranged family moment.

Thankfully, professional models are usually extremely adept at adapting to different scenarios, although some are better at group work than others. Often, you must ask them to exhibit extreme emotional closeness to complete strangers, which can be intimidating.

Encourage interaction and if necessary break the ice. Make models aware early on if they are going to be part of a group, as this allows them time to get to know one another.

It can be difficult for a group image not to appear "forced," so think about your location, the shoot environment, and what feelings they invoke. If you are trying to create a scene, for example a BBQ, get the models to actually grill something, rather than pretending to. Encourage movement and laughter, but know when to tell the models to stop and let you capture something great they're doing. Be wary of rivalries on group sets, and be inclusive of all models. Listen to your client if they prefer a certain person, but try not to leave anyone out. Sometimes it can take a shy model a while to warm up to a group scenario.

### CONTAIN THE PARTY

Photoshoots can be fun, but always remember that it is a professional working environment. On set for an advertising campaign with Peggy Sirota, DJ's were booked to keep the 20 models upbeat for a "holidays" campaign. It worked, but the models inevitably got overexcited, losing sight of the purpose of the shoot, and calling for strict disciplining from the crew.

## SHOOTING GROUPS

Taking great images of groups of models brings a raft of challenges for the photographer. Some of these are technical—such as how to effectively light more than one person— while some are about people management and how to communicate your vision. The third is more artistic, where you have to be fully focused on the image in the viewfinder to make sure everyone is doing what he or she is supposed to, but in a pleasing composition. Group shots can be a tough gig for any photographer.

When you have groups of people, communicating with them gets more complex, as not everybody likes to communicate in the same way. There could be issues with egos, or with some models being more experienced than others. It's the photographer's job to quickly assimilate all the characteristics of the models and get them to not only understand the vision, but how they can play their part in it and how they should work together.

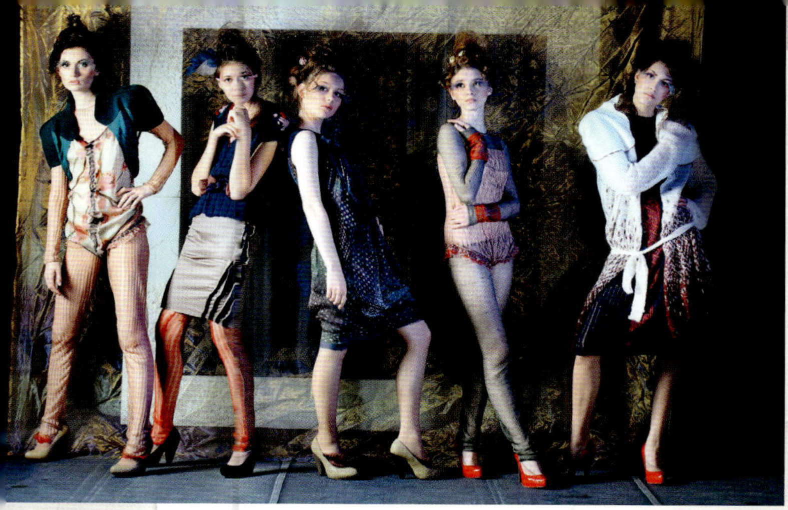

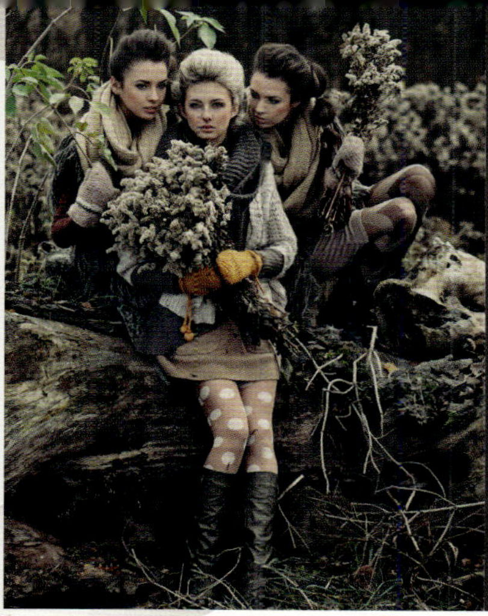



LEFT & CENTER: **GROUP SCENARIOS**
Group shots can be effective both in studio and on location, though space is often necessary. Think about the relationships you wish to portray when deciding where to shoot. Even in close quarters models can seem detached from one another, combine location and interaction to achieve the look you desire.

In many cases, shoots with lots of people in them are often more cinematic and hint at a real narrative. In other words, the people are there for a reason and there is some semblance of a story to tell. If that's the case (or it can be made to feel as if it is) then explain the roles of each of the people in the shot. It could be a boy, girl, and jilted former lover, for example, who has just appeared on the scene. Or three young girls hitting their big prom night in glamorous dresses. This would give the models a scenario to visually act out and could act as a real anchor point to keep coming back to if the shoot starts to get confused.

Of course, it could be simply several models on a seamless white background in a studio. In that case, the styling and editorial story should be able to guide the photographer and the models into the scenario or look that is wanted. The worst case is having lots of models who don't really know what they are doing or why.

Once the shooting starts, the photographer needs to be very aware of who is doing what in the frame. It often happens that three out of the four models are perfect, but the fourth looks awkward, or is obscured by the others. The photographer needs to check every person in every part of the frame each time the shutter is released. Mentally, it is far more tiring than a shoot with a single model and it is also harder to motivate multiple people to come up with something extraordinary.

Shooting a group of people also requires more space, and also some way of them being able to get close together without it being too forced. In a location, it's often good to find somewhere where there are chairs or places to rest at different levels, so the composition is not too formal and lined up. Of course, this could be the look you are going for as it creates a certain feel and sometimes tension!

Group shots are also more challenging from a technical point of view in terms of depth of field and lighting. To get everyone sharp, chances are you will have to use a smaller aperture for increased depth of field. If you are using ambient lighting, this means the shutter speed can get slower, or the ISO needs to be increased. In a studio, you'll need more flash power.

## PHOTOSHOP TO THE RESCUE!

Using editing software to "save" pictures should always be a last resort, but a clever photographer should know what can and can't be done to pull a result out of the bag. A shot with several different models can be one of those scenarios. Chances are that the best frame will have most of them, but not all of them, in an ideal position, or one of your models will have their eyes closed. The perfect shot, ruined.

However, if the shots were all taken on a tripod and the subjects moved very little between shots, a talented retoucher could potentially composite together the best bits of two or more photos into one final shot. It's not ideal, but it could turn a good shot into a great one.

# A WORD FROM THE BOYS

**THE MODELING INDUSTRY** is one of the very few where women dominate. As a male model it is much harder to make a name for yourself and it can involve long hours with little reward. You are often employed as a secondary character, generally selling a lifestyle image rather than product, as the target market and customers tend to be female. Male photographers I know have admitted to me they find it difficult and even “uncomfortable” to shoot other men, but I see this as limiting. Working solely with a male model, or shooting a couple, or working with mixed groups, it all adds to your portfolio and experience as an artist and director. As a photographer you should aspire to shoot everyone, especially when it will increase your chances of booking the latest campaign. Men’s fashion is advancing all the time, so here are a few wise words from some of the top boys in the industry:

## BARRETT PAUL

Talk to us. If something needs to be adjusted, tell me, I can figure it out. The worst is a silent photographer. If you are engaging, I will be engaging on set, in real life, and in the pictures. I’ve run into both diva photographers and models. There are lots of people that get a taste of this industry and think they are God’s gift. I think that it’s a real shame when something like modeling, which isn’t serious work, becomes anything but fun. I’ve worked with celebrities, who have been so down to earth and I’ve worked with no-name photographers who throw hissy fits. I think it says a lot about you as a person.

## MIKE FALKOW

As a male model in a female-dominated industry it can sometimes feel like you are being used merely as a prop, another accessory the client will add in or take away, like they would a bracelet or scarf, or indeed a coat rack. That being said, it has been rare for a photographer to treat me as such though. Over the years I’ve been modeling I have been lucky that very few photographers have been difficult to work with and the majority are positive people, with great energy, who treat everyone on set as equals and inspire me to want to work harder, and make the experience a lot of fun. I have shot all over the world and even when battling language barriers, passion, and creativity shine through.

Models can be more demanding. It can be enjoyable to shoot alone, but I like to create moments with others. You can see it like the job it is and not get caught up in the fact that there’s a beautiful girl standing next to you. But, models come with all kinds of personalities and sometimes we just don’t “click.” At times like this you have to remain professional and rely on the photographer to take charge. Models don’t have the right to tell each other how to work, so if someone is behaving in a negative manner, it helps if the photographer knows when to step in. A photographer is much like a director in that way. It’s his or her set. And ultimately it is he or she who sets the tone of the shoot. Creative enthusiasm is very infectious, and when a photographer understands this and “infects” the set with an upbeat disposition, it’s always a great and uplifting experience for all involved. It’s wonderful when everything flows and everybody gets on, but it takes a good photographer to lead a shoot and turn it around when the energy is stunted and the shots just aren’t working.

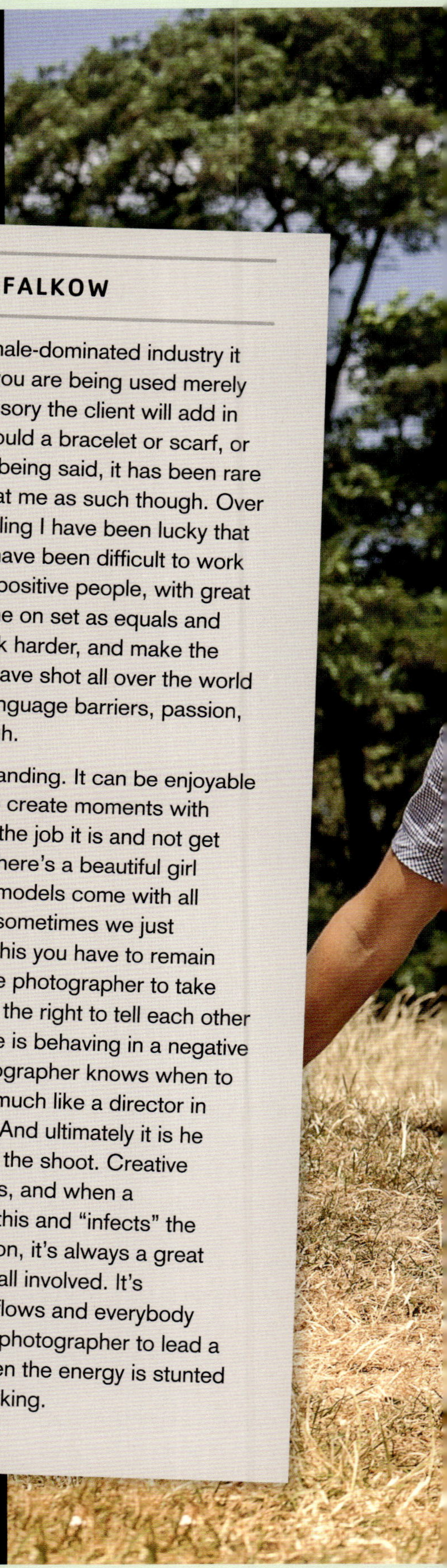

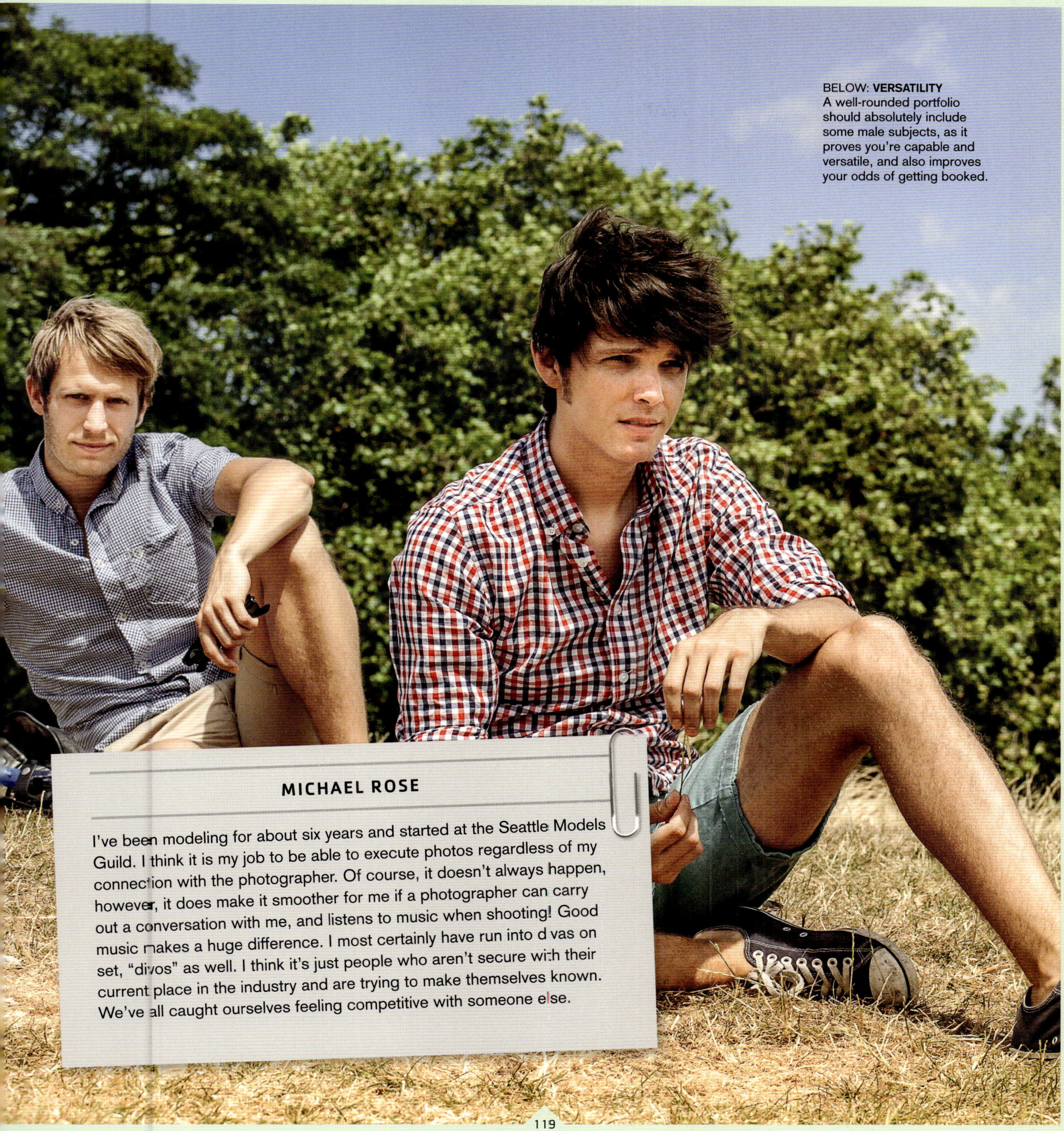

BELOW: **VERSATILITY**
A well-rounded portfolio should absolutely include some male subjects, as it proves you're capable and versatile, and also improves your odds of getting booked.

### MICHAEL ROSE

I've been modeling for about six years and started at the Seattle Models Guild. I think it is my job to be able to execute photos regardless of my connection with the photographer. Of course, it doesn't always happen, however, it does make it smoother for me if a photographer can carry out a conversation with me, and listens to music when shooting! Good music makes a huge difference. I most certainly have run into divas on set, "divos" as well. I think it's just people who aren't secure with their current place in the industry and are trying to make themselves known. We've all caught ourselves feeling competitive with someone else.

# SHOOTING GIRLS: DOUBLE TROUBLE!

Girls can be trouble—I am one and I admit it. More than one in a room together and it can be "insta-sisters" or claws may fly. Even though a photo shoot is a professional environment, the competitive nature of the industry can lead to fireworks behind the scenes. Working with multiple female models means that you're going to be dealing with issues such as jealousy, embarrassment, and spite. Egos will be bruised and self-confidence smashed to smithereens.

In smaller markets models may know each other well, have worked together previously or cast together often. This can be good or bad, depending on their history—I've been mid-shoot with two girls when they discovered they were dating the same guy. Female models will often bond immediately, at least on a professional level, but there are many things you may not realize that can affect their relationships.

Models notice things such as who gets called in first, who has their makeup done first, and who wears a certain outfit. You might not realize that one likes a dress, but the other girl gets to wear it, or one likes a particular male model but the other gets to shoot with him. Maybe you took a picture on your phone of one girl, but you forgot to snap anyone else? Models count shots, they eavesdrop to see who is being considered for the cover option, and if one outshines the other they get upset—no one likes to feel as though they're underperforming.

It's difficult, but don't let situations get petty. Try and eliminate problems as soon as possible. I am not suggesting you could or should have control over these matters, but be aware of behavioral changes throughout the day and boost confidence where necessary. Learn names and direct individually, and certainly avoid favoritism or openly comparing girls.

### DESIGNATED DRIVER

On trips away, or after a fun shoot you may celebrate with the models. Remember you might be dealing with young girls who are under the legal drinking age, though—in these situations you are the responsible adult in charge.

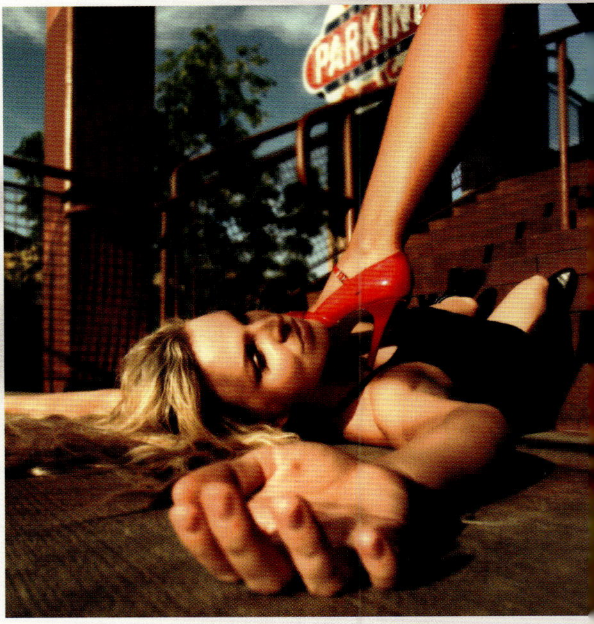


ABOVE: **EGO WARS**
Try not to let one person's ego destroy your entire shoot. If the way a model is talking or acting is visibly affecting another person, put a stop to it.

OPPOSITE: **TWO'S COMPANY, THREE'S A CROWD**
When a group of female models gang up on you it can be slightly intimidating. This is great for your shots but must be contained and controlled.

Use the energy they are giving off to enhance a shot. People can be shy of touching—some girls can be very cold and hard to act with—so encourage interaction and movement. Don't let a quieter soul fade into the background. Models seek affirmation and positivity, they will feel embarrassed if told they're doing something wrong, especially in front of their peers.

Obviously, as a fashion photographer you will be interacting with gorgeous, talented individuals. This can lead to relationships between photographers and models, but keep it professional on set and be aware that the industry

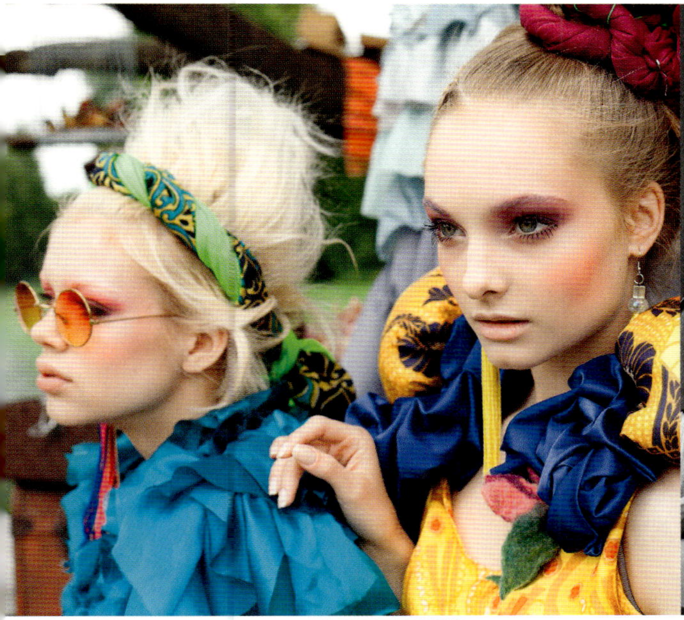

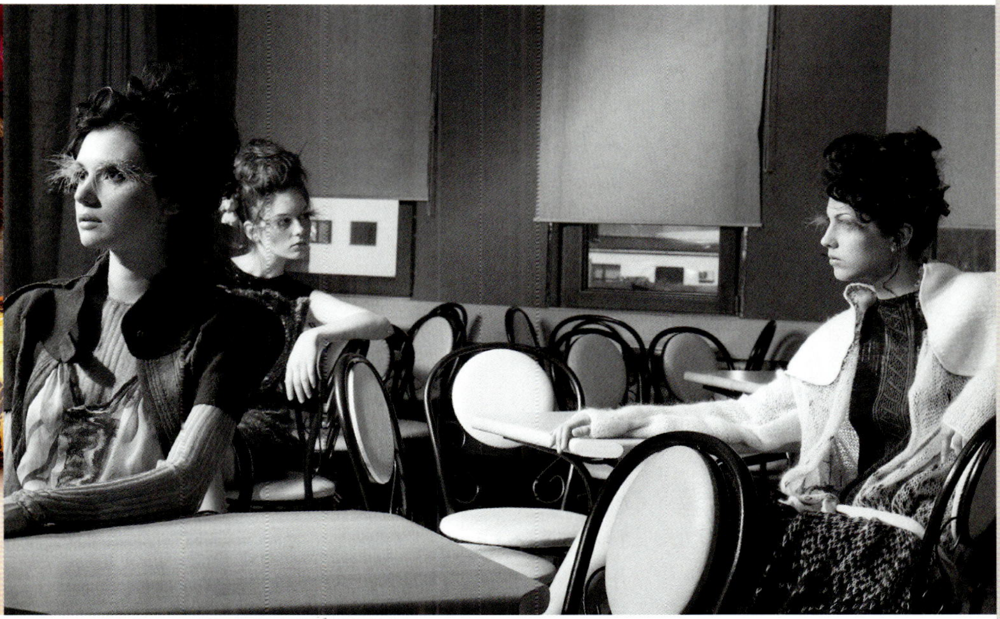

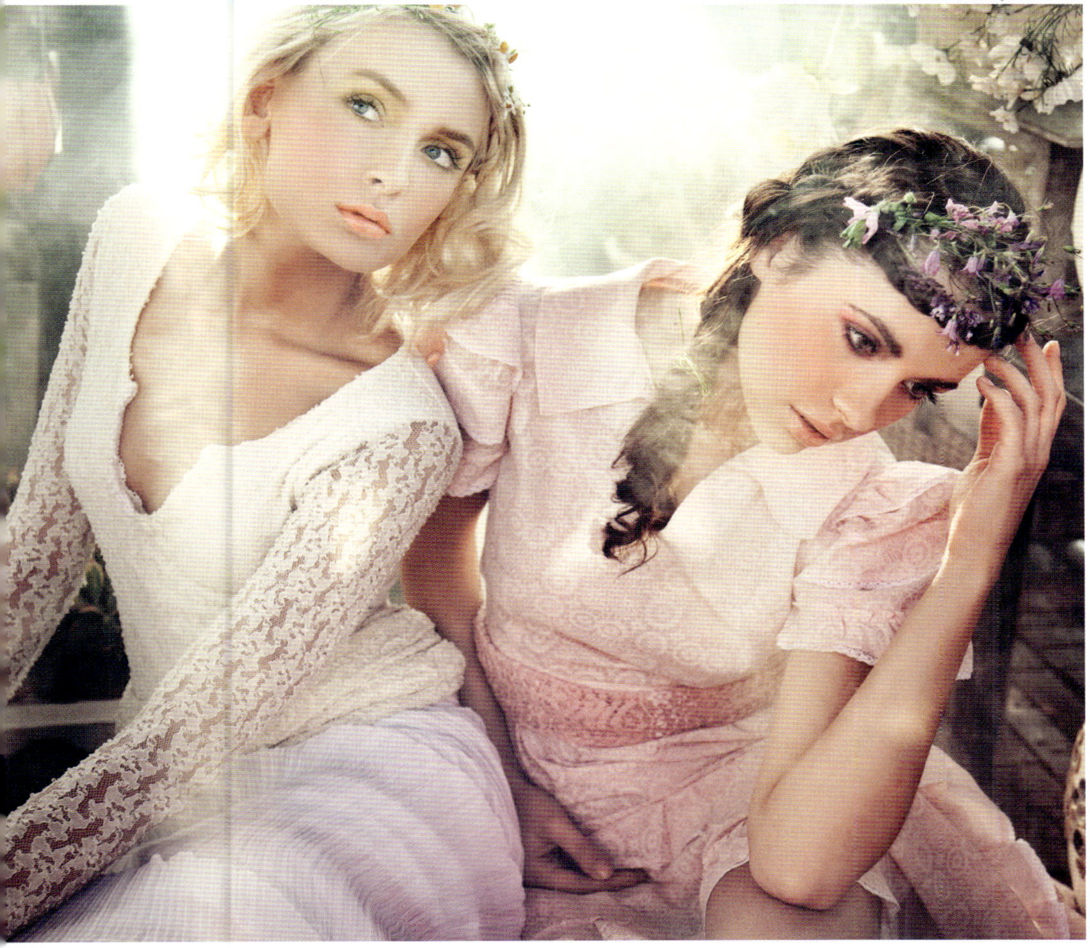

ABOVE LEFT & RIGHT: **BEHIND THE SCENES**
Become an ongoing presence behind the scenes to monitor the atmosphere and how the models and your team are interacting. Be available to answer any questions.

is small and word travels fast. It's easy to build a reputation quickly, which could affect your relationships with agency bookers and clients. If you are attracted to someone, try to wait until the shoot is finished to ask them out. And of course, be careful, models have been known to take advantage to further their career—try not to get hurt!

Most female models develop quickly into strong, powerful women, confident, controlled, and experienced in working with different people every day and creating lifelong friendships in seconds. If you are able to direct multiple models at the same time you can successfully combine their forces to shoot beautiful double, triple, or group shots that appear "real."

# SHOOTING COUPLES:
# CREATING THE "TOGETHER FOREVER" LOOK

**IMAGINE TURNING UP TO WORK in the morning, getting introduced to someone new, and no matter how you felt about them, having to act as though you are head over heels in love. It is a model's job to do this with professional integrity and it would be unusual for someone to refuse to partake in an intimate scene. However, you can make things easier in these sensitive situations by making sure that everyone is comfortable and relaxed at all times.**

Casting couples can be tricky, as you often end up with young girls working with much older guys. I have male model friends who complain about getting threats from disgruntled boyfriends, or having to act romantically with underage girls whose moms are there to supervise. To help, you could try to book older girls, or those who are more aware of their bodies and who won't act like a deer in headlights when asked to hug the male model she is supposed to be engaged to. Look for previous work of a similar nature. With the boys, aim for a more mature character who isn't salivating when you tell him he gets to lock lips with a pretty lady.

Never assume a model will be OK with kissing—that's generally considered to be crossing a line if you spring it on someone on set. Many models, including the ones with partners, are happy to act out relationships, but if you want an overly passionate image it's best to mention it during the casting process.

Although it is not compulsory to let models know before the shoot that they will be acting as a couple, on

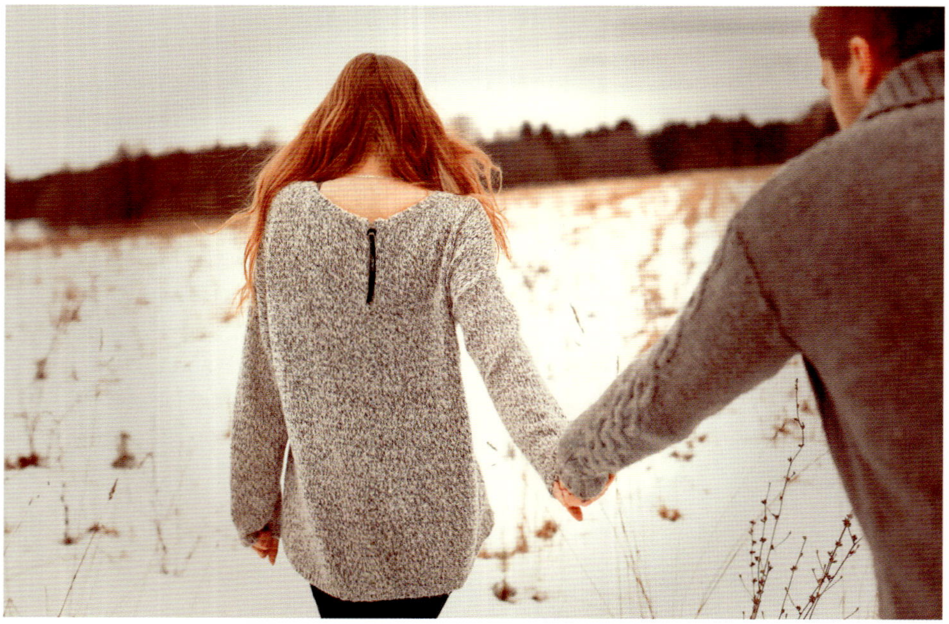

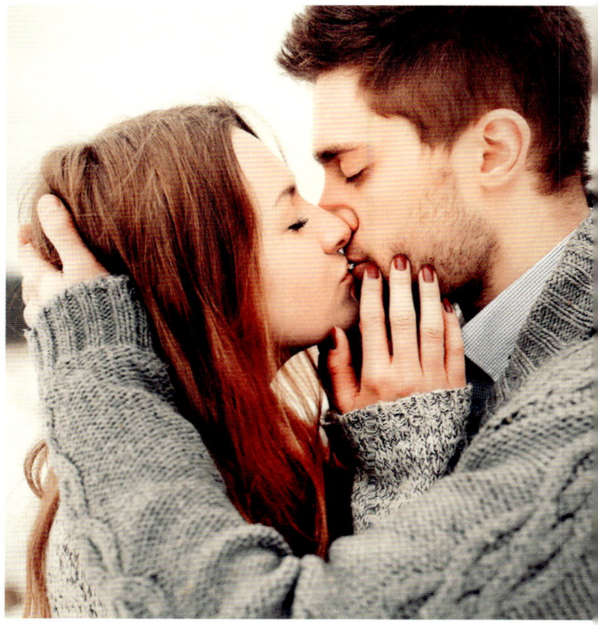

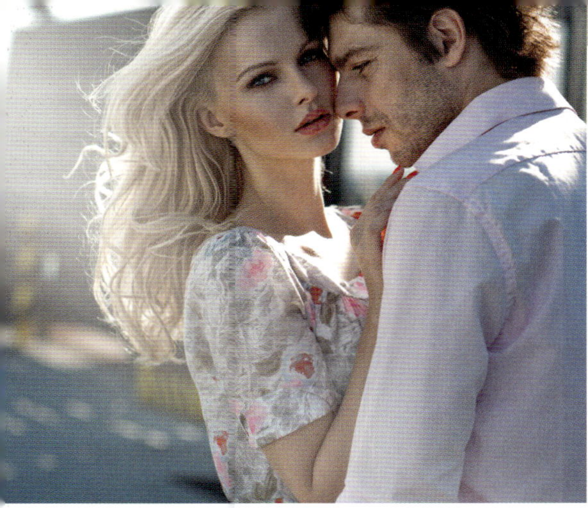

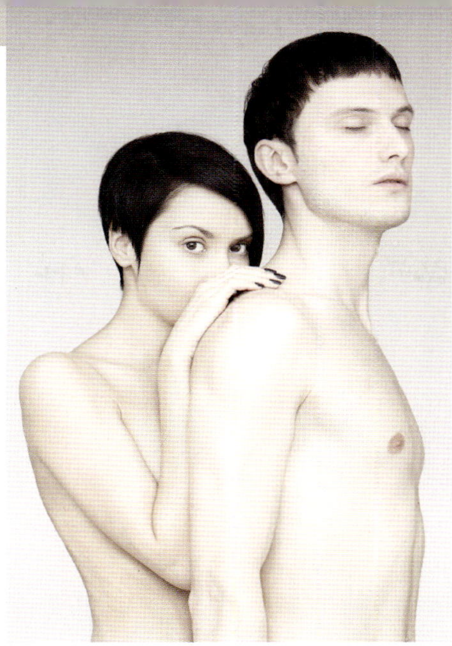

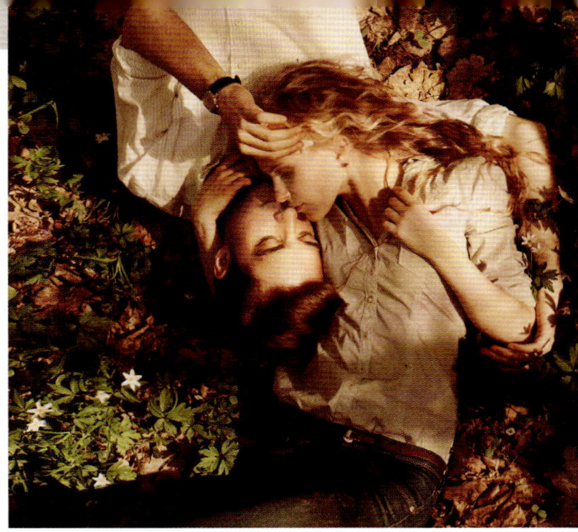

ABOVE: **PROPS!**
Often one half of a couple has been employed as a human "prop," so make sure you draw focus to the correct model.

ABOVE CENTER: **LEVEL OF PRIVACY**
Give the models the space and privacy they need to perform comfortably. Make sure you or your stylist provide clean dressing robes for models just in case they are shy or traveling in between locations.

ABOVE LEFT: **CHEMISTRY ON SET**
If you manage to find a "model couple" who spark visual chemistry, don't lose it. Close the set, make sure cell phones are off, anything so the moment can intensify rather than be interrupted.

OPPOSITE: **KISS ME QUICK**
It can be easier to ask models to lock lips with one another if you work up to the more intimate shots. First, encourage fun, friendly shots so the models can get used to each other and tension is reduced.

### OBSERVATION

On a week-long shoot for Abercrombie & Fitch with 40 models there was no shooting on the first day, only observation. As the catalog called for a lot of making out in the nude they thought it would be best to see who found each other attractive beforehand.

### TIP SHAKE IT OUT

If things are feeling forced during a shoot, and the models have lost that spark, ask them to break apart and "shake it out" or "do a little dance." Anything to make them laugh and relax the situation before embracing again. As in reality, on-camera couples sometimes fight, so have fun playing with emotions in your photography.

shoot day ensure that both are aware of the scenario in plenty of time and have the privacy they need. If underwear or nudity is involved ask wardrobe to provide robes for the models so you can position them covered up if they are feeling insecure.

Keep the shooting environment private, removing anyone from the location who doesn't absolutely need to be there. Don't allow crew to take photographs on their cell phones if the models are in compromising positions. Promote respect on your sets. Ask the models to OK touching with one other and let them know they can rely on the stylist to make them aware if anything that is not meant to show, is showing. The atmosphere needs to be light and often needs humor to break the ice, but never joke about a model or let anyone take things too far—it's easy to offend in these situations. If necessary, take models aside to talk individually, reducing the risk of embarrassing them in front of one another.

With on-camera couples, chemistry can spark flirtatious fireworks, or it can be non-existent and you'll struggle to find that "together forever" look. Convince the models that for the time you are shooting they are actors, and encourage them to move freely so they don't get stuck in an awkward position. Show them how good a few frames look to inspire confidence in their aesthetic union, and if nothing seems to be working, try and shoot them in poses where eye contact is reduced and they can both easily imagine they are cuddling the person they truly want to be with.

# CALMING DOWN THE BOYS

**MODELING IS ONE OF THE ONLY industries in the world where men get paid less than women. There are fewer jobs available and more often than not, men are used as accessories. That means becoming a successful male model can be hard work and fiercely competitive. Some will take the job incredibly seriously when you shoot and others will pass it off as a hobby. You have to roll with whatever attitude is brought to set that day.**

As with the girls, male models come in all shapes and sizes, from muscular "jock" types to skinny effeminate waifs, and with all kinds of personalities, from introverts to cocky attention-seekers. When a model is represented they are aware they are, in some way, aesthetically pleasing to society at large. It can be difficult for a person to know they are very, very, good looking, and guys deal with it differently. There will always be the odd, vain, "him-bo" type—it's unavoidable—but the majority are professional, fun to work with, and surprisingly humble. They realize they are living a lot of people's dreams, getting paid to go to great locations and have gorgeous girls in lacy lingerie draped over them.

### TIP FINDING "THE ONE"

Cast to brief. For example, for a commercial job a guy really has to smile a lot of the time. Not all boys are smilers, so find the ones with positivity in their soul, who seem permanently happy, and make it contagious. They do exist!

Of course it's not as simple as that. When shooting guys and girls together, respect the situation. If a guy has a scantily clad female model writhing around on top of him for a shot, he might need a moment to calm down afterward. Don't embarrass someone by addressing it publicly, there are styling techniques to avoid awkward situations so if necessary talk to wardrobe. Assess beforehand how mature a male model will be in a romantic scenario.

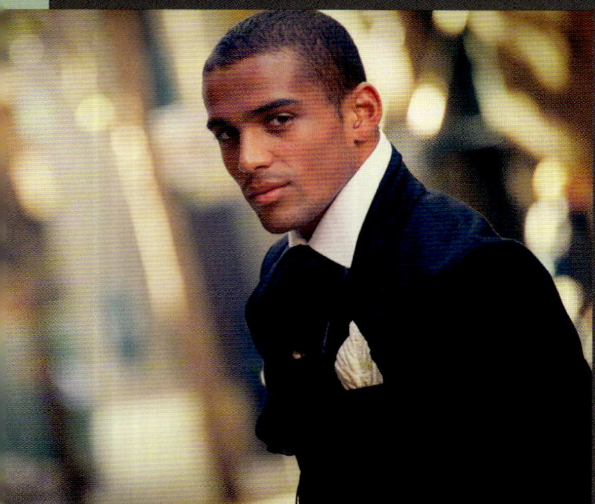

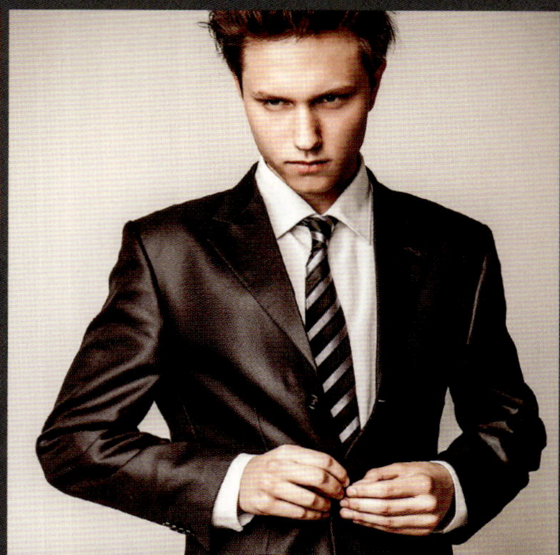

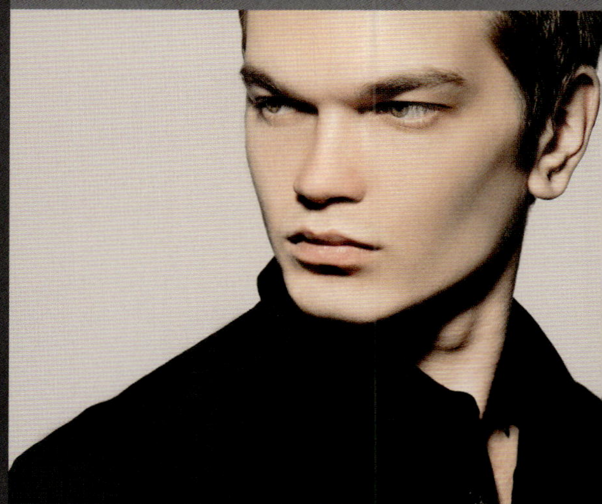

Dynamics are important and will shift significantly if there is more than one male model on set. Two or more together can boost the testosterone levels—I've witnessed push-up competitions, arguments about past sporting achievements, and loud comparisons of shoe size to name a few. Contain this behavior as it can quickly escalate—you want your models to have fun, but not too much.

Male models have to wait around a lot. It's not unusual for them to get the same call-time as a female model. This is fine if the photographer is shooting singles of them while the girl gets ready, but if not, prep can take hours. Be aware of this when scheduling. Men most definitely need makeup and styling, but on most jobs it only amounts to basic concealer, lip balm, and a hair ruffle. You want people to arrive in ample time, but let them sleep in as much as possible.

Most male models are used to substantial down time and are capable of entertaining themselves, but it's easy to get bored over a long shoot day. With larger groups distract the guys with skateboards, musical instruments, or games—cards and dice work well, but look out for the gamblers! Monitor behavior, as in my experience male models are a bit like cats—they take naps in strange places, they attempt crazy stunts like balancing on the edges of rooftops, and they tend to wander off so you spend half the day shouting for them. Attempt to keep calm and in control at all times.

## KEEPING TRIM

Male models are often pickier with their diets than most females, so can be on strict nutritional programs. Losing weight isn't easy and it is often forgotten that men are as sensitive about their appearance as women. It should also be noted that men suffer from eating disorders and can need help too.

OPPOSITE LEFT & CENTER: **SHAPES AND SIZES**
Even within agency guidelines male models range in size and body shape. From buff to lanky think about the affect on your proposed outfits. Would they suit a suit or rock a rock T-shirt?

OPPOSITE RIGHT: **BAD ATTITUDE**
Men are known to be unwilling to express their emotions. If a male model suddenly goes quiet or develops an attitude, there might be more to it than meets the eye. Take some one-on-one time.

BELOW: **BE RESPECTFUL**
If a shot is supposed to be sexually intense and intimate, but looks forced, avoid saying it out loud. Encourage. Give it time, and rather than piling on the pressure on either model, respect the awkwardness of the situation.

BELOW RIGHT: **TESTOSTERONE BOOST**
Groups of male models on set can lead to competition, one-upmanship and pranks. So much testosterone in an environment that celebrates their good looks can need containing.

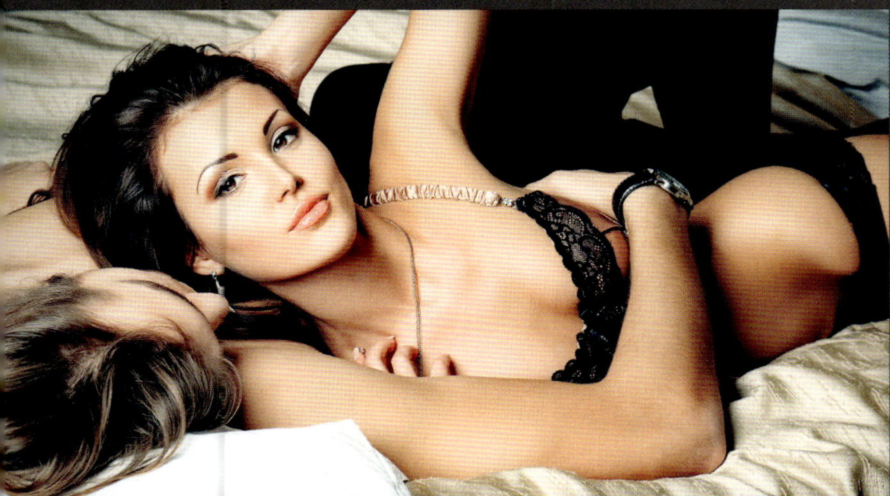

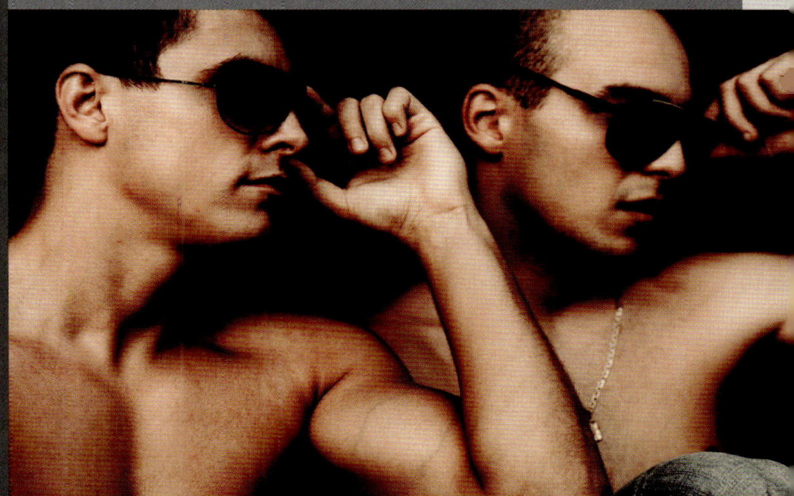

# NICHE MARKETS

**THERE ARE SMALLER subcategories associated with fashion photography that are also worth encompassing. They use many of the same techniques and require positive interaction with models to produce great shots. Larger agencies cover a range of talent, while others deal specifically with niche markets.**

## PLUS SIZE

Although their measurements might be slightly different, shooting plus-size models is no different to working with regular fashion models. On many jobs you will be shooting multiple models who range in size to cover a company's full collection. When it comes to posing and directing, it's about what looks great on camera and flatters the clothing.

There are arguments for and against shooting real plus-sized girls and slimmer models who use padding, and how natural the end result appears. It can upset girls who work hard to maintain a certain physique when others "pad." Make casting decisions based on your personal morals and beliefs (or lack thereof). Jobs that involve plus-size models are generally more commercial—a lot of catalog and online print work is available, which can mean higher day rates.

## BIT-PART

While it's not uncommon for a studio to borrow staff members to shoot isolated body parts, hand, foot, and even butt models are capable of earning thousands of dollars a day. They are frequently used in advertising when a client wants close-up shots of a specific body part wearing or handling their product.

When casting these kinds of jobs you are looking for flawless versions of that particular body part. Hand models tend to have great skin, and their hands are smooth, hairless, and unblemished, with minimal wrinkles, long, slender fingers, and attractive, manicured, nails.

They need to be posed in a relaxed, graceful fashion to avoid "The Claw" (a rigid grip often used by less experienced or nervous models), so ask them to "shake it out" if they clamp up.

Most foot models have high arches, which gives their foot a naturally graceful curve. Working fashion models are often forced to wear ill-fitting shoes on a daily basis, resulting in blisters and sores, so foot doubles are employed as they concentrate solely on their feet.

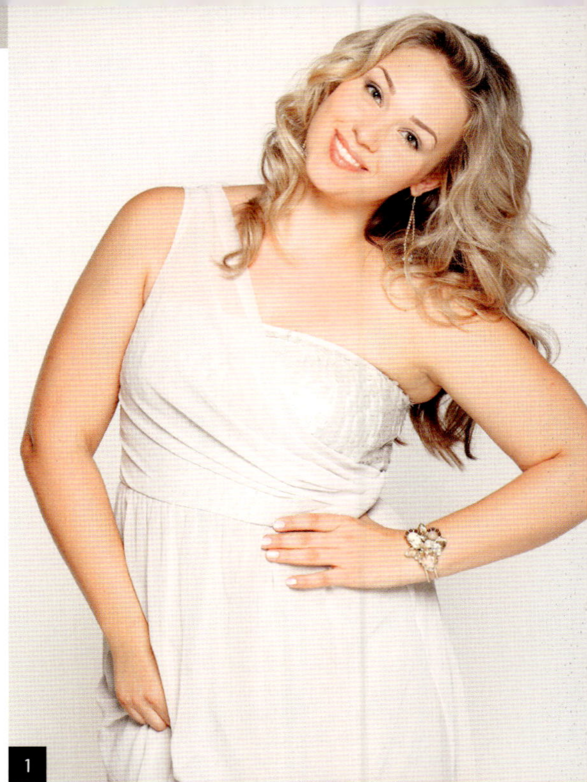
1

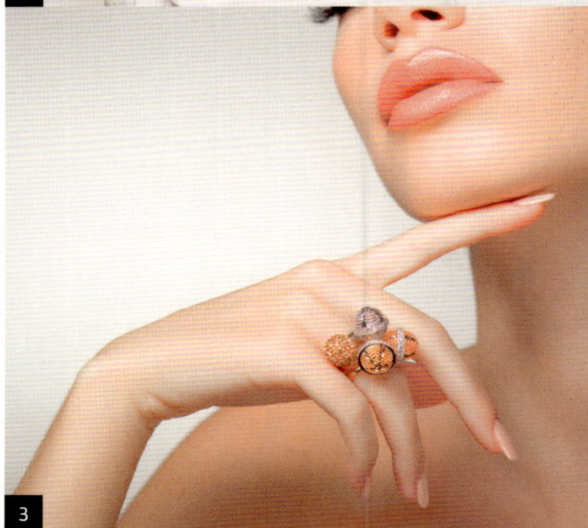
3

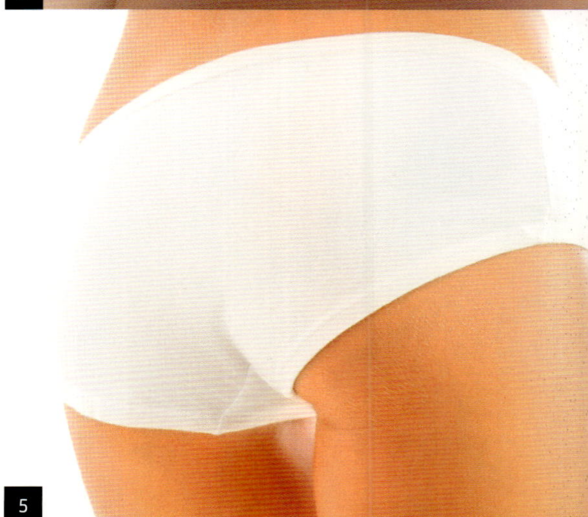
5

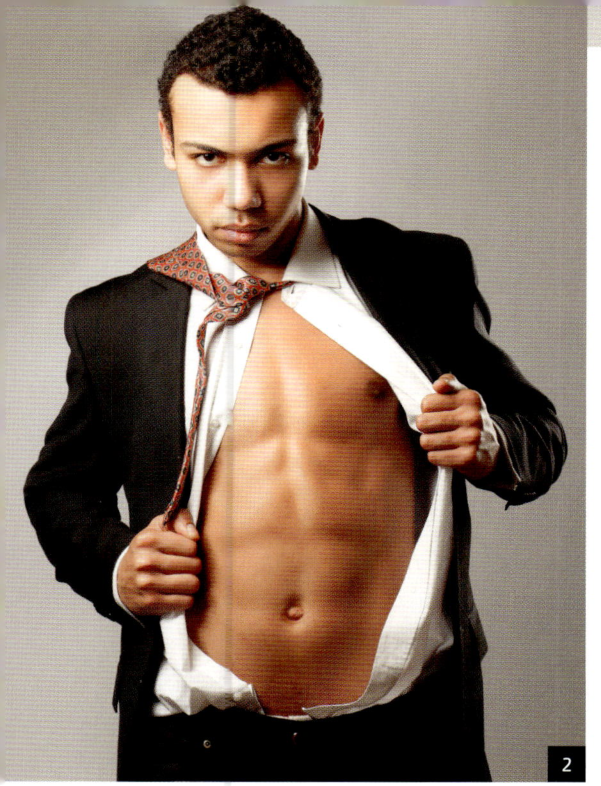

2

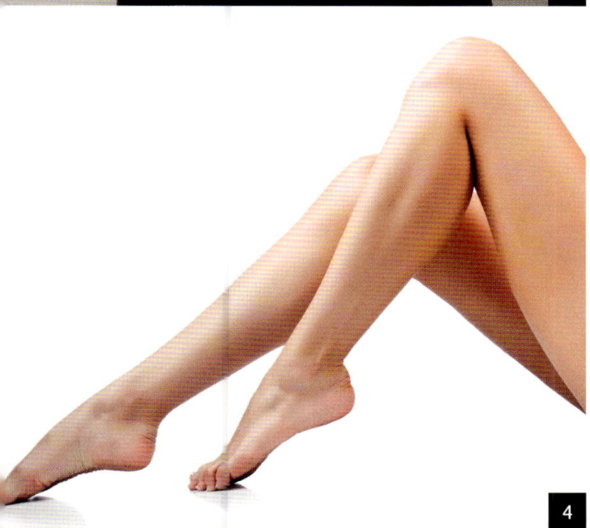

4

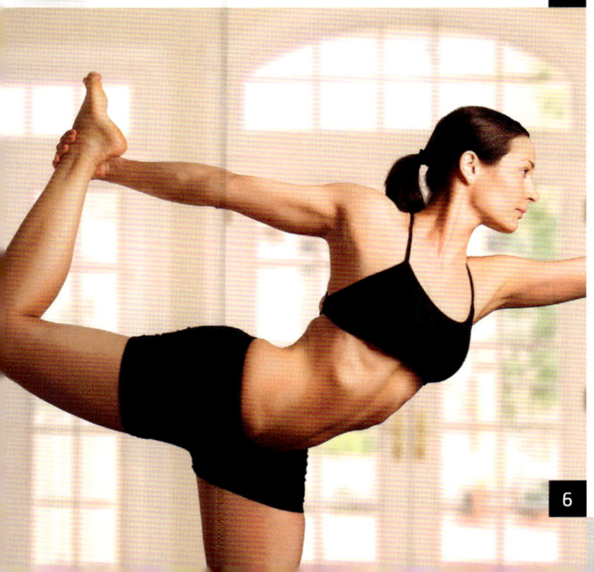

6

## CASTING BODY PARTS

Bit-part models take their jobs very seriously and work hard to produce high-end portfolios. Don't be surprised to see an entire book of a model's butt. Treat every casting the same way and maintain respect at all times.

Butt models have to keep their body fat index low and regularly get waxed, exfoliated, and spray tanned. But no matter the body part, nothing is as important as the model having the timing and patience required to hit a mark, over and over again.

## SPORT, FITNESS, & HEALTH

There are multiple fitness and health magazines and companies on the market and if you do your research you will find that there are also many high fashion models who are trained in sports, martial arts, and other fitness techniques. At times you may also be asked to shoot magazine editorials of experts in these fields. You will be relying upon them to repeatedly exhibit their skills in an attractive manner, which can be easier with athletes who are used to strict training methods. Be kind to those who are less experienced on camera and allow them time to relax and get into their zone. At castings watch out for those who cannot pose for a long time without muscle shakes, as even slight movements can translate into blurry pictures.

## GLAMOR, NUDE, AND FINE ART

Even though there are a number of high concept fashion magazines and advertising outlets that include tasteful nudity, if you cross the line too far into glamor and "fine art" photography you will lose your appeal in the more commercial markets. For advice on shooting models in more erotic situations see chapter 11.

1: **SIZE DOESN'T MATTER**
Certain photographers shy away from shooting plus-size models as they can be disregarded amongst high fashion circles. Try embracing all forms of beauty in your work to enlighten those with closed minds.

2: **TASTEFUL VS. CROSSING THE LINE**
As with all of your shoots you need to make sure you are not crossing the line into tacky or distasteful, unless that's what you are going for. If you want to get great clients, keep it classy.

3, 4, 5: **BIT PARTS**
The amount of advertising and commercial work that features a single body part is underestimated. In each of these shots a human is attached to said part and needs to be directed just like every other type of model.

6: **OUT OF BREATH**
When photographing sports or fitness remember a model needs to stagger their energy levels so they can continue to perform throughout the shoot. Don't push too hard, models vomit too.

# WORKING WITH CHILDREN & ANIMALS

**PEOPLE SAY NEVER WORK with animals or children, but in fashion you might have to work with both, at the same time. Throughout my career I have shot with all kinds of animals, including dogs, pigs, cats, donkeys, and even the odd stuffed penguin. I've worn zebra print while riding a zebra and had a monkey jump me. I've also had temporary children of all ages, and discovered that whether you are shooting with tigers or toddlers, much of the same advice can be applied.**

Keep a watchful eye at all times, as safety is your number one priority. Both children and animals have a lot of energy, are unpredictable, and can bite. Older models can be scared of either and will lie about it to get a job. When casting consider allergies—there are definitely those who would claim to be allergic to children, especially other people's! This is not the attitude you're looking for when casting a parental figure.

On set, kids and animals both have professional "wranglers" who are in charge of keeping them safe and happy whilst herding them to where they need to be. Wranglers are usually well versed in the strict regulations that apply, and although they follow guidelines that exist for a reason, it can often feel that they are making your job harder. Try to be patient in these situations. You will be asking your model to interact in different ways with the talent, so if a parent or owner challenges you at any time, listen respectfully and accommodate any issues they may have. Certain animals must be dealt with in very particular ways and you must ensure this is adhered to at all times. In an extreme case, ask someone to leave if they are unhappy or endangering your set.

As a general rule, shoot quickly. If you can, set up the shot before the talent arrives to reduce wait time. Hours are often limited and overtime can be expensive or illegal. Prioritize your shoot schedule: it's polite to let your

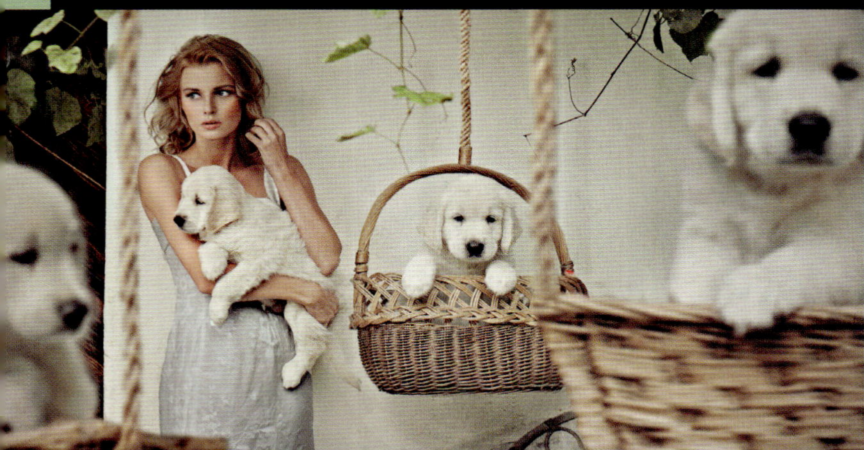

ABOVE: **SAFETY FIRST**
If you're inexperienced you might easily overlook something on set that would send a parent into shock. Keep safety in mind at all times. Amp kids up with music and games but watch out for their well being.

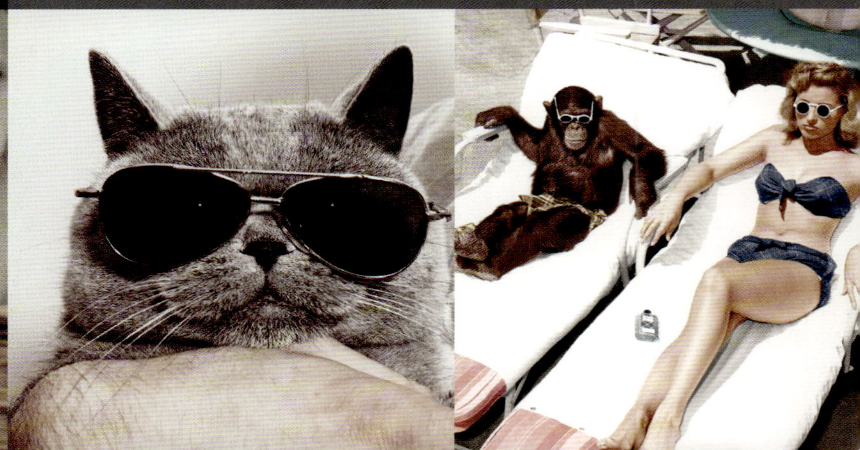

ABOVE: **SCRATCH & BITE**
If you are working with an animal that has the capability to harm a model make sure you follow all the rules and don't push any boundaries. Keep the model in mind even when you know a shot would be fantastic.

older models know what's happening, as they understand the rules and are used to rushing to get a shot or waiting around as necessary.

Most importantly, have fun. Encourage your older models to bond with their co-stars and build chemistry. Remember, everyone has an off day—sometimes the kid won't laugh or the flamingos will refuse to co-operate, but never get angry. A raised voice can spook a shy child or skittish animal. Photo shoots can be intimidating, busy, and loud, so you never know how a usually confident child might react. This is not a good time to be a control freak.

> *One time I was working on a commercial set with a Shar Pei puppy. The lead girl was introducing herself to the dog when she tripped and fell. The loud noise frightened the pup and from then on it was scared to be around her. Eventually the girl had to be cut completely.*
>
> **COKEY FALKOW,** *model and actor*

Children and animals can produce some of the most fun and emotion pictures, but you have to be ready to capture the magic when it happens, because 10 seconds later the sugar fix might run out (I've seen both kids and pigs being fed sugar cubes on set) and you'll be left with nothing. That said, never underestimate anybody either, no matter how young or hairy—the truth is, the majority of children and animals in the industry are more professional than most of the adult models.

**TIP FRAGILE!**

If you are borrowing from a friend—whether their beloved puppy or only child—make sure you look after them and return them in one piece!

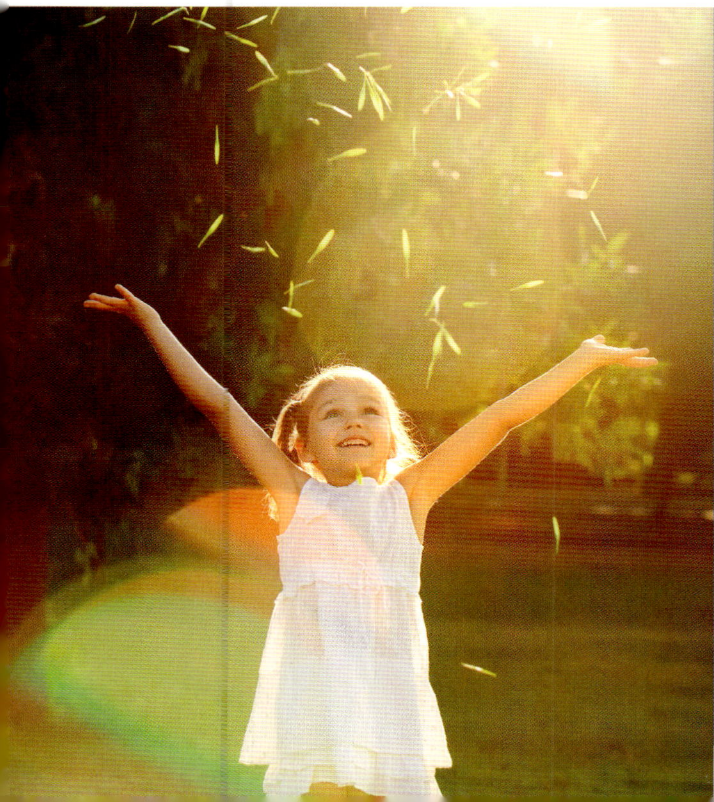

LEFT: **MAKE 'EM LAUGH**
Sometimes, getting a child to laugh can seem almost impossible. Be patient, make silly faces, and relate to them. Tell your models to do the same as well.

RIGHT: **STRANGER DANGER**
Having strangers on set, including "wranglers," can be disconcerting. Remember they are there for a reason and you can work with them rather than against. Listen and learn.

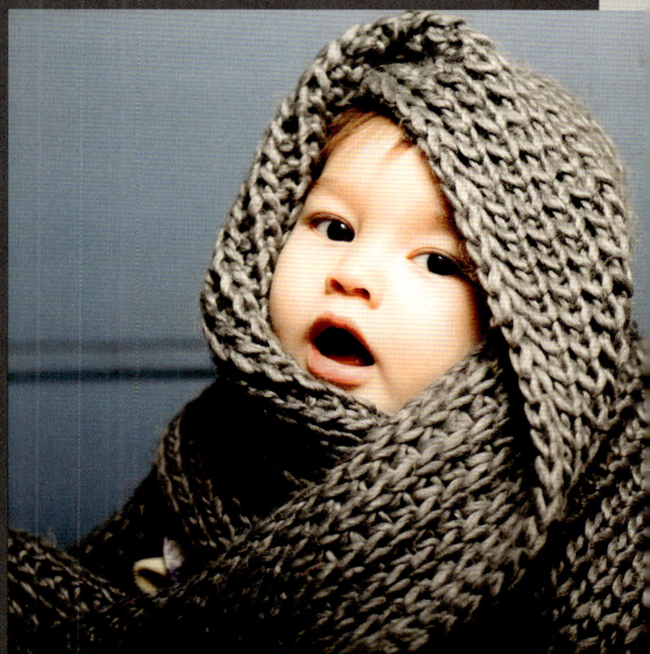

## BEHIND THE LENS WITH

# LUKE PEARSALL

"I once had a model break down in the middle of the Las Vegas desert, crying and ruining her makeup. It wasn't a fun experience. One of the biggest problems I run in to is when a model is hired and doesn't come in with a team player attitude. I don't want to work with the model that wants to be treated like a princess and pampered, I want to work with the girl or guy who is ready to roll up their sleeves and lend a hand, or at least ask to. I want someone who is cool with the crew, and who doesn't spend all day on their phone texting or acting like they are bored with the whole situation. I will never hire those models again for any job, even if their images are incredible. It's about a relationship between not just me and the model, but everyone on the crew and that means more to me then anything. I've seen one bad apple spoil the bunch and one good one make everyone hungry for more.

Unfortunately, I have met many divas. I can't stand them and neither can the clients who are usually the ones writing their checks. In my younger days I had a harder time holding my tongue with them, but as I have grown up a little I realize that sometimes it's better to just take them aside and let them know what's up and just get through it.

### BIO

Luke Pearsall is a fashion and commercial photographer, director, and producer with a diverse background in film and stills photography. He is based in Los Angeles, USA.

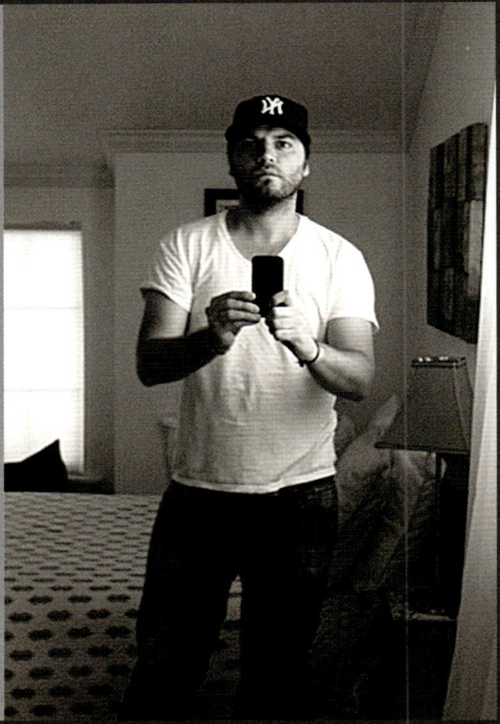

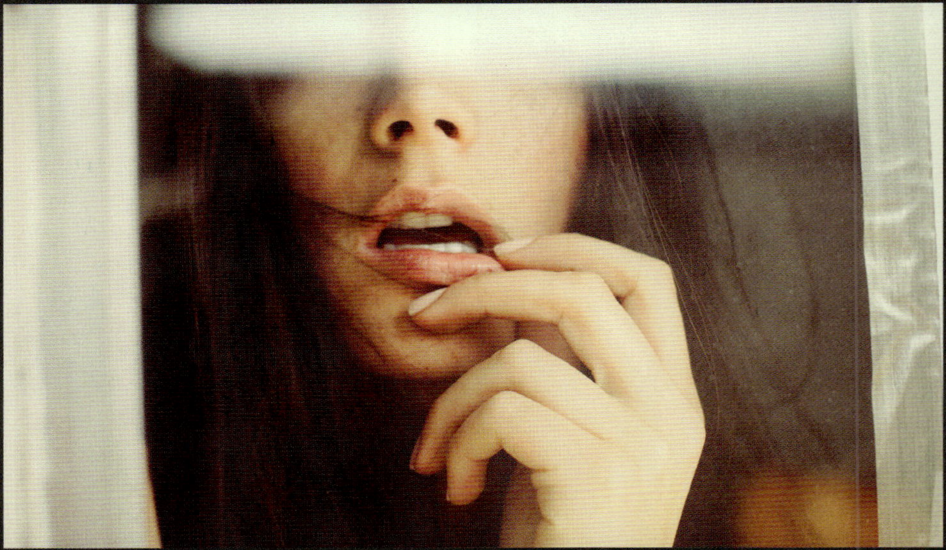

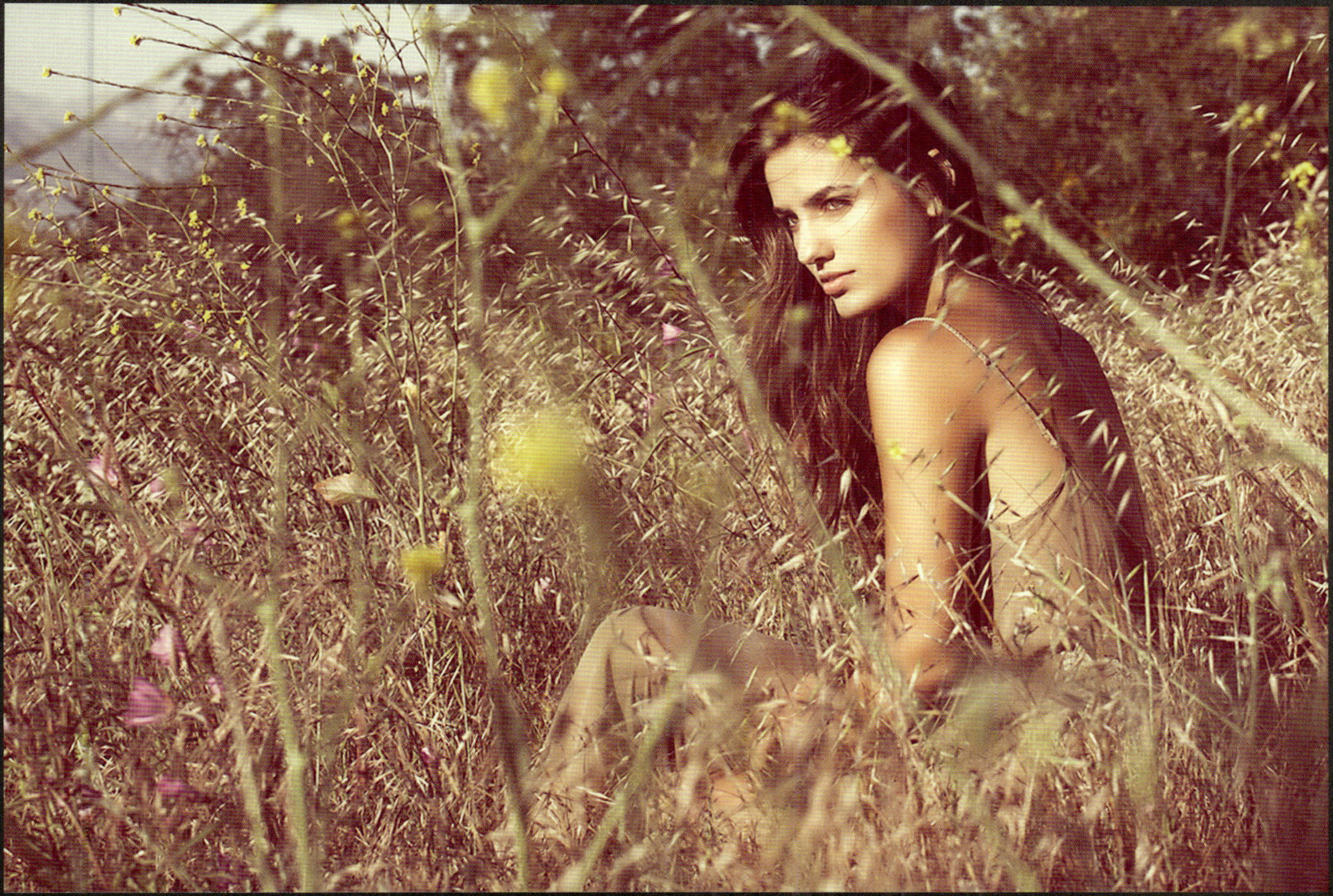

ABOVE & OPPOSITE: **LOOK UP**
Luke uses a range of locations from the nearby desert to his own apartment. This highlights the importance of being creative, of looking around you and visualizing what could work as a great backdrop as well as being realistic with a model's time constraints.

Before I direct anyone to do anything I like to chat with them and figure out what type of person they are. Shy, outgoing, flirty, sexy, or can they just do it all? I think as a photographer you have to adjust your game in every scenario. I like to laugh a lot, and I find myself being self-deprecating at times just to get a laugh. If people are laughing they are comfortable.

I like to let the model know what look and feel we are trying to go for and the good ones usually take it and run. Communication is the most important thing in the world in making a picture work. I have seen and probably been in situations where the direction being given and the response between model and photographer is just not clicking and becomes awkward beyond belief. Those days are hard on both ends for talent and artist, but a good photographer keeps trying to break the barrier and communicate more effectively.

If serious direction is needed I sometimes find it helpful to show reference images and be patient. In the film days photographers used to pretend to shoot a couple of rolls of film in empty cameras before they even shot a single frame just to get those jitters out for both the model and themselves. In the digital world we can do the same thing except we can actually shoot! ”

# 10

# IT'S ALL ABOUT THE CLIENT

**CLIENT DECISIONS AND REQUESTS can seem stifling on a shoot, but you must remember at all times that without them you wouldn't have a job. This chapter is about keeping the important people happy, focusing on poses that highlight clothing and accessories, working with fabrics, and interacting positively with your client. Included throughout is advice from top fashion stylist and creative consultant, Natalie Toren, whose styling work has appeared in countless international publications as well as editorial and advertising work.**

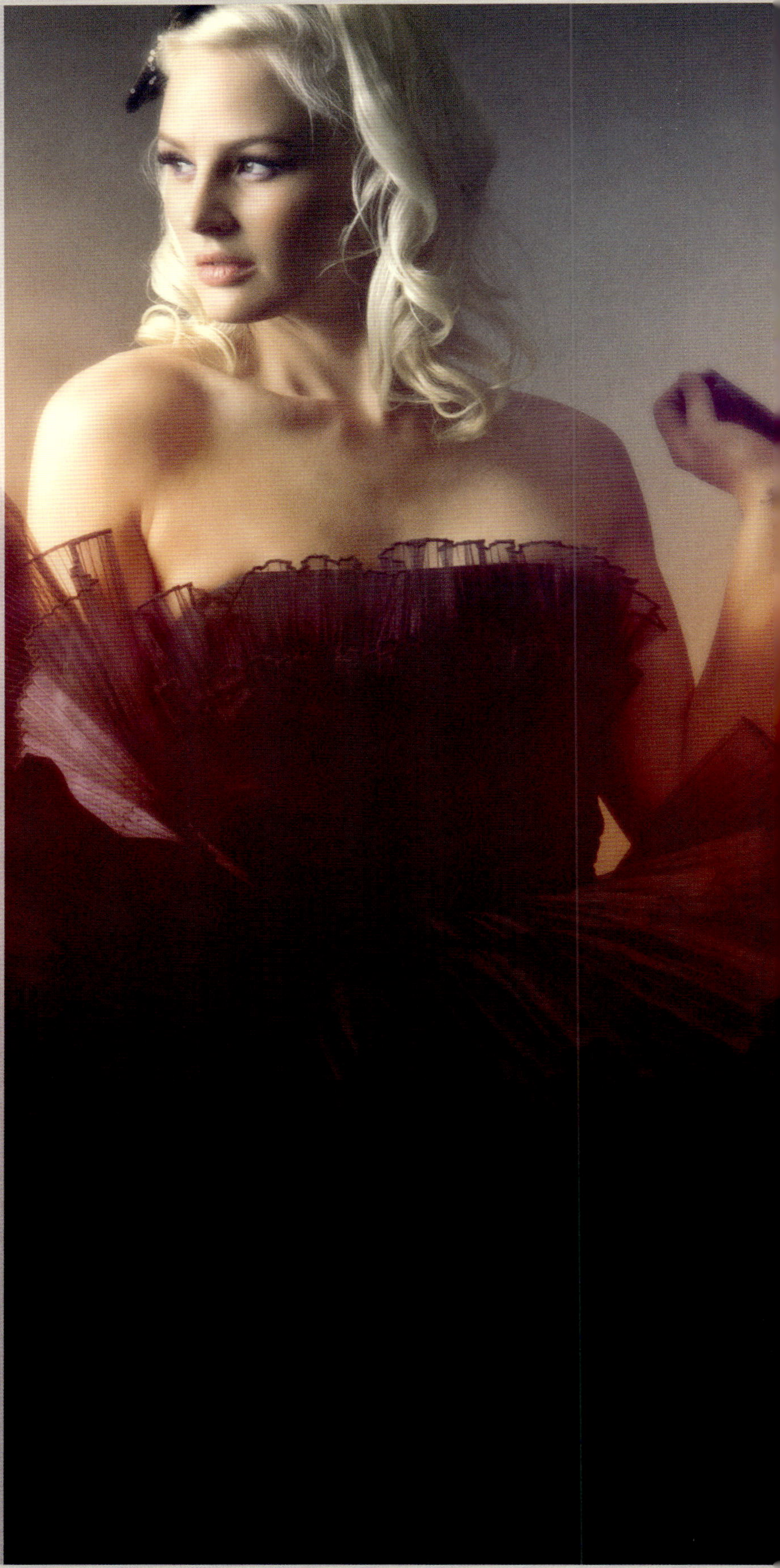

RIGHT: **MODEL BEHAVIOR**
Models can forget that they should adjust their behavior according to client, especially when present on set. If your model is acting in an inappropriate manner, let them know discreetly.

# REMEMBER THE TARGET MARKET

**FASHION COMPANIES and magazines produce photoshoots to advertise their products, expressing a particular lifestyle ideal to their individual target markets. The competition to stay on-trend and fresh is fierce. When any company spends money there must be good reason for it, with high potential for return on the investment. Therefore these shoots are not spur-of-the-moment road trips—there are specific marketing needs that must be met and consequences if the final product fails to generate profit.**

A client's presence on set can create a formal environment, but they should not be feared. It's true that they can be powerful, intimidating people who make you feel like you have absolutely no idea what you're doing, but they can also be lovely, passionate people who are willing to hand over the reigns completely. Be confident in your abilities—you were booked for a reason and if necessary respond to them in terms of their brief. Explain your decisions and how they promote the needs of the company and the image they aim to portray. Always respect their position, even when their ideas are impossible to achieve in the location and with a lighting system they themselves specified and you just spent hours setting up. Learn to roll with it. Yes, they may know nothing about photography, or cameras, or lighting, and they can decide they want to change the background or the entire set-up at any point, but the best photographers can make a client feel as though they've changed everything to suit their needs when actually only a few minor variations have occurred.

A lot of other voices on a working set want to be heard as well: art directors, producers, company CEOs, everybody wants to share their opinion and feel that their input will have a positive impact in some way. Collaborating is what makes fashion photography fun, and if you keep the overall objectives of the project in mind there is room for experimentation. Assuming you're shooting digitally, listen, quickly shoot a frame, check the difference, and then respectfully agree or disagree.

RIGHT: **TOO MANY COOKS...** Opinions can vary widely on set and at times it will seem impossible to please everybody. Don't worry, this happens to every photographer, just try to keep calm and open-minded as much as possible in this scenario.

FAR RIGHT: **KEEP CONTROL** The client has a certain amount of control behind the scenes, but only you can maintain your relationship with the model on set. You are their point of reference for direction and only your voice should be heard when shooting is in progress.

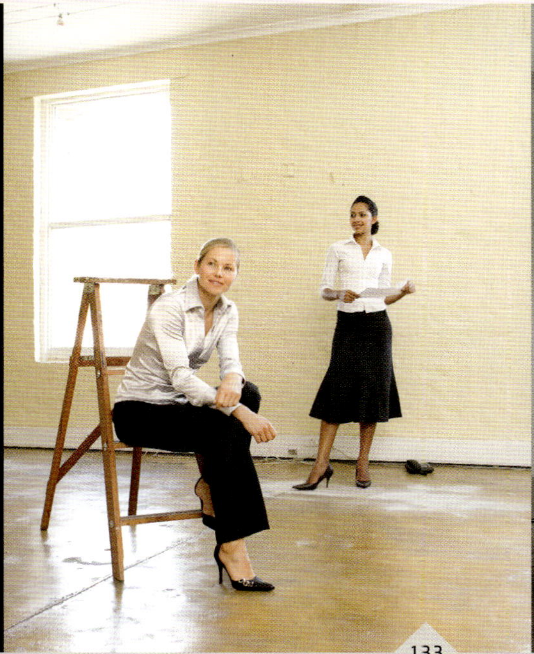

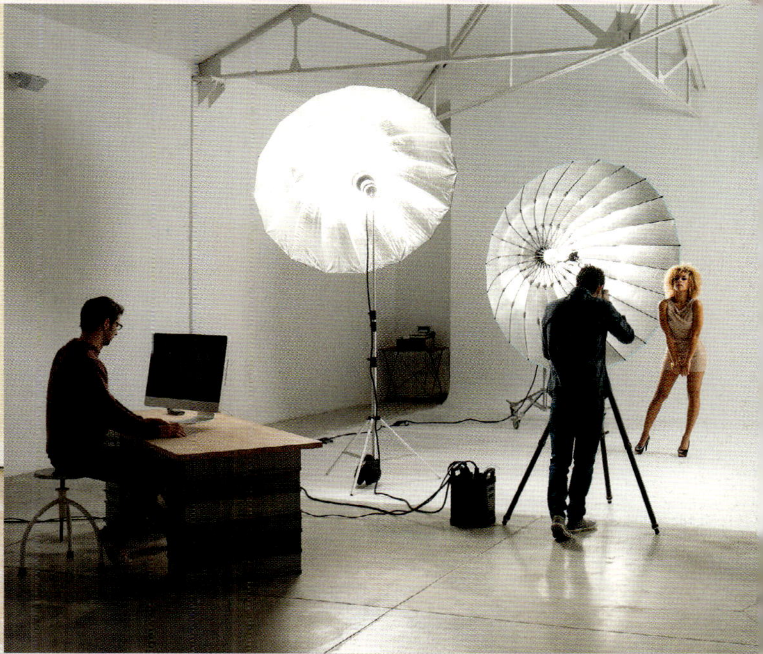

# THE PRODUCT

**YOUR PROJECT BRIEF should be as detailed as possible when it comes to product specifications. You need to know how many outfits must be shot during the day, which items are required to be featured, and whether a designer will be styling the outfits with accessories such as jewelry and shoes. You have to consider who your client is trying to appeal to—whether it's a designer trying to submit to a fashion editor, or a marketing team trying to sell press-ads to millions of teenagers. Adapt your shoot accordingly.**

Throughout the process you should be aiming to showcase pieces in the most effective way possible. There are a lot of details a photographer can overlook when it comes to clothing and accessories. There might be a logo that needs to be the focus point, or a clasp that has to be shown a certain way.

> *Even though photographers want unbridled creativity, they have to be accommodating when it comes to certain wardrobe restraints or featuring specific items. Stylists have to occasionally jump through hoops to get certain items or promise to shoot something in a specific way to continue their working relationship with a brand. For example, certain fashion houses refuse to let runway looks be modified on any way—they must be shot as a 'full look,' including accessories and shoes. A stylist can be vilified for misusing clothing—the relationships with PR are so tenuous.*
>
> **NATALIE TOREN,** *stylist*

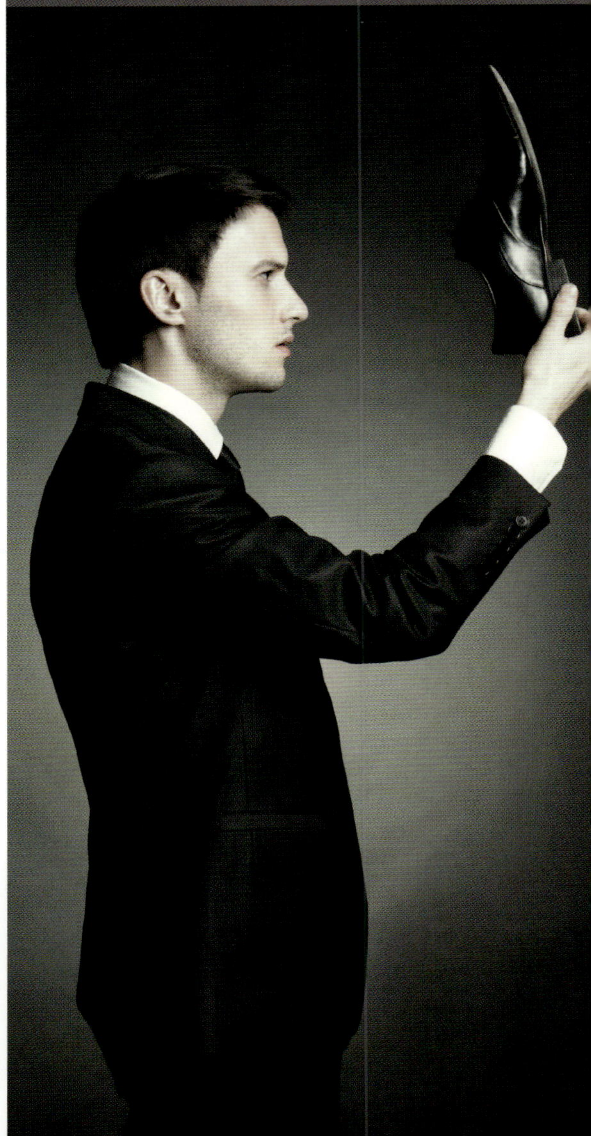

ABOVE: **ATTENTION TO DETAIL**
It is the industry expectation, especially in advertising, that there is a flawlessness in a finished image, even if something is supposed to be naturalistic. Otherwise it can read as clumsy or amateurish.

OPPOSITE RIGHT: **PERPLEXED BY PRODUCT**
Sometimes a particular bag or shoe can leave you creatively stumped. Take a look at the item from every angle. Try it isolated, featuring a great background, or ask your model to come up with quirky pose ideas.

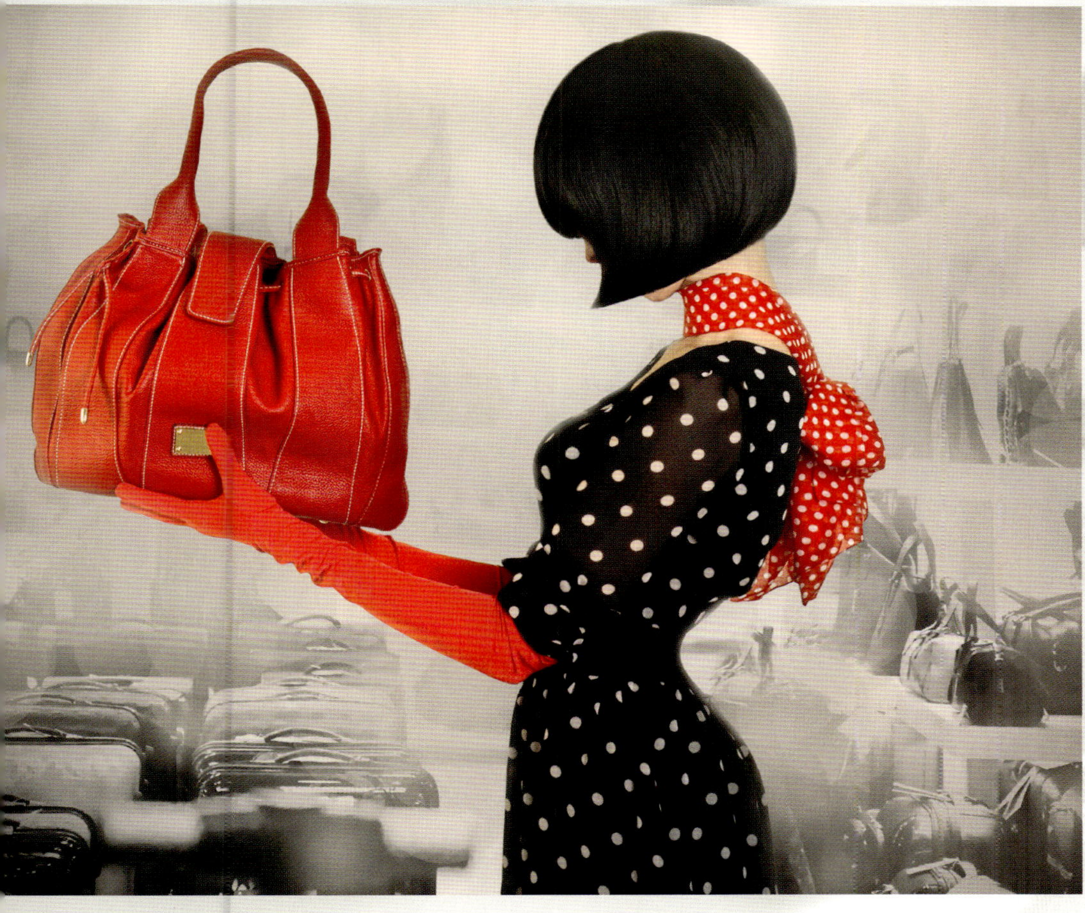

Seams, labels, and linings cannot be seen at times and a particular outfit may have to be worn in a variety of ways—with a hat and without one, for example.

When shooting, you might think you have captured the perfect image, only to discover the model was holding the handbag the wrong way round. Depending on the style of shoot the entire look might have to show, as it would naturally fall, without the model covering any part of the styling. Or, you may have more freedom, so long as you ensure that at least a piece of each item is shown. Make sure you know what is expected of you.

Think about the garment when you are setting up the shot, discuss beforehand whether a close-up, mid-length, or full-length image is necessary, or if a particular side may be favored due to the lighting. Think about whether the shoes will show or if the model will be sat, kneeling, laid down, or partially obscured in such a way that a detail or the overall cut might not show. Some shots are more difficult with certain items of clothing, such as constricting, tight outfits that restrict movement or boxy cuts that become unflattering if a model sits down. Over time, especially if you experiment with this when you are testing, you will learn which shapes and materials work well with different poses and set-ups.

## SHOOTING FABRIC

Fabrics are important to show, but can be tricky to capture. Tightly drawn patterns, checks, or thin stripes can blur and "buzz" on camera (a phenomenon known as moiré) and it's important to be aware of folds, layers, ruffles, or horizontal stripes that can widen an image, even with a skinny model.

## MAKE IT SHINE

When you're photographing garments with sequins or with a metallic finish, it's often essential that you show off the shiny finish—the unique element of the garment. To do this, it's all about controlling the reflection of the light source in the shiny part of the subject. These shiny bits act like a mirror, so you have to carefully choose your light source—whether that's an artificial source or a reflector—and then carefully watch how it reflects in the subject. Move the light or subject around until you get the desired amount of reflection. You may have to change the light source for a larger one to get a more pronounced effect.

The shape of the light source also matters, especially if the garment is very shiny, as is the case with latex. Typically, large rectangular softboxes and reflectors will give a larger reflection, with a better-defined edge. Of course, if you want to underplay the shiny parts, the converse is true. To get rid of reflections you may have to move your light source higher or further away from the camera. A polarizing filter could also be used to reduce reflections, although they also cut down the amount of light hitting the sensor by up to 2 stops.

# FINDING THE POSE

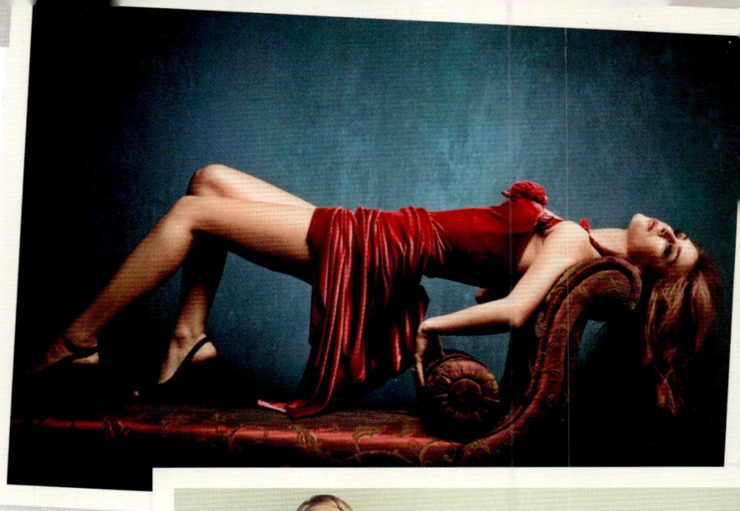

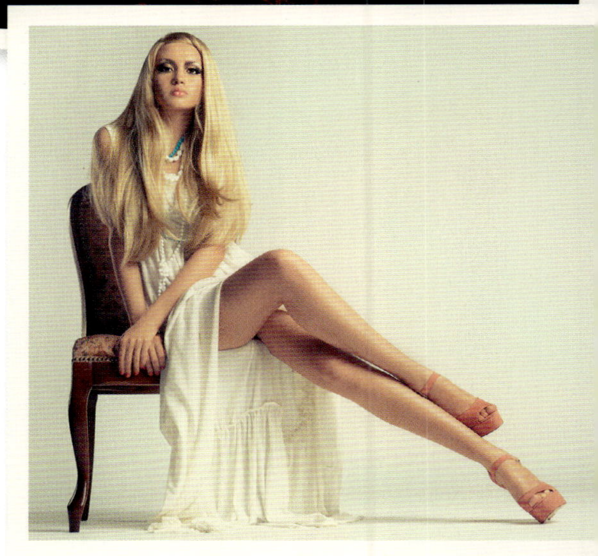

**CLOTHING IN GENERAL can baffle a photographer, which is why trusting your stylist is so important. Research fashion; the history of design, magazine editorials and fashion blogs, noting which outfits are on trend and styled in particular poses. On set, observe your model, they learn what looks and more importantly, feels good. Watch how they move before you start shooting, remember which shapes the outfit lends itself to when the model is relaxed and unaware of an audience.**

It is a fashion designer's job to experiment with cut and style. Thankfully, with most outfits a pose will be more obvious—some dresses lose their shape if a model sits, for example, so must be shot standing. However, boxy cuts, wide stripes, and baggy looks can all be tricky to shoot. If something isn't working try different positions, rather than getting stuck in one and losing momentum. Ask the model to sit, crouch, or lie down, whatever looks flattering or masks a problem area. Let the model know what works and what doesn't, so they can then flaunt it or avoid it, saving time.

Work with, not against the material and patterns. Look for details or design elements that the model can use to enhance an image, such as billowing sleeves, embroidered pockets, or fringing, which looks great with arms up and movement. If you are outside, embrace the effect wind has on a flowing outfit, or use a wind-machine in a studio to recreate this look. Direct a model to swing gently from side to side, twirl, take a step, or a small jump to breathe energy into a shot. At times the styling will be uninspiring, but try never to get bored, stay innovative, and work with a model to produce something fun and fresh.

Be sure to feature mid-length and full-length posed shots to show the clothes in their entirety. Sometimes getting overzealous with close-ups means the client and stylist wind up with a collar story, but not much else. On almost every photo shoot at least one item won't fit, but a good stylist has tricks up their sleeves—sometimes it may mean that you won't be able to shoot from the back or side, though, as maybe a zip won't fit or the sample is so big that it must be clamped.
A lot of fashion photography involves "smoke and mirrors" and making it work in whatever way you can to get the shot. There will certainly be days when you need to invite the crew for a drink afterward!

### TIME TO REFLECT

A mirror on set can be extremely useful. A model can try a few poses before shooting, to see how it makes them feel and what works. This can be particularly important on e-comm shoots where the number of shots per outfit is limited.

> *A great model will know how to carry herself to best display the clothes—for example, they know to hold a great posture for structured, corseted, or boned pieces. On a technical level, samples are cut for a specific shape and models need to morph into it, by elongating their neck or torso, angling forward or back. Photographers should always be aware of these angles, where clothing is bunching, rippling, or whiskering, or is clearly too tight in certain poses. If they can give the right direction to the model and the proper posing cue, they can save themselves hours of painstaking retouching. It also helps if they can hide any of the extensive hardware—anything from pins to clamps to foreign constructs—that the stylist implements to make the clothing fit better.*
>
> **NATALIE TOREN,** *stylist*

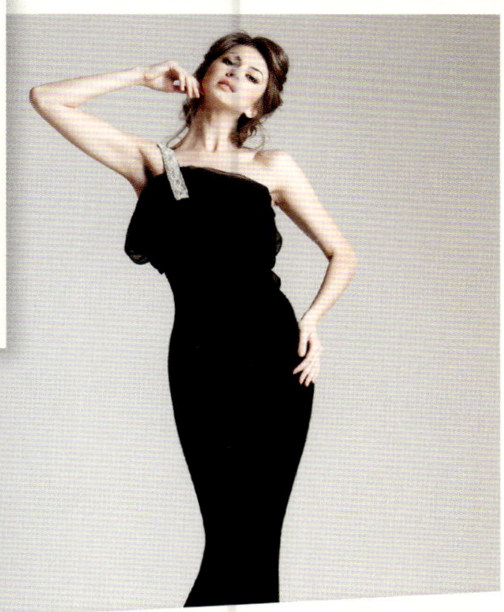

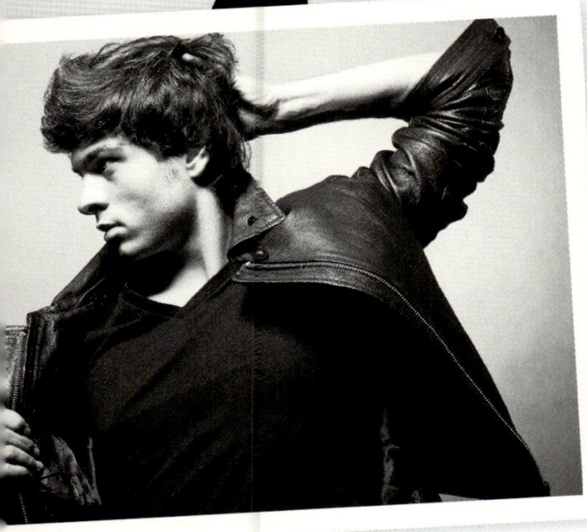

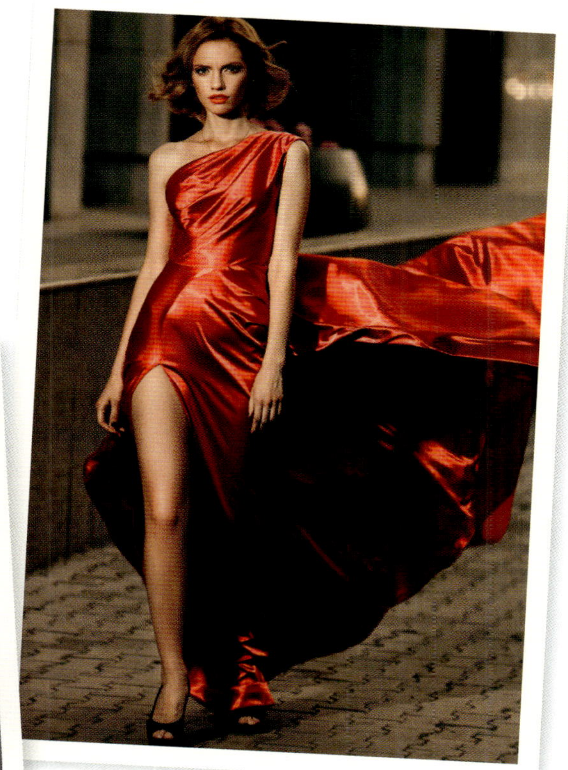

### TIP: VPL

Models are taught to wear nude underwear to shoots, but if the panty line is visible or causing lines you may have to ask them to remove it. If this is awkward, use the stylist as a go-between, as they develop close relationships with models.

LEFT & OPPOSITE: **TAKE YOUR TIME** It can often take a while to find the right pose to suit the clothing. Be patient, don't get frustrated with yourself, the product, or the model. Movements, such as a runway stride, can add dynamism. Furniture and props can provide pose inspiration and improve your overall set design. Change things up until it feels right.

# POSING WITH ACCESSORIES

Accessories can be difficult to shoot, especially if they are expected to be seen in a full-length shot. Note important items beforehand and include them as much as possible. Again, a good stylist will help you, but the more you learn about every aspect of the industry the more you can help each other. Before you begin, make sure that the model knows which items must be visible. They can easily forget when they start to move freely, so if this happens, stop and politely remind them—there is no point in wasting shots.

Let's start at the top and work our way down. Hats, headpieces, hairpins, hoods, headbands, bows, and bandanas can easily disappear at certain angles or from a distance. Hair is important, as depending on the style it can compliment or conceal an item, but don't forget that styling changes can affect your shoot time. If you are going to shoot a look with and without a headpiece, start without the piece—a finely coiffed hairstyle can be ruined by wearing a hat for just a few frames.

Unless you are specifically shooting sunglasses, be careful of including them as the model's face is hidden, which is a makeup artist's worst nightmare. They can save you at a sunny location where it's so bright the model's eyes are watering, but if they are used in every shot they can hide the model you cast completely. Instead, maybe let the model hold them, use the motion of them taking them on and off, or put them in a shirt pocket so that they are still "featured," albeit minimally. Again, watch the model's hair, especially if they are taking the glasses on and off, and also pay attention to the reflection in the lenses.

Earrings need to be photographed with a profile shot, so make sure you take a profile shot when casting. For options, work a three-quarter view and ask the model to adjust their eye-line, from ceiling to floor. If the image lacks life, ask the model to slowly sweep their hair behind the ear—this works particularly well if you need to show off a ring at the same time.

Anything that is worn around the neck has an individual hanging length that must work with the outfit—tops can be distracting or necklines too high to allow the item to fall correctly. Scarves can be worn many ways, so make sure you are shooting them the way the client wants.

Showcase a belt by tucking shirts in or asking the model to put their hands in their pockets. Gloves can be taken on and off, or simply held. Watch out for

### NAILED IT!

Manicurists are employed on sets to take care of a model's nails, fingers, and toes—you can't shoot jewelry or shoes with a dodgy nail job! Sometimes clients will ask models to get a manicure/pedicure before a shoot and invoice the cost.

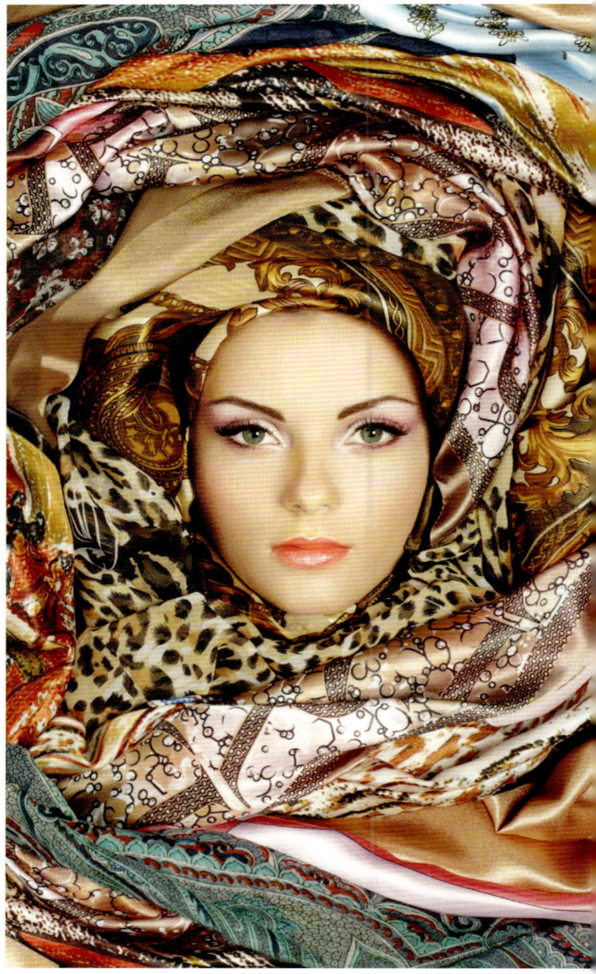

bracelets, as they can move around a lot, especially if a model lifts their arms. As they move they can twist and flip over, hiding a design or getting stuck awkwardly half way up the arm. If you are shooting a particular side, ask the model to move the bracelet to the visible wrist. This applies to rings too.

Suspenders, nylons, and hold ups—as with socks and shoes in lengthier outfits—sometimes need a skirt lift or wider stance to show. With maxi dresses a walking stride can help. A lot of shoes are borrowed and can't be used in certain locations—often they must be taped on the soles which you should definitely avoid showing. However, shoes really can make an outfit and you should try to cover the side and top views. Remember that models are miserable in ill-fitting shoes, though, so if necessary ask them to bring a selection. At least you know they will fit.

**TIP BAG LADY**

A handbag can make or break an outfit. Work bags at different heights on the arm and shoulder—they can also be swung or placed independently from a model. Bags are often stuffed to appear full, but watch for logos and clasps that need to be shown (or hidden).

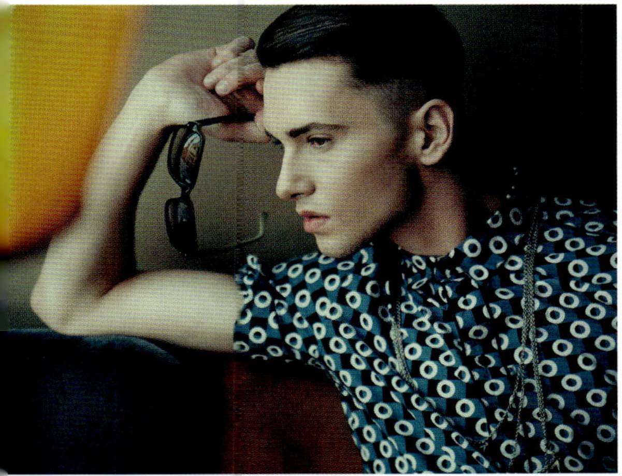

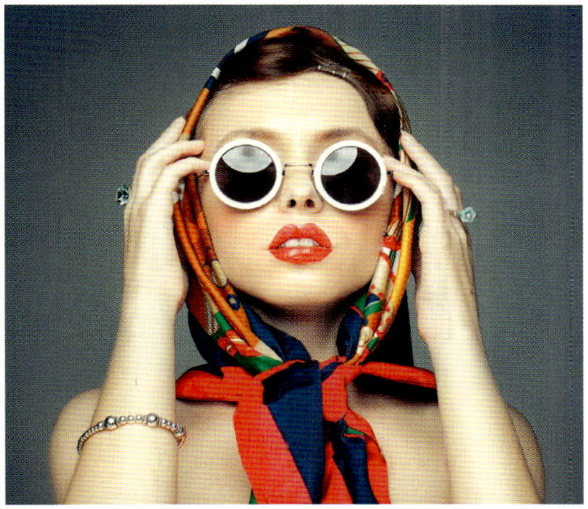

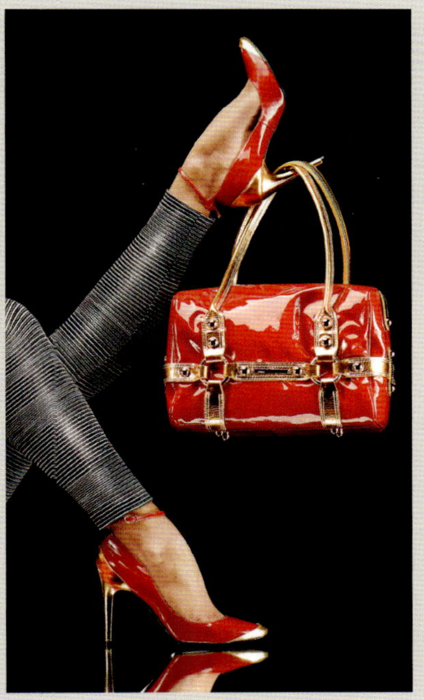

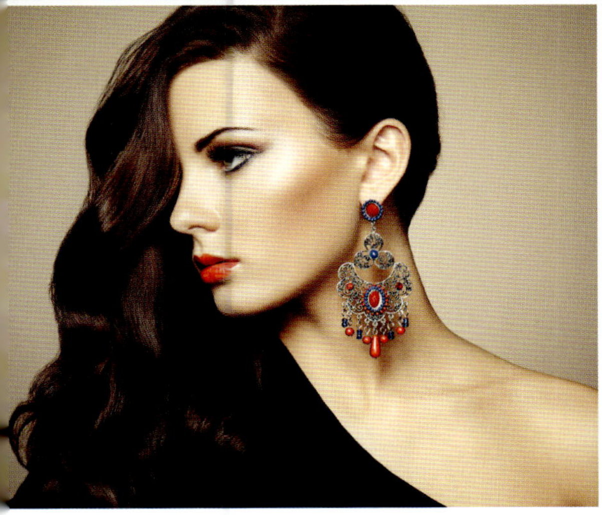

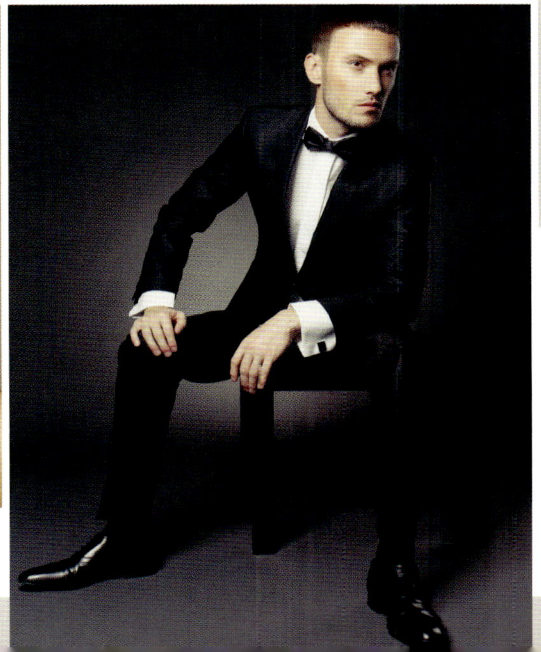

LEFT & OPPOSITE: **HIGH IMPACT**
Photographers often forget about accessories and the impact they can have. At times you will be required to highlight a pair of earrings or sunglasses, do what you can to pull focus. Position your shot and the model accordingly. Hand and head poses are usually important in these situations.

# STYLING FOR BEGINNERS

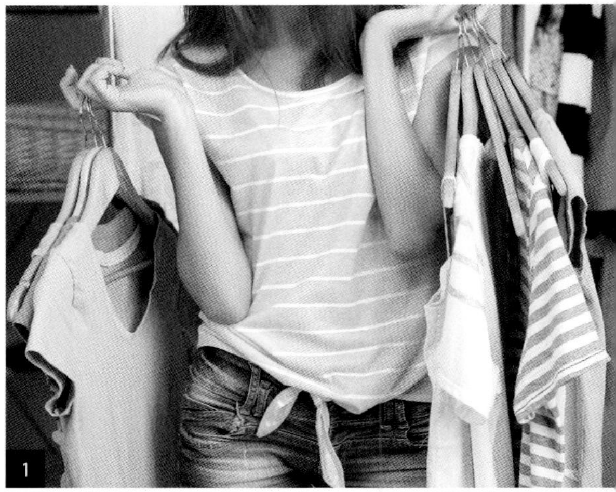
1

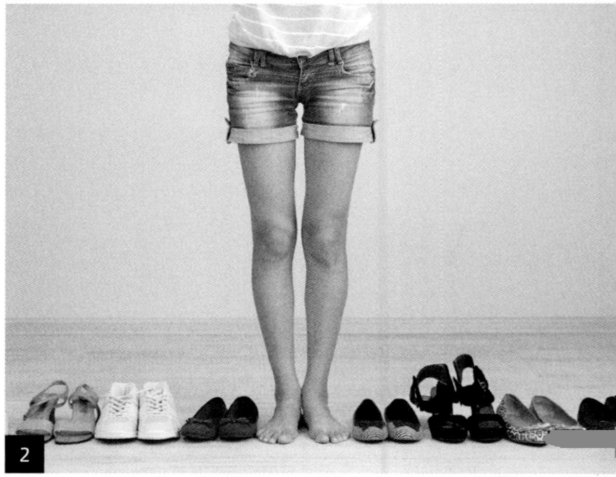
2

**WHEN YOU ARE SHOOTING tests a stylist can often be the hardest team member to find. Designers and stores rarely hand over clothes to anyone who is unestablished, so many photographers shooting tests include makeup and hair, but ask the models to bring their own clothing. This can work in your favor or have disastrous results. All models dress differently, so some will turn up with a wild and wacky wardrobe, while others will have barely any shootable items.**

If you have no idea what the model is bringing you are going to have to find inspiration on the spot. If they turn up with nothing at all, it might be time to think of an impromptu makeup story. Be flexible and choose a space that could work with a variety of outfits. Keep it raw and natural without complication. If the outfit really isn't working, concentrate on the model's face and mid-range shots rather than shooting full length.

To make life easier, you could include a list of items the model could bring on the Call Sheet. Don't make it too specific, for example don't say, "I need the model to bring floral printed, three quarter length, capri pants," as not many people have those, but "please bring a range of pants (prints if possible), jeans, skirts and any floral items you may own," would be a reasonable request. Usually a list would include denims, plain solid tanks and tees, shorts, a jacket, swimwear, and nice undergarments. Also include a selection of shoes, pumps, and sneakers, and possibly accessories too, such as jewelry, gloves, or tights. All of these are staples that people generally have in their wardrobe. Ask them to bring two dresses, or suits, but don't ask for everything they own, especially if you live in a city where models generally catch the subway.

### TIP FASHION SLANG

Be aware that foreign models may not understand the fashion terms from your home country. As a Brit working in America I had to learn that "trainers" are "sneakers," there are "pants" not "trousers," a "waistcoat" is a "vest," and "pumps" are high heels, not running shoes.

Keep it simple. Think about the number of shots you're aiming for and whether any will be close-ups. Maybe you will only need to put together three or four outfits? Models can get embarrassed over the stuff they own, and many won't have their full wardrobes with them as they are often traveling. If a model turns up with a suitcase, take some time to go through it—they probably spent a lot of time deciding what to bring. Models get attached to clothing and they might really love something that won't shoot well. People are sensitive, so if someone looks like they are getting upset, shoot a few

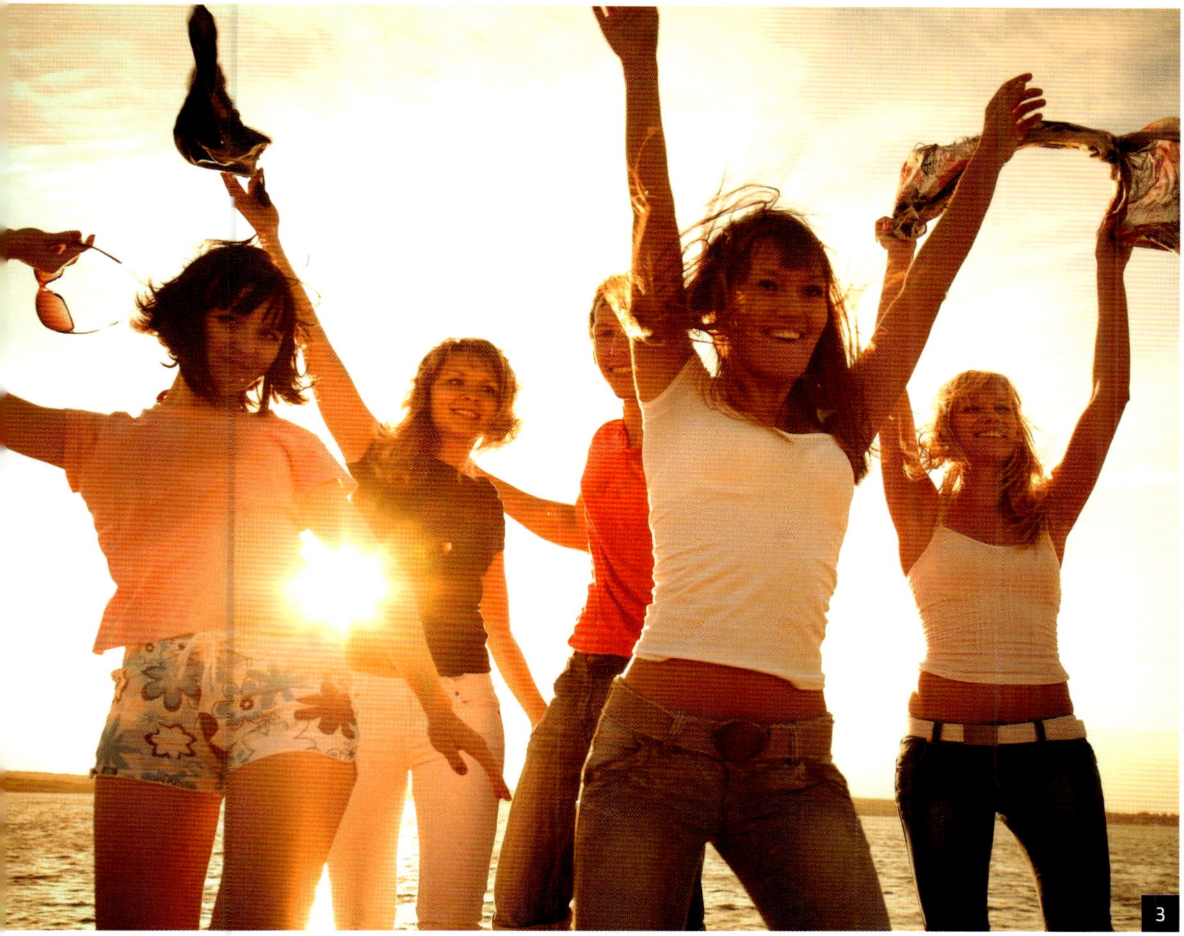
3

**1, 2: CLOSET SPACE**
Whether your model is bringing clothes or you are working with a stylist it can be important to remember you will need some space to look at outfits and hang important items. Consider purchasing a portable clothing rack and hangers.

**3, 4: LESS IS MORE**
If your clothing requirements for models and stylists become too specific it can be off putting. If you make your requirements less limiting and allow people some freedom you could end up with a mixture that just works.

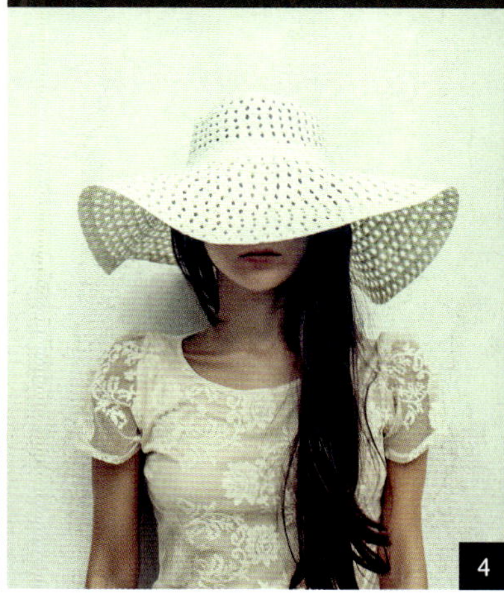
4

frames, go very close and only capture a corner, or make their pose more dramatic so it compliments an unusual item.

It can help for you to own a few pieces of wardrobe as backup. Go to thrift stores or borrow from friends, but make sure the models knows if a garment is precious so they don't smear makeup over your girlfriend's silk blouse. Buy a range of jeans in various sizes and styles—men's and women's. Denim never goes out of fashion, but not everyone is the same size so there's no need to only buy skinnies in a size zero.

Keep cuts simple and clean and buy items that a model can play with—wrap scarves, hoodies, and hats for example. In terms of styling the pieces, look at what models are wearing when you cast them, check out how fashion store mannequins are styled, and online street style blogs can help too. There's no need to spend a fortune, just sort through to find classic pieces that will suit most body shapes: simple tanks, white shirts, some shorts, and maybe a few pairs of heels in larger sizes. Make sure the clothing is freshly cleaned and, if necessary, you will be ready and able to style a model.

## WORK WITH WHAT YOU'VE GOT

Some models refuse to bring clothing to shoots. Maybe they don't have what you want, they forget, they've stayed over with a friend the night before, or they're just plain lazy. This is why backups are important. You may even end up shooting your own shirt and the shorts the model arrived in!

# 11

# SHOOTING SEXY

**THE IDEA OF SHOOTING GORGEOUS MODELS vamping in little to no clothing can be the reason many photographers are attracted to the industry. Whether this is good or bad is moot. What is important is that asking a young girl or boy to strip off and act in a sexual manner when you have only just met can be difficult and uncomfortable for everyone involved. In this chapter we talk about how to avoid creating awkward situations and promoting your professionalism both on set and at home. Focusing on the effect of gender behind the lens we also hear from some of America's more prevalent female photographers and discuss their work.**

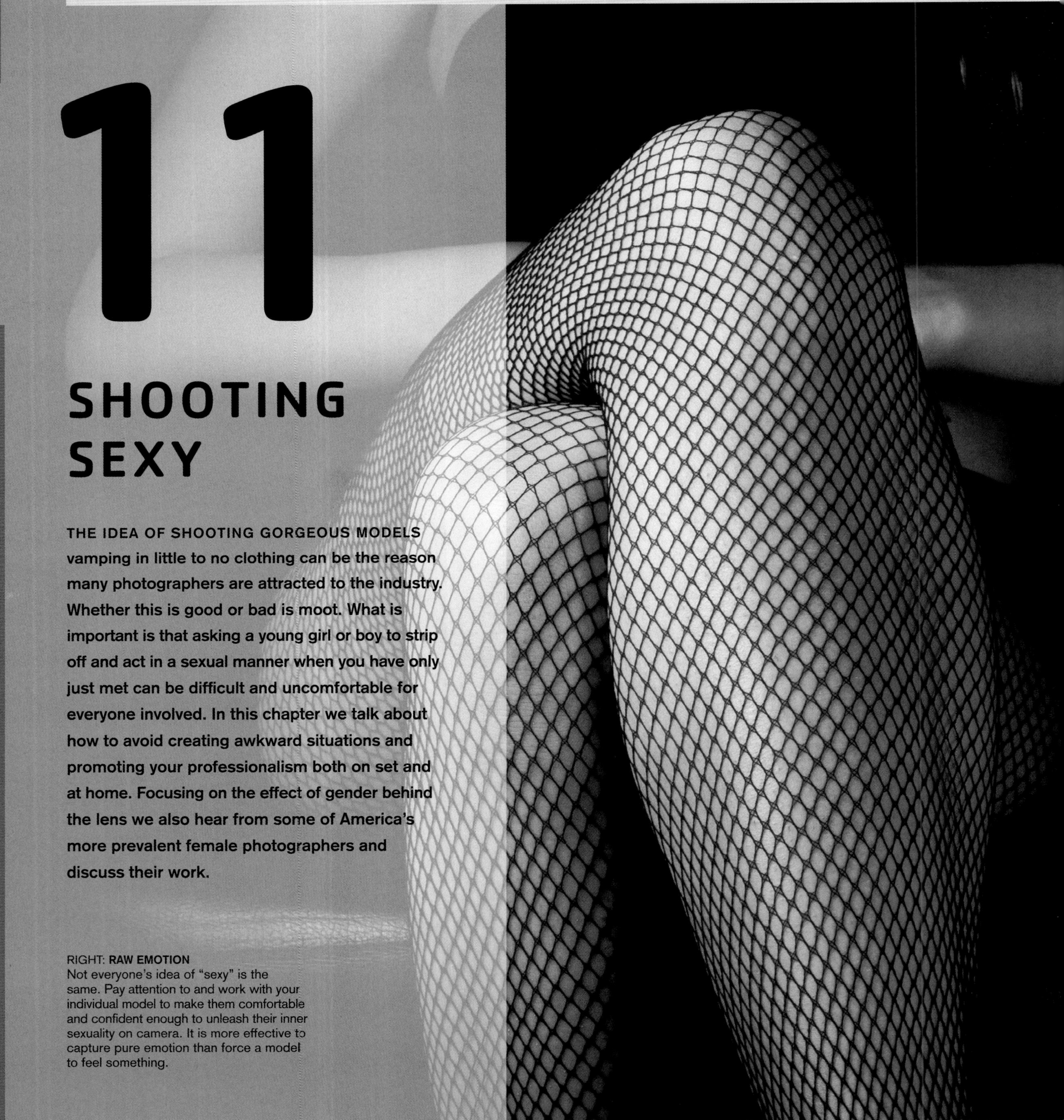

RIGHT: **RAW EMOTION**
Not everyone's idea of "sexy" is the same. Pay attention to and work with your individual model to make them comfortable and confident enough to unleash their inner sexuality on camera. It is more effective to capture pure emotion than force a model to feel something.

# STAY PROFESSIONAL

**A HIGH PERCENTAGE OF FASHION photography involves images of a sexual nature—after all, "sex sells." This encompasses a wide variety of emotional and visual stimulation, but it is important to understand the differences between high fashion and glamor. Certain poses and situations can cheapen a photograph, but it is possible to achieve "sexy" without vulgarity. To start with, be aware of your intended client base and audience—what you think is attractive might cause offense elsewhere and affect future bookings.**

When selecting a model for a sexy shoot, consider their age, experience, and body language when approached about posing provocatively in lingerie or swimwear. Older models can be easier to work with in these situations, as they are usually more aware of their bodies and feelings. A younger model may have never had a sexual experience, which can reveal itself through their poses and expressions.

Be careful when photographing models that look young, no matter their age—you want to avoid getting noticed for the wrong reasons. As with every shoot, your model might be a veteran or a newbie, but their experience level may not matter depending on their personality. Check portfolios for previous work of a similar nature, as some models will give off a natural and hypnotizing sense of self-confidence and personal freedom that just works for these kinds of jobs. Remember, it is not always the model with the "perfect" figure.

On the day, consider the model's needs. Think about how you appear to them. Shooting alone can be intimidating, and you should never ask anyone to do anything that makes them uncomfortable. Talk beforehand, provide mood boards, set any necessary boundaries, and do your best to promote your professionalism.

Be aware of low-self esteem and nerves in your model. Reassurance is particularly important, but keep it above board, never poke fun, be rude, or attempt to flirt in these situations. Invoke confidence.

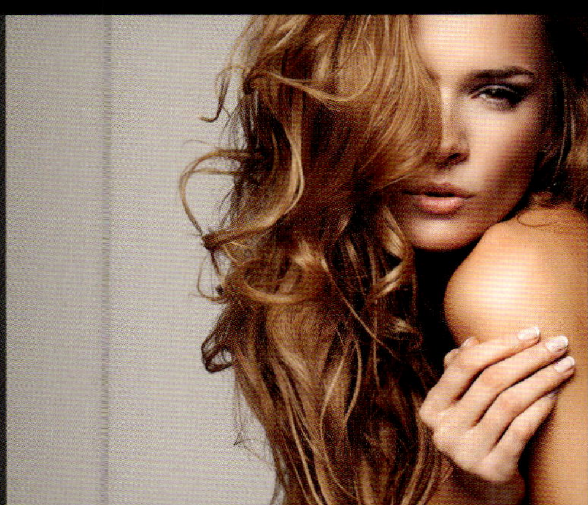

ABOVE: **POUT IT OUT**
Some models turn every shot into a sexual image. Watch out for permanent pouty "duck faces," mouths hanging open in every shot and lustful eyes.

RIGHT: **GIRL TALK**
The majority of models will turn up perfectly groomed and "tidy" to every shoot. However if you're shooting lingerie or swimwear think about giving a model prior warning. There may be issues with shaving or waxing that you might never realized existed.

FAR RIGHT: **MANSCAPING**
If you require a male model to take off their shirt check beforehand whether they wax or shave their chests and decide which look will best suit your shoot. Remember baby oil can be used to define muscle and for shine.

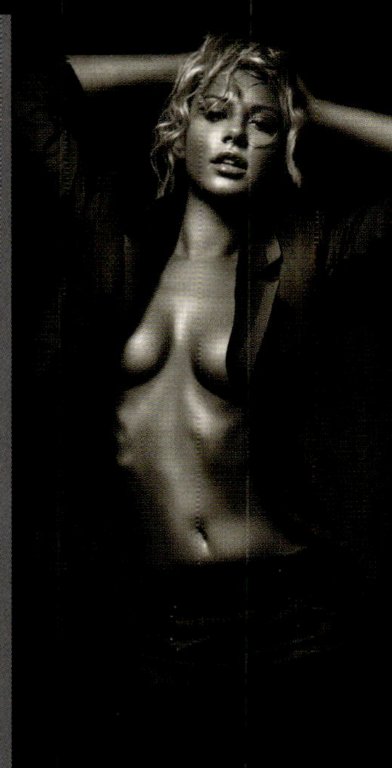

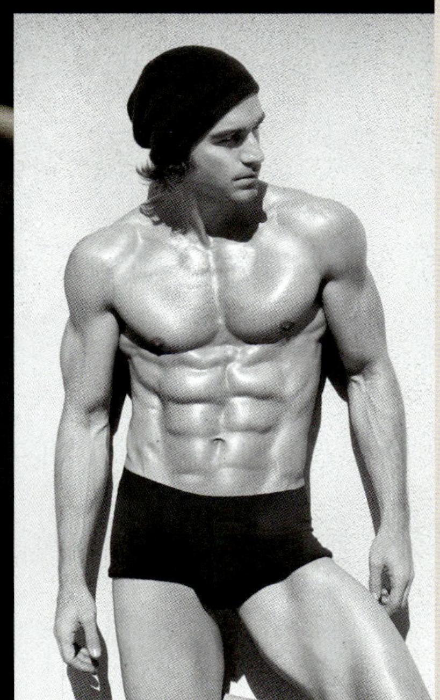

# REALLY, REALLY GOOD LOOKING

BEING TOLD YOU ARE SEXY can be a welcome compliment, but being told to act sexy can be a frightening proposition. Learn to direct scenes of this nature rather than just telling a model to "be sexier." Don't get embarrassed talking about body parts when posing a model, as they are an essential part of this process. Be confident and considerate to make your model feel comfortable—they are in a vulnerable position and are relying on you to justify what is happening at the time.

For female models, bust size can be a sensitive issue, but it is important when shooting lingerie and swimwear. The size of the cleavage will change the fit dramatically. Traditionally, models have smaller breasts, mainly to suit designer's needs, but as fashion and style have evolved over the years many of our top models now have ample bosoms.

If you are casting lingerie or swimwear of a certain size, stipulate the cup size on the brief. However, it should be noted that quite magnificent results can be achieved with the help of silicone breast enhancers placed outside the body, inside the bra, also lovingly referred to as "chicken fillets." If you find a model you love, but their chest doesn't meet the required measurements, bring them in for a fitting and ask your stylist to do their best. If you give people a chance you may be surprised at the results.

Male models shooting in their underwear have their own insecurities. Be respectful at all times and put yourself in their position. Just because they are male does not mean you are allowed to mock them—if you are uncomfortable, stop shooting particular jobs and ask yourself what your motives are.

Nipples can be another taboo subject, but they often need to be discussed openly in fashion circles. Models can have problems with their nipples being shown, even through semi-opaque clothing. Some girls refuse to take

### TIP COVER UP

Talk to your stylists and girlfriends about the latest developments in underwear. Sticky pads that sit over the nipple are now available, which flatten their imprint without the model having to wear a full brassiere with straps that can affect the lines of an outfit.

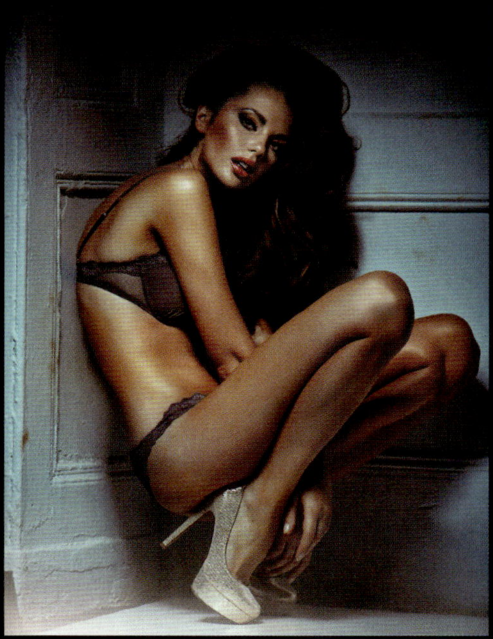

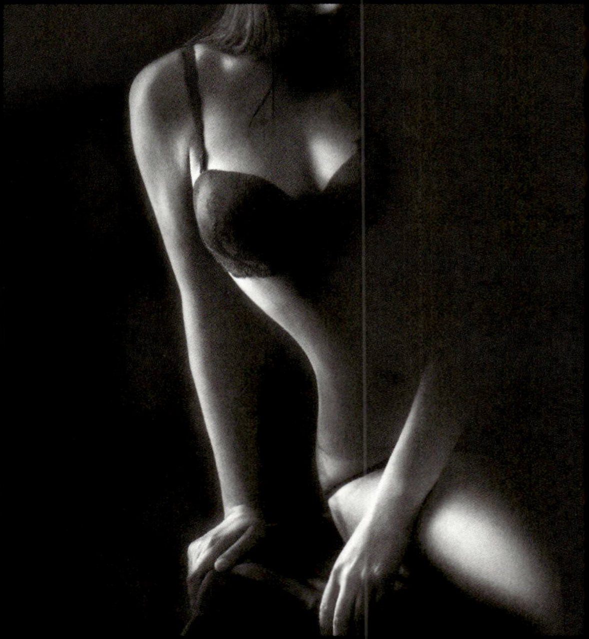

off their bras, no matter the effect on the outfit. Clients can actually be physically disgusted if you send them images where nipples are apparent underneath material because the model was cold. Know what your client wants. Some will love it if the model is happy to flash a nipple here and there. Communicate with your model and gauge the reaction of your clients using common sense to get as many of your images in print as possible.

Every professional female fashion model is taught to wear a flesh colored, seamless "g-string" to work, while most male models wear tight boxers or briefs. Many models will want to wear their "invisible" underwear underneath wardrobe underwear. This can look unsightly and cause problems in post production, but remember that you might be asking them to wear borrowed undergarments that could have been worn multiple times previous to the shoot. This is unhygienic and unacceptable. Unless it is obvious that the underwear is brand new, don't expect your model to strip off and wear it—would you?

If possible, make sure you discuss this with your stylist beforehand. Similarly, avoid asking models to try on underwear at a casting—if it's necessary, consider telling them to bring their own, or to wear swimwear underneath their clothes. If fit is particularly important, larger companies have been known to provide each model with underwear to try on, be photographed in, and keep afterward.

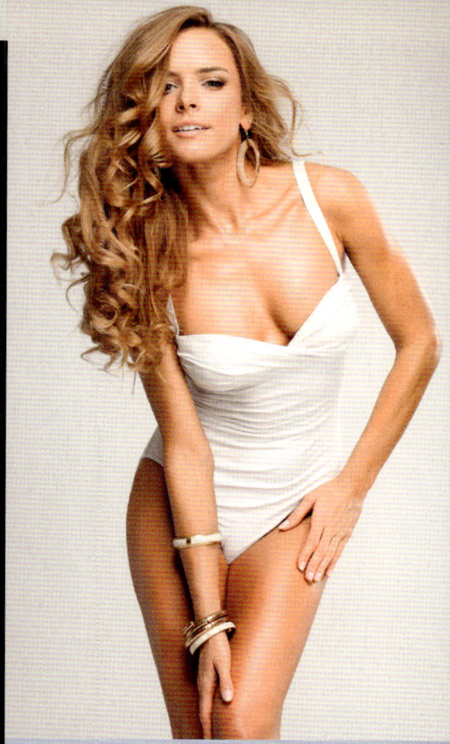

## LINGERIE VS. SWIMWEAR

Girls can have strict rules regarding lingerie and swimwear. It may seem as though a similar amount of skin is showing, but some models will refuse to model underwear as it is considered too revealing. At times like this you should abide by the model's wishes.

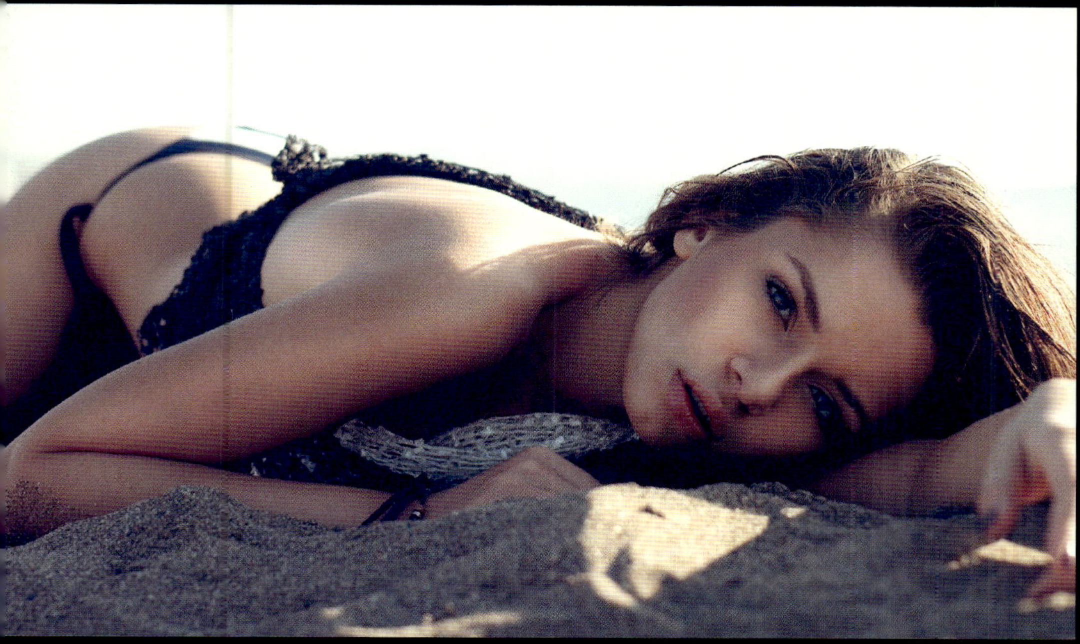

OPPOSITE : **LINGERIE**
Models generally have higher rates when shooting in lingerie, make sure you check with agencies about their policies and don't do something spontaneous and compromise your budget. Even if a model agrees, their agency rules the books.

LEFT & ABOVE: **SWIMWEAR**
Swimwear can often be associated with more commercial shoots but with recent advances in design and style, the results are not so limiting. Both one pieces and bikinis are now regularly used in high fashion and editorial work.

# MAINTAINING RELATIONSHIPS AT HOME

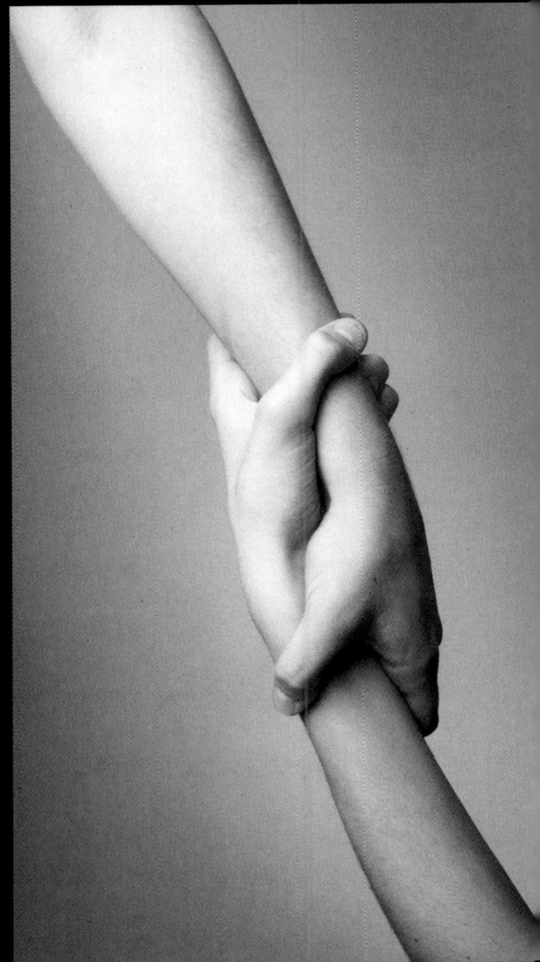

**PHOTOGRAPHERS, MODELS, makeup artists, in fact, anyone associated with the fashion industry, can develop issues with family, friends, and more often, partners. The time and effort required to succeed means that it can be a draining career, both physically and emotionally. There are unpredictable schedules, competitive pay rates, and demanding days with long hours to deal with, and you just can't always predict when you will get home. This lifestyle can be hard to explain to a long-term nine-to-fiver and difficult to maintain if it is doubled up within a household.**

### PHONE HOME

Issues may arise where the behavior you require of a model might affect their relationships at home. Maybe they have an overprotective partner or parent, or someone else they are anxious not to upset. Allow a model the time for a phone call if they have to kiss or interact provocatively with another model—it never hurts to ask.

On top of that, fashion can be an easily misunderstood industry. The images produced do not necessarily mimic the behind-the-scenes experience, but it is understandable how jealousy and mis-communication can affect a relationships if a concerned partner misconstrues the job. People get jealous, and as a photographer it can be hard to explain the instant relationships that spark while interacting all day with gorgeous members of the opposite sex.

You need chemistry to produce great shots, and there will be times when you have to go away for long periods with numerous models with whom you will be expected to dine in the evenings. Models will become your friends and you will talk about them when you get home.

They will be funny, intelligent, and beautiful, and you might hang out with them at parties and snap pictures of you together for social media sites. It won't always look like you are hard at work and you won't be able to deny that, for the most part, you are having fun. Try to communicate openly so these factors don't affect your partner or relationships with friends.

Avoid boasting, but don't be afraid to talk about what you do. It is usually better to explain than be vague or aloof. If you think it would be a positive step, invite your partner to set one day so they can witness first hand just how regimented, unsexy, and unglamorous the process can be. Reassure them.

Remember, it is not easy to date a photographer, so be considerate. You will be spending long hours away from your partner, and even longer hours on your computer staring at images of impossibly attractive humans. Ask yourself if you could cope if the

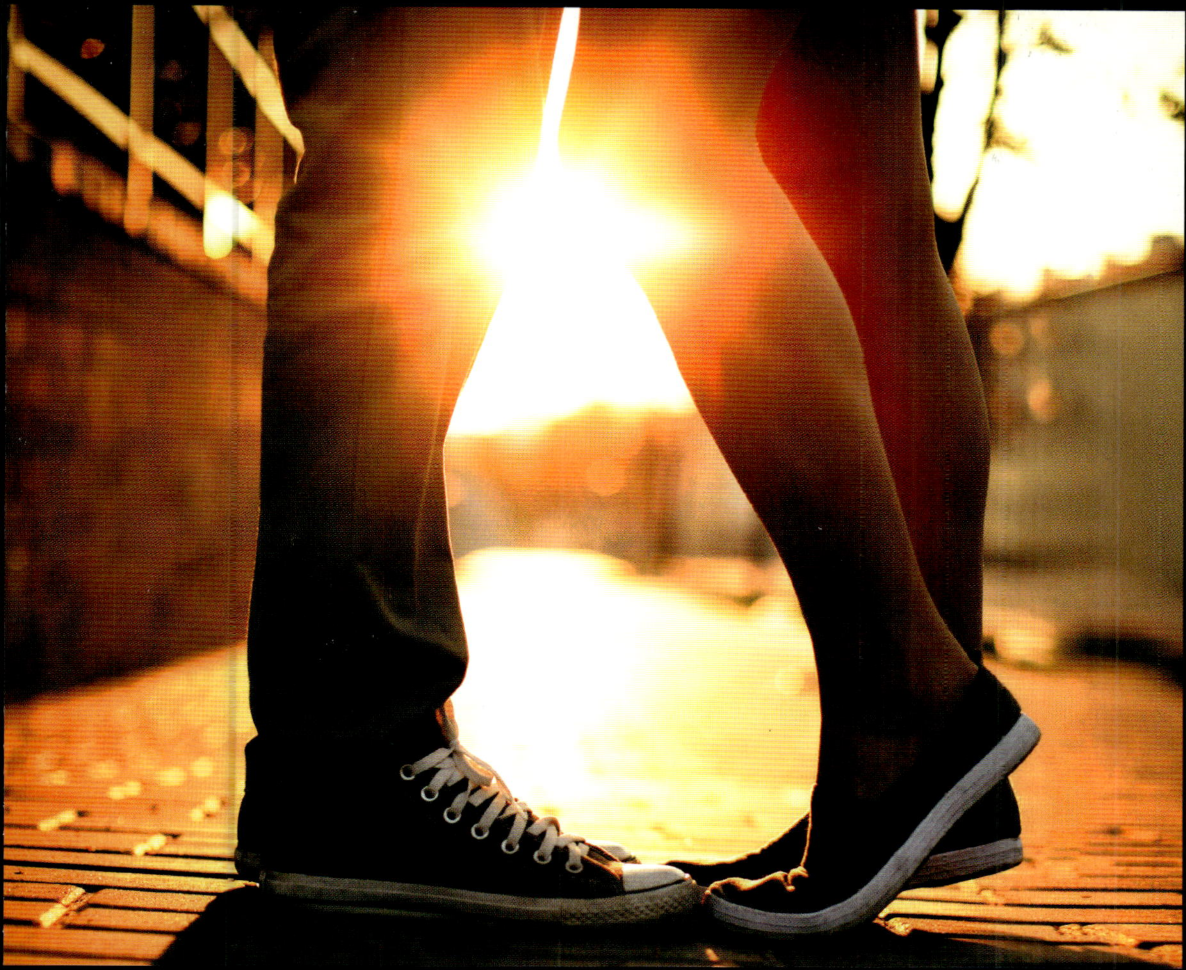

OPPOSITE: **STAY CONNECTED**
Like many people working in a creative industry, photographers can suffer from their family and loved ones believing fashion photography is not a "proper" or "real" job. Though difficult to understand, try to connect on whatever level possible. True support is hard to come by.,

LEFT & BELOW: **DO WHAT YOU LOVE**
Never let another person, even someone you love, stop you from doing what makes you happy. Whatever it takes, if you are on a path, you should not be held back by those that should be there to encourage you.

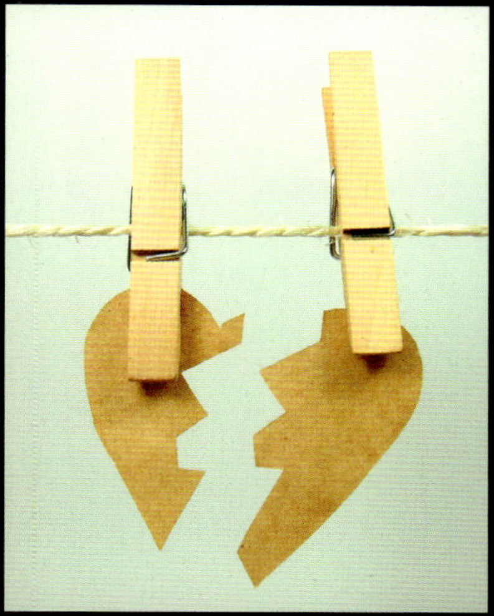

### TIP BE NICE

Whether you are single or in a relationship empathize with team members who are attached or have children. There are times they may have to leave early or cancel last minute if something important arises. Don't pander, but be nice, especially if you work together often.

situation was reversed and remember, if you date a model or another photographer, you should beware of your own green-eyed monster.

If you are changing your career path dramatically, people you love may suddenly have to change their day-to-day lives and some will find it harder to adapt than others. Try not to let your work affect your home life. Every relationship is different, but it always helps to be honest and let a person know that this might be a different way of life, but it is your passion and part of who you are—it is not a means of meeting people. The majority of fashion photographers I know are happily married. Many work as husband and wife teams, often as fellow photographers working side by side.

# THE GENDER EFFECT

**THE STEREOTYPE of "male photographer, female model," still exists, and as with most stereotypes, there is a certain truth to it. There are advantages and disadvantages to both genders working as photographers, but some of the most successful teams working in fashion today are all female, and women of all ages should feel encouraged to pick up a camera and start shooting, even if the industry is male dominated. Here are words on the subject from three prominent female photographers:**

## VIVIEN KILLILEA

To be honest, I think being female helps me shoot male models. I really do think that male models find it easier to open up when a female is photographing them. They can get their "sexy" on without being judged by another man! From an events standpoint I think it helps too. It's a male dominated industry and people tend to look twice when they see a girl holding a 10-pound camera. I shot New York fashion week and got to know the security guards—I said "hi" to them every morning and asked about their day. After the first two days they started giving me back-stage passes to the shows. My agency was happy about that too. I think it would be harder for a guy to pull moves like that with security.

## EMILIE ELIZABETH

The positives and negatives of being female behind the lens are tricky to explain. I've written several answers to this, some tactful and some downright sexist. The truth is, there's no easy way to answer this without acknowledging the fact that traditionally, men have been behind the camera and have shaped our ideals when it comes to beauty. I primarily shoot fashion, and I'm completely aware that the "male gaze" is still the standard. It's difficult to fake, but luckily female photographers such as Annie Leibovitz and Ellen von Unwerth have paved the way for women like me.

I really enjoy shooting women and several models have told me that they actually prefer working with a female photographer. I believe that being a woman has often made it easier to gain trust quickly with my subjects. Female models deal with uninvited attention coming from all directions on a pretty regular basis, so I think it's a relief for them to know that they can just focus on the job and have fun when they're with me.

As a woman I also have a genuine interest and understanding of the clothing. I know how it moves and the most flattering angle to shoot almost every silhouette because I've probably worn it myself. But most importantly I know how badly a model's feet hurt after running, jumping, and walking back and forth in sky-high heels for eight hours. I make sure she knows that I know because nothing's worse than blisters that go unappreciated!

There's still a lot of uncharted territory when it comes to female photographers in fashion, which means there's a great opportunity, challenge, and responsibility for any woman in the industry right now. I would love for female photographers to help abolish the stale clichés seen in every fashion magazine and instead, provide a unique perspective that other women can genuinely relate to."

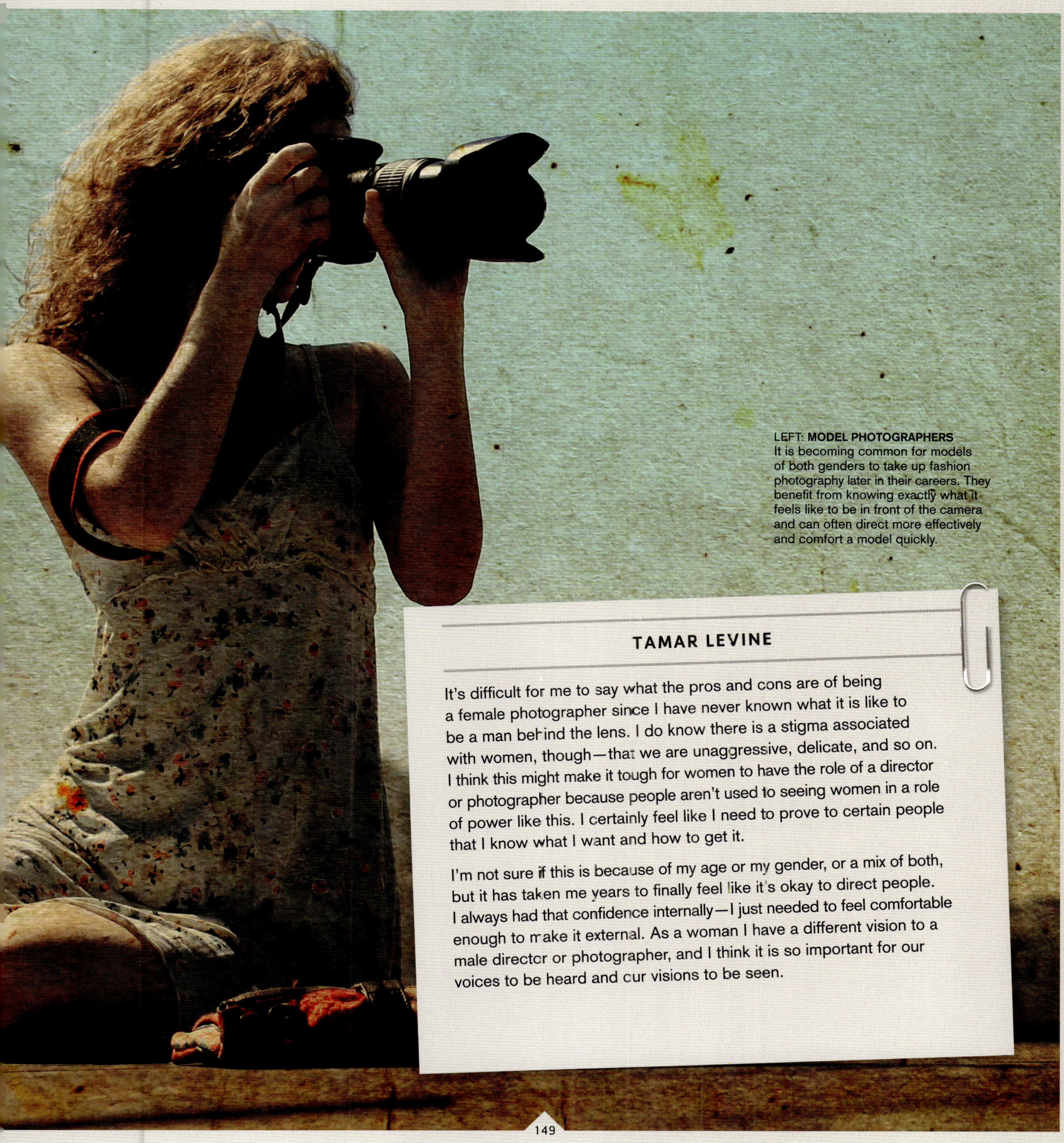

LEFT: **MODEL PHOTOGRAPHERS**
It is becoming common for models of both genders to take up fashion photography later in their careers. They benefit from knowing exactly what it feels like to be in front of the camera and can often direct more effectively and comfort a model quickly.

## TAMAR LEVINE

It's difficult for me to say what the pros and cons are of being a female photographer since I have never known what it is like to be a man behind the lens. I do know there is a stigma associated with women, though—that we are unaggressive, delicate, and so on. I think this might make it tough for women to have the role of a director or photographer because people aren't used to seeing women in a role of power like this. I certainly feel like I need to prove to certain people that I know what I want and how to get it.

I'm not sure if this is because of my age or my gender, or a mix of both, but it has taken me years to finally feel like it's okay to direct people. I always had that confidence internally—I just needed to feel comfortable enough to make it external. As a woman I have a different vision to a male director or photographer, and I think it is so important for our voices to be heard and our visions to be seen.

# 12

# FINISHING UP

**THE END OF A SHOOT can be the most important time for a photographer. Not only must you be sure that you've covered exactly what you need, but you must keep the energy up, even after a long day, until the final click. In this chapter we discuss how best to achieve this, as well as explaining how crucial the time after a shoot is completed can be to your career.**

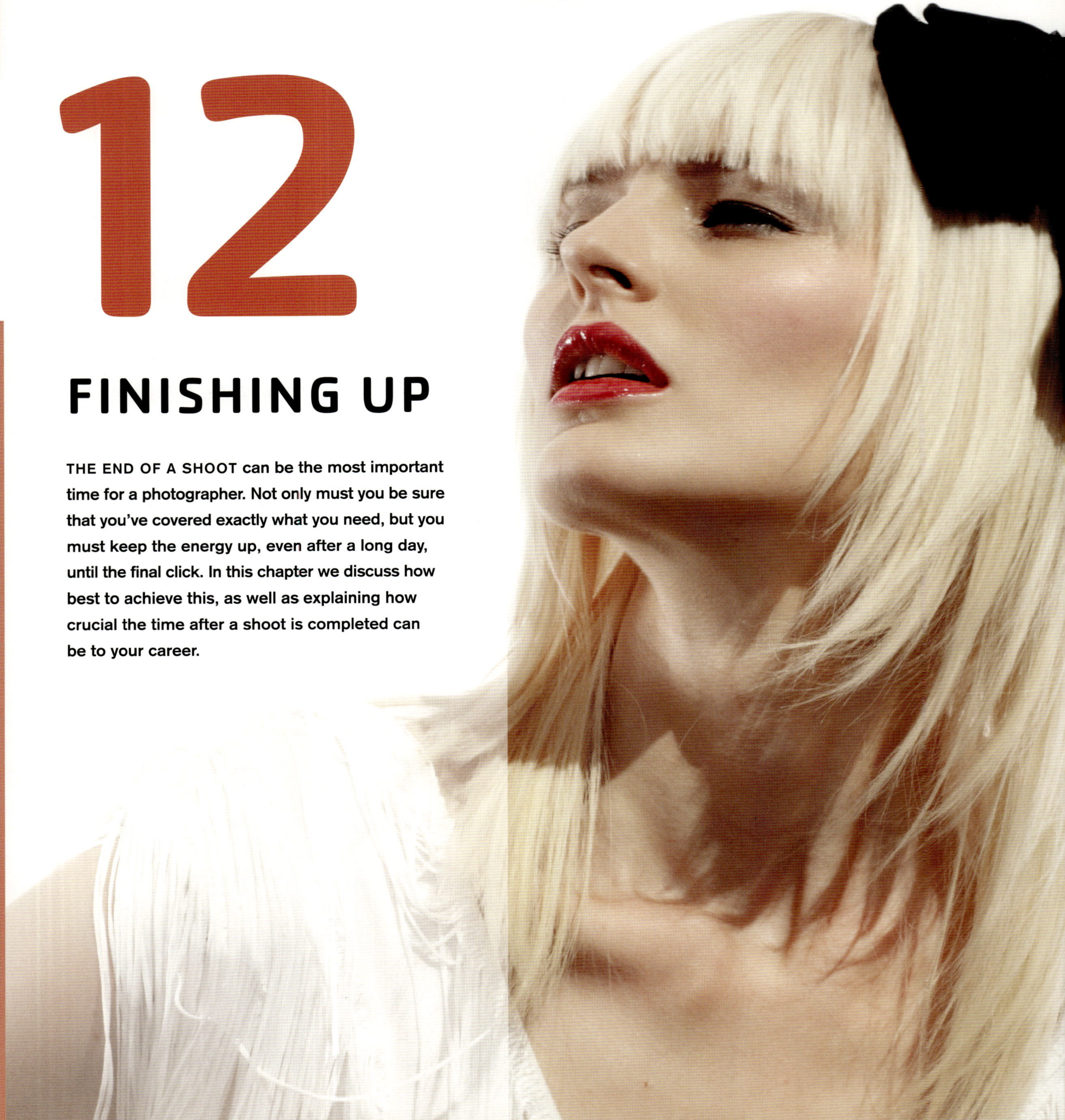

# THE FINAL CLICK

**AT SOME POINT IN EVERY SHOOT there is going to be a lull in energy, usually right after lunch or toward the end of the day. Food makes people sleepy, so order coffees after meals and provide sweet snacks and energy drinks to raise depleted blood sugar levels. Pump up music with a beat and don't let slow, melancholy tunes bring down the atmosphere in a room. Tiredness shows in pictures: models will lack energy and spirit when posing, and can become clumsy and are more likely to injure themselves. Monitor your crew when working long days, as waiting around can make people tired. Try not to overwork anyone beyond their limits and combat any signs of flailing as best you can.**

It doesn't have to be like this. Be clear on the length of the shoot, have lots of breaks, include your models and team in the creative decisions and show interest in them. Banish negativity if at all possible! One way of making sure the shoot doesn't just fade out is to schedule a fun, high-energy session toward the end of the day. As long as everyone is fed and watered well, then why not go out with a bang! Turn the music up and let the model go wild! That way, the session could end on a real high note and lots of fun that would leave a lasting impression.

Perhaps break out the wind machine and get some hair blowing. Or get the model on a swing, or trying a kiddie's bicycle for size! You could get some great shots too—far better than images of tired models just waiting for the time to go home!

Sometimes, though, you need to make quick, realistic decisions at the end of the day, especially if things start to overrun. You might have to cut a shot to avoid cramming everything into the last few minutes when everybody just wants to go home. Other times the day will be shorter than you expected. Clients may worry that a faster shoot lacks quality, so gauge the situation, but don't be afraid to call it if you have it. Make sure you have covered everything, it has transferred and downloaded correctly, and everything has been noted that needs to be noted.

You never want to call a model back to set when they've already smeared off their makeup and ruined their hair, so don't let anyone leave set until you have checked and re-checked.

RIGHT: **CLOSE-UPS**
It can be visibly noticeable when a model is fatigued. Try to take any important close-ups nearer the beginning of the shoot or just after lunch when the makeup will be fresh, yet had time to settle.

FAR RIGHT: **TIRED MODELS**
Models tire more quickly if they are cold, hungry, or dehydrated, which can be a lot of the time. Make sure to provide blankets or bring an extra coat, especially if you're shooting outside, and keep everyone hydrated and fed regularly.

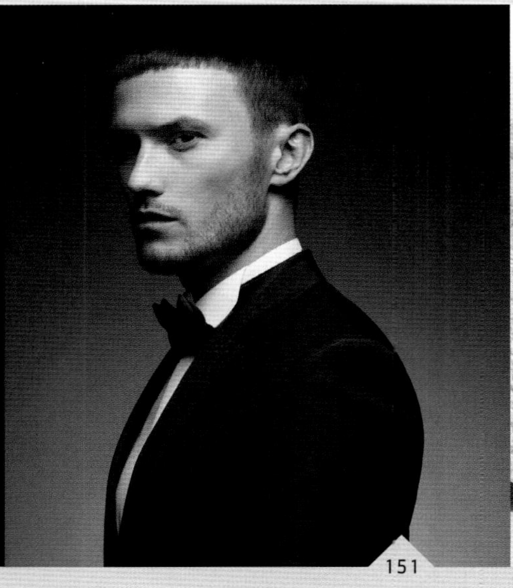

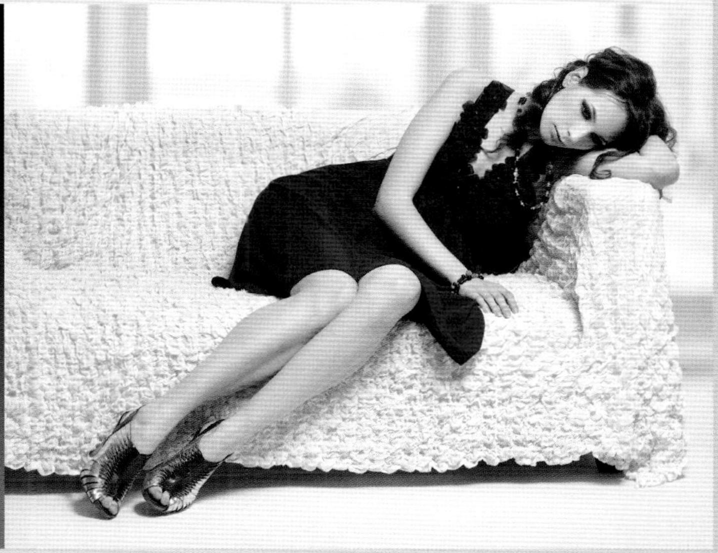

# KEEPING ENERGY UP

**THERE'S NO TWO WAYS ABOUT IT, a long photo shoot is tiring for everybody involved, especially full-day shoots which, more often than not, run far longer than a normal working day. Photographers love to go on location and use natural light, and for many that can mean an early start and late finish. The light in the middle part of the day is often the most harsh and hardest to use, but the low light in the morning and again in the evening has a wonderful quality and direction that artificial lights just can't get close to.**

Often the light of pre-dawn is used, as it can be so pure and soft, but it is also early! 3am call times are not unheard of as models must get to the location, have their hair and makeup done, and then be on set at 5am. They are then expected to turn into stunning, serene creatures rather than ones that would rather still be in their bed.

Similarly, at the other end of the day the light can be glorious and warm as the sun sets. Then, as it moves into twilight, there's a whole world of opportunities for the talented and creative photographer. But if you try to get a model and a creative team to do this—an early start plus a very late finish—you're not going to get the best results. People will be tired and very soon, as the energy levels drop, so does the quality of the shots. You may also find it tough to book models and other creatives for shoots in future if you develop a reputation for punishing shooting schedules.

Even if you are just working in the confines of a studio, a full day of shooting can be a very long day. It's not just the time you are there, but also the time you have to physically do things, such as moving lights or holding heavy cameras. The most important is concentration—while taking photos may look like a fun thing to do, when you are mentally juggling all the technical issues, as well as trying to be creative and inspire your team, it is a very grueling day. Often, the shots start out well and peter out towards the end of the day as everyone becomes more and more tired or burned out.

People do their best work when they are motivated and engaged, not tired and hungry, so it's essential when planning a shoot that people's natural needs are taken care of. Make sure you have lots of breaks, lots of fresh

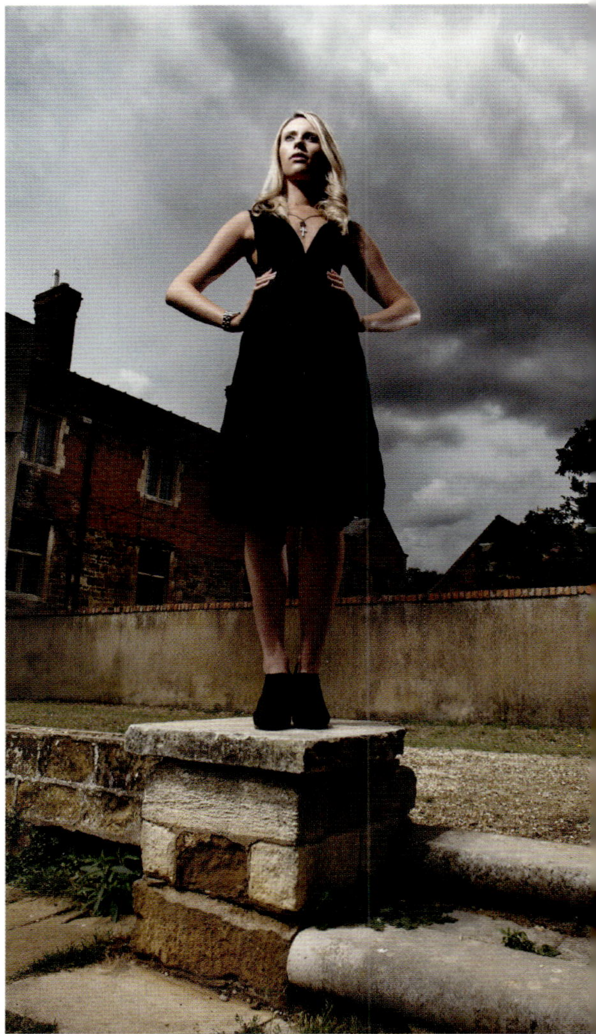

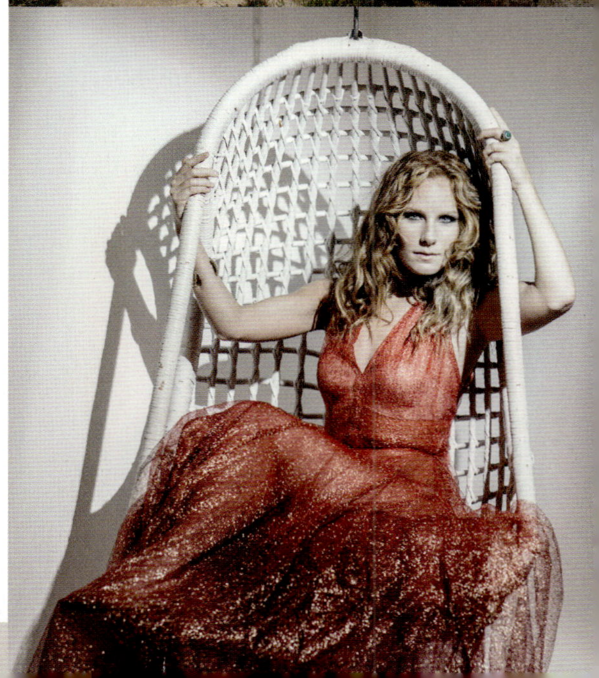

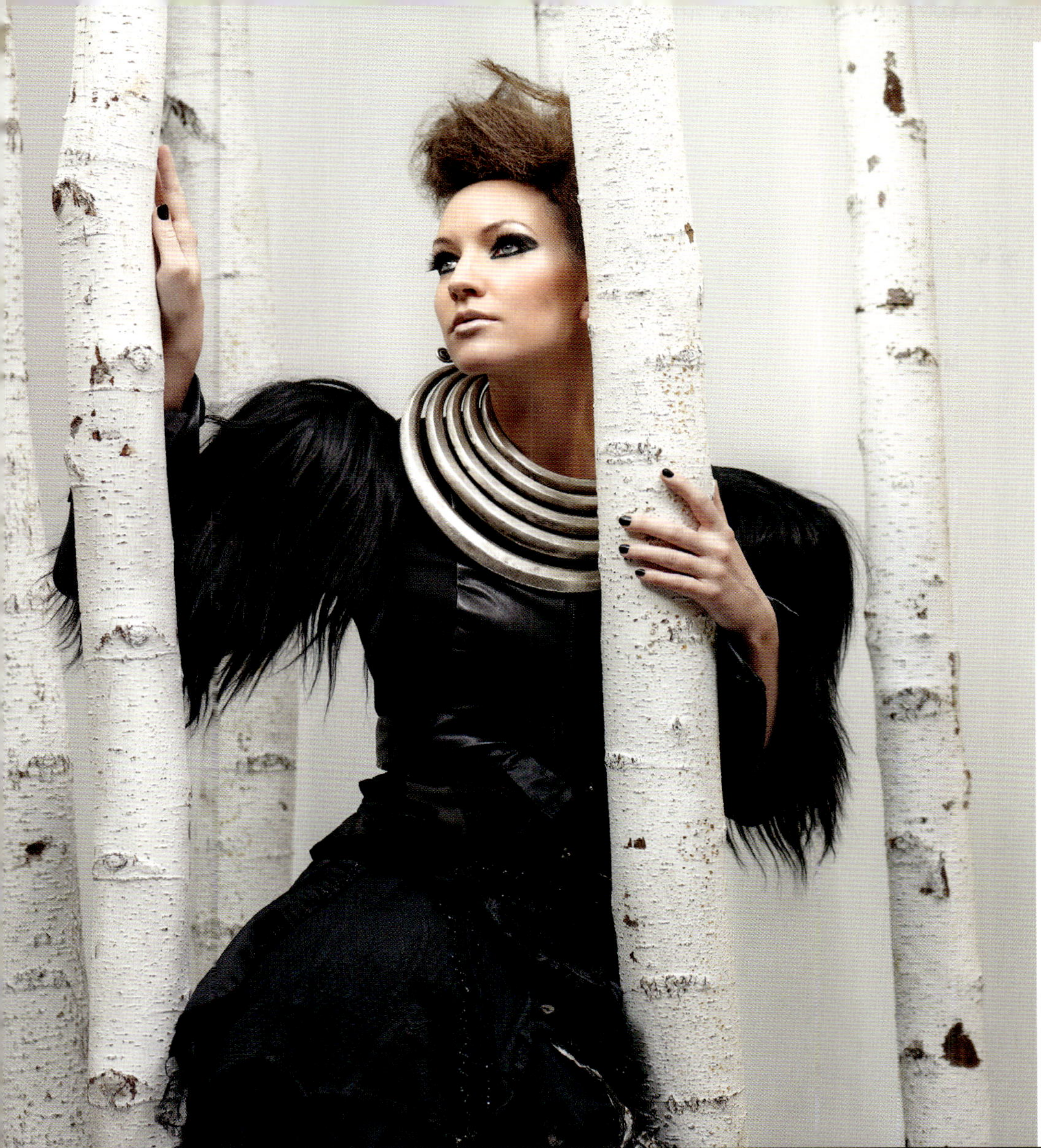



food, and a mix of hot and cold drinks. Somewhere pleasant to sit for a few minutes, away from the set, is ideal as it gives everyone a break. A break for lunch is essential, to refuel both body and mind, and this is also a great time to get to know your model better, and perhaps talk through ideas. To feel looked after like this is important, and it's the only way a photographer can get the best out of their models and team until the end of the shoot. If it's a relentless, fun-less slog, with lots of time pressure and few breaks, nobody is having a fun time, and it will show.

It's also very important to be clear on the working hours. Nobody likes to be kept for longer than they were expecting. It's not conducive to a great shots, especially toward the end of the session when tempers can fray.

OPPOSITE TOP:
**BABY IT'S COLD OUTSIDE**
A gray and overcast day can mean temperatures aren't too high, yet the model may still be asked to wear a lightweight, flimsy dress. Be aware that an uncomfortable model won't be giving the best results.

LEFT: **HANGING AROUND**
Swinging around in a comfortable chair may look like fun, but after lots of clothing changes and shots during a long shoot, it's easy for a model to get tired and lose focus.

ABOVE:
**KEEP THE MODEL HAPPY**
If the shoot is a set built in a studio under constant light like this shot, then the lighting can get hot and a model may end up glaring into a light for a long time. Always consider the model's safety and comfort.

RIGHT: **IT'S NOT ALL GLAMOUR**
A wind machine is used to make a model's hair blow and give a more dramatic shoot. But it blows dust into the eyes and can be uncomfortable as well as a bit chilly, especially with not many clothes on! Use it sparingly and make sure the model has breaks.

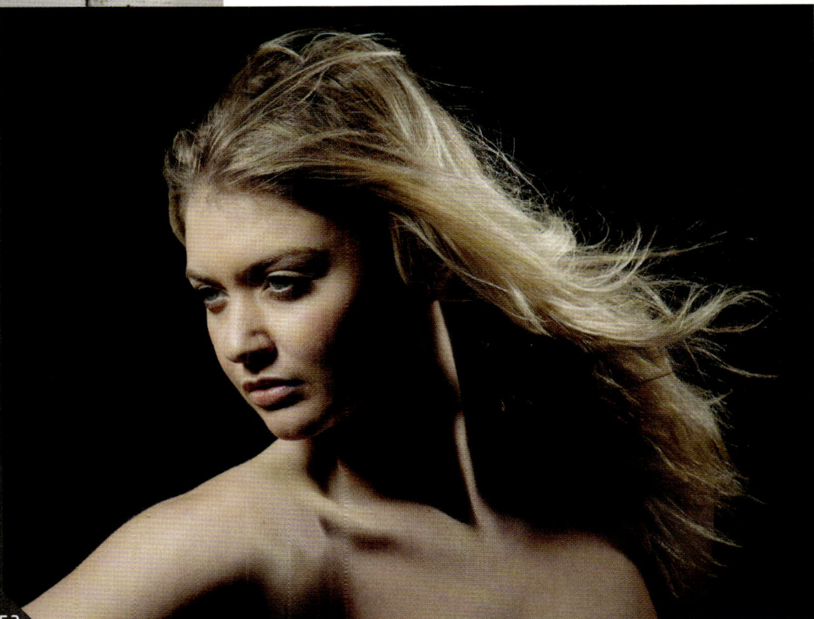

## KEEPING IN CONTACT:
# THANKING AND CREDITING

**ONCE THE DAY OF THE SHOOT is over, make sure you thank everyone involved in person. Small gestures can leave an impression. Afterward, send out short "thank you" notes via email or social media to your model, team, client, and if you went through an agency, to the booker you dealt with. Give feedback, but keep it light and positive unless a serious issue came up. It is common courtesy, but easily forgotten when you have other shoots to set-up, retouching to take care of, and deadlines looming.**

It is important to stay on top of your schedule. The most detrimental thing you can do to your career is take on too much and fail to produce high quality images on time. Be sure to send the finished images to any clients and all members of the crew, if necessary, and if you have the time available ask if anyone would like to make their own selects. However, be careful not to promise what you can't deliver. If you have personal contact with the model it is good to send them copies too, but be sure to check that their agency also received the images. Listen to feedback and learn from it, but remember that model bookers can be curt if they are busy. Try not to take it personally, though—the best indication that your work is appreciated is by repeat bookings.

If your shoot will appear in a publication or be showcased online it is crucial that you credit all those involved, correctly. Try not to forget anyone, even on your social media profiles, as people hold grudges. Check spelling and quote up-to-date representation information. Requirements differ with publication and medium, especially with specifics such as clothing, jewelry, and location credits. Make sure you check any guidelines and follow them accordingly.

### CREDITING THE TEAM

If shooting models is really a people-based business, then keeping in contact with the agency, stylists, or others you have used is even more about interpersonal skills! It's vital you keep in contact with the agency or team, not only to make them feel appreciated, but also to remind them you are there and of your skills. They often have a lot of other photographers vying to get involved, so make sure you are the one they remember for all the right reasons.

First, and most important, is to get pictures to anybody you have promised to let have them in a speedy manner. Nobody expects finished work overnight, but a few weeks or so would be seen as being timely. Make sure the images are ready to be used, rather than unprocessed Raw files—you should never let any unfinished shots out, as it can easily ruin your reputation.

Of course, it's important that you have total clarity and agreement before the shoot starts on who gets pictures, which pictures they get, and what they can and can't be used for. And also when they can be used. Without explicit instructions, models have a habit of instantly sharing any new photos on the Facebook page or Model Mayhem profile without a second thought. Get everything down in writing and stick to it.

When the shots do go out, make sure the team is credited properly, especially if it's been a test or there has not been any payment made. A good credit list includes the model's name and her agency, plus the stylist, hair, and makeup artists, assistants, clothes, and jewelry designers, and even the location. But don't leave these credits to chance—not everyone may want to be credited, so always check beforehand. Check all spellings, too.

If you are sharing the photos digitally, not only include the name of the person involved but also a link to their website or listing page (if they want it). It's also good practice to add these credits to the metadata on your photos, so that it is embedded into the image data itself. In a world where tracing the author or content of a photo can be problematic, it could be of great benefit to everyone involved.

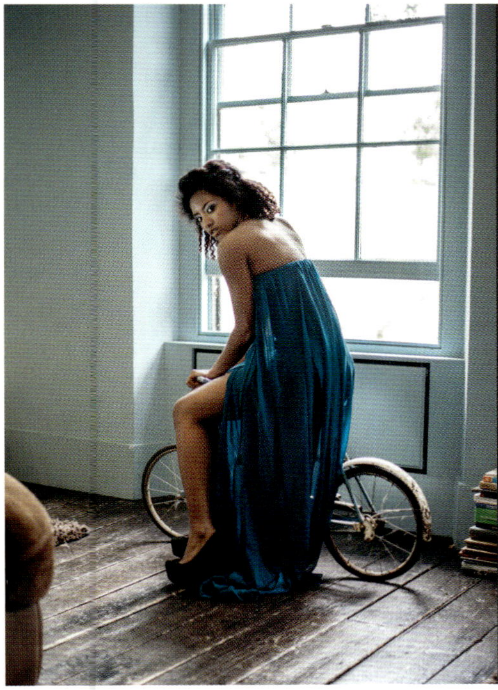

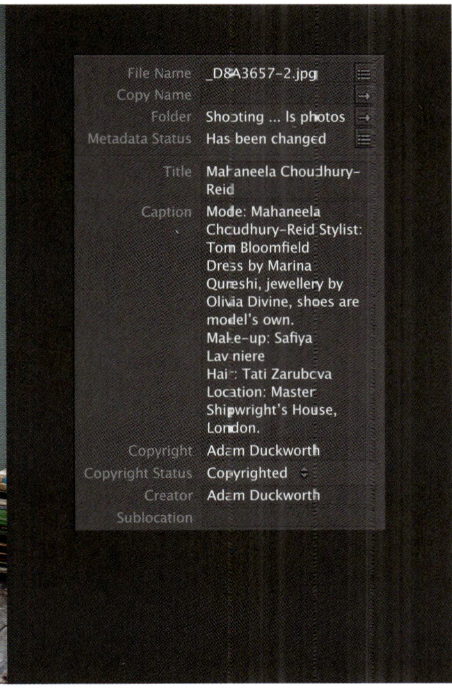


### EXAMPLE OF A GOOD CREDIT

**Model:** Mahaneela Choudhury-Reid

**Photographer:** Adam Duckworth

**Stylist:** Tom Bloomfield

**Dress:** Marina Qureshi

**Jewelry:** Olivia Divine

**Shoes:** Model's own.

**Makeup:** Safiya Laviniere

**Hair:** Tati Zarubova

**Location:** Master Shipwright's House, London.

### PREMATURE RELEASE

There can be serious rules regarding the timely release of images. If you email out your images, make sure you specify whether there are any restrictions on publication, such as not uploading them to the internet until the shoot runs. When it is time, people will crop and add filters to your pictures, try not to take offense as everyone likes to have an opinion.

### EXAMPLES OF A BAD CREDIT

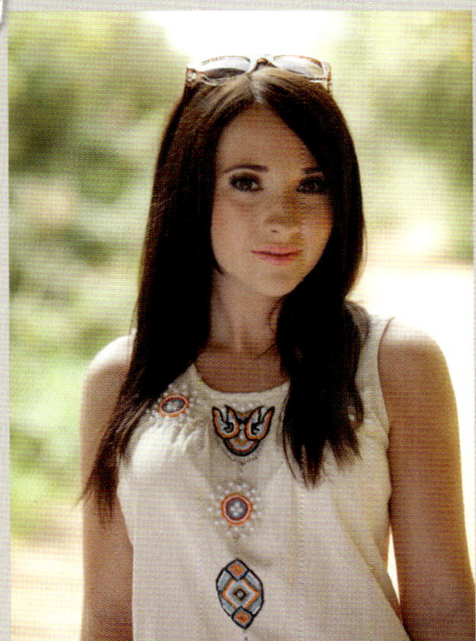

**Model:** Tamrin Leanda

**Photographer:** Adam Duckworth

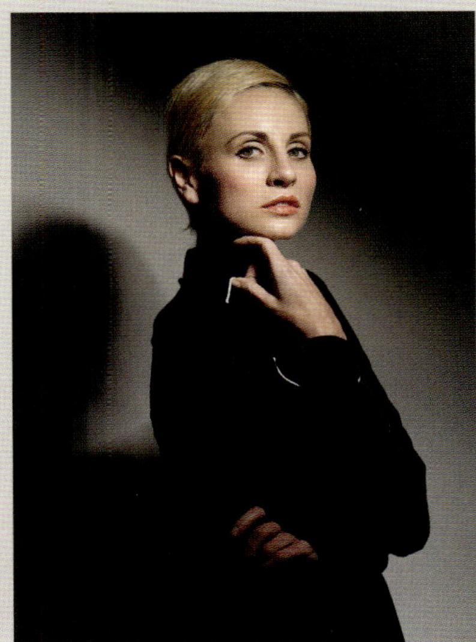

**Model:** Claire Elesabeth

**Photographer:** Adam Duckworth

# MAINTAINING YOUR REPUTATION

**TO BECOME A SUCCESSFUL, well-known fashion photographer you are going to have to work hard at building and then maintaining a positive reputation. The industry "talks" and when you combine that with high-speed internet access a negative comment can be a career killer.**

Self promote, not in an aggressive or boastful manner, but to showcase your work and try to introduce it to a larger audience. Know that any time you post something online you are opening yourself up to criticism. Be brave, though. You are never going to please everyone, so if someone has something negative to say, don't engage with them. The second you engage you start to look weak—keep your online presence positive and respectful. Agencies, clients, and models all check online profiles, so it is important to look professional at all times.

Be nice to people, especially other photographers. Avoid jealous behavior even when it seems the undeserving are prospering. You have talents to offer that others cannot and if you start to judge, your acts lose meaning. Don't get caught up in hype or believe other people's—everyone lies on their resume.

If you start to think you are more important than those around you it will probably be too late before you realize. It's easy to become egotistical when things go well, but the freelance world is a roller coaster ride and you have to take the good with the bad. There will times when you're working so hard you're wishing for a day off, but there will be dry spells as well, when you're at home on the sofa waiting for the phone to ring. Don't let this faze you, and try not to whine, complain, or publicly beg for jobs. Rather than procrastinating, test, or scout a new location. It's a crazy ride, but if you are able to enjoy the highs and roll with the lows you'll never want to get off.

Your reputation is important because agencies need to know they can trust you, that you work well with models, and that you will produce great tests and editorials on a regular basis without any negative repercussions. If they hear you are disagreeable or unreliable you will be less likely to book the job. Your team is your most important asset and they also need to trust that you will look after them. If you wrong them or one of their colleagues (it's a small world) you might not be able to find a makeup

## REPUTATION

As a model, it's great to turn up on set, see who the photographer is, and smile. Maybe it's because you know the style of modeling they prefer, or because they're funny and make you feel comfortable instantly. Maybe they're decisive and get through shots quickly. Ask your models who their favorite photographers to work with are and the reasons why.

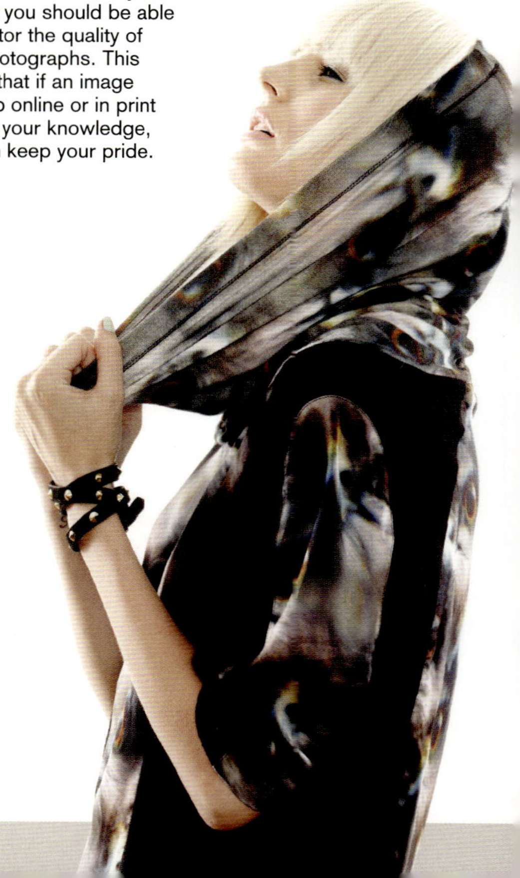

RIGHT & OPPOSITE:
**QUALITY CONTROL**
If you make sure that you produce every one of your images to the best of your abilities you should be able to monitor the quality of your photographs. This means that if an image pops up online or in print without your knowledge, you can keep your pride.

artist the next time you want to shoot. Most importantly, models must have no doubt that working with you is going to be worth their time, that you're not creepy, and your online promotion will benefit them.

Models dream about working with the best; the photographers they hear about who are world famous for creating and capturing pure magic. Every fashion photographer should aspire to consistently produce great shots, with well-cast models, in a positive and safe environment. They should dream of becoming the photographer that every agency is desperate to work with and that clients are fighting over to book. The kind of photographer that causes every model around the world to do a happy dance at the mere thought of stepping in front of their lens.

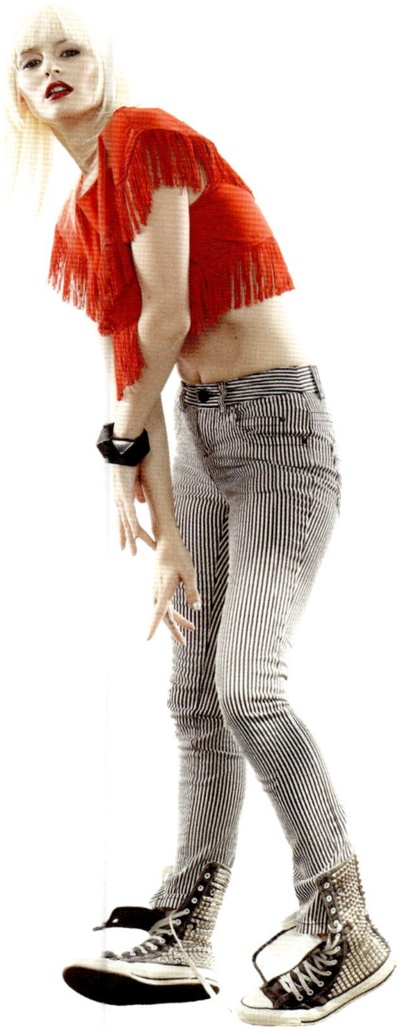

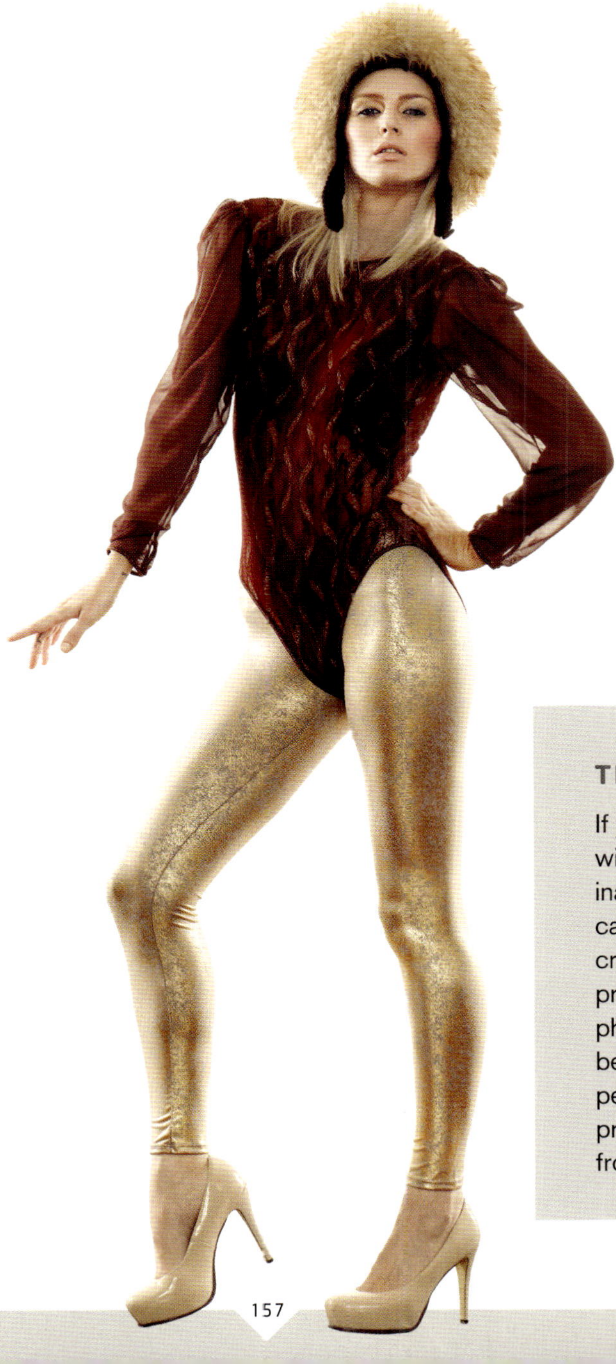

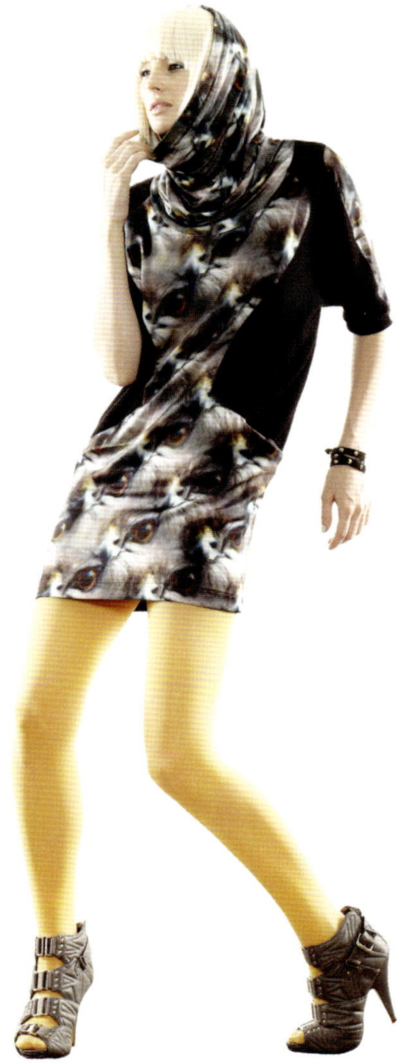

### TIP KEEP IT CLEAN

If you are connected online with friends who might post inappropriate comments or cause unnecessary conflict, create a separate web presence for your photography. It can be beneficial to divide your personal and professional profiles to prevent content from clashing.

# INDEX

# ACKNOWLEDGMENTS / PICTURE CREDITS

## From Franki

*I wrote "Shooting Models" this summer sat on planes, trains, winnebagos, makeup chairs, and for the most part, my sofa. After modeling for over ten years it was exciting to work on a project that lasted longer than a few days and involved more than turning up and having a nice lady make me look pretty. In all seriousness it feels good to have produced something I believe could help those either enter or improve an industry I adore. Information was gleaned in the moment, on set, between clicks, and through changing room walls. Thanks to a few years of experience and a valuable network of talented photographers and models I am honored to know, we were able to piece together what feels like a truly informative guide to the ins and outs of fashion photography.*

*I would especially like to thank Adam Juniper as well as the entire team at Ilex Photo publishing for believing that a blonde model could be capable of stringing a few sentences together. My editor Natalia Price-Cabrera also deserves thanks for helping me through the process when I am determined to leave everything to the last minute. I appreciate the introduction to my co-author Adam Duckworth.*

*Numerous photographers, models, makeup artists, and stylists were graciously on hand to offer advice throughout, but I must say a special thank you to friends in the industry, Natalie Toren, Scott Nathan, and Christian Bier. All of whom went above and beyond the call of duty when it came to helping out a stressed buddy. Ron Cruz also lent his photographic skills more than once and for all of this I am eternally grateful.*

*I am lucky to have a family who have understood all the crazy choices I have made in life and have supported every one of my decisions without a negative word uttered. My parents, who have dealt with me living in a different country for over a decade, truly believe whatever makes me happy makes them happy. I couldn't ask for more and cannot thank them enough for giving me the self-confidence to jump on a plane alone to New York at 18, hit the world head on, and never look back.*

*My last words of thanks belong to my wonderful husband, Cokey Falkow, who for the past three months has lived alongside his "model wife" spending an awful lot of time in front of the computer in comfy pants, with no makeup on, demanding wine. He has dealt with mood swings and meltdowns, and that was before I started writing the book. I could not be more thankful for that level of support. From reading pages to rubbing shoulders, he was there.*

*To everybody who has given images, advice, and messages of support, I thank you for taking the time to help me and hopefully help others to learn from your experience.*

## From Adam

*I would like to acknowledge my gratitude to all of the following who have helped greatly in my photographic journey.*

*Dave Beck, Gary Astill, Mark Langley and Chris Carr at Manfrotto, and Lastolite.*

*Chris and Emily Whittle, Louise O'Shea, Kev Treadwell, Brian Collier, and the crew at The Flash Centre for Elinchrom.*

*Paul Roper at JP Distribution for Pocket Wizards and Sekonic meters.*

*Nic Duckworth of Ameliorate retouching.*

*Lots of colleagues at Factory Media.*

*Terry Hope, Will Cheung, Roger Payne, and Matty Graham at Bright Publishing.*

*Miss Aniela, John Owen, Bob Q Martin and to the people in many of the photos: Amie Field, Amy Kitchingman, Ashli Rosetti, Clare Elesabeth, Katie Green, Leah Hibbert, Mahaneela Choudhuri-Reid, Maisie and Tamrin Leeanda.*

*Above all it has been thanks to Nic Duckworth who has given me the encouragement to create and for beautifully retouching my work.*

*I thank you all.*

## Picture Credits

**Cover image (c) Neil Favila**

Photo (c) t. Harrison Hillman: 4, 150, 156, 157; (c) Lotus Josephine: 6, 34 (background image), 72, 110; (c) John Owen: 7L; (c) Adam Duckworth: 7C, 7R, 16, 17, 56, 57, 86–97, 102R, 103, 108, 152–155; (c) Ron Cruz: 12, 13; (c) Jory Lee Cordy: 18, 19L; (c) Scott Nathan: 30, 31; (c) Nancy Schoenmakers: 34, 35; (c) Kesler Tran: 44, 45BL, 45BR; (c) Franki Falkow: 45T; (c) Ronald Cruz, www.ronskigfx.com, ronald@ronskigfx.com: 46, 132; (c) Nicole Le Bris: 61; (c) Nat Sin: 75, 98, 104, 105; (c) Emilie Elizabeth: 76, 84 (background image), 85; (c) Frank Gallaugher: 119; (c) Luke Pearsall: 130, 131;

**Courtesy of Shutterstock:**

Everett Collection: 8L, 8R, 9, 128R; ilolab: 8C, 38R, 39TR; Aleshyn_Andrei: 10B, 36R, 68B, 69T, 79, 120L, 123R; aaleksa: 10C; Nejron Photo: 10T; AS Photo: 11TL; Holbox: 11C; Erwin Usban: 11B; Syda Productions: 11TR, 68T; Lobke Peers: 14L; conrado: 14R, 68C, 71, 83R, 100C, 113L, 114, 116-117, 117R, 121B, 123L, 128R, 139TL, 143C, 144L; CURAphotography: 15L, 143R; dhorsey, 15R; Kiselev Andrey Valerevich: 19BC, 65BL, 117L, 121TR, 125L; Mike Laptev: 19R; Dmitry_Svetkov: 19TC; Goodluz: 21; iofoto: 22; ollyy: 24L; Peshkova: 24R; Alexey Lysenko: 25T; alekup: 25B; r.nagy: 26L; Roman Sigaev: 26R; Monkey Business Images: 27L, 41R, 133L; photobank.ch: 27C; Valeria Potapova: 27R; Anton Oparin: 28L, wavebreakmedia: 28R; Nadya Korobkova: 29; Studio10Artur: 32, 38TR; Boris Bushmin: 36L; Augustino: 37L, 67BL, 67TC; White Room: 37C, 51B; Seprimor: 37R; Edin Ramic: 38C; Darren J. Bradley: BL; Imageman: 38B; Shane Trotter: 39TL; Pindyrun Vasily: 39BR; crystalfoto: 40, 64TL; solominviktor: 41L, 82R, 122, 147L; Lipik: 41C; Kaponia Aliaksei: 42, 121TL; Mayer George: 43TL, 66R, 78T, 106, 123L, 139BC, 151L; Anton Gvozdikov: 43BL; Miramiska: 43TC; Maridav: 43TR; Surkov Vladimar: 43BR; terekhov igor, 47; BlueSkyImagr, 48, 49L; Shkvarko: 49R; Eugenio Marongui: 50T; Appear: 50B, 53, 64BL; Nataliya Naivsuper: 51T; brickrena, 52; bikeriderlondon: 54, 55; coka: 59TR, 77L, 125R, 136T; CREATISTA, 58, 59BC, 59BR; Oleg Gekman: 62, 65TR, 67BR, 137BL, 138, 139BL; Warren Goldswain, 63L; Vita Khorzhevska: 63R, 67TL; Matusciac Alexandru: 64TR, 65TL, 69C, 126C, 137TL; 101imges: 65R; Geoffrey Jones: 66L; luminaimages: 67BC; Denis Komarov: 67TR; Evgeniya Porechenskaya: 69B, 141R; Aleksandr Doodko: 70T; YuriyZhuravov: 70B, 82L, 137R; javi_indy: 73; lenaer: 77R; Maksim Toome: 78B; Subbotina Anna: 80; Malyugin: 81TL; Anna Omelchenko: 81TC; FirstLine: 81TR; Ksenjavka: 81B; Lana K: 83L; Nadya Korobkova: 84L, 136B; @erics: 99L; Charmer: 99R, 107BR; Nikita Starichenko: 100T; yurok: 100B; iko: 101T; new vave: 101C; Roxana Gonzales: 101B; kuzma: 102L; Pawel Papis: 107BL; Jose AS Reyes: 107TL; Binksi: 107TC; Sabino Parente: TR; Dmitry Raykin: 111L; wrangler: 111R, 116R; InnervisionArt: 112, 113R, 124C; Annette Shaff: 120R; Alessandro Colle: 124L; Alexander Supertramp, 124R; Serg Zastavkin: 126T, 151R; HannaMonika: 126B; lenetstan: 127T; Elnur: 127C; StockLite: 127B; Korionov: 128C; Elena Efimova: 129L; Aliyev Alexei Sergeevich: 129R; WEExp: 133R; Grachikova Larisa: 135R, 144R; artjazz: 135L; Yana Zastolskaya, 139TC; Dmitry Fischer: 139R; Africa Studio: 140; YanLev: 141L; Oliver Sved: 142; kiuikson: 143L, 145T; Dmitry_Tsvetkov: 145B; vadim kozlovsky: 146; Bogdan Wankowicz: 147R; Dubova: 148; Mihael Zhelezniak: 154